SOCIABLE LETTERS

SOCIABLE LETTERS

Margaret Cavendish

edited by James Fitzmaurice

broadview editions

NATIONAL LIBRARY OF CANADA CATALOGUING IN PUBLICATION DATA

Newcastle, Margaret Cavendish, Duchess of, 1624?-1674
    Sociable letters / Margaret Cavendish; edited by James Fitzmaurice.

(Broadview editions)
Includes bibliographical references.
ISBN 1-55111-558-1

    1. Women—Conduct of life—Fiction.   2. Epistolary fiction, English.
3. Character sketches.   I. Fitzmaurice, James, 1943-   II. Title.
III. Series.

PR3605.N2S63 2004   823'.4   C2004-901165-0

Broadview Press, Ltd. is an independent, international publishing house, incorporated in 1985. Broadview believes in shared ownership, both with its employees and with the general public; since the year 2000 Broadview shares have traded publicly on the Toronto Venture Exchange under the symbol BDP.

    We welcome comments and suggestions regarding any aspect of our publications—please feel free to contact us at the addresses below or at broadview@broadviewpress.com / www.broadviewpress.com

North America
Post Office Box 1243,
Peterborough, Ontario, Canada K9J 7H5
TEL (705) 743-8990; FAX (705) 743-8353

3576 California Road,
Orchard Park, New York, USA 14127

E-MAIL customerservice@broadviewpress.com

United Kingdom and Europe
NBN Plymbridge.
Estover Road, Plymouth PL6 7PY, UK
TEL 44(0) 1752 202301
FAX 44 (0) 1752 202331
FAX ORDER LINE 44 (0) 1752 202333
CUST. SERVICE cservs@nbnplymbridge.com
ORDERS orders@nbnplymbridge.com

Australia & New Zealand
UNIREPS University of New South Wales
Sydney, NSW 2052
TEL 61 2 9664099; FAX 61 2 9664520
E-MAIL infopress@unsw.edu.au

Series Editor: Professor L.W. Conolly
Advisory Editor for this volume: Michel W. Pharand

Cover design by Lisa Brawn
Typeset by Liz Broes & Trevor Browne, Black Eye Design

This book is printed on 100% post-consumer recycled, ancient forest friendly paper.

Printed in Canada

Contents

Acknowledgments

I have had many informal conversations with scholars on the topic of Margaret Cavendish and on subjects related to seventeenth-century England more broadly. Such conversations, some of them carried out exclusively on e-mail, have proved enormously valuable as I have assembled this book. The scholars involved include, but are not limited to, Alexandra Bennett, Sylvia Bowerbank, Mary Campbell, Stephen Clucas, Trevor Foulds, Nancy Gutierrez, Ursula Haerting, Elizabeth Hageman, Paul Hartle, Carrie Hintz, Lisa Hopkins, Leigh Hursh, Erna Kelly, Lee C. Khanna, Marika Keblusek, Marina Leslie, Kate Lilley, Trevor Lipscombe, Steve May, David Norbrook, Emma Rees, Kevin Sharpe, Anne Shaver, Brandie Siegfried, Katherine Romack, Paul Salzman, Lisa Sarasohn, Hilda Smith, Sara Jayne Steen, Mihoko Suzuki, Margaret Thickstun, Rebecca Totaro, Katie Whitaker, Gweno Williams, Tanya Wood, Suzanne Woods.

I also am indebted to library staff at the Cambridge University Library, at the University of Nottingham Library, and at the Huntington Library. Staff of the Document Delivery Department of the Cline Library at Northern Arizona University has been able to find and quickly supply me with most of the books and articles that I requested. The listserv of the Margaret Cavendish Society has proved invaluable, as have a series of biennial meetings of the society in England, France, and the United States. I have made extensive use of the search capabilities of Renaissance Women Online, a website maintained by the Brown University Women Writers Project.

Much of the work on this book was completed while I was a visiting lecturer at Nottingham Trent University and, later, while I was a senior visiting fellow at Gonville and Caius College. My thanks to those two institutions as well as to the Intramural Grants Committee at Northern Arizona University.

I have a large debt to Anne Scott, who read the introduction to this book. My largest debt, however, is to Susan Fitzmaurice, who read most of the manuscript more than once and who listened patiently to me as I thought out loud about the project in its various stages. Thinking out loud was a part of the process of composition used by Margaret Cavendish as described by her in "A True Relation," so I feel that I am in good company. This book is dedicated to my family: Susan, Anne, Stephen, Rosie, and John, as well as to the memory of Keith.

List of Illustrations

Thus in this Semy-Circle, wher they Sitt,
Telling of Tales of pleasure & of witt,
Heer you may read without a Sinn or Crime,
And how more innocentl'y pass your tyme.

Cavendish seated before a fire with her family.

[Reprinted by permission of the Huntington Library.]

Introduction

Margaret Cavendish is well known to those who read seventeenth-century British literature as the first woman in England to publish a great deal, some thirteen books printed in twenty-two editions. Her short fiction, scientific speculation, poems, novellas, plays, and letters, together with her autobiography and the biography of her husband, testify to her willingness to work with a wide variety of forms. Her writing, until the beginning of the 1990s, was generally thought to be quirky or quaint, but now it is taken seriously. Once scholars interested in matters of sex and gender found her books a puzzling mix of protofeminst and traditional positions, but such scholars have become less likely to see her as a bad writer whose bad writing derives from a patriarchal society. Rather, she generally is seen as a good writer who overcame the impediments of patriarchy to produce books that are ironic, suggestive, and discursive — as opposed to contradictory, vague, and lacking in structure.[1] Historians of science and those who trace the relationship between science and literature see her as an important author, and her connection to the Vitalist scientific movement of the seventeenth century is sometimes compared to that of Milton.[2] Her plays, once thought unactable, in recent years have been performed in Europe, North America, and Australia.

Sociable Letters

Much of what is found in *Sociable Letters* is like letters composed by actual women. Indeed, Cavendish says that she tried to imitate the written communication of two women living at a little distance from one another and that she avoided the style of artificial, "Romantical" letters (first preface to her readers in this volume, page 42). At the same time, she occasionally may be guilty of some of the manipulations that were practiced by her predecessor James Howell. Howell rewrote a number of genuine letters prior to the publication his *Epistolae Ho-Elianae* (1650) so as to make his understanding of historical events seem prescient (see *Sociable Letters*, letter 165).[3]

---

1 See Nichole Pohl, "'Of Mixt Natures': Questions of Genre in Margaret Cavendish's *The Blazing World*," *Princely Brave Woman*, ed. Stephen Clucas (Aldershot: Ashgate, 2003) 51–68.

2 John Rogers, *The Matter of Revolution: Science, Poetry, and Politics in the Age of Milton* (Ithaca: Cornell UP, 1996) 181.

3 James Howell, *Epistolae Ho-Elianae* (London, 1650).

Further, quite a few of the letters composed by Cavendish are less recognizable today as epistolary efforts and more readily understood as essays in the tradition of Francis Bacon and Michel de Montaigne (see Appendix C). Cavendish often classifies and subdivides, so that, for instance, we find men and women sorted into various categories. The topics of these essays include marriage, medicine, science, war and peace, politics, as well as English and classical literatures. A wide variety of other subjects are touched upon as well. The strength of the book is to be found less in any particular *genre* or topic, however. Rather, an on-going series of observations about life as it was lived in the seventeenth century gives the volume its power.[1] A little spice is added to the mix when one realizes that some but by no means all of the characters were actual people, hidden behind initials and anagrams. Readers of the time were invited, it appears, to find the key for who was who. In letter 173, for example, the scholar who reads aloud badly is probably the philosopher Thomas Hobbes, and C.R. in several letters seems to be King Charles II (letters 49 and 196 in particular). The situation is complicated by the facts that Cavendish sometimes pokes fun at herself under cover of the initials of her married or maiden names and that she frequently puts her own ideas into the speeches of people she discusses. Many letters are narrative in form and develop fictional characters. Indeed, it is possible to trace the beginnings of realistic characterization in eighteenth-century fiction back to *Sociable Letters*.[2] There are, finally, letters that are in no way fictional, letters written to living persons who were mostly friends and family.

The organizing principle of *Sociable Letters* is variety, and the book is discursive. On this account it is much like another book by Cavendish, *The World's Olio* (1655). An "olio" was a savory stew made from various ingredients and so, after a fashion, is *Sociable Letters*. Cavendish alternates long and short letters, comic stories with serious essays, and tries to avoid grouping letters by topic. In the first preface to her readers, she says that she had considered writing another book of plays but chose not to do so in order to offer a change of pace. She goes on to suggest that her letters are like scenes from a play, scenes that may be read independently and that

---

1   She may have borrowed from Richard Flecknoe's *A Relation of Ten Years' Travel in Europe, Asia, Affrique and America* for her approach to material taken from every-day life. See Katie Whitaker, *Mad Madge, The Extraordinary Life of Margaret, Duchess of Newcastle, the First Woman to Live by her Pen* (New York: Basic Books, 2002) 211.

2   B.G. MacCarthy, following J.J. Jusserand, makes this point in *The Female Pen, Women Writers and Novelists, 1621–1818* (New York: New York UP, 1994) 244–48. See also Robert Adams Day, *Told in Letters: Epistolary Fiction Before Richardson* (Ann Arbor: U of Michigan P, 1966).

do not require the reading of other scenes or a whole play to be enjoyed. Her interest in variety, then, is not unlike what we find with Robert Herrick in his book of poems, *Hesperides* (1648). For the most part she carries through with her intentions as stated, although some of her letters on the subject of Antwerp are clustered at the end of the book, as are the missives to her actual friends and family.

Marriage in *Sociable Letters*

The single most important topic in *Sociable Letters*, be it subject to the analysis of an informal essay or depicted in the theme of a brief narrative, is marriage. Should anyone, and women in particular, marry at all? What are the motivations for marriage? How does a person deal with the physical attraction attendant upon youth? What about money and social status in the choice of a spouse? How do children fit within a marriage? Who is dishonored by adultery and who suffers in what ways? What danger is there from mistresses and what are the consequences of divorce?

Cavendish always praises her husband and pronounces herself fortunate in her own marriage, but in *Sociable Letters* and elsewhere she is deeply dubious about the benefits of the institution for women in general. In a play within her comedy *The Convent of Pleasure* (1668), we learn that men may beat their wives, that childbirth sometimes brings about the death of the mother, and that children are frequently ingrates. Early in *Sociable Letters* (letter 4), we find three sisters who say they will not marry. The variety of their complexions as well as the differences in their temperaments mark them as representatives for all womankind, and the intent of the letter seems to be a refutation of the traditional view that women must marry before they lose their ability to attract men. "Time wears out youth and fades beauty," says the male critic of the three young women. They respond that they need not be beautiful if they can be wise. Their position is quite probably what was accepted by Cavendish, but she avoids being preachy by apparently offering a general critique of women, "When our sex cannot pretend to be fair, they will pretend to be wise." Feminists have been disconcerted by statements of the sort found here, but Cavendish is being ironic in this instance, invoking an old saw with a wink.[1]

---

1   For a treatment of irony in this passage from the perspective of the history of the English language, see Susan Fitzmaurice,"Tentativeness and Insistence in the Expression of Politeness in Margaret Cavendish's *Sociable Letters*," *Language and Literature* 9 (February 2000): 7–24.

Letter 32 tells the stories of two married women, one patient and one a shrew. Since the Griselda-like woman shows fortitude as well as forbearance and since the Kate-like woman precipitates a dish-throwing "hurley burley" in the midst of a dinner party, we may be tempted to believe that Cavendish takes the traditional view of what is proper behavior in women. Men may be rude or lose control of themselves; women must make up for these weaknesses. The story, however, is less a moral fable and more a matter of slapstick comedy. If anything, Cavendish is sarcastic in her closing, "leaving the Angelick Lady to be a Pattern to her Sex." Who, Cavendish seems to be saying, would want to follow such a pattern of spineless submission? Certainly not Cavendish, herself. As the book comes to a close, she is, for a change, very direct in describing for her sister Ann the dangers of marriage and the safety of a single life (letter 201). Should anyone have missed her point, Cavendish gives us an unequivocal statement.

If one does decide to marry, then the choice that Cavendish sees made by most of her contemporaries is between the physical attractiveness of youth and the financial gain attendant upon age. Her wry suggestion is that the old foolishly marry for beauty while the young reap monetary benefits that will be thrown away when they, themselves, become old (letter 39). Many desire marriage and therefore frequent "Hymen's markets," which include "churches, plays, masques, balls" (letter 50). Cavendish may seem cynical about the way in which women and men chose spouses during the seventeenth century, but, like Dorothy Osborne, she really is more amused than appalled.[1] Cavendish even goes so far as to suggest at least half seriously that a marriage between a man and his kitchen maid has the virtue of being a love match and that the couple will be happy (letter 42).

Cavendish has little patience with wives who are overcome with delight in being pregnant (letter 47). Such women, she says, care more about the attention that comes from being with child than for the responsibilities that go with bringing up children. She also says that children are only necessary to carry on a man's lineage and have no importance where women are concerned (letter 93). Nevertheless, she doted on her husband's grandchild Henry, and probably means that children do not perpetuate a woman's name. Cavendish, who was childless, probably believed that her own name would be carried forward on the title pages of her books. What we do know for certain is that she did not always get on well with her

---

1   See *Letters from Dorothy Osborne to Sir William Temple*, ed. G.C. Moore Smith (Oxford: Clarendon, 1928).

stepchildren and that they did not always get along with one another (see the letter from Elizabeth Cavendish Egerton in this volume).

Less than convincing are her repeated statements that a wife's adultery dishonors a husband but a husband's does not dishonor a wife (letter 201). In any event, she qualifies such statements by saying that if there is no dishonor for the wife, there is unhappiness, and, indeed, she metes out painful punishment for faithless men in her short fiction contained in *Nature's Pictures* (1656). The main issue for Cavendish, however, is not really honor. What troubles her is the threat to the stability of marriages derived from faithlessness, and she, like Jane Barker, describes wives who become slaves or are threatened with becoming slaves to their husbands' mistresses (letters 153 and 155).[1] Sometimes she makes light of the problem as with the man who is publicly "persecuted" by another man's mistress (letter 36). It makes more sense, says Cavendish wryly, for a man to be persecuted by his own "whore." Cavendish may take as a model for such outrageous wit Angel Day's enormously popular collection of form letters *The English Secretary*, for some of Days's exemplary letters are outlandishly comic. One, which according to its title is designed to console a man whose old wife has died, in fact congratulates him on being rid of her (see Appendix C). Joking aside, Cavendish was aware that any man, her husband included, could fall under the spell of a woman who was willing to become a mistress. An attendant problem with mistresses was that they might marry single men and hence damage the position of other women on the marriage market. Cavendish is especially unhappy when men of position and respect, like Pericles of Athens (letter 30), make such a choice in marriage. With King Charles II wont to put his trust in and to accord status to his mistress Nell Gwyn, Cavendish was not dealing with a hypothetical problem, but her own husband, though something of a ladies' man during his first marriage, seems to have been faithful to her. What makes *Sociable Letters* interesting is that Cavendish is more inclined to remark upon the ironies attending adultery than to offer self-righteous condemnation. She gives the courtesan Aspasia, who married Pericles, credit as a fine rhetorician, one to whom men brought their wives so that these women might hear her eloquence (letter 30). It is ironic, Cavendish suggests, that a man would want to have his wife learn anything from a woman so apparently opposed to marriage.

---

1   See "The Unaccountable Wife," *A Patch-work Screen*, rpt. in *First Feminists: British Women Writers, 1578–1799* (Bloomington: Indiana UP, 1985) 175–79.

Cavendish says that divorce is more harmful to women than men and in the unironic letter to her sister Ann (letter 201) sees divorce as dishonorable for all concerned. As with Salome in Elizabeth Cary's *Mariam*, Cavendish probably understands divorce to be a recourse open only to men.[1] She is, however, deeply sarcastic when she suggests at one point that the Lady M.L. (the initials she carried before marriage, Margaret Lucas) is only being teased by an unfaithful husband who has pretended that he wanted a divorce. Such teasing was no joke for Cavendish.

It is often the colorful and unexpected details of these letters that make them so powerful. A man is beaten by his wife in public (letter 26), not a frequent occurrence to be sure but one that gives a sense of the variety of marriages that existed in the seventeenth century. Another man throws sweet meats into a room in order to seduce a maid and the maid is unjustly blamed by his wife for enticing the husband (letter 124). Such is the stuff of marriage as understood by Cavendish.

Medicine and Science

Medicine for Cavendish is very closely connected with diet, and she often takes a scientific approach as she offers advice about this or that illness.[2] She tends to recommend various sorts of cordials and rarely sees the need for more serious intervention. In an exceptional instance she suggests a "tap-hole" to "vent" the "superfluity" of a man ill with dropsy (letter 139). Nevertheless, she is more likely to discuss the effect of new milk or brown bread on one's health and then to offer suggestions about how to avoid intestinal "obstructions" (letter 154). There is a good deal of theory of hot and cold as well as moist and dry, but in essence Cavendish is a purveyor of home remedies and common-sense medical wisdom. In accordance with practice of the time, she often recommends bleeding patients, though the court physician Theodore Mayerne thought that she bled herself and her servants too frequently.[3]

---

1   *The Tragedy of Mariam, The Fair Queen of Jewry*, Act 1, scene 4, ed. Weller and Ferguson (Berkeley: U of California P) 79 and 80.

2   For a discussion of Cavendish's medical advice as speech acts and in comparison with medical advice offered by physicians, see Susan M. Fitzmaurice, *The Familiar Letter in Early Modern English* (Amsterdam and Philadelphia: John Benjamins, 2002) 87–127 and Susan M. Fitzmaurice, "Margaret Cavendish, the Doctors of Physick and Advice to the Sick," *Princely Brave Woman*, 210–41.

3   Douglas Grant, *Margaret the First* (London: Rupert Hart-Davis, 1957) 103–04.

There is little discussion in *Sociable Letters* of science *per se* such as is found in her books on science. A notable exception is her denial of the existence of a vacuum (letter 161), which seems out of place in *Sociable Letters* and is scarcely sociable. For nonscientific readers, her science is most interesting when it is tied to other matters such as the existence of God (letter 157). Her admission, at one point, that she is much taken with science is quite revealing. Science is a "dish" that she loves "to feed on" but the "meat is hard and not easily to be digested" (letter 199). It may be that she sometimes felt the need to keep this love under control.

War, Peace, and Politics

Cavendish often denies that women should concern themselves with matters of war and peace. Indeed, she frequently admonishes them to stay clear of politics in general. The Lady N.P. (letter 9) may well be an actual woman who meddled in "designs and plots" of national importance and who is advised against the practice. Nevertheless, Cavendish cannot resist remarking on current events and shows a distinct bitterness as regards the fortunes of those military men who make sacrifices early in a war. Her husband financed a substantial portion of the army that was defeated by Oliver Cromwell at Marston Moor, a defeat that was less the fault of the husband than the result of meddling with orders and command by Charles I. With his financial base seriously damaged, William Cavendish retired to exile on the Continent. After the Restoration, he resumed control of his pillaged estates and received what he felt was too little compensation from the new King for his loyal service. He never complained openly and Margaret Cavendish never blamed anyone directly, but she repeatedly tells her readers that it is best financially to come in at the end of a war on the winning side. If she plays the part of the traditional woman in saying that she leaves decisions about wars to men, she probably reveals what she really thinks when she points out that it is women and children who suffer the most when the battles are over (letter 120).

English and Classical Literatures

Cavendish often claimed that what she wrote derived from her own fancy and not from imitation of classical or English sources.[1] In an age still dom-

---

1 Sylvia Bowerbank, in "'The Spider's Delight': Margaret Cavendish and the 'Female Imagination,'" has examined a favorite image used by Cavendish to evoke literary creativity, a spider that spins a web from the inside of itself.

inated by the notion that composition was best when based on *imitatio* of ancient masters, hers was an unusual though not unique position.[1] In a preface to the 1662 *Plays*, Cavendish describes the situation as follows:

> But Noble Readers, do not think my Playes,
> Are such as have been writ in former daies;
> As Johnson, Shakespear, Beaumont, Fletcher writ;
> Mine want their Learning, Reading, Language, wit:
> The Latin phrases I could never tell,
> But Jonson could, which made him write so well.
> Greek, Latin Poets, I could never read,
> Nor their Historians, but our English Speed;
> Nor could not steal their Wit, nor Plotts out take;
> All my Playes Plots, my own poor brain did make:
> From Plutarchs story I ne'r took a Plot,
> Nor from Romances, nor from Don Quixot,
> As others have, for to assist their Wit,
> But I upon my own Foundation writ.[2]

She is quite misleading in admitting to so little indebtedness to earlier writers. The truth is that she had considerable familiarity with the Greeks and Romans in translation as well as with French romance and English history beyond what is contained in John Speed's *History of Great Britain*.[3] Further, she was not above borrowing from Shakespeare, as with her retelling of the story of Lysimachus and Marina from Shakespeare's *Pericles*. The reworking of Shakespeare's plot occurs at the beginning of "Assaulted and Pursued Chastity," found in *Nature's Pictures*.

While it may be true that Cavendish was less given to imitation of the ancients than her contemporaries and it is doubtless the case that she did not read the classics in Greek and Latin, she both read and gave considerable thought to what she found in translation. She certainly was familiar with many of the lives from Plutarch, though she was also irreverent

---

1   See Achsah Guibbory, "Imitation and Originality: Cowley and Bacon's Vision of Progress," *SEL, Studies in English Literature* 29 (1989): 99–111.

2   Sig. A7v.

3   *The World's Olio* (1655), in particular, shows careful thought about and comic rereadings of classical stories of virtuous women. Much the same is true of the book's approach to Tudor history. As for romance, Cavendish repeatedly ridicules the improbabilities of its plots even as she reproduces such improbabilities in her own fiction: See *Nature's Pictures*, Sig. C2r.

enough to joke about Plutarch's "lies" rather than *Lives* (letter 30). It is from Plutarch that she gets the tale of Pericles and the courtesan Aspasia, and Plutarch provides her with the story of Julius Caesar, whom she admires, as well as that of Cato, whom she does not (letter 187).

> Cato ... perceiving his Country was like to be Govern'd as a Monarchy, which was before a Republick, Kill'd himself, although he knew the old Government was so Corrupted, as it caused great Riots, Tumults, Seditions, Factions, and Slaughters, Killing and Murdering even in the Market-place, so as it could not be Worse what Chance soever came.

As a royalist, Cavendish has a little fun overturning an old and widely accepted interpretation of a well-worn story.

Perhaps most interesting is her assessment of the literary worth of three important writers, Ovid, Virgil, and Shakespeare. She feels a special kinship with Ovid, whom she credits with wit and, more in keeping with her own professed interests, with fancy.[1] We also know that she composed "baby books" before she was married and it is clear that she was interested in what might be called serious literature when she was young, probably in addition to romance. She absorbed what others had to say about Virgil and Ovid most significantly after she was married and had come in contact with her husband's literary coterie.[2] She notes in passing what she has "heard" about Virgil and Ovid, and bases much of her judgment of their works on the lives of the men. Virgil was a flatterer who found worldly reward. Ovid had more integrity and hence was "Unhappy," particularly in his banishment from Rome. Nevertheless, she is careful to say that she is in no position to comment on the power of Virgil's language, since she is limited to reading a translation (letter 146). She tells us that Ovid was not as "palpable an imitator as Virgil." In so saying, she may give Virgil his due as an imitator of nature, or she simply may mean that he slavishly followed Homer. With Ovid, the situation is more clear. She not only admires his fancy but praises his variety. In being a collection of stories rather than a continued narrative, *The Metamorphoses* is more like *Sociable Letters* than it is *The Aeneid*.

What Cavendish has to say about Shakespeare is strikingly modern and quite out of keeping with the time in which *Sociable Letters* was published.

---

1   See letter 162.

2   See the special volume on the Cavendish Circle in *The Seventeenth Century* 9.2 (Autumn 1994).

Halliday in *The Cult of Shakespeare* gives ample evidence of Restoration distaste for the lower-class characters to be found in Shakespeare's plays. Cavendish, contrary to Restoration standards, mentions Doll Tearsheet, Mistress Quickly, and Nan Page in the same breath with Cleopatra (letter 123). The point, again, seems to be variety. Shakespeare was not limited to depicting any one social class. In her own plays, Cavendish concentrates on the upper classes, but not to the exclusion of servants. Dick, in *The Convent of Pleasure*, is more than a match for his master intellectually. The poorest and least privileged get serious treatment, again in *The Convent of Pleasure* and even more markedly in a manuscript play probably by Cavendish, *The Lotterie*.[1] Cavendish was not merely the first woman to launch a serious and sustained critique of Shakespeare. She was the first person to do so.

Miscellaneous Topics

Sociable Letters covers a wide variety of subjects, espousing viewpoints that are sometimes surprising for modern readers. For instance, Cavendish condemns drinking and gambling, but gambling for her includes large wagers laid on tennis matches (letter 101). Clearly tennis was not the focus for most gamblers of seventeenth-century England, who concentrated their attention on cards and dice, but one man did manage to lose 500 pounds. In the words of Cavendish he is like many men who "Toss away their Estates & Lives with a Ball." She wryly suggests that the man take up chess, where his losses would be less, or, better yet, fox and geese, a harmless board game. Again she surprises, when she asserts that tennis has no redeeming value as exercise because it is too strenuous.

She follows Ben Jonson in showing her disdain for religious extremism, and, like him, is content to poke fun at Puritans rather than take them seriously (letter 17). Other topics include musical and spoken performance (letters 202 and 173), reason and belief (letter 37), and the relationship between envy and friendship among women (letter 158).

Letters from Margaret Cavendish to William Cavendish

The love letters sent by Margaret to William were not written for print, though such letters, as everyone at court knew, could fall into the wrong

---

1 See *The Lotterie*, in James Fitzmaurice,"English Lotteries and 'The Lotterie,' a Manuscript Play Probably by Margaret Cavendish," *Huntington Library Quarterly* 66 (2003): 155–67.

hands and be read by persons other than the intended recipient. Any letter needed to be written with care. Margaret's love letters were composed nearly twenty years before the publication of *Sociable Letters*, when she was about twenty-two and had yet to publish a book. They are, nonetheless, carefully crafted and sometimes self-consciously mannered for comic effect. For an account of their contents, see the introduction to the section in this book containing them (page 89).

The Context of Family and the Context of Women's Letters

It is instructive to read Cavendish's letters, both the love letters and *Sociable Letters* within the context of correspondence composed by family members and in light of letters written by other women of the time. The letters composed by Elizabeth Cavendish Egerton, Margaret's stepdaughter, and Christiana Cavendish, Margaret's cousin by marriage, are as often as not similar in style and general appearance to what is found in Margaret's love letters.

Sociable Letters concerns itself with two topics that were of interest to women letter writers of the Cavendish family: health and family relationships. Elizabeth and Christiana both bring up the topic of health, and Christiana goes into some detail on the subject. Elizabeth's anger with her brother Henry and with his wife reminds us that sometimes comic scenes in *Sociable Letters* provide ways to describe tensions that built up within the Cavendish family. The love letters of Dorothy Osborne and Aphra Behn form a context for Margaret's letters to William. Osborne is by turns romantic and pragmatic, while Cavendish tends to blend the two approaches to love. Behn mostly provides a contrast with Cavendish, as Behn's love for her correspondent, John Hoyle, was not returned. We need to remember, however, that Behn was able to use her letters to put distance between herself as unrequited lover, on the one hand, and herself as professional writer, on the other.

In a preface to the marquis of Newcastle found in *Sociable Letters* (page 38), Cavendish defends herself against the likes of Lord Denny, who viciously attacked Lady Mary Wroth as a woman who wrote. Denny believed that women should "work" — cook and sew, look after the house — rather than put together books. Indeed, intelligent, articulate, capable women, in his view, should keep themselves busy with domestic chores and not commit their thoughts to paper. They should not circulate manuscripts as many women did, including Elizabeth Cavendish Egerton, and they should not write for print, as was the case with Margaret. He might have gone on to say that they should not concern themselves with court politics and should not issue reports in writing, as did Christiana. Osborne's articulate, insightful letters would have made him nervous. Behn's success as a commercial writer would have been met by him with disbelief. These five women were far too wise to follow such advice as he gave, though it was everywhere to be found.

The Life of Cavendish

Early Life

"A True Relation," the autobiographical excursus to be found at the end of the first edition of *Nature's Pictures*, reminds us of how important Cavendish's early years were to her. Mostly we learn that she admired the strength and versatility of her widowed mother and that she formed a permanent bond with her siblings. She was particularly close to Catherine, whom she calls "sister Pye" (letter 200). "A True Relation" was not reprinted in the second edition of *Nature's Pictures* perhaps because it had been intended, in part, as an introduction of the author to the world rather than as a record of her early years and courtship. By the second edition, Cavendish and her writing were widely known.

"A True Relation" opens with a statement that is both important to our understanding of Cavendish and frequently overlooked:

> My Father [Thomas Lucas] was a Gentleman, which Title is grounded and given by Merit, and not by Princes: and 'tis the act of Time, not Favour; Though my father was not a Peer of the Realm, yet there were few Peers who had much greater Estates, or lived more noble therewith.[1]

It is sometimes suggested that Cavendish was a pampered aristocrat, who was out of contact with the worries of day-to-day life. Cavendish neither started out nor did she end up in this manner. Although her father boasted a heritage that included a member of Parliament for the borough of Colchester, he had no title. It is true that there was substantial wealth in the family, but it became vulnerable at the death of her father,

---

1   "A True Relation," *Nature's Pictures* (London, 1656) 368. See also *Paper Bodies: A Margaret Cavendish Reader*, ed. Sylvia Bowerbank and Sara Mendelson (Peterborough, ON: Broadview Press, 1999) 41–63.

and the family estates were literally attacked during the English Civil Wars. Elizabeth Leighton Lucas, her widowed mother, took charge and deftly worked to protect the family assets from abuses that were common when an heir was a minor, as was the case with Cavendish's older brother, John. Nor had the widow enjoyed an easy life prior to marriage, for the man who was to be her husband, having killed another man in a duel, was banished by Queen Elizabeth. At the time, the then Elizabeth Leighton was pregnant, and the exile of Thomas Lucas effectively blocked her marriage until after the baby was born. The autobiography does not discuss these events, but it is fully engaged in matters of this world and in particular offers observations about the problems of running a household, including the management of employees. Following her mother's example, Cavendish went on to be both practical and humane in this regard. In *Sociable Letters*, Cavendish tells us that she does not pry in the personal lives of those who work for her nor does she allow them to openly display behavior that will bring disrepute upon the household.

> I Hear by your last Letter, that the Lady H.W. doth Entertain [retain] a Maid-servant that hath lately Served in my House, and therefore desires you to write to me, to send her word whether she was a Good Servant when she Served me, and whether she was Trusty and Chast; first, she must Excuse me, for I will not Dispraise a Servant out of my Service, unless it were as a Punishment to some Notorious Faults; for Servants may be Better and Worse in Several Services. (letter 179)

In a frank statement that seems very modern, she goes on to say that she is not a "Porter, or Spy of [her] Maids Lower Parts." At the same time she warns employers not to be too permissive or to be ruled by those they employ.

Marriage

Quite possibly the most important decision that a person could make during the seventeenth century was the choice of a mate. In the summer of 1645, the then Margaret Lucas was a Maid of Honor to Queen Henrietta Maria and had followed the Queen into exile at St. Germain near Paris after England had become too dangerous for the Queen's household during the English Civil Wars. William Cavendish, then marquis of Newcastle and recently made a widower, found Margaret attractive and may have tried to seduce her. Letters from Margaret to William printed in this volume show that she was strongly drawn to him as well, but she had no intention of becoming an amorous conquest of the sort associated with Cavalier poetry. Rather, she desired marriage, though the Queen sided with those who felt that Margaret's social position was too humble for William. In fact, Margaret's family was on the rise socially, and one brother, Sir Charles, became a Civil War hero while another brother, Sir John, had recently joined the House of Lords as Baron Lucas of Shenfield. William had risen socially himself, and liked to joke that he had become a peer in lieu of payment for a bad debt. Thus, both Cavendish and her future husband knew what it was to move up to higher social status. More important than this common experience was the fact that the couple was also drawn together by a mutual interest in literature, for Margaret had composed her "baby books" and William was the author of poetry and plays.[1] There was a thirty-year difference in age between the two, but they appear to have been very happy. Unsurprisingly, Margaret's fiction contains many stories that end with the union of an older man and a younger woman.

After her marriage, Margaret spent the fifteen years of William's banishment from England mostly together with him in Antwerp in a large and beautiful house, which had been owned by the painter Peter Paul Rubens and which is now a museum. Several of the letters from the final quarter of *Sociable Letters* make specific reference to daily life in this period and give details about the city. The canals froze over one winter and provided an opportunity for ice-skating (letter 192); a mountebank offered entertainment with his medicine show (letter 195); carnival came and went (letter 194). It was also during this period that Cavendish began to publish. She was not the first woman to have a book of poems in English appear in print, for verses by the American Anne Bradstreet were published at the behest of someone other than the author a little before Cavendish's *Poems and Fancies* appeared in 1653. Cavendish was, however, the first Englishwoman to seek print and to have a great many books printed.

It was at about this time that she began to be known for eccentric dress, and she explains in *Nature's Pictures* and *Sociable Letters* (letter 178) that she designed her own fashions. A reputation for eccentricity may have had special benefits. Given Lord Denny's attack on Lady Mary Wroth, we may imagine Cavendish was happier to be thought of as an

---

1   See in particular Kate Lilley, "Contracting Readers: 'Margaret Newcastle' and the Rhetoric of Conjugality," *Princely Brave Woman*, 19–50.

eccentric than as a "hermaphrodite" or a "monster."[1] Her interest in fashion, however, was not merely a protective camouflage for her writing. She clearly enjoyed having a distinctive style of living, and went on to become something of a celebrity.

Life During the Restoration

With the Restoration of Charles II in 1660, Margaret and William returned to England. At first William hoped to be a force in the new government, but came to have the role of old friend to the King rather than trusted advisor. Margaret and William retired to the midlands and set about repairing their estates in Nottinghamshire, Derbyshire, and elsewhere. Margaret often writes of her satisfaction with her life of retirement in *Sociable Letters*, though we might wonder if, in fact, she longed for the general excitement and literary ferment of London. It is clear that as the 1660s progressed she became increasingly active in managing the family estates. She augmented her own jointure several times, to the dismay of the spouse of William's heir, Henry. By the end of the decade she and her most trusted financial advisor, Francis Topp, had regularized the collection of rents. The result was a poison pen letter in which the two were accused of adultery by a corrupt steward and two tenants. The tenants signed a written confession, now housed at the University of Nottingham Library, a confession that lets us know just how engaged Cavendish was in the mundane world of accounts and ledgers.[2] In 1667, Cavendish published the *Life* of her husband. This book is less a testimony to her devotion to her spouse, though it is that, and more a triumph for the author as a historian. It, too, shows her interest in lands and rents, for she devotes a full chapter to the details of the revenue lost during the fifteen years of William's banishment. If one adds in, as she does, interest compounded at six percent and if one does not forget to count destruction of forests, then the total loss accepted by the *DNB* and elsewhere is nearly a million pounds.

Cavendish and her husband, however, did not spend the decade completely hidden away in their two residences, Welbeck Abbey and Bolsover Castle. In 1667, they passed the winter and spring in London. They saw plays, including William's *The Humorous Lovers*, and visited the royal

---

1 Lady Mary Wroth, *The Poems of Lady Mary Wroth*, ed. Josephine Roberts (Baton Rouge: Louisiana State UP, 1983) 34.

2 Grant, 231–35.

family. Margaret become a celebrity on the visit, and without a doubt enjoyed the role. The diarist Samuel Pepys followed her coach around London in the vain attempt to catch sight of what he knew to be a "comely" and an exotically dressed lady.[1] It was also during the spring of 1667 that she was invited to view scientific experiments at the Royal Society, and in so doing she became the first woman to enter this bastion of learned men, whose grasp of science was not so very different from her own.[2] It is sometimes suggested that she was awed by the scientific experiments performed on her behalf, but she clearly awed the society itself with her entourage.[3] The year 1667 also saw the publication of her *Life* of William, which Elizabeth Pepys recommended, to the consternation of her husband.[4] William's long-time rival Edward Hyde, earl of Clarendon, fell from power in part by failing to gain the support of "old Cavaliers" like William. William's political career was largely over, however, and he, together with Margaret, retired once more to the midlands.

As the 1670s began, Cavendish was nearing fifty and William was almost eighty. Thus, it might have been expected that she would survive to inherit and enjoy her enhanced jointures. However, she unexpectedly died in December of 1673. In January of 1674, she was given a large state funeral, with a procession through London and burial in Westminster Abbey.

Literary Reputation

Over the last three hundred and fifty years, Margaret Cavendish and her writing have elicited a variety of reactions. In a letter composed in response to a personal encounter with Cavendish, Mary Evelyn, wife to another seventeenth-century diarist, pronounced her hostess, as "rambling as her books, aiming at science, difficulties, high notions, terminating commonly in nonsense, oaths, and obscenity." Mary Evelyn's view was colored, perhaps, by worries that her husband was paying too much attention to Cavendish, but Mary's criticism is tame when compared to that associated

---

1 April 11 and May 1, *The Diary of Samuel Pepys*, ed. Latham and Matthews, vol. 8 (London: Bell and Sons, 1974) 163, 164, 196.

2 See Lisa Sarasohn, "A Science Turned Upside Down: Feminism and the Natural Philosophy of Margaret Cavendish," *Huntington Library Quarterly* 47 (Autumn 1984): 299–307. For Pepys's view, see Latham and Matthews, eds., vol. 8, 243.

3 Evelyn both ridicules and is awestruck by Cavendish in a poem quoted in part by Grant, 24–26.

4 Latham and Matthews, eds., vol. 9, 123.

with John Stansby.[1] Stansby, whose poem on Cavendish is in the style of Restoration manuscript satire, includes a report from a lower-class man who brands her "an atheist" as well as a "whore."[2] This poem, though often cited by those who study Cavendish, is an anomaly. At the same time, Cavendish was offered sincere as well as cloying praise by many learned men, as may be seen in a volume of letters compiled by her husband after her death.[3] For most people, however, she was a harmless eccentric, who might be admired for having written such a detailed account of her husband's war years. In the eighteenth century, anthologists of women's writing tended to trivialize and sentimentalize both the woman and the writing. George Ballard, the most important anthologist of the time, chose poems that characterize Cavendish as a creature of moods, who was given to creating delicate verses about fairy folk.[4] Cavendish did, indeed, write about melancholic moods and fairies, but those poems do not begin to tell the whole story of her life or her writing. The earlier portions of the nineteenth century saw little change in Cavendish's reputation, though for Charles Lamb, Cavendish was delightfully odd, "the thrice noble, chaste, and virtuous, — but again somewhat fantastical, and original-brain'd, generous Margaret Newcastle."[5] Later in the nineteenth century, her life of her husband, again became the focus of attention. Accordingly, she came to be viewed less as a poet and more as a biographer. At the beginning of the twentieth century, Virginia Woolf cast Cavendish as a writer with no literary self-control. Woolf gave credit to Cavendish for "passion for poetry," but her final and much quoted judgment was that "[Cavendish was] giant cucumber [that] spread itself over all the roses."[6]

1   *Diary and Correspondence of John Evelyn*, ed. William Bray, vol. 4 (London: J.M. Dent, n.d.) 8 and 9. On the evening to which this quotation seems to refer, John gave her cause to feel anxious. He provides the relevant evidence himself: "To London; dined with the Duke of Newcastle, and sat discoursing with her Grace in her bed-chamber after dinner, till my Lord Marquis of Dorchester with other company came in, when I went away" ([May 8, 1667], *Diary of John Evelyn*, ed. William Bray, vol. 2 [London: Everyman, 1907] 25). After her visit to the Royal Society on May 30, 1667, John walked Margaret to her coach. John, more notoriously, developed a serious and time-consuming Platonic friendship with the young Margaret Blagg. Women other than his wife seem to have been an important part of his life.

2   Grant, 199.

3   *A Collection of Letters and Poems* (London, 1678).

4   *Female Poets of Great Britain*, ed. Frederick Rowton (Detroit: Wayne State UP, 1981) 79–82.

5   *Essays of Elia* (New York: J.M. Dent, 1906) 89.

6   *A Room of One's Own* (London: Hogarth, 1929) 65.

Although some scholars today would agree with Woolf's view that Cavendish lacked discipline, since about 1990 Cavendish has come to be appreciated as a writer of intelligence and insight. Her utopian novel, *The Blazing World*, is widely read and discussed. Her scientific thought provides puzzles for those who study early science, and certain portions of her fiction, "The Contract" and "Assaulted and Pursued Chastity," from *Nature's Pictures* are frequently studied. Much of this interest derives from what has been called "archeological" work with early women writers, that is, a commitment by a good many scholars to rereading and even rescuing women authors long dismissed as having little importance. There is, in particular, an increased interest in the nature of early fiction that is evidenced in books like Paul Hunter's *Before Novels*. Aphra Behn, Jane Barker, and Eliza Haywood, as well as Cavendish, are all receiving renewed attention as writers of narrative. In any event, it is most important to remember that *Sociable Letters* is a literary "olio" rather than a work of some other kind.

Margaret Cavendish: A Brief Chronology

1561	Francis Bacon born.
c. 1573	Thomas Lucas, father to Margaret Cavendish is born. Thomas was the son of Sir Thomas Lucas, with whom he is sometimes confused.
1586	*English Secretary* by Angel Day published.
1593	Baptism of William Cavendish, later husband to Margaret. William was the son of Charles Cavendish and Elizabeth Ogle.
1597	Thomas Lucas kills Sir William Brooke, a favorite of Queen Elizabeth, in a duel and goes into exile to escape being tried for murder. Elizabeth Leighton is carrying the child of Thomas and because of the exile cannot marry him.
1603	Death of Queen Elizabeth. Thomas Lucas pardoned by James I.
1604	Marriage of Thomas Lucas and Elizabeth Leighton.
1620	William Cavendish joins the House of Lords as the earl of Mansfield, a title he receives in lieu of an uncollectible debt.
1623	Margaret Lucas, afterwards Cavendish, born at St. John's Abbey near Colchester as the eighth and final child to Thomas Lucas and Elizabeth Leighton.
1626	Francis Bacon dies.
1627	Birth of Dorothy Osborne.
1625	Thomas Lucas dies. Death of James I and accession of Charles I.
1629	William revives his mother's title and becomes baron Ogle.
1630s	Christiana Cavendish, countess of Devonshire, corresponds with William Cavendish about his bid to become governor to Charles, prince of Wales.
1632, 3	William Cavendish stages two lavish entertainments in honor of Charles I, scripts written by Ben Jonson.
1640	Aphra Behn born at about this year.
1642	Home of Margaret Lucas plundered in the Stour Valley Riots. Beginning of the English Civil Wars.
1643	Margaret Lucas goes to Oxford to live with her sister Catherine Pye, later joins the court of Queen Henrietta Maria. Death of Elizabeth Cavendish, first wife to William. William becomes marquis of Newcastle.
1644	William Cavendish defeated by Oliver Cromwell at the Battle of Marston Moor, takes up residence in Hamburg. Sir John

Lucas, brother to Margaret, enters House of Lords as baron Lucas of Shenfield.

1645   William Cavendish meets Margaret Lucas in Paris (St. Germain) at the court of Henrietta Maria. Margaret writes love letters to William and he responds with poetry. Margaret and William marry in December.

1646   Margaret and William reside first in Rotterdam and then in Antwerp. Antwerp home once belonged to the painter Peter Paul Rubens.

1647   Death of Elizabeth Lucas, mother to Margaret Cavendish.

1648   Sir Charles Lucas, brother to Margaret Cavendish, executed after the Battle of Colchester. Family tombs violated by Parliamentary troops.

1649   Charles I executed. Publication of two plays by William, *The Country Captain* and *The Variety*.

1650   James Howell's collection of letters, *Epistolae Ho-Elianae*, published.

1651   Margaret Cavendish travels with William's younger brother, Sir Charles, to London to meet with the Parliamentary committee for compounding. Request for financial support from husband's sequestered estates are denied.

1652   Dorothy Osborne begins correspondence with William Temple.

1653   First books by Margaret Cavendish, *Poems and Fancies* and *Philosophical Fancies*, appear. Margaret returns to Antwerp.

1654   Sir Charles Cavendish dies.

1655   *World's Olio*, by Margaret Cavendish, appears.

1656   *Nature's Pictures* appears. Includes autobiographical piece, "A True Relation."

1657   William given title of prince while on the Continent. Margaret by the same token becomes princess.

1658   Death of Oliver Cromwell. Ball given by Margaret and William for Charles I in Antwerp.

1659   William's son Charles, earl of Mansfield, dies. Elizabeth Cavendish Egerton writes to Jane Cavendish Cheyne about the new heir, Henry.

1660   Restoration of Charles I. Staging of *The King's Entertainment* (probably by William) and *The Lotterie* (probably by Margaret) for Charles I in London. Cavendishes in residence first at Clerkenwell in London, afterwards at Welbeck and Bolsover in Nottinghamshire.

1662   *Orations* and *Plays* by Margaret Cavendish published.

1664   *Sociable Letters*, *Philosophical Letters*, and the second edition of *Poems and Fancies* published.

1665   William and Margaret become duke and duchess of Newcastle.

1666   *Observations upon Experimental Philosophy* published. Plague year, great fire of London.

1667   Margaret and William spend the spring in London. William's play *The Humorous Lovers* produced and mistakenly attributed to Margaret by Samuel Pepys. Margaret visits the Royal Society and publishes her *Life* of William, which is recommended by Elizabeth Pepys. Clarendon falls from power. Milton's *Paradise Lost* published.

1668   *Plays Never Before Published*, *The Blazing World* and the second edition of *Poems and Fancies* printed.

1670   Aphra Behn begins to write plays during the 1670s and meets John Hoyle, to whom she writes love letters.

1671   Confession by John Booth of his part in a conspiracy concocted by Andrew Clayton to brand Margaret an adulteress. Second edition of *Nature's Pictures* printed without "A True Relation." Second edition of *The World's Olio*.

1673   Margaret Cavendish dies unexpectedly in December.

1674   Body of Margaret Cavendish entombed in Westminster Abbey after elaborate funeral procession in London.

1676   *Letters and Poems* in honor of Margaret Cavendish published by William. William dies.

1689   Death of Aphra Behn.

1695   Death of Dorothy Osborne.

A Note on the Text

Sociable Letters was transcribed from University Microfilms copy. Original spelling and punctuation have been retained. Use of italics has been modernized except in the case of poetry. The numbering of letters has been changed to Arabic.

The letters from Margaret Lucas to William Cavendish and his poems in reply were transcribed from Grant's *The Phanseys of William Cavendish* (London: Nonesuch, 1956) and checked against Battagelli's *Margaret Cavendish and the Exiles of the Mind* (Lexington: UP of Kentucky, 1998). Spelling and punctuation are modernized, with the exception of contractions and contracted forms like "exprest." "Then," where used for "than," is modernized.

The letter from Elizabeth Cavendish Egerton was transcribed from Huntington Library manuscript MS EL 8048. Spelling and punctuation are modernized and quotation marks added where appropriate. Transcription published by the kind permission of the Huntington Library.

The letters from Christiana, Countess of Devonshire, were transcribed from the University of Nottingham Libraries, Portland Papers as follows: letter 1 from Pw 1. 56; letter 2 from Pw 1. 62; letter 3, Pw 1. 63. Spelling and punctuation have modernized quotation marks added where appropriate.

Here the *i* and *j*, as well as the *u* and *v* have been regularized. The long *s* is represented by the short *s*.

The letters written by Dorothy Osborne were transcribed from Edward Abbot Parry's edition, *Letters from Dorothy Osborne to Sir William Temple, 1652–54* (London: Sherratt and Hughes, 1903). They have been modernized for punctuation here.

The letters from Aphra Behn were transcribed from *The Histories and Novels of the Late Ingenious Mrs. Aphra Behn, Together with the Life and Memoirs of Mrs. Behn, Written by One of the Fair Sex* (London: Printed for S. Briscoe, Covent-Garden, 1696), Huntington Library Rare Book 58250. Spelling and punctuation have been modernized.

Angel Day's letters were transcribed from *The English Secretorie* (London: Thomas Snodham, n.d.), Huntington Library 600338. Checked against Huntington 435332. Spelling and punctuation have been modernized.

Francis Bacon's "Of Marriage and the Single Life" was transcribed from *The Essays or Counsels Civil and Moral and Wisdom of the Ancients* (London, William Pickering, 1845). Punctuation has been modernized.

Studious She is and all Alone,
Most visitants, when She has none,
Her Library on which She looks
It is her Head her Thoughts her Books.
Scorninge dead Ashes without fire
For her owne Flames doe her Inspire.

Cavendish at her writing table.

[Reprinted by permission of the Huntington Library.]

SOCIABLE LETTERS

TO THE LADY

MARCHIONESS

OF

NEWCASTLE

ON HER BOOK OF

EPISTLES.

When all Epistles you have read, and seek,
Who write in Latin, English, French, or Greek,
Such Wolful things, as they are only fit
To stop Mustard-pots, to this Ladie's Wit,
Nay, were they all Alive, I swear, I think,
They'd Burn their Books, and Throw away their Ink,
Make Pick-Tooths of their Pens, and for their Paper,
Only to light Tobacco, and each Taper;
Y'have Spoil'd Commerce, Intelligencers, Trade,
None now dares write a Letter, so Afraid
To be thought Fools, and is the Carriers Curse,
To find his Empty Budget, and Lank Purse,
Nay all the Post-house's Ruin'd, and will Complain,
From their Vast Gettings now they have no Gain;
Or Gilded Nutmegs,[1] or each Tavern-token,
Nick'd Sticks for Merchants, Why would you Undo
Your self at once thus and the whole World Too?
After my Hearty Commendations, This,
The Style of States-men still Applauded is;
Your Fames of Wit, this Age may think a Sin,
A Proclamation then may call it in.

                                    W. Newcastle

---

1   Nutmegs covered with saffron. See William Shakespeare, *Love's Labours Lost*, ed. H.C. Hart,
    3rd ed (London: Methuen, 1930) 167.

TO HIS EXCELLENCY

THE LORD

MARQUIS

OF

NEWCASTLE.

My Lord,

It may be said to me, as one said to a Lady, Work Lady Work, let writing Books alone,[1] For surely Wiser Women ne'r writ one; But your Lordship never bid me to Work, nor leave Writing, except when you would perswade me to spare so much time from my Study as to take to the Air for my Health; the truth is, My Lord, I cannot Work, I mean such Works as Ladies use to pass their Time withall, and if I could, the Materials of such Works would cost more than the Work would be worth, besides all the Time and Pains bestow'd upon it. You may ask me, what Works I mean; I answer, Needle-works, Spinning-works, Preserving-works, as also Baking, and Cooking-works, as making Cakes, Pyes, Puddings, and the like, all which I am Ignorant of; and as I am Ignorant in these Imployments, so I am Ignorant in Gaming, Dancing, and Revelling; But yet, I must ask you leave to say, that I am not a Dunce in all Imployments, for I Understand the Keeping of Sheep, and Ordering of a grange, indifferently well, although I do not Busie my self much with it, by reason my Scribling takes away the most part of my Time. Perchance some may say, that if my Understanding be most of Sheep and a Grange, it is a Beastly Understanding; My answer is, I wish Men were as Harmless as most Beasts are, then surely the World would be more Quiet and Happy than it is, for then there would not be such Pride, Vanity, Ambition, Covetousness, Faction, Treachery, and Treason, as is now; Indeed one might very well say in his Prayers to God, O Lord God, I do beseech thee of thy infinite Mercy, to make Man so, and order his Mind, Thoughts, Passions, and Appetites, like Beasts, that they may be Temperate, Sociable, Laborious, Patient, Prudent, Provident, Brotherly-loving and Neighbourly-kind, all which Beasts are, but most Men not. But leaving most Men to Beasts, I

---

1   An allusion to Lord Denny's poem on Lady Mary Wroth. For a transcription of Denny's poem, see *The Poems of Lady Mary Wroth*, 33–34.

return to your Lordship, who is one of the Best of men, whom God hath fill'd with Heroick Fortitude, Noble Generosity, Poetical Wit, Moral Honesty, Natural Love, Neighbourly-kindness, Great Patience, Loyal Duty, and Celestial Piety, and I pray God as Zealously and Earnestly to Bless you with perfect Health and Long Life, as becomes

Your Lordships
Honest Wife and
Humble Servant
M. Newcastle.

TO ALL

PROFESSORS

OF

LEARNING AND ART.

MOST FAMOUSLY-LEARNED,[1]

I Wish I could Write so Wisely, Wittily, Eloquently and Methodically, as might be Worthy of your Perusal; but if any of your Noble Profession should Humble themselves so Low as to Read my Works, or part of them, I pray Consider my Sex and Bredding, and they will fully Excuse those Faults which must Unavoidably be found in my Works. But although I have no Learning, yet give me leave to Admire it, and to wish I were one of your Society, for certainly, were I Empress of the World, I would Advance those that have most Learning and Witt, by which I believe the Earth would rather be an Heaven, since both Men and government would be as Celestial, for I am Confident that Wisdom, and for the most part Virtue is Inherent in those that are Masters of Learning, and Indued with Wit; And to this sort of Persons I do Offer my Works, although to be Condemned on the Altar of their Censure, and rest Satisfied with the Honour that they thought them Worthy to be Judged. Thus, whether my Works Live or Dye, I am Devoted to be

Your Servant M.N.

---

1   Cavendish sent presentation copies of many of her books to the various colleges at Oxford and Cambridge as well as to important scholars in England and Europe.

THE

PREFACE.

Noble Readers,

I Hope you will not make the Mistake of a Word a Crime in my Wit, as some former Readers have done, for in my Poems they found Fault that the Number was not Just, nor every Line Matched with a Perfect Rime; But I can answer for that Book, that there be but some such Errors in it, and those as were by Chance; besides, in some Languages as Latin and Greek, which are accounted the Chief, they regard not Rimes in their Poems, but only an Exact number of Feet and Measures;[1] however Rimes and Numbers are only as the Garments, and not as the Body of Wit; but I have been more Exact in my other Book call'd *Natural Descriptions,*[2] wherein most Verses are Just both for Number and Rimes. As for my Work, *The World's Olio,* they may say some Words are not Exactly Placed, which I confess to be very likely, and not only in that, but in all the rest of my Works there may be such Errors, for I was not Bred in an University, or a Free-School to Learn the Art of Words; neither do I take it for a Disparagemente of my Works, to have the Forms, Terms, Words, Numbers, or Rhymes found Fault with, so they do not find Fault with the Variety of the Subjects, or the Sense and Reason, Wit, and Fancy, for I leave the Formal, or Wordative part to Fools, and the Material or Sensitive part to Wise men. Concerning my *Philosophical Opinions,* some did say I was too Obscure, and not Plain Enough for their Understanding; I must confess, I writ that Book at first at the same time when I wrote my *Poems,* but to my Reason it was as Plain as I could write it, and if some Readers could not Understand it, I am not Nature to give them Witt or Understanding; yet have I since not only Over-viewed, and Reformed that Book, but made a great Addition to it, so that I believe I have now so clearly Declared my Sense and Meaning therein, that those which Understand it not must not only be Irrational, but Insensible Creatures. As for my Book of *Playes,* some find Fault they are not made up Exactly, nor the Scenes placed Justly, as also I have not in some Playes caused all the Actors to be of an Acquaintance, but this same Fault they find, I have Express'd in one of the Epistles before that Book, which they fling back upon my Work. As for my *Orations,* I have heard, that some

---

1   Milton attacked the use of rhyme in a preface to *Paradise Lost* some three years later.

2   *Nature's Pictures* (1656). Books mentioned below are as follows: *The World's Olio* (1655); *Philosophical and Physical Opinions* (1655); *Poems* (1653); *Plays* (1662).

do Censure me for speaking too Freely, and Patronizing Vice too much,[1] but I would have them not be too Rash in Judging, but to Consider, first, whether there be a sufficient Reason that may move them to give such a Censure, for truly I am as much an Enemy to Vice as I am a Friend to Virtue, & do Persecute Vice with as perfect an Hatred, as I do Pursue Virtue with an Intire, and Pure Love, which is Sufficiently Known to those that Know me; and therefore, it is not out of Love to Vice that I plead for it, but only to Exercise my Fancy, for surely the Wisest, and Eloquentest Orators, have not been Ashamed to Defend Vices upon such Accounts, and why may not I do the like? for my Orations for the most part are Declamations, wherein I speak *Pro* and *Con*, and Determine nothing; and as for that Part which contains several Pleadings, it is Fit and Lawful that both Parties should bring in their Arguments as well as they can, to make their Cases Good; but I matter not their Censure, for it would be an Endless Trouble to me, to Answer every ones Foolish Exception; an Horse of a Noble Spirit Slights the Brawling of a Petty Cur, and so do I. As for the Present Book of Letters, I know not as yet what Asperions they will lay upon it, but I fear the'l say, they are not written in a Mode-style, that is in a Complementing, and Romantical way, with High Words, and Mystical Expressions, as most of our Modern Letter-writers use to do; But, Noble Readers, I do not intend to Present you here with Long Complements in Short Letters; but with Short Descriptions in Long Letters; the truth is, they are rather Scenes than Letters, for I have Endeavoured under the Cover of Letters to Express the Humors of Mankind, and the Actions of a Man's Life by the Correspondence of two Ladies, living at some Short Distance from each other, which make it not only their Chief Delight and Pastime, but their Tye in Friendship, to Discourse by Letters, as they would do if they were Personally together, so that these Letters are an Imitation of a Personal Visitation and Conversation, which I think is Better (I am sure more Profitable) than those Conversations that are an Imitation of Romantical Letters, which are but Empty Words, and Vain Complements. But the Reason why I have set them forth in the Form of Letters, and not of Playes, is first that I have put forth Twenty Plays already, which number I thought to be Sufficient, next, I saw that Variety of Forms did Please the Readers

---

1   Perhaps in response to such criticism, Cavendish removed from the second edition of *Nature's Pictures* a passage that placed several notorious Biblical figures happily in Elysium. The passage included observations concerning Lot's incest with his two daughters, about which Cavendish writes: "Lot and his Daughters were more merrily disposed than the rest: I asked the reason; and it was answered me, that as they fell in love in the World, so they should there continue for ever." Quoted from *RWO, Renaissance Women Online*.

best, and that lastly they would be more taken with the Brevity of Letters, than the Formality of Scenes, and whole Playes, whose Parts and Plots cannot be Understood till the whole Play be Read over, whereas a Short Letter will give a Full Satisfaction of what they Read. And thus I thought this to be the Best Way or Form to put this Work into, which if you Approve of, I have my Reward.

UPON HER

EXCELLENCY

THE

AUTHORESS.

This Lady only to her self she Writes
And all her Letters to her self Indites;
For in her self so many Creatures be,
Like many Commonwealths, yet all Agree.
Man's Head's a World, where Thoughts are Born and Bred,
And Reason's Emperour in every Head;
But in all Heads doth not a Caesar Reign,
A Wise Augustus hath not every Brain,
And Reason in some Brains from Rule's put out
By Mad, Rebellious Thoughts, and Factions Rout;
And Great Disorder in such Brains will be,
Not any Thought with Reason will Agree;
But in her Brain doth Reason Govern well,
Not any Thought 'gainst Reason doth Rebell,
But doth Obey what Reason doth Command,
When 'tis his Will, doth Travel Sea and Land,
As some do Travel out to Kingdomes far,
And Guided are by Observation's Star,
They bring Intelligence from every State,
Their Peace, their Wars, their Factions, and their Hate,
And into every City Travel free,
Relate their Customs, Trafficks, Policy,
Observe each Magistrate, their Formal Face,
And what Authority they bear, or Place,
Whether they Covetously do Extort,
Or are Ambitious, giving Bribes at Court,
To Raise to Places, or to Hide their Crime,
For thus Men do to Wealth and Office Clime,
And some into the Churches go to see
Who Kneels in Pray'r, or comes for Company,
Implores her Favour, and makes his Complaint
Be Known, Or who doth turn her eyes about,

To shew her Face, or see, a Lover out;
And some to Balls, and Masks, and Playes do go,
And some within Kings Courts do get a Place,
Observe the Grandeur, and the Courtly Grace,
The Ceremony and Splendor of a court,
Their Playes, Balls, Masks, and every several Sport,
And all their Amorous Courtships which they make
And how the Ladies do each Courtship take,
The Antick Postures of the Younger Race,
Their Mimick Gestures, and Affected Pace,
Their Amorous Smiles, and Glancing Wanton Eyes,
All which do Noble Souls Hate and Despise;
And some amongst the Privy-Counsel get,
Where round a Table Prince and Nobles sit,
Hear what they say, Observe their Cross Debates,
And mark which speakes through Faction, which through Hates
Some Lord that is in Favour more than he,
For in State Matters seldom they Agree.
And thus Her thoughts, the Creatures of her Mind,
Do Travel through the World amongst Mankind,
And then Return, and to the Mind do bring
All the Relations of each several thing;
And Observation Guides them back again
To Reason, their Great King, that's in the Brain;
Then Contemplation calls the Senses straight,
Which Ready are, and Diligently Wait
Commanding Two these Letters for to Write,
Touch in the Hand, as also the Eye-sight,
These Two the Soul's Clerks are which do Inscribe,
And Write all Truly down, having no Bribe.

TO THE

CENSORIOUS

READER.

Reader, you'l think, perchance, my Wit in Fault,
Like Meat that's too much Brin'd, and Over-salt,
But better Poets far than I have been,
Have written Sharper, and with Greater Splene,
Yet they have much been Prais'd for writing so,
And on Advancing Stigues[1] of Fame do go;
But my Poor Writings they no Malace know,
Nor on a Crabbed Nature did they Grow;
I to Particulars give no Abuse,
My Wit Indites for Profitable Use,
That Men may see their Follies, and their Crimes,
Their Errours, Vanities, and Idle Times,
Not that I think they do not Know them well,
But lest they should Forget, Im' Bold to tell,
For to Remember them, like those that Ride,
Not thinking on their Way, may chance to Slide,
Or Fall into a Ditch, so I for Fear
Bid them take Heed, Beware, and have a Care,
For there are Stumps of Trees, or a Deep Pit,
Or Dangerous Passages where Thieves do sit
And Wait, or Ravenous Beasts do lye for Prey,
Of such a Lane where's Foul and Dirty Way
And so of Waters, and each Dangerous place:
But I write not to any mans Disgrace;
Then Censure not my Satyr wit for Crime
Nor putting this Epistle into Rime.

---

1   Sticks, i.e., legs (?).

SOCIABLE

LETTERS.

LETTER 1

Madam,

You were pleas'd to desire, that, since we cannot converse Personally, we should converse by Letters, so as if we were speaking to each other, discoursing our Opinions, discovering our Designs, asking and giving each other Advice, also telling the several Accidents, and several Imployments of our home-affairs, and what visits we receive, or entertainments we make, and whom we visit, and how we are entertaind, what discourses we have in our gossiping-meetings, and what reports we hear of publick affairs, and of particular Persons, and the like; so that our Letters may present our personal meetings and associatings. Truly, Madam, I take so much delight in your wise, witty, and virtuous Conversation, as I could not pass my life more pleasing and delightfully; wherefore I am never better pleased, than when I am reading your Letters, and when I am writing Letters to you; for my mind and thoughts are all that while in your Company: the truth is, my mind and thoughts live alwayes with you, although my person is at distance from you; insomuch, as, if Souls die not as Bodies do, my Soul will attend you when my Body lies in the grave; and when we are both dead, we may hope to have a Conversation of Souls, where yours and mine will be doubly united, first in Life, and then in Death, in which I shall eternally be,

Madam,
Your faithful Friend and humble Servant.

LETTER 2

Madam,

The Lady C.E. ought not to be reproved for grieving for the loss of her Beauty, for Beauty is the light of our Sex, which is Eclips'd in Middle age, and Benighted in Old age, where-in our Sex sits in Melancholy Darkness, and the remembrance of Beauty past, is as a displeasing Dream. The truth is, a young beautiful face is a Friend, when as an old withered face is an Enemy, the one causes Love, the other Aversion: yet I am not of Mrs. U.R's. humour, which had rather dye before her Beauty, than that her

Beauty should die before her: for I had rather live with wrinkles, than die with youth; and had rather my face cloth'd with Time's sad mourning than with Death's white hue; and surely it were better to follow the shadow of Beauty, than that Beauty should go with the Corps to the Grave; and I believe that Mrs. U.R. would do, as the tale is of a woman, that did wish, and pray she might die before her Husband, but when Death came, she intreated him to spare her, and take her Husband; so that she would rather live without him, than die for him. But leaving this sad discourse of Age, Wrinkles, Run and Death, I rest,

> Madam,
> Your very faithful Friend and humble Servant.

LETTER 3

Madam,

I Do not wonder, there are great factions between the three families C.Y.O. by reason they have no business, or imployment to busie their heads about, and their servants & followers have as little to do, which makes them censure, backbite, and envy each other; for Idleness and Poverty are the creators of Faction, and Pride and Ambition the disturbers of Peace. Wherefore Idleness should be banish'd out of every family, which will also be a means to be rid of Poverty, for Industry is the way to thrive: Besides, when men have something to do, they will have the less time to talk; for many words from discontented persons increase hate, and make dissentions: the truth is, words for the most part make more discord than union, and more enemies than friends; wherefore Silence is more commendable than much Speaking, for the liberty of the tongue doth rather express men's follies, than make known their wit; neither do many words argue much Judgement; but as the old Saying is, The greatest talkers are the least actors, they being more apt to speak spitefully, than to act mischievously; another Saying is, That musing men rather study to do evil, than contemplate on good; But I am not of that opinion, for if men would think more, and speak less, the world of mankind would be more honest and wiser than they are, for Thoughts beget Consideration, Consideration begets Judgement, Judgement begets Discretion, Discretion begets Temperance, and Temperance begets Peace in the Mind, and Health in the Body, for when men want Temperance, they are subject to Insatiable Appetites, unruly Passions, and wandring Desires, which causes Covetousness and Ambition, and these cause Envy and Hate, which makes Faction and

Strife, which Strife I leave to Busie Natures, Restless Minds, Vain Humours, and Idle Fools, and rest,

> Madam,
> Your faithful Friend and Servant.

LETTER 4

Madam,

The other day was here the Lady J.O. to see me, and her three Daughters, which are call'd the three Graces, the one is Black, the other Brown, the third White, and all different coloured beauties; also they are of different features, statures and shapes, yet all three so equally handsom, that neither Judgment nor Reason can prefer one before another: Also their behaviours are different; the one is Majestical, the other Gay and Aery, and the third Meek and Bashful; yet all three graceful, sweet and becoming: Also their Wits are different; the one Propounds well, the other Argues well, the third Resolves well; all which make a harmony in discourse. These three Ladies are resolv'd never to marry, which makes many sad Lovers; but whilst they were here, in comes the Lord S.C. and discoursing with them, at last he asks them, whether they were seriously resolv'd never to marry? they answered, they were resolv'd never to marry. But, Ladies, said he, Consider, Time wears out Youth, and fades Beauty, and then you will not be the three young fair Graces; You say true, my Lord, answer'd one of them, but when we leave to be the young fair Graces, we shall then be the old wise Sibyls. By this answer you may perceive, that when our Sex cannot pretend to be Fair, they will pretend to be Wise; but it matters not what we pretend to, if we be really Virtuous, which I wish all our Sex may be, and rest,

> Madam,
> Your very faithful Friend and Servant.

LETTER 5

Madam,

In my opinion the marriage between Sir A.G. and Mrs. J.S. is no ways agreable, wherefore not probable to be bless'd with a happy union, though she is likelyer to be the happier of the two; for 'tis better to have an old doting fool, than a wanton young filly; but he will be very unhappy through

Jealousie, what with his Dotage, and her Freedom, which will be like fire and oyl, to set his mind on a flame, and burn out the lamp of his life; Truly, I did wonder, when I heard they were married, knowing her nature and his humour, for she loves young masculine Company, and he loves onely a young female Companion; so that he cannot enjoy her to himself, unless she barr her self from all other men for his sake, which I believe she will not do, for she will not bury her Beauty, nor put her Wit to silence for the sake of her Husband; for, if I be not mistaken, she will love a young Servant better than an old Husband; nay, if her Husband were young, she would prefer variety of Servants, before a single Husband, insomuch, that if she had been made when there was but One man, as Adam, she would have done like her Grand mother Eve, as to have been courted by the Devil, and would betray her Husband for the Devil's sake, rather than want a Lover. But leaving the discourse of Jealousie, Age, Courtship, and Devils, I rest,

Madam,
Your very faithful Fr. & S.

LETTER 6

Madam,

In your last Letter you sent me word, that Sir F.O. was retir'd to write his own Life, for he saies, he knows no reason, but he may write his own life as well as Guzman;[1] and since you desire my opinion of his intended work, I can onely say, that his Life for anything I know to the contrary, hath been as evil as Guzman's, but whether his Wit be as good as Guzman's, I know not, yet I doubt the worst, and to write an Evil life without Wit, will be but a dull and tedious Story, indeed so tedious and dull, as I believe none will take the pains to read it, unless he himself read of himself: but it is to be hoped, that he will be tir'd of himself, and so desist from his self Story. And if he do write his own Life, it will be as a masking Dolphin,[2] or such like thing, where the outside is painted past-board or canvas, and the inside stuff'd with shreds of paper, or dirty raggs, scrap'd from dunghils: and if he set his Picture before,

---

1 Guzman is the central character of a picaresque novel translated by James Mabbe, *The Rogue: Or the Life of Guzman de Alfarache: Written in Spanish by Matheo Aleman* (1622).

2 There may be an allusion here to the famous masking dolphin that was presented before Queen Elizabeth at Kenilworth in 1575. "The Dolphyn was conveyed upon a boate, so that the owers seemed to be his finnes" (John Nichols, *The Progresses, and Public Processions of Queen Elizabeth*, vol. 1 [London, 1788] 68).

as a Frontispiece to his Book, it will be like an ill-favour'd masking Vizzard. But if he have any Friends, surely they will perswade him to imploy his time about something else; but some are so unhappy, as they have nothing to imploy Time with; they can waste Time, but not imploy Time; and as they waste Time, so Time wasts them.[1] There's a saying, That men are born to live, and live to dye; but I think some are onely born to dye, and not to live; for they make small use of life, and life makes small use of them; so that in effect they were ready for the Grave, as soon as they came forth from the Womb. Wherefore if Sir F.O. go forward with his work, he will dig his Grave through the story of his Life, and his Soul-less Wit will be buried therein. But leaving his dead Wit to his paper Coffin, and his unprofitable Labours to his black mourning Ink, I rest,

Madam,
Your faithful Fr. and S.

LETTER 7

Madam,
I am sorry to hear, Wit is so little known and understood, that Sir W.T. should be thought Mad, because he hath more Wit than other men; indeed Wit should alwayes converse with Wit, and Fools with Fools; for Wit and Fools can never agree, they understand not one another; Wit flies beyond a Fools conceit or understanding, for Wit is like an Eagle, it hath a strong wing, and flies high and far, and when it doth descend, it knocks a Fool on the head, as an Eagle doth a Dotril,[2] or a Woodcock, or such like Birds; and surely the world was never so fill'd with Fools, as it is in this age, nor hath there been greater Errours, or grosser Follies than there hath been in this age: It is not an age like Augustus Caesar's when Wisdom reign'd, and Wit flourished, which was the cause of Plenty & Peace throughout the whole world; but in this age Debauchery is taken for Wit, and Faction for Wisdom, Treachery for Policy, and drunken Quarrels for Valour: Indeed the world is so foolishly Wicked, & basely Foolish, that they are happiest who can withdraw themselves most from it: But when I say the world, I mean the world of Men, or rather the Bodies of Men, for there doth not seem to be many Rational Souls amongst them, they

---

1 Compare Shakespeare's *Richard II*, "I wasted time and now doth time waste me" (V.v).

2 The dotrel was a proverbially dimwitted bird. The male lead in Jonson's *The Devil is an Ass* is a foolish squire named Fitzdottrel.

are Soul-less men, Bodies of men that have only Senses and Appetites. But you say, every Particular complains of the world, as I do in this Letter, yet None helps to mend it. Let me tell you, Madam, it is not in the power of every Particular, nor in a number, But the Chiefest persons must mend the world; *viz.* they that govern the world, or else the world will be out at the heels. But in some ages the world is more tatter'd and torn, than in other ages; and in some ages the world is patch'd and piec'd, but seldom new and suitable; and it is oftener in a Fools-coat than in a Grave Cassock. Wherefore, leaving the motley, I rest,

> Madam,
> Your faithful Friend and Servant.

LETTER 8

Madam,

You were pleas'd to invite me unto a Ball, to divert my Melancholy Thoughts, but they are not capable of your Charity, for they are in too deep a Melancholy to be diverted; like as bodies that are starved, and almost dying for hunger, so weak as they cannot feed, at least that want strength to nourish or digest, having not life enough to re-kindle the vital fire, which want of food hath neer put out. Thus, Madam, I do not refuse your Charity, but I am not capable to receive it; Besides, my very outward appearance would rather be an Obstruction to your Mirth, than any Addition to your Pleasures, and for me, it would be very improper; for a grieved heart, weeping eyes, sad countenance, and black mourning garments, will not be suitable with dancing legs; In truth, my leaden Spirits have soder'd up my Joynts so stiff that they will not move so agilly, as is requir'd in Dancing; I am fitter to sit upon a Grave, than to tread measures on a Carpet; and there is such an Antipathy in my mind to light Aires, that they would sooner stop my Ears as Discord, than enter into my Hearing as harmony; indeed my Senses are as closed or shut from the world, and my Mind is benighted in Sorrow, insomuch as I have not one lighted thought, they are all put out with the memory of my Loss. Thus, Madam, Memory hath made an Oblivion; but though it hath buried for the present the worldly Joys of my Life, yet it hath not buried my grateful Thanks for your Favours, for which I am,

> Madam,
> Your most humble S.

LETTER 9

Madam,

In your last Letter I perceive that the Lady N.P. is an actor in some State-design, or at least would be thought so, for our Sex in this age, is ambitious to be State-Ladies, that they may be thought to be Wise Women; but let us do what we can, we shall prove our selves Fools, for Wisdom is an enemy to our Sex, or rather our Sex is an enemy to Wisdom. 'Tis true, we are full of Designs and Plots, and ready to side into Factions; but Plotting, Designing, Factions, belong nothing to Wisdom, for Wisdom never inter-meddles therein or therewith but renounces them; it is onely cheating Craft and Subtilty that are the managers thereof; and for deceiving Craft, Women are well practised therein, and most of them may be accounted Politicians; for no question but Women may, can, and oftimes do make wars, especially Civil wars; witness our late Civil war, wherein Women were great, although not good actors; for though Women cannot fight with warring arms themselves, yet they can easily inflame men's minds against the Governours and Goverments, unto which Men are too apt even without the perswasion of Women, as to make innovation through envy and emulation, in hopes of advancement in Title, Fortune and Power of which Women are as ambitious as Men; but I wish for the honour of our Sex, that Women could as easily make peace as war, though it is easier to do evil than good, for every fool can make an uproar, and a tumultuous disorder, such as the wisest can hardly settle into an order again. But Wo-men in State-affairs can do as they do with themselves, they can, and do often make themselves sick, but when they are sick, not well again: So they disorder a State, as they do their Bodies, but neither can give Peace to th'one, nor Health to th'other; but their restless Minds, and unsatiable Appetites, do many times bring Ruin to the one, and Death to the other; for Temperance and Quietness are strangers to our Sex. But leaving the Lady N.P. to her pretty Designs, and weak Plots, I rest,

Madam,
Your very faithful Fr. and S.

LETTER 10

Madam,

In your last Letter you were pleased to tell me for news, that C.U. was newly made a Lord; truly he deserves it, and if his Title were to be measur'd, it would be far short of his Merit, but it is a greater honour to have more Merit than Title, than to have more Title than Merit. Indeed Title ought to be but as a Sign; as the King's Arms or Picture to a Shop of rich Merchandise; so Title should be but to have it known there is a worhty Person, who is full of Noble Qualities, Moral Virtues, Sweet Graces, Divine Influences, Learned Sciences, Wise Counsels, and the like, which ought to be commenced and traffick'd within the world, for their own and others good, benefit and pleasure; for the riches of the Mind must do as other riches, which is to disperse about, not to lie unprofitably hid, and horded up from all use; but they ought to be as Staple Commodities, and not as Trifles of Vanity, which wear out, or are laid by, as mens humours change, and are more for fashion than benefit. But some men seem to be richer than they are, and some to be poorer than they are; they that seem richer than they are, lay all in their outward Shops, and those that seem poorer than they are, lay all in their inward Ware-houses; Those that lay all in their outward Shops are vain-glorious Persons, those that lay all in their inward Ware-houses are magnanimous Persons; But womens Minds or Souls are like Shops of small-wares, wherein some have pretty toyes, but nothing of any great value, I imagine you will chide me for this opinion, and I should deserve to be chidden, if all Women were like to you; but you are but one, and I speak of Women, not of One woman; and thus I am neither injurious to You, nor partial to our Sex; but I wish with all my heart our whole Sex were like to you, so I might hope to be one of your Copies, and though you are an example not to be pattern'd, yet I will endeavour to imitate you as much as I can, by which I may be so much the more worthy to be

> Your Ladiships
> Humble Servant.

LETTER 11

Madam,

I Hear the Lady B.A. and the Lady C.D. are gone to be Courtiers, but I believe they will neither agree with the Court, nor the Court with them; for the one hath been bred fitter for a Nunnery than a Court, and the other bred to good huswifry, fitter for the Countrey than a Court; the truth is, Sparing is unnatural for a Courtier, and Praying is not usual for a Courtier, yet those Ladies that are Beautiful are made Saints there, and the men are their Devouts, which offer them Vows, Prayers, Praises, and sometimes Thanksgiving, and many times they are Penitents; but when the

Ladies Beauties decay, the men become Apostates. Thus you may see many of our Sex are made Saints, though they be Sinners, but they are Sainted for their Beauty, not for their Piety, for their outward Form, not for their inward Grace: Indeed they are worldly Saints, and the Court is their Heaven, and Nature their Goddess, which indues them with attractive Graces; to which I leave them, and rest,

Madam,
Your faithful Fr. and S.

LETTER 12

Madam,
I Hear the Lady D.C. makes Politick feasts and entertainments, feasting the Courtiers, and entertaining them with dancing and carding, to whom she doth Politickly lose her mony, and causes her husband to lend them mony out of a Policy, and 'tis likely she will Politickly ruin her husband; for I believe she is more Politick with her husband than with the Courtiers, and they more Politick with her than her husband. But many wives will perswade their husbands to invite company, pretending some Designs, whenas their chief Design is, to have Company; and they will be very free and frolick with their guests, making their husbands believe they are so onely to compass, or bring their Designs to pass; so as they make their husbands Pimps to Cuckold themselves, who think their wives wise women, both in their Counsels and Actions: Such, and the like inventions and excuses wives have to be in company; and it is to be observed, that those wives that love freedom and company, will be so very kind to their husbands when they bring home company, or are with such company as they like, that not onely strangers, but their husbands think them for that time the best wives in the world; whenas being all alone, to their husbands, the Furies are no more turbulent, nor worse nature'd than they; But in much company all is as their husbands please, whether to dance or play; upon which kind words and humble behaviour, their husbands are so ravish'd with joy, as then it is what their wives please; nay, they intreat their wives to please themselves, and approve of all they say or do. Other wives, to get, or be in company, will insinuatingly flatter, and perswade their husbands, that they are the wisest, or wittiest men in the world, and that there is none that knows how to entertain company but he; that for their own parts they hate much company, as nothing so tedious and troublesome, and onely take delight to see their husbands entertain guests,

and love to hear them discourse with strangers, their wit and behaviour being so far above others; and to encourage their husbands, or to flatter them the more, they will repeat their Discourses when they are alone together, as how well such or such a question was resolv'd, or how wittily such or such a one was answere'd, and the like; whereupon the husband often invites company, onely for his wife to hear his supreme Wit, wise Sentences, and to see his grave Entertainments, whenas his wife laughs in her mind to hear what a Fool, and to see what a formal Coxcomb, and how self-conceited he is. Thus most husbands, are either deluded with Politick wives, or forced to obey, or humour their Turbulent and Peevish wives, or deceived by their Insinuating and Flattering wives, to betray themselves. But fearing I should divulge too much of the nature of our Sex, I stop here, and rest,

Madam,
Your faithful Fr. & S.

LETTER 13

Madam,
Most of Mrs. L.A's. discourse is of her self, indeed every one is apt to speak of himself, as being full of self-love, which makes most tongues discourse of a self-theme; but her theme, is to tell how good a Wife she will make when she is married, although the proof will be after she is married, if she can get a Husband; for I believe she wants one, and desires one, because she talks so much of a Husband, and promises so well for a Husband. Truly, it is to be observed, that all Maids love to talk of Husbands, all Widows of Suters, and all Wives of Lovers: for men may marry, nay do often marry, yet not for Love, but for Interest as for Posterity, or the like; and Suters may woo, yet not for Love, but Interest, as for Wealth, or the like; But when Amorous Lovers plead, it is for no other design, but to lie with the Woman they make their address to; and married Wives are more apt to yield than Maids or Widows, having a cloak to cover their shame or reproach, and a husband to father their children; and they are more fond of amorous Courtships than Maids or Widows, because they are more barr'd, as being bound in Wedlock's-bonds: besides, it requires more secrecy and difficulty; both which Women love. But when Maids, Widows, and Wives talk of Husbands, Suters and Lovers, they are so delighted with the Discourse, as you may perceive, not only by their Speech, being then quicker, and their Wit sharper, and

Words fluenter, but also by their Looks, their Eyes being livelier, their Countenances pleasanter, and their Behaviour gayer or wantoner, than in any other Discourse, especially if it be upon particular Persons, such as they fancy, or think they fancy them. But as for Mrs. L.A. who discourses so much of a Husband, I do verily believe, she will make a very good Wife, not that she says so, but that she hath been bred strictly and retiredly, and is of a sober, and stay'd Nature, not apt to run into Extravagancies, nor to desire variety of Company, but is Huswifly and Thrifty, and of an humble and obedient Behaviour, and not onely Attentive to good Advices, but Tractable and practive to them; all which makes her deserve a good Husband, and I wish her one with all my heart; but she must take her fortune, whether none or any, bad or good; but many a good Batchelour makes an ill Husband, and many a wild deboyst[1] Batchelour makes a good Husband; and as for Widowers, many men that were good Husbands to their first Wives, are ill Husbands to their second, or third, or fourth, or to some good, and some bad; and some that have been ill and unkind Husbands to their first Wives, are very good, & fond Husbands to their second: the like for Maids, Wives and Widows; so as none can make a wise choice in hap-hazard; for hap-hazard, as chance, barrs out Wisdom's prudence, it blindfolds Wisdom, having no sunlight into Chance; so as a Fool blinded with Ignorance, may choose in the Lottery of Husbands and Wives, as well as the Wisest, being blinded with the inconstancy of Mankind. But leaving Mrs. L.A. to the Lottery, and her Matrimonial Contemplations and Discourses, I rest,

> Madam,
> Your faithful Friend and Servant.

LETTER 14

Madam,

I am of your opinion, that Philosophers & Poets certainly should be the wisest men, for they having so deep an insight, as to pierce even into the Secrets of Nature, it should be easie for them to have an insight into the Designs, Counsels, and Actions of Men, & to forsee the Effects of Things; for they that can Judge of Hidden and Invisible Causes, and can find out their Effects, may easily Judge of Visible Actions or Businesses amongst Mankind; and there is no man that can be Wise, that hath not a deep piercing insight,

---

1 Debauched.

and a clear fore-sight to conceive and fore-see, what is, and what may probably be; for 'tis not History that makes men Wise, nor Law, nor Logick, nor
to be Learn'd in all the Sciences, but to have a Natural Ingenuity, as to conceive Rationally, to judge Solidly, to understand Perfectly, to perceive
Readily, to distinguish Clearly, to compare Rightly, to search Narrowly, to
examine Strictly, to observe Generally, to consider Seriously, of all that hath
been, is, or is not, or what may be, or cannot be; In all which Natural Philosophers, and Poets are the most Ingenious men; But of this sort of men the
world hath not many, indeed so few, as the rest of mankind doth not understand them, for they think them rather Fools than Wise men; for though
Wisemen know Fools, yet Fools know not Wise men, nay Fools do not
know Fools, but Wise men know Wise men; for how should a Fool know
a Fool, when he knows not Himself? But if any fault be in Natural Poets and
Philosophers, 'tis that they are so delighted with Transcendency, as they will
not Descend to consider, or regard the Actions and Designs of Men, no, not
the outward and ordinary works of Nature; they are of Nature's privy
Counsel, wherefore they scorn to be in Temporal or Human Counsels of
Men; they are Natural States-men, and will not be Temporal Statesmen,
neither will they attend Temporal Princes, being Nature's Chief Courtiers;
and when they chance to observe the Actions and courses of other men, they
view them with a despising smile, to see their gross Errours, ridiculous
Follies, painful Pleasures, foolish Vices and unprofitable Labours; also Natural
Philosophers and Poets are not only the Wisest, but the Happiest men; not
only in pleasing themselves with their vast Knowledge, supreme Wits, subtil
Conceptions, delightful Imaginations, and curious Fancies, having all the
Delights of the Mind, and Pleasures of Thoughts, but in that they can
Conquer their Unruly Passions, Unsatiable Appetites, and order their Minds
according to their Fortunes; they are Happy in any Condition, having their
Happiness always with them, when other men's Happiness lies alwayes without and their Unhappiness within them, their Minds are alwayes like troubled Waters, and every cross Accident is apt to make a Storm, when Poets
and Philosophers Minds are like the fixt Stars, having onely a twinkling
motion; or rather like the Sun, which keeps a constant Course, and never
alters, but yet moves swiftly about the world, and views every corner, and
peirces into the very bowels of the Earth, and their Sun-like Mind is the light
of their Thoughts; like as the rest of the Planets receive light from the Sun,
so the Thoughts from the Mind; and as the Sun hath Heat and Light, so hath
the Mind Reason and Knowledge; and as the Sun inlivens several Creatures,
so their Mind conceives several Causes and Effects, and creates several
Fancies, and as the Sun shews the World, and the World of Creatures, so the

Mind finds and shews the Truth of Things. But leaving them to true Knowledge, Wisdom, Wit and Happiness, I rest,

> Madam,
>> Your faithful Fr. and S.

LETTER 15

Madam,

Yesterday was the Lord N.W. to visit me, where amongst other Discourses we talk'd of the Lady T.M. not sooner was her name mentioned, but he seem'd to be rapt up into the third Heaven, and from thence to descend to declare her Praises; and to repeat his Expressions, they were so extraordinary, as they will not easily go out of my Memory, so as you shall have them word for word. First, he said, She was a Lady fit to be the Empress of the whole World,[1] for though Fortune had not given her a Temporal Crown, Dignity and Title, as neither by Inheritance,[2] Victory, nor Choice, nor had not advanced her to a Temporal Imperial Throne, nor held she a Temporal Imperial Scepter, yet she was Crown'd at her Birth the Empress of her Sex; for though Fortune had not Crown'd her Body, yet Nature had Crown'd her Soul with a Celestial Crown, made of Poetical Flame, instead of Earthly Gold that Crown's the body; and instead of Diamonds, Pearls, and other pretious Stones set in Golden Crowns, her Celestial Crown was set with Understanding, Judgement and Wit, also with clear Distinguishings, oriental Similizings, and sparkling Fancies, a Crown more glorious than Ariandne's Crown of Stars; and though she was not advanced on a Temporal Imperial Throne, yet she was set higher, as on a Throne of Applause; and though she posses'd not a Temporal Imperial Scepter, yet she had a powerful Perswasion and the tongue of Eloquence; and though she was not adorn'd with Imperial Robes, yet she was adorn'd with Natural Beauty;[3] and though she had not a Temporal and Imperial Guard, yet she was

---

1 The letter offers various autobiographical possibilities. Cavendish often speculated about what she might do if she were empress of the world. See the letter to "All the Professors" at the beginning of this volume and letter 197. She also enjoyed anagrams, and N.W. are her husband's initials written backwards. Likewise T.M. are the first and last letters of Margaret reversed. See the note to letter 33.

2 Cavendish stresses her humble origins in her autobiography, "A True Relation" (to be found as part of *Nature's Pictures*).

3 Samuel Pepys and others testify to her beauty. See Pepys, [April 26, 1667], ed. Latham and Matthews, vol. 8 (London: Bell and Sons, 1974) 186–87.

guarded by Virtue; and though she was not attended, waited and served with and by Temporal and Imperial Courtiers, yet she was attended, waited on, and served by and with the sweet Graces, and her Maids of Honour were the Muses, and Fame's house was her Magnificent Palace. Thus was she Royally Born, and Divinely Anointed or Induded, and Celestially Crown'd, and may Reign in the memory of every Age and nation to the world's end; and not onely Reign, but Reign Happily, Gloriously, and Famously. But when he had said what I have related, I could not chuse but smile to hear such Poetical commentations of a Woman, doubting none of our Sex was worthy of such high, and far-fetch'd praises he ask'd me why I smil'd? I told him, I smil'd to observe how the Passion of Love had bribed his Tongue; he said, he was not guilty of partial Bribes, but Justice had commanded his Tongue to speak the Truth; I told him, I was glad to find, at least to hear, that there was Justice in Men, and Merit in Women, as the one to Praise, the other to be Praise-worthy; but I pray'd him to give me leave, or to pardon me, if I told him, that his Speech shew'd, or express'd him a Temporal and Imperial Courtier, as to praise one Lady to another, and to give so many Praises to an absent Lady, as to leave no Praises for the present Lady: He pray'd me to pardon him that Errour, and that hereafter he would alwayes Praise the Lady he was present with. But Madam, those Praises given the Lady T.M. had I been apt to Envy, it had turn'd me all into Vinegar, or dissolv'd me into Vitriol; but being unspotted, and free from that speckled Vice, I am heighten'd with joy to hear any of our Sex so Celestial, as to deserve a Celestial Praise: And leaving you to the same Joy, I rest,

Madam,
Your faithful Friend and Servant.

LETTER 16

Madam,

I Hope I have given the Lady D.A. no cause to believe I am not her Friend; for though she hath been of Ps. and I of Ks. side, yet I know no reason why that should make a difference betwixt us, as to make us Enemies, no more than cases of Conscience in Religion, for one may be my very good Friend, and yet not of my opinion, every one's Conscience in Religion is betwixt God and themselves, and it belongs to none other. 'Tis true, I should be glad my Friend were of my opinion, or if I thought my Friend's opinion were better than mine, I would be of the same; but it should be no breach of Friendship, if our opinions were different, since God is onely to be the Judg: And as for the matter of Governments, we Women understand them not, yet if we did, we are excluded from intermedling therewith, and almost from being subject thereto; we are not tied, nor bound to State or Crown; we are free, not Sworn to Allegiance, nor do we take the Oath of Supremacy; we are not made Citizens of the Commonwealth, we hold no Offices, nor bear we any Authority therein; we are accounted neither Useful in Peace, nor Serviceable in War; and if we be not Citizens in the Commonwealth, I know no reason we should be Subjects to the Commonwealth: And the truth is, we are no Subjects, unless it be to our Husbands, and not alwayes to them, for sometimes we usurp their Authority, or else by flattery we get their good wills to govern; but if Nature had not befriended us with Beauty, and other good Graces, to help us to insinuate our selves into men's Affections, we should have been more inslaved than any other of Natur's Creatures she hath made; but Nature be thank'd, she hath been so bountiful to us, as we oftener inslave men, than men inslave us; they seem to govern the world, but we really govern the world, in that we govern men: for what man is he, that is not govern'd by a woman more or less? None, unless some dull Stoick, or an old miserable Userer, or a cold, old, withered Batchelor, or a half-starved Hermit, and such like persons, which are but here and there one; And not only Wives and Mistresses have prevalent power with Men, but Mothers, Daughters, Sisters, Aunts, Cousins, nay, Maid-Servants have many times a perswasive power with their Masters, and a Land-lady with her Lodger, or a she-Hostess with her he-Guest; yet men will not believe this, and 'tis the better for us, for by that we govern as it were by an insensible power, so as men perceive not how they are Led, Guided, and Rul'd by the Feminine Sex. But howsoever, Madam, the disturbance in this Countrey hath made no breach of Friendship betwixt us, for though there hath been a Civil War in the Kingdom, and a general War amongst the Men, yet there hath been none amongst the Women, they have not fought pitch'd battels; and if they had, there hath been no particular quarrel betwixt her and me, for her Ladiship is the same in my affection, as if the Kingdom had been in a calm Peace; in which Friendship I shall always remain hers, as also,

Your Ladiships
most Humble and Devoted S.

LETTER 17

Madam,

The pure Lady, or Lady Puritan,[1] is so godly, as to follow all those
Ministers she thinks are call'd and chosen by the Holy Spirit, to preach the
Word of God, whereas those Ministers preach more their own words,
than God's, for they interpret the Scripture to their own Sense, or rather
to their Factious Humours and Designs, and after their Sermons, their
female Flocks gossip Scripture, visiting each other to confer Notes, and
make repetitions of the Sermons, as also to explain and expound them; for
first the Minister expounds the Scripture, and then the Women-hearers
expound the Sermon; so that there are expoundings upon expoundings,
and preaching upon preaching, insomuch as they make such a medly or
hash of the Scripture, as certainly the right and Truth is so hidden and
obscur'd, that none can find it; and surely the Holy Spirit, whom they talk
so much of, knows not what they mean or preach, being so much and
such Non-sense in their Sermons, as God himself cannot turn to Sense;
but howsoever, it works on some to a good effect, and causes as much
Devotion amongst many, as if they preach'd Learnedly, Eloquently, and
interpreted Rightly, and to the true sense & meaning; for many sorrowful & penitent tears are shed, but whether they be bottled up in Heaven,
I know not; certainly *Mary Magdalen* could not Weep faster for the time,
or fetch deeper Sighs, or stronger Groans for her Sins, than they do, which
shews that they have been grievous Sinners; but whether their Sins were
of the same kind as hers were, I cannot tell, and I think they would not
confess, for Confession they account Popish. But truly, and verily, the
Lady Puritan who hath been to visit me this afternoon, hath so tired me
with her preaching Discourse, as I think I shall not recover my weary
Spirits and deafned Ears, this two dayes, unless a quiet sleep cure me; nay,
she hath so fill'd my head with words, as I doubt it will hinder my silent
Repose; howsoever I'le try: and so taking my leave as going to bed, I rest,

> Madam,
> Your faithful Fr. and S.

---

1   Cavendish and her husband were both long-standing Royalists. Ridicule of Puritans is to be
found in the plays of Jonson and became a staple of Restoration drama.

LETTER 18

Madam,

I Observe there is an emulation between the Lord V.A. and the Lord G.V. for Worth and Merit, striving which shall excell each other in Virtue, Noble Qualities, Practicable Arts, Learn'd Sciences, Witty Poetry, and the like;[1] as for Justice, Temperance, Valour, Fortitude, Generosity, Gratitude, Fidelity and Loyalty, as also, for Courtesie, Civility, and Obligements; for wise Forecasts, prudent Managements, industrious Ingenuities, noble Commands, and honest and conformable Obedience; likewise for graceful Behaviours, and handsom Demeanours; also, for Fencing, Riding, Vaulting, Wrestling, and the like; for proper and fit Sciences for Noble Persons to be learn'd and known, as Fortification, Navigation, Astronomy, Cosmography, Architecture, Music, and History; and for Wit, as Scenes, Songs, Poems, and the like: and this Emulation makes them Admire, Love, Respect, and Praise each other, and watch all opportunities to Oblige each other, thinking and esteeming it a Happiness so to do; for the effects of Emulation are quite different from the effects of Envy, for Envy is full of Dispraise and Detraction, either covertly or openly, and watches all opportunities to do Mischief, and to obscure the Beauty of Virtue, and the grace and becoming demeanours of Virtuosoes; whereas Emulation rejoyces when Virtue is visibly Seen, and justly Praised, and Virtuosoes highly Commended: indeed, Emulation dwells with the Worthiest Persons, Envy with the Basest. But, Madam, 'tis a wonder in an age so basely Bad, there should be two persons so noble Good; when most men spend their time so idely Vain, that they should spend their time so ingeniously Prudent; when Vice is advanced, and Virtue disgraced, that they, should Shun that advancement, and imbrace Virtue; when Treason is Rewarded and Loyalty Punished, that they should loyally Suffer, and not basely Betray; when Flattery is heard, and Truth rejected, that they should choose to be Silent, or Speak what they think. They covet not Office, Authority and Wealth, nor do they ambitiously strive to Command, but when they are employed, they do not grow proud with their Authority and Place, nor richer by taking Bribes; nor do they partially Favour their Friends, nor are they Unjust to their Foes; they use no Malice nor Favour, but are Upright and Just; and in their Commands in War, or Governments in Peace, although

---

1   The distinction between envy and emulation is made by Aristotle in *Rhetoric*, II, 10 and 11. Cavendish writes in a "A True Relation," "I repine not at the gifts that Nature or Fortune bestows upon others, yet I am a great emulator" (*Nature's Pictures*, 315). Cavendish may have her husband in mind for the man of many accomplishments. See *Paper Bodies*, 61.

they are carefully Strict, they are not Imperious nor Cruel; but, in short, they endeavour to serve their King Loyally, their Country Faithfully, and every particular Man Generously, if it lie in their power. But leaving these two Nobles to their Glorious Emulatings, I rest,

Madam,

Your faithful Fr. & S.

LETTER 19

Madam,
As the Emulation between the Lord V.A. and the Lord G.V. was Commendable, and worthy of great Praise, so the Envy between the Lord P.R. and the Lord M.A. is Discommendable, and worthy to be Condemn'd; for they strive not to imitate equally, or surpass each other for Worth and Merit, for Courtesie and Civility, for Valour and Generosity, for Learning and Poetry; but strive to imitate equally, or surpass each other in Expences and Bravery, for Shew and Vain glory, for Offices and Honour, for Vice and Vanity, as which shall make more luxurious Feasts, delicious Banquets, masking Scenes, dancing Balls, gay Shews, as brave Cloaths, gilded Coaches, laced Liveries, many Pages, Lackies, hackny Horses, and handsom Mistresses; also they strive for Court Preferments, each would have All Offices and Honours, although, perchance, neither could well discharge any One Place or Office Wisely, if Honestly, nor be worthy the Least Title they are ambitious of; also they strive to be out-Flattered, which Flatterers they maintain at great charge, and to compass their each out-stripping, or out-reaching Designs, they will crouch Basely, flatter Grosly, bribe Liberally, wait Diligently, watch Carefully, and attend Patiently; But I foresee their Fate, which is, they will die despised Beggars, for if they get their Designs, they will be Losers, for the Bribes they give for them, and their Presents and Entertainments, are more than their Designs are worth, and more than they shall gain by them, if gotten; but if their Designs fail them, they will be double losers, besides the expence of their gay Vanities; so what with out-braving, out-bribing, and out-spending each other, they will both be soon out of their Estates; for if they spend upon their Stocks, or Credits, or both, they will have nothing left to spend, and when they are both Poor, Envy may chance to make them Friends, as it doth now, being Rich, Enemies; for though Envy is a following Enemy to Wealth and Prosperity, yet 'tis a Friend to Poverty, and

for the most dwells with Poverty; to which I'le leave these two Envious
Persons, and rest,

> Madam,
> Your faithful Fr. and S.

LETTER 20

Madam,

I Remember you told me, that formerly, you thought Time troublesome,
and every Place wearisome; as in the Spring, you would wish for Summer,
and when Summer came, you would wish for Autumn, and in the
Autumn you would wish for Winter, a cold wish; nay every Day, every
Hour, every Minute, you thought Tedious and Long. Indeed Time runs so
fast upon Youth, as it doth oppress Youth, which makes Youth desire to
cast it by; and though the Motion of Time is swift, yet the Desire of Youth
is swifter, and the Motions of Thoughts are as far beyond the Motions of
Time, as the Motion of Time is beyond the Motion of Nature's Architecture; so as Youth through it's Sharp, Greedy, Hungry Appetite, devours
Time, like a Cormorant doth Fish; For as he never stays to chew, but
swallows down whole Fishes, so Youth swallows, as it were, whole Dayes,
·Weeks, Months, Years, untill they surfeit with Practice, or are fully satisfied
with Experience: The same reason makes Youth weary of every Place or
Company, for they are not satisfied, because they have not had enough
variety of Knowledge, they know not the right use of Time, the
unprofitable use of Vanity, the restless motions of Variety, nor know they
the Deceits, Abuses, and treacheries of their own Kind, as Mankind, neither do they know their own Natures and Dispositions, they know not
what to Choose, nor what to Leave, what to Seek, nor what to Shun; neither have they felt the heavy burthens of Cares, nor oppressions of Sorrows
for Losses and Crosses; they have not been pinched with Necessity, nor
pained with long Sickness, nor stung with Remorse; They have not been
terrified with bloody Wars, nor forsaken of Natural Friends, nor betrayed
by feigned Friendships; they have not been robbed of all their
Maintenance, nor been banished their Countrey.[1] Thus being tenderly
Young, they are Opprest with the quick repetitions of Time, and their

---

1   Cavendish probably is thinking of her husband, for he was one of the few Royalists banished
     from England by Cromwell's government after the Civil Wars were over. The repeated use
     of the word "motion" reminds us that she, like other amateurs, wrote on science.

Senses being Sharp and their Appetites Hungry, they greedily Devour Time though in the end Time devours them, the Meat, the Eater; also the desire of Knowledge makes every Place and Company wearisom, for Youth takes delight in that which is New, they being New themselves, for Youth is like Garments new made, and being new themselves, they Sympathetically delight and love new things, as new Clothes, new Houses, new Vanities, new Sports, new Countries, new Companies, new Lovers, new Friends, and any thing that is new to them, insomuch as they would rather have a new Enemy, than an old Friend; and thus will youth do, until Time turns its back, whereupon are written all the Follies of Youth, which Folllies they could not see to read whilst Time was before them, for while Times face is towards them, they onely see their childish desires, which are all written upon Times breast. But, Madam, I believe, that Time, as troublesom as it hath seem'd to you, you would be glad now of its stay; but Time doth as all Courting Amorosoes do, they run to imbrace Youth, though they tire Youth with their troublesom kindness, but when the gloss of Youth is past, they leave off their Amours, nay, they hate those they made love to, and strive to get away from them as fast as they can, and as far off; Just so doth Time, it makes love to all, and then forsakes all it hath made love to. But Madam, it hath but newly turn'd its head from you, but it will turn its whole body; at first it will seem to pace slowly from you, but it will mend its pace, and at last run from you, yet let it run without your repining, or grieving for its neglects, for no perswasion will make it stay. But, Madam, you will be happier in Times neglects, than in its imbracements, and will make more advantage from Times heels than from its head, for Times head is fill'd with Vanity, and on Times heels is Experience; yet although Time runs from you, Wisdom will stay with you, for Wisdom is the Son of Time, and became Wise by his Fathers Follies, which are written upon his Fathers back; for Wisdom waits alwayes behind his Father, and neither Wisdom the Son, nor Time the Father, do meet face to face; and you will find more happiness in wisdom's Company than in Times Courtships, for Wisdom's Conversation is Comfortable and Pleasing, it speaks with the Tongue of an Oratour, the Wit of a Poet, and the Advice of a Friend; then who would be troubled with the fantastical humours, apish Actions, flattering Speeches, and subtil Deceits of Time? but lest this Letter should be as tedious as formerly Time was, I'le stop here, and rest,

Madam,
Your Ladiships faithful Fr. and S.

LETTER 21

Madam,

I Am sorry that Mrs. P.L. hath had so great a loss at cards, as the grief of the loss caused her to weep; But Gamesters are like Merchant-adventurers, and for the most part have the same fate, as to die Bankrupts, for more are impoverish'd by their losses, than inriched by their gettings, but gaming was never so much practised by our Feminne Sex, as it is in this age, and by their losses, (I know not for their skill) they seem Masculine gamsters, and I believe they quarrel as much in their play, onely they fight not Duels, unless with their Tongues. But I observe that cards is one of the chief pastimes of our Sex, and their greatest delight, for few or none of our Sex loves or delights in Poetry, unless a Copy of Verses made in their praise, wherein for the most part is more Flattery than Wit; neither doth our Sex delight or understand Philosophy, for as for Natural Philosophy they study no more of Nature's works than their Faces, and their greatest ingenuity is, to make them Fairer than Nature did; and for a Moral Philosophy, they think that too tedious to learn, and too rigid to practise; yet I make no question but they have heard of Temperance, though few are acquanted with it, and Prudence they scorn to accompany, they dispise her as a mean, plain Huswife, and Fortitude can get no entrance, for strong Fears keep her out; as for Justice, I think our Sex doth onely resemble the Emblem or Moral, as Justice is blinded with a band to keep out Partiality, so our Sex is blinded with Ignorance, which keeps out Knowledge; and though our Sex holds no Sword in their hands to cut off Offences, yet they hold as sharp a Weapon in their mouths, to cut off good Fame, and will make more Offences, than the Sword of Justice is able to cut off; and as for the Balance of Justice, which is Judgement, they never use it, for they seldom Weigh any thing and for Faith, Hope, and Charity, they seem to have no more Faith than to believe their own Praises, and their onely Hope is for pre-eminence of Beauty of Title, for Place or Wealth and for Vanities; and as for Charity, they spend so much upon themselves, as they are so far from governing their Passions and Appetites, as their Passions and Appetites govern and rule the whole courses of their Lives; neither doth our Sex take much delight in true History, for naturally our Sex is too lazy to look back into past Times, neither have they the peircing foresight to see into Future times, they only regard the Present; neither doth our Sex take much pleasure in harmonious Musick, only in violins to tread a measure; the truth is, the chief study of our Sex is Romances, wherein reading, they fall in love with the feign'd Heroes and Carpet Knights,[1] with whom their Thoughts secretly commit Adultery, and in their Conversation and manner, or forms or phrases of Speech, they imitate the Romancy Ladies: And our Sexes chief Pastime is Gaming of all kinds or sorts, but most Cards, whereby they lose more money than get reputation; indeed, Carding is their Work, for they make it rather a Labour with long and tiresome Sitting, careful Playing, and painful Vexing and Fretting, than a Pleasure and Recreation; and our Sexes chief Exercise is Dancing, not alone, amongst themselves, for that they hate, but in masculine Company, and this they love so well, as to dance themselves into a firie heat, if not a Fever; and their onely delight is in Love and Courtships, and their only pleasure Luxury, insomuch as they are for the most part Eating, whether Sitting, Walking, or Dancing. But leaving our Sex to their Banquets, Courtships, Dancing and Gaming, I rest,

Madam,
Your faithful F. & S.

LETTER 22

Madam,
You said in your last Letter, that Sir G.A. doth so brag of his own gallant Actions, as he saves his neighbour the labour to report them; I am sorry to hear gallant men should brag of their own Actions, for their bragging takes off the gloss of their Courage; for as Time takes off Youth or fresh Colour off Beauty, so Self-praise takes off the Esteem and Honour of Merit: But as some will boast of their own Worth, so others will boast of their own Baseness, as what subtil Cheats they have practised, or whom they have Betrayed, or how ingenious they were in telling Lies, or how many Robberies they have committed; as also of their Disobedience, Disloyalty, and the like; others will boast of their Debaucheries, as how often they have had the French Disease, how many Women they have Debauch'd, how much they can Drink before they are Drunk, and how long they can sit a Drinking, what Monies they have Won or Lost at Play, how Vain and Expensive they are, or have been, and many the like, which I wonder at, that men should Glory and take a Pride in that which is Base or Foolish: But this argues some men to have mean Souls and foolish Brains, full of idle

---

1   Cavendish teases her readers, for she, herself, wrote romances. Often the heroines of her romances have too much "good sense" to read such romances as they inhabit.

Discourses, wanting Judgement and Wit; also unprofitable Lives, and when they Die there is a good riddance, for they were but as Rubbish in the World, which Death, like as an honest painful Labourer, takes up like as Dunghils, and throws them into the Grave, and buries them in Oblivion, not being worthy of a monument of Remembrance, in which Grave I leave those that are Dead, and those that Live I wish may be Reformed to more Purity, so I rest,

> Madam,
> Your faithful Friend and Servant.

LETTER 23

Madam,

It is not strange that the Lady L.T. and the Lady A.M. should fall out, so, as to be Enemies, although they were such fond friends as not to be pleased in each others absence, but Friendship that is made out of fond Humours,[1] seldom lasts long, especially when they live and bord together; for first, Fondness wears away with Use and Acquaintance, next, being borded together, Faults or Neglects are committed, and Exceptions taken; Self-love of the one person will be served first, and Self-love of the other person will not suffer it; besides, many cross Humours, and sometimes little Envies, will appear betwixt equal Persons that live together, especially Women, and the sooner, if either or both have Husbands or Lovers; for Women will be sooner jealous of their Husbands or Lovers for their She-friends, than Men will be of their Wives or Mistresses for their He-friends: but Houshold Friends for the most part are Home-lovers, that is, the He-friend makes love to the Wife, or the She-friend is Courted by the Husband; and if they be both married, 'tis likely they Cuckold each other; and thus, for Example, these Ladies are become Enemies through Jealousie, for though the Lady L.T. profes't to love her Friend the Lady A.M. dearly well, yet it seems, she will not have her to Share with her of her Husbands Love or Courtship, although Sir T.O. the Lady L.Ts. Husband, could be no less than a Servant to his Wifes dear Friend; Besides, it is a temptation to an Husband, to see two She-friends Imbrace, and Kiss, and Sport, and Play, which makes the Husband to desire to do the like, not with his Wife, but his Wifes Friend, for the temptation is from that which men are not accustomed to, or to do as they see others do; but 'tis likely, when the

---

1   There is a pun here on "fond" in the sense of "foolish."

jealous Humour of the Lady L.T. is over, they will be Friends again, till the Jealous Humour return again. Thus they may be Friends and Enemies all their Life time, and perchance take a pleasure in being so, for Women for the most part take delight to make Friendships, and then to fall out, and be Friends again, as so to and fro, which is as much Pastime and Recreations to them, as going abroad and staying at home. But I wish all Friends were as constant Friends as your Ladiship and I, who are insepa-rably united, for as long as I live I shall be,

> Madam,
> Your Faithful Fr. and S.

LETTER 24

Madam,

In your last Letter I perceive the Gallants of the Time, I mean Gallants for Youth and Bravery, for Vice and Vanity, for Expence and Prodigality, for foolish Quarrels, and rash Duels, these Gallants, it seems, condemn Age as unfit for State-affairs, as neither to Govern, Command, Direct, nor Advise; but certainly those States or Kingdoms that have young Governours and Counsellers, shall have more Combustions and Disorders committed by their Ignorance and Follies, than the most experienced Age can Rectifie: indeed such Kingdomes and States are rather govern'd by Chance than Wisdom. 'Tis true, Fools have Good Fortune sometimes, but not so often as Bad, which shews they neither have a Politick Ulysses, nor a Counselling Nestor, for though Young men may Fight as Achilles, yet they can neither Counsel as Nestor, nor Speak as Ulysses; not but that some Old men may be Fools, but it is against Nature for Young men to be Wise, wherefore they are fitter to Obey than to Command, and to be Advised, than to give Counsel, for it is a wonder whenas young Counsellers keep Peace, or young Generals be Conquerours; and it makes them more Famous, because not Usual, especially when Fortune favours them, as she doth many times their Rash Adventures, or haughty and Ambitious Enterprises; for good Fortune makes Youth appear more Glorious than Age; but Fortune many times favours Youth, as she favours Fools, for a time, and in the end leaves them to their own Ruin; but where Fortune hath little or nothing to do, as in wise Counsels, there their Ignorance and Follies, Passions and Partialities, Factions and Emulations appear, especially in the success of their Counsels; wherefore Young men may better and more safely be trusted with an Army than a City, for 'tis more safe to leave them to Fortune, than to trust them with Prudence; for Young men can tell better how to make Wars, than to keep Peace, being easier to Lead an Army, than to Rule a Kingdom, to Fight a Battel, than to Order a Commonwealth, to Distribute Spoils, than to Do Justice, for Fortune hath more power in Victory than Right. 'Tis true, sometimes there's such a Concurrence and Conjunction in Affairs of State, as also in Armies, as the Wisest or Valiantest men cannot make better, nor Fools nor Cowards worse, which is the cause that many times Wise or Valiant men, or both, may be thought Fools and Cowards, and Fools and Cowards Wise or Valiant men; and many times Fools are too hard for Wise men, by reason there be numbers of Fools for few Wise men, nay, numbers of Fools for One Wise man, which Wise man may be buried in the Rubbish of Fools; but if a Wise man be not overpower'd, he treads down their Follies and Triumphs in Peace and Prosperity: But Aged men most commonly are assisted and attended by Mercury and Pallas, and Young men by Mars and Venus. The truth is, 'tis against Sense and Reason, that Young men can be so Wise, or proper for Affairs of a Commonwealth, either to Command, Govern, or Counsel, as Aged men, who have had long Experience, and great Observations, by Seeing, Hearing, and Knowing much, so as there is nothing New, or Unacquainted to them, neither in Varieties, Changes, nor Chances; for Nature, Fortune, and Time, is their long Acquaintance, by which they know the Appetites, Passions, Humours, Dispositions, Manners, and Actions of Men, with their Defects, Errours and Imperfections; also the Revolutions of Time, the Casualties of Chance, the Change of Fortune, and the Natural Course, Causes, and Effects of several Things in the World, all which makes Aged men Wise, and want of such Experience and Observation, makes Young men Fools in comparison of Aged men; for Young men can have but a Relative, and not an Experienced Knowledge, nor can they have very much by Relation or Reading, having not time enough for Instruction & Learning; whereas Aged men have Read, Heard, Seen, Convers'd and Acted in and of several Ages, Societies, Nations, Men, and Business; also in several Places of several Subjects, and several Matters, to several Men, at several Times: But Young men are so Conceited, and Opinionative of themselves, as they think, they neither want Wit, Judgement, Understanding, nor Knowledge, and that Antient men rather Dote than Know; but though Young men cannot be Wise in Nature, unless by Inspiration, yet those are nearest to Wisdom that have been Bred up, Instructed, and Educated by Wise Age, and so much Better and more Knowing they are than others which have been Bred, Instructed, and Educated by Young Pedants or Governours, as the first shall be as Old men, although but

Young, and the others shall be as Boyes when they are Young Men, and Young Men when they are Old, or rather Boyes all their life time, although they should live long; so that one may say, Happy is Youth that lives with Age: But leaving as well Aged as Young men, to Knowledg and Ignorance, Wisdom and Folly, Prudence and Fortune, I rest,

Madam,
Your very faithful Friend and Servant.

LETTER 25

Madam,

The Lady P.R. was to visit the Lady S.I. and other Ladies with her, whose Conversation and Discourse was according to their Female Capacities and Understandings, and when they were all gone, the Lady S.Is. Husband ask'd his Wife, why she did not Talk as the rest of the Ladies did, especially the Lady P.R. so Loud and Impertinently? She answered, she had neither the Humour, Breath, Voice, nor Wit, to Speak so Long, so Loud, and so Much of nothing: He said, her Answer liked him well, for he would not have his Wife so Bold, so Rude, and so Talking a Fool. Thus, Madam, we may perceive how Discourse in Conversation is Judged of, and for the most part Condemned by the Hearers, when perchance the Ladies imagine that they are Applauded and Commended for their Wit and Confident Behaviour; for Self-love thinks all is well Said or Done, that it self Speaks or Acts, so that Self-love doth alwayes Approve it self, and Dispraise others. But leaving Self-love to Self-admiration, and that Admiration to others Condemnation, I rest,

Madam,
Your faithful Fr. & S.

LETTER 26

Madam,

We have no News here, unless to hear that the Lady C.R. did beat her Husband, and because she would have Witness enough, she beat him in a Publick Assembly, nay, being a woman of none of the least Sizes, but one of the largest, and having Anger added to her Strength, she did beat him Soundly, and it is said, that he did not resist her, but endured it Patiently; whether he did it out of fear to show his own Weakness, being not able to

Encounter her, or out of a Noble Nature, not to Strike a Woman, I know not; yet I believe the best: and surely, if he doth not, or cannot tame her Spirits, or bind her Hands, or for Love will not leave her, if she beat him Often, he will have but a Sore life. Indeed I was sorry when I heard of it, not onely for the sake of our Sex, but because she and he are persons of Dignity, it belonging rather to mean born and bred Women to do such unnatural Actions; for certainly, for a Wife to strike her Husband, is as much, if not more, as for a Child to strike his Father; besides, it is a breach of Matrimonial Government, not to Obey all their Husbands Commands; but those Women that Strike or Cuckold their Husbands, are Matrimonial Traitors, for which they ought to be highly punished; as for Blows, they ought to be banished from their Husbands Bed, House, Family, and for Adultery, they ought to suffer Death, and their Executioner ought to be their Husband. 'Tis true, Passion will cause great Indiscretion, & Women are subject to Violent Passions, which makes or causes them so often to err in Words and Actions, which, when their Passion is over, they are sorry for; but unruly Passions are onely a cause of uncivil Words and rude Actions, whereas Adultery is caused by unruly Appetites; wherefore Women should be Instructed and Taught more Industriously, Carefully, and Prudently, to Temper their Passions, and Govern their Appetites, than Men, because there comes more Dishonour from their unruly Passions and Appetites, than from Mens; but for the most part Women are not Educated as they should be, I mean those of Quality, for their Education is onely to·Dance, Sing, and Fiddle, to write Complemental Letters, to read Romances, to speake some Language that is not their Native,[1] which Education, is an Education of the Body, and not of the Mind, and shews that their Parents take more care of their Feet than their Head, more of their Words than of their Reason, more of their Musick than their Virtue, more of their Beauty than their Honesty, which methinks is strange, as that their Friends and Parents should take more Care, and be at greater Charge to Adorn their Bodies, than to Indue their Minds, to teach their Bodies Arts, and not to Instruct their Minds with Understanding; for this Education is more for outward Shew, than for inward Worth, it makes the Body a Courtier, and the Mind a Clown, and sometimes it makes their Body a Baud, and their Mind a Courtesan, for though the Body procures Lovers, yet it is the Mind that is the Adultress, for if the Mind were Honest

---

1   Education of women is an issue in "The Contract" and "Assaulted and Pursued Chastity," longish stories found in *Nature's Pictures* and reprinted by Kate Lilley. The heroine of the first studies moral philosophy, history, and poetry, while the second heroine disdains moral philosophy in favor of mathematics and books of plays.

and Pure, they would never be guilty of that Crime; wherefore those Women are best bred, whose Minds are civilest as being well Taught and Govern'd, for the Mind will be Wild and Barbarous, unless it be Inclosed with Study, Instructed by Learning, and Governed by Knowledg and Understanding, for then the Inhabitants of the Mind will live Peaceably, Happily, Honestly and Honourably, by which they will Rule and Govern their associate Appetites with Ease and Regularity, and their Words, as their Household Servants, will be imployed Profitably. But leaving the Lady C.R. and her Husband to Passion and Patience, I rest,

Madam,
Your faithful Friend and Servant.

LETTER 27

Madam,
Yesterday I employed my time in reading History, and I find in my self an Envy, or rather an Emulation towards Men, for their Courage, Prudence, Wit, and Eloquence, as not to Fear Death, to Rule Commonwealths, and to Speak in a Friend's behalf, or to Pacifie a Friend's Grief, to Plead for his own Right, or to Defend his own Cause by the Eloquence of Speech; yet this is not in all Men, for some men have Courage and no Wit, and some have Wit and no Conduct, and some have neither Wit, Courage, nor Conduct; but mistake me not, for I do not Envy or Emulate a Stubborn Obstinacy, nor a Desperate Rashness, nor an Inslaving Policy, nor Fine Words and Choice Phrases; but to Fight Valiantly, to Suffer Patiently, to Govern Justly, and to Speak Rationally, Movingly, Timely and Properly, as to the purpose, all which I fear Women are not Capable of, and the Despair thereof makes me Envy or Emulate Men. But though I love Justice Best, and trust to Valour Most, yet I Admire Eloquence, and would choose Wit for my Pastime. Indeed Natural Orators that can speak on a Sudden and Extempore upon any Subject, are Nature's Musicians, moving the Passions to Harmony, making Concords out of Discords, Playing on the Soul with Delight. And of all the Men I read of, I Emulate Julius Caesar most, because he was a man that had all these Excellencies, as Courage, Prudence, Wit and Eloquence, in great Perfection, insomuch as when I read of Julius Caesar, I cannot but wish that Nature and Fate had made me such a one as he was; and sometimes I have that Courage, as to think I should not be afraid of his Destiny, so I might have as great a Fame. But these wishes discover my Aspiring Desires, and all those Desires are but

Vain that cannot be Attained to; yet although I cannot attain to Julius Caesar's Fame, it suffices me, to have attained to your Favour, and to the Honour to subscribe my self,

Madam,
Your faithful Friend and Servant.

LETTER 28

Madam,

In your last Letter you were pleased to Condemn me for Admiring Words, so much, as to prefer Eloquence before all other Musick; but pray, Madam, mistake me not, for I do not Admire the Words, but the Sense, Reason, and Wit, that is Exprest, and made Known by Words; neither do I Admire Formal Orators, that speak Premeditated Orations, but Natural Orators, that can speak on a Sudden upon any subject, whose Words are as Sweet and Melting as Manna from Heaven, and their Wit as Spreading and Refreshing as the Serene Air, whose Understanding is as Clear as the Sun, giving Light of Truth to all their Hearers, who in case of Perswasion, speak Sweetly, in case of Reproof, Seasonably, and in all cases, Effectually. And, Madam, if you do Consider well, you cannot chuse but Admire, and Wonder at the Power of Eloquence, for there is a strange hidden Mystery in Eloquence, it hath a Magical Power over mankind, for it Charms the Senses, and Inchants the Mind, and is of such a Commanding Power, as it Forces the Will to Command the Actions of the Body and Soul, to Do, or to Suffer, beyond their Natural Abilities, and makes the Souls of men the Tongue's Slaves; for such is the power of an Eloquent Speech, as it Binds the Judgement, Blindfolds the Understanding, and Deludes the Reason; also it Softens the Obdurate Hearts, and causes Dry Eyes to Weep, and Dryes Wet Eyes from Tears; also it Refines the Drossy Humours, Polishes the Rough Passions, Bridles the Unruly Appetites, Reforms the Rude Manners, and Calms the Troubled Minds; it can Civilize the Life by Virtue, and Inspire the Soul with Devotion. On the other side, it can Enrage the Thoughts to Madness, and Cause the Soul to Despair. The truth is, it can make Men like Gods or Devils, as having a Power beyond Nature, Custom and Force, for many times the Tongue hath been too Strong for the Sword, and often carried away the Victory; also it hath been too Subtil for the Laws, as to Banish Right, and to Condemn Truth; and too hard for the Natures of Men, making their Passions its Prisoners: and since Eloquence hath such Power over Arms, and Laws, and Men, as to make Peace or War, to Compose or Dissolve Commonwealths, to Dispose of Souls and Bodies of Mankind, wherefore those men that are indued with such Eloquence and overflowing Wit, are both to be Fear'd and Lov'd, to be highly Advanced or utterly Banished; for those whose Eloquent Wit out-runs their Honesty, are to be Punished, but those that employ their Eloquent Wit and Elegant Graces, to the service of the Commonwealth, are to be Esteemed, Respected, and Relied upon, as Pillars of the Commonwealth. But to conclude, Wit makes a Ladder of Words, to climb to Fame's high Tower, and the Tongue carries men further than their feet and builds them a Statlier, and more Lasting Palace than their Hands, and their Wit, more than their Wealth, doth Adorn it. But now, leaving Words and Wit, I rely upon Love and Friendship, and rest,

Madam,
Your faithful Friend and Servant.

LETTER 29

Madam,
I Heard by your last, that the Lady S.P. was to visit you, where, amongst her other Discourses, she spoke of me, and was pleased to Censure and Condemn, as to Censure the Cause, and Condemn the Manner of my Life, saying, that I did either Retire out of a Fantastick Humour, or otherwise I was Constrain'd, in not having the Liberty, that usually other Wives have, to go Abroad, and receive what Visitors they please:[1] But if she did but know the sweet Pleasures, and harmless Delights I have by this Retirement, she would not have said what she did; and to answer to what she said, This course of Life is by my own voluntary Choice, for I have liberty to do any Thing, or to go any Where, or to keep any Company that Discretion doth Allow, and Honour Approve of; and though I may err in my Discretion, yet not in cases of Honour, for had I not onely Liberty, but were Perswaded or Inticed by all the World's Allurements, or were Threatned with Death, to Do, or Act anything against Honour, or to do any Thing or Act, Honour did not Approve of, I would not Do it, nay, I would Die first: But in that which is called Honour, are many Ingrediencies, as Justice, Chastity, Truth, Trust, Gratitude, Constancy, and

---

1 Cavendish often defended her life of seclusion, but she was probably more social than this letter suggests. In "A True Relation," she writes, "as for my humour, I was from my childhood given to contemplation" (*Nature's Pictures*, 310; *Paper Bodies*, 59).

many the like. Next I answer, That it is not out of a Fantastick Humour, that I live so much Retired, which is to keep my House more than go Abroad, but out of Self-love, and not out of Self-opinion, and it is Just and Natural for any one to Love himself: Wherefore, for my Pleasure and Delight, my Ease and Peace, I live a Retired Life, a Home Life, free from the Intanglements, confused Clamours, and rumbling Noise of the World, for I by this Retirement live in a calm Silence, wherein I have my Contemplations free from Disturbance, and my Mind lives in Peace, and my Thoughts in Pleasure, they Sport and Play, they are not Vext with Cares nor worldly Desires, they are not Covetous of worldly Wealth, nor Ambitious of empty Titles; they are not to be catch'd with the Baits of Sensual Pleasures, or rather I may say, Sensual Follies, for they Draw my Senses to them, and run not out to the Senses; they have no quarrelling Disputes amongst them; they live Friendly and Sociably together; their onely Delight is in their own Pastimes and harmless Recreations; and though I do not go Personally to Masks, Balls, and Playes, yet my Thoughts entertain my Mind with such Pleasures, for some of my Thoughts make Playes, and others Act those Playes on the Stage of Imagination, where my Mind sits as a Spectator. Thus my Mind is enter-tain'd both with Poets and Players, and takes as much Delight as Augustus Caesar did to have his Mecaenae, the Patron of Poets, sit and hear Virgil and Horace read their Works unto them; so my Mind takes Delight in its dear Mecaenae, which is Contemplation, and to have its Poetical Thoughts, although not like Virgil or Horace, yet such as they are, it is pleased to have them Repeat their Poems, and other Works which they make; and those my Mind likes best, it sends them forth to the Senses to write them down, and them to send them out to the publick view of the World; and many times the Senses send in Objects to the Mind, who straight com-mands his Poetical Thoughts to take them for Plots of Playes, or causes the Grave Philosophical Thoughts to Discourse of them, or his Oratorical Thoughts to practice their Eloquence on them, or his Critical Thoughts to Dispute and Argue with them, which done, all their several Discourses, Disputes, Arguments, Poems, Playes, and the like, made on those Objects, are sent back to the Senses to write them down, so that the Mind and the Thoughts imploy the Senses, and the Senses imploy the Mind and Thoughts, and thus I take as much Pleasure within my self, if not more, as the Lady S.P. doth without her self; indeed none enjoyes truly himself, but those that live to themselves, as I do, and it is better to be a Self-lover in a Retired Life, than a Self-seeker in a Wandring Humour, like a Vagabond, for they go from Place to Place, from one Company to another, and never are at rest in their Minds nor Bodies; and how should it be otherwise? for they lose themselves in Company, and keeping much Company, they know not where to find themselves, for as for their Dwelling-place, they are sure to miss of themselves there; but indeed they have no constant Dwelling, for going much Abroad, they dwell Every where, and yet to speak Metaphorically, No where. But every ones Delights are different, for the Lady S.P. delights her self with Others, and I delight my self with my Self; Some delight in Troubles, I delight in Ease, and certainly much Company and Conversation cannot chuse but be Troublesome; for in much Company are many Exceptions, much Envy, much Suspicion, much Detraction, much Faction, much Noise, and much Non-sense, and it is impossible, at least improbable, for any particular Person to please all the several Companies they come into, or are visited by, if the Resort be many, by reason every one hath as different Humours as Faces, wherein some will be Displeased, if others should be Pleased, and most commonly they are so far from pleasing All, as None is Pleased; for if any particular Person should Praise Every one, it would be thought Flattery, if he should Praise None, it would be conceived to be Envy, if he should Praise but Some, it would be judged to be Partiality; the like for Discourse; if one should Address his Discourse to any One, or to Some more than to Others, it would be taken as a Disrespect, if Generally, to the whole Company, it would be accounted Pride, as taking ones self to be the onely Singular Person that must have a General Audience; neither can any one Person fit his Discourse to every one's Humour, Fancy, Capacity, Understanding, Knowledge or Delight, nay, most commonly, whatsoever is Spoken, is Interpreted to the worst Sense, at least, Contradicted, and when they are parted, their Words or Discourse is Repeated to their Disadvantage, and Commented on, and Interpreted to an evil Sense; and if they say Nothing, or but Little, they are accounted Ill-natured, or thought Fools, and yet they love not to hear any one speak but themselves, every one desires to be heard, yet takes it ill not to be spoken to; also if particular Persons make an Entertainment, if they invite not those they have no acquaintance with, as well as those of their Acquaintance, if they are within the distance of coming to the Entertainment, they take it for an Affront, but if they should leave out any Acquaintance, it is a Breach for ever, and they become their Enemies: also if particular Persons be accoustred Bravely, they are Envied, if they be attired in plain, mean Garments, they are Despised; and if any Woman be more Beautiful than commonly the rest are, if she appears to the World, she shall be sure to have more Female Detractors and Slanderers, to ruin her Reputation, than any Monarch hath Souldiers to fight an Enemy, & if any Woman be Ill-favoured, it is mentioned as a Reproach, although it be Nature's fault, and not hers, and if she be indifferently Handsom, they speak of her as Regardless; if she be in Years, they will say, she is fitter for the Grave than Company, if Young, fitter for a School than Conversation, if of middle Years, their Tongues are the Fore-runners of her Decay; if she have Wealth, and no Titles, she is like Meat, all Fat and no Blood, and if great Title with small Wealth, they say, she is like a Pudding without Fat, and if she hath both Wealth and Title, they Shun her as the Plague, they Hate to see her, as Owls hate the Light, and if she hath neither Wealth nor Title, they Scorn her Company, and will not cast an eye towards her; and thus the Generality is to every Particular: wherefore it is impossible for any Particular either to Please the Humours, or Avoid the Slanders or Reproaches of the Generality, for every One is against Another; indeed, every One is against All, and All against every One, and yet through the itch of Talk, Luxury, Wantonness and Vanity, they will Associate into Companies, or rather I may say, Gather into Companies, and Frequent each others Houses, whereas those that endeavour to be truly Happy, will not be Troubled with such Follies, nor Disturbed with such Toyes: But I am not so Retir'd, as to bar my self from the Company of my good Friends, or such as are free from Exception, as not to Translate harmless and simple Words, to an evil Sense or Meaning, or such as are so Noble, as not to Dispraise, or Detract from such Persons as they are pleas'd to take the pains to Visit, or from such as will not take it for a Neglect, if I do not punctually return their Visit, or perhaps not Visit them at any time, but will Excuse or Pardon my Lazy Humour, and not account it a Disrespect, as truly it is none, for I do Honour and Admire all Civil, Worthy, and Honourable Persons, and would be ready at all times Honestly to Serve them. But this Retired Life is so Pleasing to me, as I would not change it for all the Pleasures of the Publick World, nay, not to be Mistress of the World, for I should not desire to be Mistress of that which is too Big to be Commanded, too Self-willed to be Ruled, too Factious to be Govern'd, too Turbulent to live in Peace, and Wars would Fright, at least Grieve me, that mankind should be so Ill-natur'd and Cruel to Destroy each other. To conclude, I am more Happy in my Home-retirement, than I believe the Lady S.P. is in her Publick Frequentments, having a Noble and Kind Husband, who is Witty and Wise Company, a Peaceable and Quiet Mind, and Recreative Thoughts, that take harmless Liberty; and all this I have declar'd to you, that you may let the Lady S.P. know that my Retirement from the publick Concourse and Army of the World, and Regiments of Acquaintance, is neither through Constraint, nor Fantastick Humour, but through a Love to Peace, Ease, and Pleasure, all which you Enjoy; which is the fulfilling of your Ladiships faithful Friend and Servant's Happiness.[1]

LETTER 30

Madam,

Yesterday, being not in the Humour of Writing, I took Plutarch's Lives, or as some call them, Plutarch's Lies, but Lives or Lies or a mixture of both, I read part of the day in that Book, and it was my chance to read the Life of Pericles the Athenian, in which Story he is Commended for his Gravity, Government, and Wisdom; this Pericles I did much Admire all the time I read of him, until I did read where it was mentioned of his marrying Aspasia, a famous Courtesan, and then I did not think him so Wise a man as I did before, in that he would not rule his Passion better, but to marry a Whore; neither doth Gravity and Wantonness suit well together, for to my imagination a Grave Cuckold doth appear most Ridiculous: And although she was Constant to him, yet the Lewdness of her former Life could not but be a great Blemish to him, as to marry the Dregs and Leavings of other men; But it seem'd that she had an Attractive Power, especially on such as they call Wise men, as Statesmen, Philosophers, and Governours, and all this Power lay in her Tongue, which was a Bawd for the other end; nay, so well (it is said) she could Speak, that not only such men as forementioned did come to hear her, and to learn to speak Eloquently by her, but many also brought their Wives to hear her, which in my opinion was Dangerous, lest they might learn her Vice with her Rhetorick; but it seems the Graecians were not like the Italians concerning their Wives, although they were like them concerning their Courtesans; but honest Women take not so much care to Speak well as to do that which is Virtuous. And so leaving Aspasia and Pericles in Plutarch's History, I rest,

Madam,
Your faithful Friend and Servant.

---

1 Oddly, there is no formal closing to this letter.

LETTER 31

Madam,

I Cannot wonder if I hear that men which are Advanced to Power and Authority should be Dispraised, because it's usual; but rather I should wonder, if I should hear such men Praised or Applauded, although their Lives and Actions were Blameless, nay Wise and Honest; for I have observed, that if any man have more Wealth, Merit, Power, or Wit, than his Neighbour, he is sure to be privately Hated, and publickly Rail'd or Exclaim'd against, and to shew their Hate and Dispraise is against his Merit, Wealth, Power, Wit, or the like, if this man fall from those Favours either of Fortune or Nature, he is not onely Pittied, but dearly Beloved, and highly Praised; and this Ill and Inconstant Nature and Humour is so frequent in all Ages and Nations, as it may very easily be believed, that it was Created in the Essence of mankind, insomuch, that had Men been created before the Angels Fell, they would have Envyed their Glory, and Accused God of Partiality, in making such difference between Men and Angels, but whenas those Angels were cast from Heaven to Hell for their Wickedness, they would Censure God for being too Severe in their Punishment; Yet, Madam, mistake me not, to believe all men are so Envious and Ill-natur'd, but some; for surely though many Angels fell through Spiritual Pride, Envy, and Ambition, yet many remained in Heaven, as Pure as when first Created; and so likewise many Men by the Mercie of God are bred to Virtue, and blest with Piety, to which I leave them, and rest,

> Madam,
> Your faithful Friend and Servant.

LETTER 32

Madam,

Sir, D.D. and his Lady had invited a great many of their Friends to a Feasting Dinner, and being Set, they fell to Eating, and soon after to Talking, for Talking accompanies Eating and Drinking, especially at a Feast; but amongst other Discourses, they were speaking of Marriage, Husbands and Wives, where Sir D.D. said somewhat that his Wife had great reason to take Unkindly, knowing her Virtue had deserv'd more loving Expressions from him, especially in an open Assembly, which unkindness forced Tears through her Eyes, but they were becoming

Tears, for they did not cause the Feature in her Face to be Distorted, for she appear'd in her Countenance Sweet and Admirable, as if there had been no Discontent in her Mind, neither did she shew any Discontent in her Words or Behaviour, for she neither Complain'd, nor Rail'd at her Husband, nor Quarrel'd with him, nor rose from the Table in a Passion, to the Disturbance of the Company, as most Women would have done, and often do, when they are Displeased or Anger'd, but she wip'd the Tears from her Eyes and Addrest her self, as she did before, to Entertain her Friends Civilly and Courteously, and when they had all Dined, and the Cloth taken away, she ask'd pardon of her Friends for her Tears, saying her Tears had made their meeting appear rather as a funeral Condoling, than a merry Feasting: But truly, said she, I could not help it, for they would not be restrain'd do what I could, for some words my Husband spoke caused a Storm of Grief in my mind, which rais'd up Billows of Tears that overflow'd my Eyes, yet, said she, the Dearest and Loving'st Friends will both Take and Give Cause of Exception some-times, for not any Man or Woman is so Perfect as not to Err; and thus her Discretion did not suffer her Passion to Disturb her Guests, and her good Nature did Excuse her Husband's Folly, and her Love did Forgive his Disrespect to her; But the lady C.C. did not behave her self so, for her Husband Sir G.C. and she had invited many of their Friends to a Feasting dinner, and she, as the Mistress, to order all affairs belonging to a Wife, took upon her to order the Feast, and being a Mode-Lady, would have a Mode-Feast; but the Cook knowing his Master loved rost Beef, sent in a Chine of rost Beef to the Table, and when her Guests were all Set, and beginning to Eat, she spied the Chine of Beef, whereat she was very angry, to have, as she thought, her Feast disgraced with an old Countrey fashion, and not only an Old, but a Countrey fashion, to have Beef serv'd to their Table; wherefore she, to shew her self a Courtier, rather than a Country-Lady,[1] commanded one of the waiters to take the Beef from the Table, Sir G.C. her Husband desired not to have it taken away, for said he, I love Beef better than any other Meat, but she to express she had a Ladies Nice Stomack, or rather a Nice Ladie's Stomack, said, the Beef was fulsom to her Eyes, and made her Stomack sick to see it, her Husband bad her to look upon some of the other meat, and to give him leave to eat of what he lik'd; but she would not agree to that, for, said she, the very Smell was Offensive to her, and therefore she would have it taken away, he said it should not be taken away, untill he had eaten as much as he

---

1 Cavendish was, herself, a country lady at the time of the printing of *Sociable Letters*.

would; but in fine, their words Multiplied, and gathered together in an outragious Tumult, raised their voices into an Uproar, and then from Words they went to Blows, flinging whatsoever came next to hand at one anothers head; their Guests being in danger to be Hurt, rose from the Table, and Sir G.C. and his Lady rose also, and went to Cuffs but their Friends did soon part them, and the Lady went Crying into her Chamber, and was Sick, because she had not her will, at least Feign'd her self Sick; As for their Guests, they were rather invited to Fast than to Feast, as it fell out, for all the fine Quelquechose was spoil'd and overthrown in the hurly burly, but the Beef was so Substantial and Solid, as it strongly kept its place on which the Guests might have Fed; but Fright, Noise and Disorder, had taken away their Appetitte to Eating. Thus, Madam, I have related these Feasts and Entertainings, to let you know the different Humours and Behaviours of these two Ladies, the one having cause to be Angry, did Patiently and Discreetly pass over her Injury, appearing Celestial, the other out of a vain Humour, fell into a raging Passion, the truth is, she shew'd her self a Fool, and behav'd her self as Mad. But leaving the Angelick Lady to be a Pattern to her Sex, I rest,

> Madam,
> Your Faithful Fr. & S.

LETTER 33

Madam,
I Do not wonder, that the Lord C.R. should delight in Effeminate Pastimes, as Dancing, Fidling, Visiting, Junketing, Attiring, and the like, because he is an Effeminate Man, fitter to Dance with a Lady, than to Fight with an Enemy; nor do I wonder that the Lord N.W. practices Riding, Fencing, Vaulting, Shooting, Hunting, Fortifying, Navigating, and the like, because he is an Heroick man, fitter to Conquer a Nation, than to Dance a Galliard or Courrant;[1] nor I do not wonder that Lord A.M. Drinks, Whores, Games, and the like, because he is a Debauch'd Man, apter to

---

1   A marginal note in the Emmanuel College, Cambridge, copy of *Sociable Letters* identifies N.W. as William Newcastle, husband to Cavendish. William published on riding and had been in charge of the King's armies in the North during the Civil Wars. See letter 15 for more on N.W. Margaret Cavendish may tread on thin ice with the Lord C.R., since the King was widely known by those initials and was frequently considered to be uxorious. Possibly, she means a tease of the sort one finds in the opening lines of Dryden's *Absalom and Achitophel*.

Quarrel than to Fight; neither do I wonder that the Lord L.U. Studies, Reads, Writes, Travels, Inquires and Searches for Right and Truth, because he is a Wise Man; nor do I not wonder at the Lord F.O. that loves Amourous Courtships, because he is an Idle Man; nor I do not wonder at the Lord C.H. that Prayes to God, Sends to the Sick, and Relieves the Poor, because he is a Good Man; nor do I wonder at the Lord W.I. who Extorts, Exacts, and Deceives, because he is a Wicked Man; neither do I wonder at the Lord C.C. who Visits the Meritorious, Applauds the Worthy, Assists the Industrious, and the like, because he is a Generous Person; nor I do not wonder at the Lord G.R. that he Speaks false with his Tongue, Dissembles in his Countenance, Betrayes in his Actions, because he is a Base Man. Thus, Madam, we may divide Mankind into eight parts or rather into four, for those four, as the Effeminate, Idle, Wicked, and Base, are but the Slime and Dung of Mankind, and onely the Heroick, Wise, Good, and Generous, are the Soul and Body of Mankind; the first are neither good for Citizens, Magistrates, nor Commanders, but rather fit to be set in the fore-fronts of Battles to be Destroyed, or to fill up Breaches, being but Rubbish; but then you will say, this were the way to Destroy most Men in the World, the truth is, if it were not for such Men and Ravenous Beasts, the World would be rather a Heaven than a World. But leaving them and Beasts, I rest,

Madam,
Your faithful Friend and Servant.

LETTER 34

Madam,
You were pleased to Express to me in your last Letter, that you have been in the Country to see the Lady M.L. who seems Melancholy since she was married, which is a sign she is not pleas'd with the Condition of her Life;[1] I believe one of the causes of her Melancholy is, that she is in the Country, wherein is little Resort, especially of courting Gallants, for most Women love Variety of Company, and much Company, even married Wives as well as Maids, neither do all Widows shun Company; As for Maids, they have an excuse to get them Husbands, and Widows are at liberty to make a second, third, or fourth Choice, when their Husbands are

---

1 Perhaps intended to recall the initials of Margaret Lucas, maiden name of the author. Cavendish sometimes teases herself about her tendency towards melancholia.

dead, but Wives have no excuse for the Company of Courting Servants, and merry Meetings, but onely the Splene, which nothing can cure but Company and Jollity, to divert Melancholy, and to remove the Splenetick Obstructions and Crude Vapours, for which Dancing, Feasting, Gaming, and the like, is the best Cure, *Probatum est*;[1] Whereas the lone Company of a Husband is so far from working any Cure, as it is many times the Cause of the Disease; But if her Melancholy proceed from want of Variety of Company, I pitty both her Husband and Attendants, for most commonly a Peevish Frowardness[2] doth attend that Melancholy, they will Quarrel with every Thing, and not be Pleased with Any, take Exceptions at every Word, complain of being Sick, but know not where their Pains are, even as Weary of Themselves, which makes their Husbands many times Weary of Them, and to Divert the Grief of their Wives Troubles, they Solace with their Wives Maids, who are more Pleasant Company, being not troubled with the Splene, as not having a Husband, nay, when they do Marry, their minds are so employ'd about getting a Livelihood, as they have not time to think of their Splenes, besides, they are forced to Labour and Work for their Living, which keeps them from such Obstructions or Disease, and the Splene is a Disease which is onely amongst the Noble and Rich, whose Wealth makes them Idle, and their Idleness begets an appetite to Variety of Diets, Clothes, and Company, whereas Poor, Laborious People know not such Disease. But leaving this Theme, give me leave to welcom you out of the Country, and to acquaint you, that I will shortly Personally wait upon you, as is the duty of,

> Madam,
> Your faithful Friend and Servant.

LETTER 35

Madam,
Sir W.C.'s Wife you know hath a Conversable and Ingenious Wit, yet not being very handsom, her Husband hath got him a Mistress, who is very beautiful and handsom, but yet she is a Fool; a Friend of his ask'd him why he chose a Fool for his Mistress? he said, he did not Court her for her Wit, but for her Beauty; for, said he, now I have a Mistress for Delight, and a

---

1   It is proven. The phrase, from medieval Latin, is something of a joke given Cavendish's views on scholastic philosophy.

2   Perverseness.

Wife for Conversation, I have a Mistress to Look on, and Admire, and a Wife to Listen to and Discourse with, and both to Embrace at my Pleasure; but, said his Friend, if your Wife should come to know you have a Mistress, you will not take much Pleasure in her Conversation, unless you account mourning Complaints of, or to you, Exclamations and Curses against you, cross Speeches, opposite Actions, and hideous Noise, to be Conversable and Delightful; for the truth is, said he, your Wife's words will be so Salt, Sharp, and Bitter, as they will Corrode your Mind, Leaven your Thoughts, and make your Life Unpleasant. My Wife, said Sir W.C. shall not know I have a Mistress; his Friend replied, your often Absence will Betray you, or else some other will tell her, for Adultery is like Murder, it seldom escapes finding out; and since that time Sir W.C.'s Lady hath heard of her Husbands Mistress, but she seems not to be Angry at it, but talks of it with great Patience, saying, that if her Husband takes Pleasure in Variety, he will be more delighted with her Wit, than with his Mistress's Beauty, and will sooner be tired with gazing on One Object, than in hearing Divers Discourses and Diversions of Wit, Sense, Reason, Judgement, Fancy, and Speech; Besides, said she, Wit attracts the Mind more to Love, than Beauty to Admiration, and if my Husband Loves me Best, said she, I am well content he should Admire her Beauty Most, as also to Imbrace her as much as he pleases, for I am so Delighted, and Wedded to my own Wit, that I regard not my Husbands Amours nor Imbracings, for Wit is Spiritual and not Corporeal, it lives with the Mind, and not with the Body, being not subject to the gross Senses, for though Wit, said she, may be known by Words and Actions, yet those are but the Pictures of Wit's Works, not Wit it self, for that cannot be Drawn, it is beyond all Draughts; and so much Difference, said she, is between my Husband's Mistress and his Wife, as a Picture and an invisible Spirit, which Spirit can both Help and Hurt, Delight and Terrifie, Damn and Glorifie; But howsoever, said she, my Wit shall not be my Husbands Evil Spirit, neither to Reproach him, nor to Disgrace, Reprove, Delude, or Anger him, but it shall be always ready to Defend, Commend, Inform, Delight, and if it could, to Reform him; but I believe, said she, that is past the power of my Wit, for it is a hard matter to Restrain Nature from Liberty, especially of the Appetites, for the Passions of the Mind are more easily Govern'd, than the Appetites of the Body, for they are Sensual and Brutal, wherefore Time is a better Reformer of the Appetites than Reason. But, Madam, this is to let you know the Lady W.C.s Wit, Discretion, and Temper, which is more than most of our Sex hath; and so leaving her to her Wit, and her Husband to Reformation, and his Mistress's Beauty to Time, I rest,

Madam,
Your most faithful Friend and Servant.

LETTER 36

Madam,

You were pleased in your last Letter to express, how Mr. P.C. is persecuted by another man's Whore, which is not usual, for though many men are Persecuted by their own Whores, both in Body, Mind, Course of Life, and Estate, Diseasing the One, Vexing the Other, Opposing the Third, and Spending the Fourth, yet not usually by any other man's, but their own, at least believing them to be onely theirs; but I believe Mr. P.C. will not easily clear himself from her, for Courtesans are often assisted by the Powerful, insomuch as in any Law-sute or petitioning Request, they shall be heard, and their Sute granted, although against all Law or Right; Such Power and Favour hath Concupiscence, as to corrupt Magistrates, bribe Judges, see Lawyers, flatter Courtiers, and the truth is, intice, allure, and perswade most of Mankind; but although there be in all Ages and Nations, Courtesans, and Men liable to be Tempted, yet men have not been frequently tempted, perswaded, or allured to Marry Courtesans, unless in this Age, wherein Courtesans are so Prevalent and Fortunate, as they do not onely get themselves Husbands, when Beauty and Lovers begin to leave them, but marry more Richly and Honourably for Dignities, than Honest, Chaste Widows, or Pure and Innocent Virgins, which is apt to make Honest and Chast Women to doubt, their Honesty and Chastity is not blest with such good Fortune as Dishonesty is, insomuch as those that are not Honest, merely, and for no other end, than for Honestie's sake, may be Corrupted through hopes of good Fortune; but where Virtue takes a thorow Possession, it never leaves the Habitation; yet many that have been Base, Wicked, and of Beastly Lives, may be Reformed, so as to become very Honest, Worthy, and Pure, and such Reclamed Persons ought to be Esteem'd and Respected, for I am not of Mrs. F.Rs. Humour, who Hates a Reformado. But some Men are of that Humour, as they Hate Honest, Chast Women, not onely out of a Despair of their Enjoyments, but that they love the Company and Conversation of Wanton and Free Women, insomuch that a Courtesan shall have a greater and stronger Power to Cause and Perswade Men to do Actions not onely to the Ruin of their Estates and Families, but to the Ruin of their Honours and Reputation, nay, to make them Unnatural, Extravagant or Base, than an Honest Chast Wife hath to Perswade her Husband to keep his Estate, Honour, or Honesty; for many a Worthy and Honourable Person hath Degenerated from his Birth and Breeding, from his Natural Courage and Generosity, from his Loyalty and Duty, from his Natural Affection and Sacred Vows, from his Honour and Reputation, through the Perswasion of Whores; nay, many Men love a Whore so much more than an Honest and Chast Woman, as many make better Husbands, and are more Fond and Kinder to their Wives if they be Libertines, than if they were Honest and True to their Marriage-Bed; But leaving such men to their own Heads, and their Wives to their Neighbours Beds, I rest,

Madam,
Your faithful Friend and Servant.

LETTER 37

Madam,

You were pleas'd to tell me in your last Letter, that there was a great and earnest Dispute between O.G. and C.O. in Divinity, as to prove many things which are easier to be Believed than Proved; for though Proof makes Knowledg, yet Belief doth not make Proof; for though many thousands of men Believe alike one Thing or Things a thousand years, yet neither the number of Men, nor of Years, doth prove it to be true, it only proves that so many Men did believe it for so many Years; for though there be many things in Nature that may be Conceiv'd, and Demonstrated to Reason, at least, to have a Probability in Reason, but cannot be Demonstrated to the Senses, yet the Conceptions do oftener deceive, not onely the Reason, but the Senses, than the Senses do the Reason or Conception, for though the Senses may, and are oftentimes Mistaken and Deluded, yet they are the most certain and surest Guides and Informers we have; But Divinity is above all Sense and Reason, as also all Demonstrations, wherefore Faith is required in all Religions, for what cannot be Conceived or Apprehended, must be Believed, and if the chief Pillar of Religion is Faith, Men should Believe more, and Dispute less, for Disputations do argue Weakness of Faith, nay, they make a Strong Faith Faint, for all Disputes in Divinity are Enemies to Faith, and are apt through Contradictions and Different Opinions, to Destroy Religion, making the Thoughts and Mind Atheistical, and the Words Sophistical, Men spending more time in Disputing than Praying, rather striving to Express their Wit than to Increase their Knowledge, for

Divine Mysteries are beyond all Natural Capacity, and the School-men have rather taught Men Contradictions than Truth, and Church-men rather Division than Union. But all Disputes and Arguments in Divinity are onely fit for Church-men, whose Profession is to be Teachers and Instructors in the Divine Laws, and not for Lay-men, unless they intend to be Church-men: for as all National Laws have Judges, Serjeants, Barresters, Attornies, and the like, to Perform and Execute the Common and Civil Laws, that have been Prudently Enacted for the Good and Benefit of the Bodily Life and Commonwealth; so there are Bishops, Deans, Deacons, Parish-Priests and Curats, to Perform and Execute the Divine Laws, which have been Spiritually Enacted for the Salvation of mens Souls; and as Lawyers are Informers of the National Laws, and Pleaders of Causes, so Ministers are Informers of the Divine Laws, and Teachers of good Life, and all Spiritual Causes should be Decided by the Bishops, as all National or Human Causes by the Judges, otherwise there would be a Confusion both in Church and State; wherefore those that are not of that Profession, ought not to meddle therewith, or Dispute thereof, but to Submit to that which our Fore-fathers thought fit to Enact, Order, and Dispose, for the good of their Successors, and Succedent Times; And so leaving O.G. and C.O. to agree if they can, I rest,

Madam,
Your faithful Fr. and S.

LETTER 38

Madam,
You were pleased to desire, that one of my Servants should inquire for Sir N.G. and give him a Letter, or to leave the Letter at his Lodgings. Madam, I must tell you what I hear, which is, that he may be Enquired for, but before he can be Found, or his Lodgings Known, he will be gone out of the Town; not that he obscures his Lodging, but that he Stayes not any where, for he is like a Shadow, or a Ghost, when you think it is so near as to speak to it, it straight appears afar off, or Vanishes away; and he is not onely in this City, but in every Town, for he rides from Town to Town, as Birds flie from Tree to Tree, and his onely business is for Divertisement for Health, so that his Life is as if it rid Post; but let him ride from Death as far as he can, and do what he can to Shun it, yet Death will Meet him at his Journeys end, and there Arrest him, and Imprison his Body in a Grave, for Time hath laid an Action of Battery against him, and hath now

threescore and fifteen years Summoned him to Appear, but as yet he keeps out of Sight, and will as long as he can, as we may perceive by his riding, and short stay in every place he comes to. Indeed Nature hath been his Friend, and seems to be so still, and as long as she Protects him, Death cannot get him; nay, she hath Favour'd him more than many of his Neighbours, or Acquaintance, for he never stayes so long in one place, as to make a Neighbourhood, but hath Acquaintance in every place; neither doth he trouble any Acquaintance with long Visits, but onely as to ask how they do, and so farewel; he doth not stay to examin the long Welfare of his old Acquaintance, nor to make tedious Complements with new Acquaintance, nor stayes to inquire for those Acquaintance he sees not, but he will make new Acquaintance at first sight; and this Advantage he hath by riding to several places, if it be any, that he hears more News than any other man, for he meets News in every Town, which his Memory like a Portmantua carries with him, and as in every Town he takes up some News, so in every Town he leaves some; But such a Posting Life, were I a Man, would be Wearisom to me, for it would soon Tire my Life, or Rid me out of the World, at least to my thinking, although to him it is a Sport and Pleasure, or else he would not do so, since he is not Constrain'd thereto. Wherefore, as for your Letter, it must either be sent back to you again, or else it must lie here as a Watch to Take him, for it is impossible it should Overtake him, nor can any one tell where to find him, except those that are in the same place he is, which soon changes to Is not, so as one may say, he Is, and Is not, he is like a Juglers Ball, 'tis here, 'tis gone; but he is no Jugler himself, for I hear he is a very Worthy Person, and his Honest and Harmless Endeavour to Prolong his Life, shews him a Wise man; and so leaving him and your Letter to meet, though I know not when, I rest,

Madam,
Your faithful Friend and Servant.

LETTER 39

Madam,
I May give the Lady F.L. Joy of her second Marriage, for I hear she is Married again; but I fear it will be applyed to her, what is said of another Lady, who Married first very well for Title and Wealth, her Husband being in Years, but she very Poor, and amongst much Company it was told, she seem'd to be a Crafty, Witty Woman, that she could get such an Husband;

no, said one man, it was not the Wit or Craft of the Lady, that got her such a Husband, but the Folly of the Man that Married such a Wife; and after he Died and left her very Rich, she married a Young man that had no Estate, and then they said, that it seem'd her second Husband was a Wise Man, that he could get so Rich a Wife; no, said the former Man, it was not the Wisdom of the Man, but the Folly of the Woman, that caus'd that Match; so she was even with her first Husband in Folly, for he play'd the Fool to Marry her, and she play'd the Fool to Marry her second Husband. Thus most of the World of mankind is mistaken, for what they Attribute to some men's Wit, is other men's Folly, but for Marriages, the truth is, that Folly makes more Marriages than Prudence; as for Example, Mr. A.B. hath Married a Common Courtesan, if she had been Particular, it had been more Excusable; but all men are not so foolish, for I hear that Sir W.S. will rather indure the Persecution of his own Courtesan, than Marry her. But leaving the Lady F.L. to her new Husband, and Mr. A.B. to his new Wife, and Sir W.S. to his pursuing Whore, I rest,

Madam,
Your most faithful Friend and Servant.

LETTER 40

Madam,
I Have observed, that in time of Peace, most men study the School-men and Fathers, and in times of War they study Martial-men and Poets, or rather Practise what former Martial-men have Taught, and Repeat what former Poets have Written, for when they are in Garrisons, or have any spare time from Fighting, as Assaulting, or Defending, they will chuse to read Homer, Virgil, and Lucian, rather than St. Ambrose, St. Hierome, St. Augustin, St. Chrysostome, or the like, or rather than they will read Books of Controversies, as Scotus, Thomas Aquinas, and others, they will read Caesar's Commentaries; the truth is, though School-men and Books of Controversies do not Fight Combats, yet they make Quarrels and Disputations, so that there are More, Oftener, and Continual Wars in Schools than in the Field, onely that their Weapons they use in Schools, are not so deadly as those that are used in the Field, for there is great difference between Tongues and Swords, Words and Blows; The truth is, Scholars and Women quarrel much alike, as after the same manner, wherein is more Noise than Danger, and more Spite than Mischief; but yet different Opinions in Religion and Laws in a Commonwealth, cause Cruel Civil

Wars, making Factions and Parties, with Disputations and Arguments, and nothing will decide the Quarrel but Blood and Death, nor end the War, but Destruction of the Whole, or Conquering Victory of the one Party over the other, whereof the late Wars in this Country are a woful Example, all being brought to Confusion with Preaching and Pleading, on the one side Preachers and Pleaders became Souldiers, on the other side, Souldiers became Preachers and Pleaders, so that the Word and the Sword made great Troubles, and grievous Calamities in these Nations, and though there hath been much Blood Shed, many Lives Lost, Men Banish'd, and Families Ruined, yet there are Divisions still; But leaving War and Strife, and Praying for Peace and Quiet, I rest,

Madam,
Your faithful Friend and Servant.

LETTER 41

Madam,
'Tis now become a fashion for men to brag of their Fortunes or Estates, to get Credit, as to Borrow, or run on the Score, for they think if Trades-men believe they are able to Pay, they will be willing to Trust, and if they can get Trust, they'l spend as long as their Credit will last, and when they ow Most, they bear up Highest, for Tradesmen for fear of Losing what they have Trusted or Lent, will Trust or Lend more in hope to be paid All at last, so as they fling the Handle after the Hatchet; and whereas at first the Borrowers are Humble to get Credit, at last the Creditors become Humble Petitioners for their Own, and Wait for an Answer with their Caps in their hands, and the Borrower, like a proud Favorite, will hardly be Seen or Spoken to, nay, when he vouchsafes them his Presence and Answer, he gives them Words for Pay, and Promises more than he is able to Perform, and sometimes they have Frowns and Checks, for being so Presumptuous to Come before they were Sent for, or so Bold to Ask for what was justly Owing them; But certainly Creditors deserve good Words for their good Deeds, though they can get no Mony for their Wares. But in these needy times Tradesmen must venture to Trust, or else they will hardly put off their Commodities, for where one payes ready Mony, five, nay twenty, run on the Score; the reason is, there is not so much Mony *in Specie*, not in all Europe, nay, in the World, as to pay readily for all that is Bought, for there are more Commodities than Mony, I may say, more Paper than Mony, for Paper and Parchment payes more than Mony; a

little Mony sprinkled amongst many Bills and Bonds, keeps up Commerce and Trading throughout the World, more than Exchange of Commodities doth. But those live most at Ease that Borrow not, and those that Lend not have the most Friends, for ther's an old Saying, Lend your Mony, and Lose your Friend; the truth is, a man shall sooner lose a Friend with a Debt, than get a Friend by a Gift. But leaving Debts and Gifts to the Poor and the Rich, I rest,

Madam,
Your faithful Friend and Servant.

LETTER 42

Madam,

I Am sorry Sir F.O. hath Undervalued himself so much below his Birth and Wealth, as to Marry his Kitchin-maid, but it was a sign he had an Hungry Appetite, or that he lived a Solitary Life, Seeing no better Company, or Conversed not with Women of Quality;[1] or else he hath been too Privately Kind, and was loth to have it Publickly Known; or he hath tried her Virtue, and so Married her for Chastity, though many Women will Deny some, and Grant to others; or else he Married her for Beauty, or Wit, or both, although the Inferiour or meaner sort of People, especially Women, are oftener owners of Beauty than Wit, and if they have some Wit, it is onely Sharp Replies, which are a kind of a Scolding; and I have heard that the Way or Manner of Courtship amongst the Inferiour sort of People in E. is Scolding, they Scold themselves into Matrimony, or at least, make Love[2] in a rough, rude Style; But perchance Sir F.O. Married his Kitchin-maid in hopes she would make a Nimble and Obedient Wife, which he might fear one of Equal Birth would not be; Indeed he hath chosen one out of the humblest Offices, or Houshold Imployments, for the Kitchin for the most part is the lowest Room in a House; Yet I write not this as believing he may not be Happy in his Choice, for 'tis likely the Match may be more Happy than Honourable, and if he thinks it no Disgrace, or cares not for Disgrace, all is well, for it only concerns himself, as having no Parents living to Grieve or Anger, nor no former Children to Suffer by. But

---

1 Perhaps the best-known marriage of this sort took place between George Monck, Duke of Albemarle, and a laundress named Nan Clarges. Such unions were often lampooned. See George De F. Lord, *Anthology of Poems on Affairs of State* (New Haven: Yale UP, 1975).

2 Conduct a courtship.

though her Office and Birth were both Dripping and Basting, yet his Dignity and Wealth hath made her a gay Lady; and so leaving him to his dish of Brewess, I rest,

Madam,
Your faithful Friend and Servant.

LETTER 43

Madam,

You were pleas'd to desire me to send you my opinion of Mrs. R.E.s Wit, truly I cannot judge of her Wit until I have a longer Acquaintance with her, for there are many several Degrees, and divers Sorts of Wit, as from a Pint to a Tun, or Teirce, or Pipe of Wit, all which may be drawn Dry, and their Brains be as Empty Barrels; and some have Rivers, or Seas of Wit, which sometimes Ebb and sometimes Flow, wherein some have Double Tides; and others have Springs of Wit, which issue out into small Streams, but make great Flouds, by reason they constantly Flow without Intermission. But there are not many Seas, nor Rivers, nor Flouds, nor Springs of Wit, for there are more Bottels than Springs, and more Barrels than Seas of Wit. As for Spring Wit, it is Fresh, Sweet, Calm, Smooth, Pure, Bright and Clear, whereas Sea Wit is Salt, Sad, Fomy, Rough, Boisterous, Unsteady, & sometimes Dangerous. And as there are several Degrees of Wit for Quantity, and Sorts of Wit for Quality, so there are Several Weights of Wit, for Salt Wit is Heavy and Searching, it Presses to the Centre, and Peirces to the Quick, and opens the Obstructions of the World of Mankind, like as Mineral Waters do the Splene, or the like parts of the Body, whereas Fresh Spring Wit is Light and Airy, Running with a Smooth and Quick Motion, Refreshing the World of Mankind, Bathing the Soul, Cleansing the Thoughts, and Quenching the Drought of Time, which is Overheated with Running; but least my Pen should become Dry with Writing, having not Wit enough to Moisten it, I'le take my leave, and rest,

Madam,
Your faithful Fr. and S.

LETTER 44

Madam,

As it was formerly the Fashion, or Custom of those that received Visits, if they were Weary of their Visitors, to look in their Watches, or to Gape, or Yawn; so now it is to have alwayes, or for the most part, Pen, Ink, and Paper lying upon the Table in their Chamber, for an Excuse they are writing Letters; as for the first, it is Rude, and the last for the most part is False; wherefore methinks it would be an Honester and Nobler Custom to speak the Truth, as to say, they Desire not to be Visited, at such Times as they would not have Company, or from such Persons as they Care not for, or to tell them truly, that they cannot Entertain them, having some Occasions which require their Attendance or Imployment, or that they are not Well, and Company would be Troublesome to them; But to receive their Visits, and then not Entertain them Handsomly, Civilly, Courteously, but Dissemblingly, Carelesly or Disrespectfully, is neither fit for Persons of Quality to do to any Company, if they will think them worthy to receive a Visit of them; neither fit for Persons of Quality to suffer from any Person; But the Visited and Visitors do not always know how to Behave themselves, for Noble Births may have Mean Breeding, for some are Nobly Born and Meanly Bred, and some are Humbly Born and Nobly Bred, and some are Nobly Born and Nobly Bred, but those are Few, and some are neither Well Born nor Well Bred, and those are Many, but very Few are Bred so Exactly, as to know Punctually how to Behave themselves to every particular Person, and in every several Company, much less in every Action of their Life, which are almost Innumerous, and as Different. Wherefore those are most to be Commended, that can go through the Course of their Life with fewest Errours; a Busie Nature is apt to commit Most, and they that meddle least in the Affairs of the World, and are most sparing of Speech, commit Fewest. 'Tis true, every living man commits some, but those are Happy that can Reckon their Errours, that they are not past Account. But if I write my Letter longer, I shall add one Errour more to those many that are past, although I am sure you will pardon those wherewith I have offended you, as believing they were not willingly, but ignorantly committed by,

Madam,
Your faithful Friend and Servant.

LETTER 45

Madam,

Since I writ to you that Letter of the first of the last Month, I have several times Conversed with Mrs. R.E. and I find her Wit runs in Parts, like as Musick, where there must be several Parties to Play or Sing several Parts; she is not a whole Consort herself, neither can she Play the grounds of Wit, but yet she can make a shift to fill up a Note; and it is to be observed, that Wit in several Persons runs on several Subjects, but few have general Wits, as to Play Musically upon every Subject, especially without making a Fault, for I have known some, on some particular Subjects, will be wonderful Witty, and on others mere Dunces and Idiots. And for parts of Wit, some have Gossiping Wit, as Midwife and Nurse Wit, also Wafer and Hippocras[1] Wit, Ale and Cake Wit, as in Christning, Churching, Lying in, and other Gossipings; Others have Bridal Wit, Gamesome Wit, also Gaming Wit, Tavern-Wit, Brothel-Wit, and some have Court-Wit, which is a Jeering, Scoffing Wit, but all these are but Scums or Dregs of Wit, onely Scum-Wit swims on the top, which soon boyls over, and Dreg-Wit lies at the bottom, and is hardly stirr'd without much motion to raise it up. Thus several sorts of Wit run about amongst Mankind, and Mrs. E.Rs. Wit is a Platonick Wit,[2] as loving Friendships, and the conversation of Souls, but take her from the Platonicks, and she is gone, both from Wit and Understanding, or those are gone from her; and so leaving her to her single-Self, and her Wit to her Platonick-Lover, I rest,

Madam,
Your faithful Friend and Servant.

LETTER 46

Madam,

I Have observ'd, that in all Combustions and Wars, those get more Favour and Profit that enter into them Latest, for those that are at the Beginning, for the most part, are Losers, either in Lives, or Estates, or both, and are least Favoured by those they Fight or Adventure for, nay most commonly

---

1 Cordial or tonic.

2 Cavendish may allude to Platonic love as it was fashionable in the court of Queen Henrietta Maria. Cavendish, as a young woman, was a Maid of Honor to Henrietta Maria both in Oxford and later in the Queen's exile in Paris.

they are Disfavour'd;[1] wherefore, if Honour and Honesty would give leave, were I a Man, I would not enter until the last course, for that is Sweetest, like a Banquet; But because Honour and Honesty would Exclame against me, for preferring Profit and Promotion before Them, therefore a Man ought to do his Endeavour in a Just Cause, for Honour and Honestie's sake, although he were sure to lose his Liberty, Estate or Life. But leaving War, Loss, Disfavour and Preferment to Worthy Persons, and Unjust States and Princes, I rest,

> Madam,
> Your faithful Friend and Servant.

LETTER 47

Madam,

Th' other day the Lady S.M. was to Visit me, and I gave her Joy, she said she should have Joy indeed if it were a Son, I said, I bid her Joy of her Marriage, for I had not seen her since she was a Wife, and had been Married, which was some four Weeks ago, wherefore I did not know she was with Child;[2] but she rasping wind out of her Stomack, as Childing Women usually do, making Sickly Faces to express a Sickly Stomack, and fetching her Breath short, and bearing out her Body, drawing her Neck downward, and standing in a weak and faint Posture, as great bellied Wives do, bearing a heavy Burden in them, told me she had been with Child a fortnight, though by her behaviour one would not have thought she had above a Week to go, or to reckon; But she is so pleased with the Belief she is with Child (for I think she cannot perfectly Know her self, at most it is but breeding[3] Child) as she Makes or Believes her self Bigger than she Appears, and says, she Longs for every Meat that is Difficult to be gotten, and Eats and Drinks from Morning till Night, with very little intermission, and sometimes in the Night; whereupon I told her, if she did so, I believ'd she would be bigger Bellied and greater Bodied, whether she were with

---

1 There seems to be a good deal of sarcasm in this letter, sarcasm based on the fact that William Cavendish, husband to Cavendish, was an early supporter of Charles I in the Civil Wars. In the *Life* of her husband, Margaret calculates the personal losses of her husband due to this support at about £1,000,000. When the monarchy was restored, the losses sustained by him were not much regarded by the new king. For more on the topic, see letter 84 and note.

2 Cavendish was a stepmother but herself childless.

3 Fertile but not pregnant.

Child or not; besides Eating so much would make her Sick, if she were not with Child; she answer'd, that Women with Child might Eat Any thing, and as Much as they would or could, and it would do them no Harm. But I have observ'd, that generally Women take more Pleasure when they are with Child, than when they are not with Child, not onely in Eating more, and Feeding more Luxuriously, but taking a Pride in their great Bellies, although it be a Natural Effect of a Natural Cause; for like as Women take a greater Pride in their Beauty, than Pleasure or Content in their Virtue, so they take more Pride in Being with Child, than in Having a Child, for when they are brought to Bed, and up from their Lying in, they seem nothing so well Pleased, nor so Proud, as when they were great with Child; and to prove they are Prouder, and take more Pleasure in Being with Child, and in Lying in, than in Having a Child, is their Care, Pains, and Cost, in Getting, Making, and Buying Fine and Costly Childbed-Linnen, Swadling-Cloths, Mantles, and the like; as also fine Beds, Cradles, Baskets, and other Furniture for their Chambers, as Hangings, Cabinets, Plates, Artificial Flowers, Looking-glasses, Skreens, and many such like things of great Cost and Charge, besides their Banquets of Sweet-meats and other Junkets, as Cakes, Wafers, Biskets, Jellies, and the like, as also such strong Drinks, as methinks the very Smell should put a Childbed-Wife into a Fever, as Hippocras and Burnt-Wine, with Hot Spices, Mulled Sack, Strong and High-colour'd Ale, well Spiced, and Stuff'd with Tofts of Cake, and the like, all which is more chargeable than to bring up a Child when it is Born; nay, they will rather want Portions for their Children, when they are grown to be Men or Women, or want sufficiency of Means to pay for their Learning and Education, than want these Extravagancies of Luxury and Vanity at their Birth; and their Children being Christ'ned, are like some Brides and Bridegrooms, that are so Fine on their Wedding-day, as they are forc'd to go in Raggs all their lives after, which methinks is very strange, that for the Vanity and Shew of one day, they will spend so much as to be Beggars all their lives after; But as I said, this Proves that Women take a greater Pride and Pleasure in Being with Child, than in Having Children well Bred, and well-Bestow'd or Maintain'd, when grown to Years; and that which makes me wonder more, is, that Wise Men will suffer their fooliish Wives to be so Foolishly and Imprudently Expensive, wherefore such men are worthy to be Impoverished, that will suffer their wives to be so Vain, for it shews them to be better Husbands than Fathers, Kinder to their Wives than Careful of their Children, also it shews them Fonder Husbands than Loving Children, because they Ruin their Fore-fathers Posterity, by Impoverishing their own Succession, and that onely to

Please their Wives Humours, and to Expend for their Wives Vanities. But leaving the Lady S.M. to her Breeding Pride or Pride of Breeding, to her Sick Pleasure or Pleasurable Sickness, to her Luxurious Feeding, and Vain Providing, and wishing her a good Gossiping, I rest,

Madam,
Your faithful Friend and Servant.

LETTER 48

Madam,
It requires Experience, Skill, and Practice, for Men, Civilly, yet Courtly, to Entertain and Accompany Women in Visiting, or the like; they must sit within a Respectful Distance, with their Hats off, and Begin a Discourse, but let the Woman Follow it, which they will do until they are out of Breath; also they must not Interrupt them in their Talk, but let them Speak as Much, or as Long as they will, or rather Can, for our Will to Talk is beyond our Power, but though we want not Words, yet we want Understanding and Knowledge to Talk Perpetually; Neither must Men Contradict Women, although they should Talk Nonsense, which oftentimes they do, but must seem to Applaud and Approve, with gentle Nods and Bows, all they say; also they must View their Faces with Admiring Eyes, although they were Ill-favour'd, but those that are Beautiful, their Eyes must be Fix'd on them, or else seem to be Dazled; likewise they must seem to Start at their Calls, and Run with an affrighted hast, to Obey their Commands. Such, and many the like Ceremonies and Fooleries there are of this kind, from Men to Women, but these are rather from Strangers than Domestick Acquaintance. Wherefore setting aside antick Follies, yet a Civil Respect and Regard is due to the Female Sex from the Masculine, even from the Greatest to the Meanest; and so leaving Men to their Constrain'd Civilities and Feign'd Admirations, I rest,

Madam,
Your faithful Friend and Servant.

LETTER 49

Madam,

I Do not wonder that C.R. will not trust E.D. in any business of great Concernment, although an Able man to manage great Affairs, by reason he hath been False, although he seems now Faithful and True;[1] but Wise men are as Jealous of those men that have been Dishonest in the matter of Trust, as of those women that have been Dishonest in the matter of Love; for though they may be true Converts, yet those that are Wary will fear they do but Dissemble, for those that are Evil do not so Easily nor Suddenly turn to Good, as those that are Good are Apt to turn to Evil, for though Repentance doth cast forth the flowing part of Evil, yet many times there are Dregs, which lie lurking in the Mind or Soul, which in time, with the help of Opportunity and Advancement, may Increase again into their former Evil Condition; and Wise men know that there is less Danger in trusting an Honest Fool than a Subtil Knave; the truth is, it is pitty that Honesty and Ingenuity or Ability should not Inhabit together, for, for the most part they live asunder, as Ability and Ingenuity with Dishonesty, which Impowers and Inables such men to do the greater Mischiefs, for Subtil Wit and great Knavery take delight to do what is Worst, and Fortune many times favours them Best, and the Actors Glory most in their Wicked Deeds; But leaving C.R. to his Wisdom, and E.D. to Truth or Dissembling, I rest,

Madam,
Your faithful Friend and Servant.

LETTER 50

Madam,

I Cannot wonder that Mrs. F.G. is so desirous of a Husband, for I observe, that all Unmarried Women, both Maids and Widows, are the like, insomuch that there are more Customers that go to Hymen's Markets, which are Churches, Playes, Balls, Maskes, Marriages, etc., than there are Husbands to be Sold, and all Prices are bidden there, as Beauty, Birth, Breeding, Wit and Virtue, though Virtue is a Coin whereof is not much; but Husbands are so scarce, especially Good ones, as they are at such great Rates, that an indifferent Price will not Purchase any one, wherefore those

---

1   It is tempting to connect the C.R. of this letter to Charles II, who used these initials. In that case, E.D. might be Edward Hyde, earl of Clarendon, who was, indeed, an "Able man to manage great Affairs." See also letters 33 and 196.

that will Buy them, must be so Rich as to be able to bestow an extraordinary Price of Beauty, Birth, Breeding, Wit or Virtue, and yet much ado to Purchase any one, nay, some cannot be had without all those joyn'd into One; But Venus's Markets, which are also Publick Meetings, (for all Markets are Publick) are so well stor'd of all sorts and degress of Titles, Professions, Ages, and the like, as they are as Cheap as stinking Makrel, and all Coins are current there, but Virtue, wherefore that is never offer'd; 'tis true, the Markets of Hymen and Venus are in one and the same City or Place, yet Hymen and Venus Sell apart, like as several Grasiers bring their Beasts to one Market or Fair; I call them several Markets, to make a Distinction of which belongs to Hymen, and which to Venus; but for better Distinction's sake, I will put them into Shops apart, or into as many Pews in one Church, or Compare them to several Scenes in one Mask, several Acts in one Play, for as many Stalls or Shops there are in one Market, and several Magistrates in one City, so many Shops hath Hymen and Venus in one Market; but the Cheapest that are to be sold out of Hymen's Shops, are young Novices; and although there is much scarcity in Hymen's Shops, yet the Price of Gold or such Riches, if they be offer'd, buyes any man that is there to be sold, which are Batchelours and Widdowers, for there's no Married man in Hymen's Shops, unless unknown that they were bought before, and once Discover'd, they are Punish'd, for Married men can neither be Bought nor Sold by Hymen or his Customers, until they be Widowers; but in Venus Shops there be as many, if nor more, Married men than Batchelours or Widowers; but both in Hymen's and Venus's Shops there are of all sorts, Better and Worse, as Mean Persons and others of Quality, Handsom and not Handsom, Old and Young, and of middle Years; And as for Women, few are Sold in Shops, for they are the Buyers, and Married Women are the best Customers Venus hath; & though Married Women go to the Publick Market, which are Publick Meetings, as Fine as they can be Drest, and to the Publick View, out of pretence to meet there, and speak with such of their Friends that are Hymen's Customers, as also to help those Friends to Choose and Bargain for a Husband, or to keep them Company, yet when they go to Venus Shops they go Covered with their Veils, or rather Follies, for fear they should be known of their Husbands that lye there to be sold, for though they go Uncovered to Hymen's Shops, as with their Friends, to Assist them, yet to Venus's Shops they go alone. Thus Married and Unmarried take some occasion to be at the Market, and thus there is more Trade, Traffick and Commerce, in this Market than in any other; But such Persons as will live Single and Chast, never come there, unless some few;

and this sort of Persons for the most part live in Diana's Court, which are Cloisters or Monasteries; also some few Married Wives that live Retired, do not Frequent this Market, but if they do, they never come into any of the Shops, but stand in the midst of the Market-place, that it may be known they Buy nothing there; But Madam, I will leave this Discourse, and though I am one of Hymen's Subjects, being a Married Wife, yet I am none of Venus's Customers, but,

Madam,
Your faithful Friend and Servant.

LETTER 51

Madam,

Yesterday Mrs. P.I. was to Visit me, who pray'd me to present her Humble Service to you, but since you saw her she is become an Alt'red Woman, as being a Sanctified Soul, a Spiritual Sister, she hath left Curling her Hair, Black Patches are become Abominable to her, Laced Shoes and Galoshoes are Steps to Pride, to go Bare-neck'd she accounts worse than Adultery; Fans, Ribbonds, Pendants, Neckcloaths, and the like, are the Temptations of Satan, and the Signs of Damnation; and she is not onely Transform'd in her Dress, but her Garb and Speech, and all her Discourse, insomuch as you would not know her if you saw her, unless you were inform'd who she was; She Speaks of nothing but Heaven and Purification, and after some Discourse, she ask'd me, what Posture I thought was the best to be used in Prayer? I said, I thought no Posture was more becoming, nor did fit Devotion better, than Kneeling, for that Posture did in a manner Acknowledg from Whence we came, and to What we shall return, for the Scripture says, from Earth we came, and to Earth we shall return; then she spoke of Prayers, for she is all for Extemporary Prayers, I told her, that the more Words we used in Prayer, the Worse they were Accepted, for I thought a Silent Adoration was better Accepted of God, than a Self-conceited Babling; Then she ask'd me, if I thought one might not be Refined, by Tempering their Passions and Appetites, or by Banishing the Worst of them from the Soul and Body, to that Degree, as to be a Deity, or so Divine, as to be above the Nature of Man; I said no, for put the case Men could turn Brass or Iron, or such gross Metals, into Gold, and Refine that Gold into its height of Purity, yet it would be but a Metal still; so likewise the most Refined Man would be but Human still, he would be still a Man, and not a God; nay, take the Best of Godly Men, such as have been

Refined by Grace, Prayer and Fasting, to a degree of Saints, yet they were but Human and Men still, so long as the Body and Soul were joyn'd together, but when they were Separated, what the Soul would be, whether a God, a Devil, a Spirit, or Nothing, I could not tell; with that she Lifted up her Eyes, and Departed from me, Believing I was one of the Wicked and Reprobate, not capable of a Saving Grace, so as I believe she will not come near me again, lest her Purity should be Defiled in my Company, I believe the next news we shall hear of her, will be, that she is become a Preaching Sister; I know not what Oratory the Spirit will Inspire her with, otherwise I believe she will make no Eloquent Sermons, but I think those of her Calling do defie Eloquence, for the more Nonsense they Deliver, the more they are Admired by their Godly Fraternity. But leaving her to her Self-denying, I return to Acknowledg my self,

Madam,
Your very faithful Friend and Servant.

LETTER 52

Madam,
I Do not wonder that there are Pimps or Bawds, for Base Vices and Wicked Baseness are too Frequent in this Age, to be Wonder'd at, and certainly the like is in every Age, for the Composition of Mankind is not so Pure, but there are both Scum and Dregs, the which are for the most part the Inferiour sort of People, but which I wonder at, is, that the Lord P.B. should be a Pimp, and the Lady B.B. a Bawd, Persons of such Quality, where it was more likely that some Inferiour Persons should Pimp and Bawd for Them, than they should be so Low, as to Pimp and Bawd for Others; But perchance some can tell, that they do make use of such Inferiour Persons for their Own turn, as they are for the turn of Others; howsoever, the Actions of this Lord and Lady shew, that their Births were better than their Breeding, or that Fortune hath Favour'd them more with Titles, than Nature hath Indued them with Noble Dispositions, and thus having more Honour from Fortune than Nature, more Antiquity by Birth than Virtue by Breeding, 'tis the Cause that the Practice of their Lives is not answerable to the Degree of their Dignities; but for the most part such Base Actions are produced either out of Extreme Poverty, or Covetousness of Presents, or Ambition of Preferments, for Bauding and Pimping is seldom done *Gratis*; But those that are truly Noble, that is, have Noble Souls and Honourable Natures, can never be Forced,

Perswaded, or Inticed to do a Base Action, insomuch as they will rather choose to do a more Wicked Action (as we hold it) which is not mixt with Baseness, as Heroically to Kill themselves, than Basely Betray Chastity, and Beastly Procure Wanton Amours, for where Honour and Virtue takes a thorow Possession, they never leave their Habitation, no more than my Friendship with your Ladiship, for I am, and will ever be,

Madam,
    Your Ladiships faithful Friend, and humble Servant.

LETTER 53

Madam,

Mrs. W.S. doth not Approve of Sir C.R. she absolutely Refuses him for a Husband, she sayes he is Effeminate, and she Hates an Effeminate Man, as Nature Abhors Vacuity; she sayes, she had rather have a Debauch'd Man for a Husband,[1] by reason Debauchery had some Courage, although the worst part of Courage, for it durst Encounter Fevers, Gouts, Stone, Pox, and many the like Diseases, not but that Effeminacy and Debauchery are some-times joyn'd in one Person, but not commonly; but, she sayes, she will never Marry, unless she may have a Valiant, Wise man, such a man that will not Rashly or Foolishly Quarrel, but Warily and Resolutely Fight, that doth not onely measure his Sword, but his Quarrel, by the Length and Breadth of Honour, a man that is not outwardly Formal, but inwardly Rational, that weighs not his Words by the Number, but by the Sense, whose Actions are Levelled by the Rule of Honesty and Prudence; such a Man she will have for a Husband. The Lady P.E. hearing her, said, she could help her to an Husband that had the Reputation of Valour and Wisdom, but he was Severe; Mrs. W.S. said, she had rather have a Severe Wise man, than a Facil Fool; but said the Lady P.E. if you have this man, he will keep you strictly to a Wife's Obedience; she said, she was Content, were he never so Severe, nay, did his Severity extend to the Verge of Cruelty, for she had rather be Beaten by a Wise man, than Kiss'd by a Fool; But leaving her at this time without a Husband's Kisses or Blows, I rest,

Madam,
    Your faithful Friend and Servant.

---

1   If Cavendish has Charles II in mind for C.R., the reference is ironic, because "debauchery" was a word to be associated with him. See letters 33, 49, and 196.

LETTER 54

Madam,

Th' other day the Lady D.C. and the Lady G.B. came to Visit me, and being both met together, as Visitants, they fell into a Discourse of History, and so of former Times, and Persons of both Sexes, at last they fell into a Discourse of Married Wives, giving their Opinions of Good and Bad Wives that had lived in former Ages, and the Lady D.C. said, that Lucretia was the Best Wife that ever History mentioned, in that she Kill'd her self to save her Husbands Honour, being a Dishonour for a Husband to have an Abused, as a Ravished Wife, for though her Husband was not a Cuckold through her free Consent, yet was he a Cuckold through her Inforcement, which was a Dishonour in the second Degree; The Lady G.B. said, that though she did believe Lucretia was a very Chast Woman, and a Virtuous and Loving Wife, yet whether she Kill'd her self to save her Husbands Honour or her Own, she could not Judge, unless she had the Effect of a God, to know the Minds and Thoughts of human Creatures, for perchance Lucretia might know, or verily believe, that when her Husband should come to know the dishonourable Abuse that was done unto her, he would have Kill'd her himself, not so much through a Jealous mistrust of her, but for the Dishonour or Disgrace of the Abuse, and if so, then the Cause of Lucretia's Killing her self, was as much through Prudence & Wisdom as through Virtue, for in Killing her self she gain'd an Immortal Fame, for by Dying by her Own hand she seem'd Innocent, whereas, had she Dyed by her Husband's hand or command, the World being Censorious, would have thought her a Criminal;[1] wherefore, since Lucretia must Dye, she chose the best way, to Dye by her own voluntary Act, but had Lucretia been Unmarried, said she, and had been so Abused, she had been a Fool to have Kill'd her self, before she had endeavoured to have Kill'd her Abuser, for it would be more Justice to have Kill'd the Murderer of her Honour, than to have Murdered her Innocent Self, onely the Revenge ought in Houour to have been Executed in some Publick Place and Assembly, and then the Private Abuse Declared, if it had not been Known already: But these two Ladies arguing whether Lucretia Kill'd her self for her Husband's Honour or for her Own, at last grew so Earnest in their Discourse, as they fell to Quarrel with each other, & in such a Fury they were, as they

---

1 In *The World's Olio*, Cavendish writes that Lucretia's husband was to blame for his wife's death, since he praised her in public and thus caused her rapist to become sexually aroused (33).

were ready to Beat one another, nay, I was afraid they would have Kill'd each other, and for fear of that Mischief, I was forced to be a Defender of both, standing between them, and making Orations to the one and then to the other; at last I intreated them to Temper their Passions, and to Allay their Anger; and give me leave Ladies, said I, to ask you what Lucretia was to either of you? was she of your Acquaintance or Kindred, or Friend, or Neighbour, or Nation? and if she was none of these, as it was very probable she was not, Living and Dying in an Age so long afore this, nay, so long, as the Truth might Rationally be questioned, if not of the Person, yet of the Manner of the Action, for perchance the clear Truth was never Recorded, Falshood having been written in Histories of much later Times than that of Lucretia; therefore Allay your Passions, for why should you two Ladies fall out, and become Enemies for Lucretia's sake, whom you never knew or heard of, but as in an old Wife's Tale, which is an old History. But howsoever, Good Ladies, said I, leave Lucretia to live and dye in History, and be you two Friends in present Life, Abuse not your selves with Rage, concerning Tarquin's Abusing Lucretia with Lust. Thus talking to them, at last I calmed their Passions, and made them Friends again, but making Peace between them, I spent more Breath and Spirits, than the Peace of two Foolish, at least, Cholerick Ladies was worth, for although there is an old Saying, Happy is the Peace-maker, yet I am happy I am quit at this present of their Company, and that I can subscribe myself,

Madam,
Your faithful Friend and Servant.

LETTER 55

Madam,
You were pleased in your last Letter to tell me, that you had been in the Country, and that you did almost Envy the Peasants for living so Merrily; it is a sign, Madam, they live Happily, for Mirth seldom dwells with Troubles and Discontents, neither doth Riches nor Grandeur live so Easily, as that Unconcerned Freedom that is in Low and Mean Fortunes and Persons, for the Ceremony of Grandeur is Constrain'd and bound with Forms and Rules, and a great Estate and high Fortune is not so easily man-ag'd as a Less, a Little is easily order'd, where Much doth require Time, Care, Wisdom and Study as Considerations; but Poor, Mean Peasants that live by their Labour, are for the most part Happier and Pleasanter than great

Rich Persons, that live in Luxury and Idleness, for Idle Time is Tedious, and Luxury is Unwholsom, whereas Labour is Healthful and Recreative, and surely Country Huswives take more Pleasure in Milking their Cows, making their Butter and Cheese, and feeding their Poultry, than great Ladies do in Painting, Curling, and Adorning themselves, also they have more Quiet & Peaceable Minds and Thoughts, for they never, or seldom, look in a Glass to view their Faces, they regard not their Complexions, nor observe their Decayes, they Defie Time's Ruins of their Beauties, they are not Peevish and Froward if they look not as Well one day as another, a Pimple or Spot in their Skin Tortures not their Minds, they fear not the Sun's Heat, but Out-face the Sun's Power, they break not their Sleeps to think of Fashions, but Work Hard to Sleep Soundly, they lie not in Sweats to clear their Complexions, but rise to Sweat to get them Food, their Appetites are not Queazie with Surfeits, but Sharp'ned with Fasting, they relish with more Savour their Ordinary Course Fare, than those who are Pamper'd do their Delicious Rarities; and for their Mirth and Pastimes, they take more Delight and true Pleasure, and are more Inwardly Pleased and Outwardly Merry at their Wakes, than the great Ladies at their Balls, and though they Dance not with such Art and Measure, yet they Dance with more Pleasure and Delight, they cast not Envious, Spiteful Eyes at each other, but meet Friendly and Lovingly. But great Ladies at Publick Meetings take not such true Pleasures, for their Envy at each others Beauty and Bravery Disturbs their Pastimes, and Obstructs their Mirth, they rather grow Peevish and Froward through Envy, than Loving and Kind through Society, so that whereas the Countrey Peasants meet with such Kind Hearts and Unconcerned Freedom as they Unite in Friendly Jollity, and Depart with Neighbourly Love, the Greater sort of Persons meet with Constrain'd Ceremony, Converse with Formality, and for the most part Depart with Enmity; and this is not onely amongst Women, but amongst Men, for there is amongst the Better sort a greater Strife for Bravery than for Courtesie, for Place than Friendship, and in their Societies there is more Vain-glory than Pleasure, more Pride than Mirth, and more Vanity than true Content; yet in one thing the Better Sort of Men, as the Nobles and Gentry, are to be Commended, which is, that though they are oftener Drunken and more Debauch'd than Peasants, having more Means to maintain their Debaucheries, yet at such times as at great Assemblies, they keep themselves more Sober and Temperate than Peasants do, which are for the most part Drunk at their Departing; But to Judg between the Peasantry and Nobles for Happiness, I believe where there's One Noble that is truly Happy, there are a Hundred Peasants; not that there be More Peasants than Nobles, but that they are More Happy, number for number, as having not the Envy, Ambition, Pride, Vain-glory, to Cross, Trouble, and Vex them, as Nobles have; when I say Nobles, I mean those that have been Ennobled by Time as well as Title, as the Gentry. But, Madam, I am not a fit Judg for the several Sorts or Degrees, or Courses of Lives, or Actions of Mankind, as to Judg which is Happiest, for Happiness lives not in Outward Shew or Concourse, but Inwardly in the Mind, and the Minds of Men are too Obscure to be Known, and too Various and Inconstant to Fix a Belief in them, and since we cannot Know our Selves, how should we know Others? Besides, Pleasure and true Delight lives in every ones own Delectation, but let me tell you; my Delectation is, to prove my self,

Madam,
Your faithful Fr. and S.

LETTER 56

Madam,
In your last Letter you writ how much the Lord N.O. doth Admire Mrs. B.U. and what Addresses he makes to her, for he being in Years hath seen much of the World, and many and Different Beauties, and hath Convers'd with many and Different Wits, and hath found and observed many and Different Humours, and hath made many and Different Courtships to many and Different Women: yet I have observ'd that men in Years would seem Lovers and Admirers, but are not;[1] and Young men are Lovers and Admirers, and would not seem so; Men in Years Praise all the Young Women they meet withall, but think not of them when they are out of their Companies, but Young men Praise some Particulars, and when Absent, are more Fond and Deeper in Love than when they are personally Present; and it is to be observed, that the chiefest Imployment of the most part of Men is to make Love, not that they are Really in Love, but Feignedly make themselves so, and Amorous Courtships are the most general Actions in the World, and the most general Imployments of the Thoughts in mens Minds; and the same is also amongst Women; so that most of mankind are Amorous Lovers, for Love is the Subject of their Thoughts, & Courtly Addresses the Action of their Time, & the Chief Business of their Lives; but if it were a Noble Love, it were Commendable, for then their Time, Industry, and Actions of their Lives would be Imployed

---

1 Cavendish was her husband's junior by thirty years.

in Acts of Charity, Friendship, Humanity, Magnificence, Generosity, and the like, but being Amorous Lovers, their Time is Idly Wasted in Adorning, Fashioning, Flattering, Protesting and Forswearing; besides, Amorous Lovers are Inconstant, Prodigal, Fantastical, and the like. But leaving them to their Complemental Adresses, I rest,

Madam,
Your faithful Friend and Servant.

LETTER 57

Madam,
Here is no News, onely I read a Gazet that speaks of a Courtesan, which hath been the Ruin of many Gentlemen's and Noble Men's Estates, by presenting her with Rich Gifts, and maintaining her in Bravery, and 'tis likely she hath Ruined their Bodies, if not their Souls, as she hath done their Estates; yet it is to be hoped, that all is not Truth that is Printed in a Gazet, for it is to be observed, that Gazets are fuller of Lies than Truths, which makes some Histories that are lately Printed and Published, to have so many Falshoods in them, being for the most part Compiled and Form'd out of Gazets; But if this part of the Gazet be true, as concerning the Courtesan, it shews that she hath a Superiour Art of Allurements, not onely to insnare one or two, but many, which Art hath a Magick Power to Transform Rational Men to Beastly Adulterers, Simple Asses, and Prodigal Fools; for certainly it cannot be merely Beauty alone that can have such Power, for mere Beauty takes oftener the Eye than the Heart, it hath more Admirers than Doting Lovers, and the greatest Gift Beauty hath given, are Praises, which Praises last not Long, by reason Beauty soon Decayes; But when Beauty is attended with Insinuating Arts, as Behaviour of Person, Pleasant Speech, and Harmonious Voice, as also the Arts of Musick, Dancing, Dressing, and the like, it becomes Victorious, and makes its Triumphs in many Hearts, like as in many Nations; But many times those Arts are Victorious without Beauty, whereas Beauty is seldom or never Victorious without them; Indeed Women Skilful in these Arts are like Juglers, which Deceive Sense and Reason, making an Appearance of that which is not Really so; and thus most of our Sex Juggle with Men, they Delude them with Artificial Shews and Insinuating Flattery, and 'tis their chief Study and Endeavour so to do; But few Arrive to that Artificial Perfection, as the Courtesan mentioned in the Gazet; wherefore it would be well if Wives had more of that Art to keep their Husband's Affections, or at least to keep them from seeking after

Variety; and for Courtesans to have less, that they might not Draw and Intice Husbands from their Honest Wives, nor Batchelors and Widowers from lawful Marriage: But for the most part Courtesans with their Arts Usurp the Wives Rights and Maids hopes; and so leaving the famous Courtesan to her Lovers, and her Lovers to their Ruins, I rest,

Madam,
Your faithful Friend and Servant.

LETTER 58

Madam,

In your last Letter you sent me word, you were not of my Opinion, that all men ought to wear their Swords at all Times, and in all Places and Companies, for you say it is not fit that Drunkards, or Mad-men, or Lovers, should wear Swords; for Drunkards will use their Swords to the hurt of Others, by reason they are Quarrelsome and Abusive; and Mad-men will use their Swords to the hurt of Themselves, either through a Frantick Despair or Conceit; and Lovers will Affright their Mistresses with them. Madam, you have forgotten two or three Words added thereto, for I said, that all Gallant Gentlemen ought to wear Swords, at all Times, and in all Places and Companies; but Drunkards and Mad-men, though they may be Gentlemen, yet they cannot be said Gallant men whilst they are Mad or Drunken, because they want their Reason to Distinguish, for the Gallantry of the Mind or Soul is Valour, Generosity, Humanity, Justice, Fidelity, and the like, all which cannot be, at least, not in force in Irrational Creatures, which Mad-men and Drunkards are for that time. And for Lovers, it is very Requisite they should wear Swords to guard their Mistresses, for she is but a Foolish Mistress that will be afraid of her Safety; But a Gallant man wears his Sword for his Honour, King, and Country; as for his Country, it includes Piety, Friendship, and Natural Affection; for his King, it includes Fidelity and Loyalty; for his Honour, it includes Truth, Right, Love, Generosity and Humanity. In truth, Generosity and Humanity is like the Sun and the Air, for Humanity doth like the Air spread equally to all, it enters every where, and fills up all Vacuities; and Generosity like the Sun, shines every where, and on every Creature, although not at one Time, yet in such a Compass of Time as it hath strength and motion to extend it self; also his Benefits are General, he Disputes not Who or What deserves his Light or Heat, but knows his Light and Heat is Beneficial to all Creatures, which if they Abuse to Evil Uses, it is none of his Fault. Thus Generosity shines in the Air of Humanity, and Fortitude is like Heaven, which no Enemy can Enter, it Defends and Guards the Distressed; and Valour is the Sword of Justice, to Cut off Offenders, and the Sword of Valour is a sharp metal'd Blade, that Gallant Gentlemen should alwayes wear about them, and have Skill to Manage it, and Judgment and Discretion to know When, and on Whom to Use it. But, Madam, lest the mentioning of a Sword should Fright you, I'le leave it, and rest,

Madam,
Your faithful Friend and Servant.

LETTER 59

Madam,
As for the Lady P.Y. who, you say, spends most of her Time in Prayer, I can hardly believe God can be Pleased with so many Words, for what shall we need to Speak so many Words to God, who knows our Thoughts, Minds and Souls better than we our selves? Christ did not teach us Long Prayers, but a Short One, nay if it were lawful for Men to Similize God to his Creatures, (which I think it is not) God might be Tired with Long and Tedious Petitions or often Repetitions; but, Madam, Good Deeds are Better than Good Words, in so much, as One Good Deed is better than a Thousand Good Words, As for Example, One Act of Upright Justice, or Pure Charity, is better than a Book full of Prayers, a Temperate Life is better many times than a Praying Life; for we may be Intemperate even in our Prayers, as to be Superstitious or Idolatrous; Indeed every Good Deed is a Prayer, for we do Good for Gods sake, as being pleasing to him, for a Chast, Honest, Just, Charitable, Temperate Life is a Devout Life, and Worldly labour is Devout, as to be Honestly Industrious to Get, and Prudent to Thrive, that one may have where with all to Give; for there is no Poor Begger, but had rather a Penny than a Blessing, for they will tell you, that they shall Starve with *Dieu vous assiste*, but be Relieved with a *Denar*. Wherefore the Lady P.Y. with her much Fasting and long Praying will Starve her Self, and Waste her Life out before the Natural Time, which will be a Kind of Self-murder, and we hold Self-murder the Greatest Sinn, although it should be done in a Pious Form or Manner; but to Help a Friend in Distress is Better and more Acceptable, than to Pray for a Friend in Distress, to Relieve a Beggar in Want, is better than to Pray for him, to Attend the Sick is better than to Pray for the Sick; But you will say, both do Well, I say it is Well Said, and Well when it is Done, but the One must not Hinder the Other, wherefore we ought not to

Leave the World to Pray, but to Live in the World to Act, as to Act to Good Uses, and 'tis not enough to Give for the Poor, but to see that the Poor be not Cousen'd of their Gifts, wherefore they ought to Distribute their Gifts Themselves, and to be Industrious to Know and to Find out those that do Truly and not Feignedly Want, neither must their Gifts make the Poor Idle, but set the Idle Poor awork, and as for those that cannot Work or Help themselves, as the Old, Sick, Decrepit, and Children, they must be Maintain'd by those that have Means and Strength and Health to Attend them; But perchance if the Lady P.Y. heard me, she would say, I were one of those that did Speak more Good Words, than Act Good Deeds, or that I neither Spent my Time in Praying nor Pious Acting; Indeed I cannot, as the Proud Pharisee, Brag and Boast of my Good Deeds, but with the Poor Publican, I must say, Lord have Mercy on me, a miserable Sinner, yet I must say thus much Truth of my Self, that I never had Much to Give; for before the Warrs of this Country I was too Young to be Rich, or to have Means in my Own Power of Disposing, and since the Warrs all my Friends being so Ruined, and my Husband Banished from his Native Countrey, and Dispossest of his Inherited Estate, I have been in a Condition rather to Receive, than to Give: Yet I have not done much of either, for truly I am as Glad not to Receive, as Sorry not to Give, for Obligation is as great a Burden to me, as not be Able to Oblige is an Unhappiness, not that I account it so great an Unhappiness to be in such a Condition, as to be fit to Receive, but to Receive in such a Condition, as not to be Able to return the Obligation, for the Truth is, I had rather Suffer for Want, than Take to be Relieved; But I thank God, I have not had many of those Burdens of Obligations, some few I have had, but those were from my near Relative Friends, not from Strangers, which is a Double, nay, a Treble Blessing; but my Condition is fitter for Prayer, as having not sufficient Means to do Good Works, my Husband being Rob'd of all his Estate, than the Lady P.Y.s who hath Saved all she can lay Claim to; Wherefore leaving her to her Prayers of Thanksgiving, and I to Prayers of Petitioning, I rest,

Madam,
Your very faithful Friend and Servant.

LETTER 60

Madam,
I Am sorry to hear there is such a Difference betwixt the Lady F.O. and her Husband, as they are upon Parting, I wish their Humours and Dispositions

were more Agreeable, and their Froward Passions less Violent; I cannot Condemn Either, nor Excuse Both, for if they Anger each Other, they have Both cause to be Angry, and are Both to be Blamed for so Doing, and so Both together they ought to be Condemned, but Each apart to be Excused: But Marriage is a very Unhappy Life when Sympathy Joyns not the Married Couple, for otherwise it were better to be Barr'd up within the Gates of a Monastery, than to be Bound in the Bonds of Matrimony; but whenas Sympathy Joyns Souls and Bodies in Marriage, then those Bonds are like Diamond-Chains to Adorn, not to Inslave them, and Heroick Honour and Chastity are the two Thrones whereon a Married Couple is Placed, Heroick Honour is the Throne of the Husband, and Chastity the Throne of the Wife, on which Love Crowns their Lives with Peace, and Inrobes or Inclothes them with Happiness, which Happiness you Enjoy, which is also the Joy,

Madam,
Of Your faithful Friend and Servant.

LETTER 61

Madam,
I Am sorry to hear you have lost so Good a Servant as E.L. was, for she was Faithful, Trusty, Loving, Humble, Obedient, Industrious, Thrifty, and Quiet, Harmlessly Merry and Free, yet full of Respect and Duty, which Few Servants are in this Age, for most are Idle, Cousening, Wastful, Crafty, Bold, Rude, Murmuring, Factious and Trecherous, and what not that is Evil?[1] But truly, Madam, the Fault ought to be laid on the Masters and Mistresses, who either give their Servants ill Examples by their Evil or Idle Life, or through a Credulous Trust, which is a Temptation to a Poor Servant, and it is a part of our Prayer, Lead us not into Temptation; or through a Neglect of Governing, for there is an old true Saying, The Masters Eye makes the Horse Fat;[2] or through a Timorous Fear of Commanding, for many Masters are Afraid to Command a Peremptory Servant, being more in Aw of the Servant than the Servant of the Master; or

---

1   Cavendish managed the family estates in the late 1660s and was able to catch a steward who took bribes.

2   "The Maisters eye maketh the horse fat," according to Camden's *Remains* (London, 1614) 283. In "A True Relation," Cavendish writes that her mother was an excellent manager both of people and of agricultural matters: "She was very skillful in leases, and in setting of lands [planting], and court [farm-yard] keeping, ordering of stewards, and the like affairs" (*Nature's Pictures*, 294; *Paper Bodies*, 49).

through much Clemency, giving their Servants their Wills so much as they neglect their Duties; or through their Prodigality, when to Inrich their Servants they make themselves Poor, so as the Servant becomes Greater than the Master, which makes them so Proud, that they Slight their Commands and Neglect their Services, Forgetting who Advanced them, and are apt to Rebel against them, just like the Devils, when they were Angels, who perceiving they were so Glorious Creatures, Rebell'd against their Creator, and would be as God himself; Just so are Poor Servants when their Master gives them fine Cloaths to Adorn them, or Money to Inrich them, or Offices to Advance them, they streight would be their Masters, nay, they will Envy their Master if they see him have any thing Better than they. This I have Known by Experience, but They will not Know it, untill they become to be like Devils, that is, in a miserable Condition, which they deserve for their Ingratitude; but a Good Servant is a Treasure, sayes Solomon; and so I think is a Good Master to a Servant, if the Servant have Wit to perceive it, But a Good Master is to know How to Command, When to Command, and What to Command; also When to Bestow, What to Bestow, & How much to Bestow on a Good Servant; also to fit Servants to Imployments, and Imployments to Servants; also to know How and When to Restrain them, and when to give them Liberty; also to observe, which of his Servants be fit to be Ruled with Austerity or Severity, and which with Clemency, and to Reward and Punish them Properly, Timely and Justly; Likewise when to make them Work, and when to let them Play or Sport; as also when to Keep them at a Distance, and when to Associate Himself with them; And truly, I should sooner chuse to Associate my Self with the Company of my Servants, had they good Breeding, or were Capable to Learn and Imitate what did belong to good Behaviour, than with Strangers, for Good Servants are Friends as well as Servants, nay, Servants are a Guard to their Masters, for Good & Faithfull Servants will Dye for the Safeguard of their Masters Life, and they will indure any Torments rather than Betray their Masters; and it is the Duty of Servants so to Do, for Servants ow almost as much Duty to their Masters, as Children to their Parents, or Subjects to their Natural Prince, for Servants are not only Govern'd, but Instructed, Fed, and Maintain'd; and what greater Crime is there, than to be a Traitor to their Governour, Tutor, and Nourisher of their Life? And every Master, the Meanest that is, is a Father and a King in his own Family, Wherefore to my Reason they are very unwise that will go out of their own Dominions, and leaving their own Obedient Subjects, which are their Servants, Travel into other Kingdoms, which are other Families, wherein they have neither Power nor

Obedience, leaving their own Servants without Rule or Guide, for when a Master is from Home, his Family is like a Body without a Head, like as a King should Travel into Forein Countries, and leave his Subjects and Kingdom and State-Affairs at Random, or to a Deputy, 'tis likely his Subjects would Rebell against him through Dislike to the Deputy, as Scorning to be Ruled or Govern'd by a Fellow-Subject, or else the Deputy will get away their Love from their Prince, and then will strive to thrust the Right Owner out; The same is with a Master and his Servants; wherefore a Wise, Loving Master will keep Home, and go no oftener Abroad than Occasion requires, but will Entertain himself with his own Family, and his Family will Entertain him with Sports and Pastimes, like as Subjects do their Princes, and whenas a Servant doth Rebell, although the Master hath not Power to Banish him the Country or Kingdom, as Princes have, yet hath he Power to turn him out of his Service, and Banish him from his House, if his Fault do deserve it; but some may think it strange, that there are as few Masters that know how to Govern their Families Wisely, as there are Kings that know how to Rule their Kingdoms Wisely; but that is no wonder, for first, where there is One King of a Kingdom, there are Thousands of Masters of Families, and a King is the Master of all those Families, insomuch as a King hath more Masters to Govern and Rule, than the Richest Master of his Kingdom hath Servants; but if Servants were as they should be, Masters would not onely Thrive by the Trusty Labours of their Servants, and Servants by the Wealth of their Master, but Masters and Servants would live Easily, by the Diligence of the One, and the Prudence of the Other; also they would live Delightfully, by their Sports and Pastimes, where the Master would sit as a Kingly Spectator, whilst his Servants were Pleasant Actors, in all which both Masters and Servants would be very Happy, so as this World would seem an Earthly Paradise. But, Madam, if I write any more, I shall go near to make you a Servant to your Servant, in a Laborious reading her Long Letter, but it was your Command in your last Letter, that I should write you Long Letters, and I believe in this I have Fully Obey'd you, which is my Desire to all your Commands, to let you Know that there is none more Truly and Faithfully

Your Ladiships
Servant than I.

LETTER 62

Madam,

Mrs. C.R. is very much troubled in her Mind with Doubts and Fears, since she hath heard that the Lady S.P. did Publickly and Privately Praise her, for, she sayes, she is afraid the Lady S.P. hath observ'd some Error in her Behaviour, or hath heard her Speak Foolishly, or hath found out some Decayes of Beauty in her Face, or some Deformities in her Shape, or some of the Masculine Sex have Dispraised her Beauty, Wit, Person, Behaviour, or the like, otherwise, sayes she, she is Confident she would never have Praised her, for, sayes she, it is so Unusual for one Woman to Praise another, as it seems Unnatural; wherefore she doth not Delight to be Prais'd by her own Sex, and since that time she received your last Letter, she will sit in a Silent Musing Posture, Considering and Examining her self, as Searching to find out what Faults she hath, or what Crimes she is Guilty of, that the Lady S.P. should Praise her, and so Peevish and Froward she is for it, as I believe she will never be Quiet, or at Rest and Peace in her Mind, until she hear that the Lady S.P. hath Spoken Spitefully of her, or hath Dispraised her some wayes or other. The Truth is, she doth Confess as much, for she sayes, She shall never think her Self Handsome, Conversable, nor Vertuous, but Ill-favoured, Foolish, Base, or Wicked, unless she be Disprais'd by her own Sex, wherefore if you Hear, as certainly you cannot chuse unless you will stop your Ears, any Femal Discommendations concerning Mrs. C.R. Pray send her Word of them, by which you will Infinitely Oblige her, and in the mean time I shall Endeavour to Pacifie her Thoughts, and Settle her Mind in Peace and Quiet, Resting

> Madam,
> Your faithful Friend and Servant.

LETTER 63

Madam,

I Have observed, there are amongst Mankind as often Mode Phrases in Speech, as Mode Fashions in Cloaths and Behaviour, and so Moded they are, as their Discourse is as much Deckt with those Phrases as their Cloaths with several Coloured Ribbands, or Hats with Feathers, or Bodyes with Affected motions, and whosoever doth Discourse out of the Mode, is as much Despised, as if their Cloaths or Behaviours were out of Fashion, they are accounted Fools or Ill-bred Persons; indeed most Men and

Women in this Age, in most Nations in Europe are nothing but Mode, as mode-Minds, mode-Bodyes, mode-Appetites, mode-Behaviours, mode-Cloaths, mode-Pastimes or Vices, mode-Speeches and Conversations, which is strange to have Minds according to the Mode, as to have a mode-Judgment, for all will give their Judgments and Opinions according to the Mode, and they Love and Hate according to the Mode, they are Cour-agious or Cowardly according to the Mode, Approve or Dislike according to the Mode, nay, their Wits are according to the Mode, as to Rallery, Clinch,[1] Buffonly Jest, and the like, for Better Wit is not usually the Mode, as being alwayes out of Fashion amongst mode-Gallants, but True and Good Wit lives with the Seniors of the Time, such as Regard not the Mode, but Chuse or Prefer what is Best, and not what is Most in Fashion, unless that which is Best be in Fashion, which is very seldom if ever Known, for that which is Best or Good, is not General, especially Wit, for the Right True and Best Wit keeps to Particulars, as being Understood by Particulars; Some Moders have oftener Wit in their Mouths than in their Brains, that is, they Speak the Wit of Others, but have none of their Own. But Grave, Experienced and Wise men give their Judgment or Opinion, not according to the Mode or Fashion, but according to Probability, Sense and Reason; neither do they say, such or such a Thing Will or Shall be, or Is so, Why? because it is the General Opinion, but they say, such or such a Thing May be, or 'tis Likely Will be, or Is so, Why? because there is a Probability or Reason for it: Neither do the Just and Wise Hate or Love, Approve or Dislike, because it is the Mode, as to Hate what is not Generally Loved, or Love what is not Generally Hated, or to Despise what is Generally Disliked, or Admire what is Generally Commended, but they Hate what is Really Bad, Wicked or Base, and not what is Thought so; and Love what is really Good, Vertuous and Worthy, not for the general Opinion, but for the Truth, and they Admire and Commend, Despise or Scorn, Dislike or Disapprove that which is Despisable or Discommendable or Scornable, and so the like; neither are they Couragious or Cowardly according to the Mode, but they are Valiant or Cautious according to the Cause or Quarrel; they do not Fight out of or in a Bravado, but for Honour, or in Honour's Quarrel; nor do they Pass by Injury, or Cover an Anger or Affront with a Rallery or Jest, but because the Person that did the Injury, or gave the Affront, was either Drunk, Mad, or a Base, Inferiour Person, fitter for his Man's Quarrel, than for his Own; and for Wise men, they Speak not with Mode-Phrases, but such Words as are most Plain to be

---

1   A repartee involving a twist or pun.

Understood, and the Best to Deliver or Declare Sense and Reason, and their Behaviours are those which are Most Manly and Least Apish, Fantastical or Constrain'd; and their Clothes are such as are most Useful, Easie and Becoming; neither do their Appetites Relish Mode-Meats or Sauces, because they have the Mode Haut Goust, but they Relish Best what is most Pleasing or Savoury to their Taste; and so for Drinks Compounded, as Chocolata, Limonada, and the like, they will not Drink them because of the Mode; neither do they Affect Mode-Songs or Sounds, because they are in Fashion to be Sung or Play'd, but because they are Well-Set Tunes, or Well-Compos'd Musick, or Witty Songs, and Well Sung by Good Voices, or Well Plaid on Instruments; neither do they follow Mode-Vices or Vanities for Fashion, but for Pleasure, or their own Humour or Fancy; nor do they use those Exercises that are in Mode, but those they like Best. Thus a Wise Man Follows not the Mode, but his own Humour, for if it be the Mode to Play at Tennis, or Paille-maille,[1] or the like, if he like better to Ride or Fence, he will let alone the mode-Exercises and Use his Own; if it be the mode-Pastime to Play at Cards or Dice, if he like better to Write or Read, he will leave the mode-Pastime and Follow his Own; and if it be the mode-Custom to Dine and Sup, and Meet at Ordinaries[2] or Taverns, if he like better to Sup and Dine at Home alone, he will not go to Ordinaries or Taverns; if it be the Mode to make General Courtships, if he Like, or is better pleased with a Particular Mistress, he will not follow the Mode; neither will he Ride Post because it is the Mode, but because his Affairs Require it; neither will he Journey from Place to Place to no Purpose, because it is the Mode, but will Wisely Sit still or Rest at his own Home, because it is Easie, Peaceable, Quiet, and Prudent, as not so Chargeable. But leaving the Modists to their mode-Clothes, Oaths, Phrases, Courtships, Behaviours, Garbs and Motions, to their mode-Meats, Drinks, Pastimes, Exercises, Pleasures, Vanities and Vices; to their mode-Songs, Tunes, Dances, Fiddles and Voices; to their mode-Judgements, Opinions and Wits; to their mode-Quarrels and Friendships, to their Mode-Lying and Dissembling, I rest,

Madam,
Your faithful Friend and Servant.

---

1   A game played with a wooden ball and a mallet.

2   Taverns serving meals at fixed prices.

LETTER 64

Madam,

'Tis usual for Men to Brag, onely some Brag more Obscurely or Neatly, and some more Grosly than others; and it is Natural for Women to Brag; but all Bragging proceeds from Self-Love, to Covet the World's good Opinion, Esteem and Respect, for through fear of Obscurity Men Divulge their own Worth, Wealth, Birth, Qualities, Abilities, Favours and Graces, and those Actions they believe are Worthy of Praise: but for the most part all Brags are heightened by the help of Self-partiality or Self-opinion beyond the Truth; so that Brags are like Romances, the Ground is True, but the Elevation False; indeed a Brag is nearer a Lie than a Truth, for to speak pure Truth is not so much a Brag as a Vain-glory, at least, a Vanity, which most of Mankind Delight in, although the Speaker is more Delighted than the Hearer, for few or none Delight to Hear a Self-praiser, unless it be those that have near Relations, as Parents, Children, Brothers, Sisters, Husbands and Wives, whose Affections are Delighted with their Friends Perfections and Good Fortunes, but Strangers and Visiting Acquaintance Dislike that Vain Truth, and are soon Tyred with such a Relation, nay, have an Aversion to the Sound of a Bragging Tongue, not their Own Tongues, for no Discourse Pleases them Better, than to Discourse of Themselves, but the Tongues of Others, which beget rather Envy and Malice in the Hearers, than Love and Admiration. But leaving this Natural Defect and Vain Effect, I rest,

> Madam,
> Your faithful Friend and Servant.

LETTER 65

Madam,

I Do not wonder that the several Cities and Towns in N. do Dislike their Governours and Government, by reason the Commons strive to Out-brave the Nobles in their Building, Garnishing, Furnishing, Adorning and Flourishing in Gold and Bravery, for even the Mechanicks in this City, and I believe in the rest, are Suffer'd to have their Coaches, Lacquies, Pages, Waiting-maides, and to wear Rich and Glorious Garments, Fashioning themselves in all things like the Nobles, which causes Envy in the Nobility, and Pride in the Commonalty, the One, to see their Inferiors Outshine them, the Other, that they can Equal or Out-brave their Betters;

This Pride and Envy causes Murmur, and Murmur causes Faction, which may in time make an Alteration in the State and Government, for when the Commons once get so High as to Justle the Nobility, a thousand to one but the Nobles Fall, and with them Royalty, by reason they are the Pillars of Royalty, or Royal Government; Wherefore the Commons should be kept like Cattel in Inclosed Grounds, and whensoever any did Break out of their Bounds, they should be Impounded, that is, the Commons should be kept Strictly, not to Exceed their Rank or Degree in Shew and Bravery, but to Live according to their Qualities, not according to their Wealth;[1] and those that will be so Presumptuous, should be Imprison'd and Fined great Summs for that Presumption, this would keep the Commons in Aw, and the Nobles in Power to uphold Royal Government, which is certainly the Best and Happiest Government, as being most United, by which the People becomes most Civil, for Democracy is more Wild and Barbarous than Monarchy; But this is fitter for Monarchs to Consider, than for Women to Speak of, and therefore leaving the One to the Other, I rest,

> Madam,
> Your faithful Friend and Servant.

LETTER 66

Madam,

I Was so Surprised with the Lady A.Ns. Letter, as I was Astonish'd, it being such a Bitter and Angry Letter; but she had Reason to be Angry, because I had committed a very great Fault by a Mistake, for I one day sitting a Musing with my own Thoughts, was Considering and Pondering upon the natures of Mankind, and Wondering with my Self, why Nature should make all Men some wayes or other Defective, either in Body, or Mind, or both, for a Proof I Chose out One whom I thought the freest from Imperfections, either in Mind, or Body, which was the Lady A.N. and I took Pen and Paper, and Writ down all the Defects I could Think or had Observed in her, and upon an other all the Excellencies she was Indued with, by Nature, Heaven and Education, which last Pleased me so Well, as I was resolved to send her a Copy in a Letter; but when I was to

---

1   In this passage, Cavendish is much like her husband, who mistrusted commoners as a group. See *Ideology and Politics on the Eve of the Restoration: Newcastle's Advice to Charles* II, ed. Thomas P. Slaughter (Philadelphia: American Philosophical Society, 1984).

send her the Letter, both the Papers lying upon my Table together, I mistook the right Paper that was in her Praise, and sent that which was in her Dispraise, never reading it when I sent it, and when she did Receive it, it seem'd she was in as much Amaze, as I at her Answer, but afterwards she fell into a very Angry Passion, and in that Passion Writ me an Answer, which I opened with great Joy, thinking she had been very well pleased with my former Letter, but when I did read it, and found out the mistake in sending the wrong Letter, I was as if I had been Thunder-stricken, my Blood flushing so violently into my Face, as to my thinking my Eyes flash'd out fire like Lightning, and after that there fell such a Showr of Tears, as I am confident there were more Tears shed than Letters Written, where I wish'd that every Letter might have been buried in the watery Womb or Toomb of every Tear, but it was in Vain, they being too fast fixt to be Drowned, for they were fixt in her Memory, and so in Mine, but yet my Tears may wash out my Fault, and my Love will ask her Pardon in the Humblest and Sorrowfull'st words as I can Speak; Wherefore pray Madam, make my Peace if you can, go to her and speak for me, and let her Know how it was, (for I dare not Write to her again,) and so in my stead Beg my Pardon, for I dare swear by Heaven, as I would have it guard my Innocency, prove the Truth, and save my Soul, I am not guilty of a Crime to her, for I was free from Malice or Envy, or any Evill Design, when I writ it, and not only free from any Evill to her, but I was full of Love and Admiration of her, and I hope she will Pardon me, since I onely writ it as a Philosopher, and not as an Enemy, and since there is none that lives but hath some Faults or Defects, though she hath the Least and Fewer than any other of Natures Creatures, and it is some Praise to have the Least; but since we are all Guilty in one kind or other, pray her to Pardon my Mistake, and Philosophical Contemplation of her, and so hoping a Good Success of your Petition in my Behalf, I rest,

Madam,
Your faithful Friend and Servant.

LETTER 67

Madam,
You were pleased in your last Letter to Ask my Opinion, Judgement, and Advice of that which you Spoke of when I last Saw you; truly, when any one asks my Opinion of Causes or Effects, or my Judgement of Affairs, or of any thing concerning the Actions of the World, as their Successes to

Good or Bad, or Desires my Advice of any Concernment to Particulars, let me tell you, as first, for Causes and Effects, my Reason Studies, and Observation Watches, to find out the Cause by the Effects, or to Foresee the Effects by the Causes; and as for the Success of several Affairs and Actions in the World, I put all the Probabilities in one Scale, and all the Impossibilities, or at least Unlikelyhoods, in another, and Weigh them both, and which soever Scale Weighs Downward, I give my Judgement; and as for Advice to Particulars, I Examin their Means, Abilities, Strength, Power, Right, Truth, and Justice, according to all which I give my Advice, for I Search the Bottom, Stirring up the very Dregs, or Fathoming the Depth; like as Sailers cast their Line and Plummet to Fathom the Sea, for fear of Quick-sands, Shelves, or the like, and then Draw up their Line to see the Depth, or at least take Notice how much the Line sinks down; so do I concerning my Opinion, Judgement, or Advice; but you must Pardon me if I give not my Judgment or Opinion in a Publick Letter, concerning Publick Affairs, in which I ought not to meddle, being a Woman; neither ought those of the Masculine Sex to give their Opinions, or Judgments, or Advices Publickly, unless they were Desired and Required so to do, as also not Impertinently, Busily, or Intrudingly, to Meddle, or Censure, or Speak of that which they have nothing to do, or at least, where they cannot Help or Mend. But pray believe, I am not so Vain as to think I can Reason, Judg, or Advise Wisely, no, I onely Endeavour, or at least, Desire so to do; and since you have not mentioned under your hand-writing, that which you would have me give my Opinion, Judgment, or Advice of, I will not give it under my hand, but leave it till such time as we Meet, for Friends may Talk as freely as Think, fearing no Treachery, and so I rest,

> Madam,
> Your faithful Fr. and S.

LETTER 68

Madam,

I Am Sorry that Sir C.A. is Kill'd, and as Sorry that V.A. hath Kill'd him,[1] for by Report they were both Worthy and Right Honourable Persons,

---

[1] This letter may have some connection with an actual incident in which Newcastle was asked by Edward Hyde, later earl of Clarendon, to stop a duel between Aubrey de Vere, earl of Oxford, and a Colonel Slinger (*Historical Manuscripts Commission*, 13th Report, *Portland Papers*, vol. 2 [London: Stationary Office, 1893] 140). V.A. works well for the initials of Aubrey de Vere reversed. C. might stand for Colonel and A. for Slinger's unknown first name.

which causes me to wonder how such two Persons could Fall out, for surely they were such men as would be as Unwilling to Give an Offence as to Take an Affront, and if the Offence was Unwillingly given, as by Chance, they being men of Honour and Merit, would not be Grieved, at least, not Angry at or for it: but many times a Third man will make a Quarrel betwixt Two others, and leave them to Fight it out. You may say, that sometimes Quarrels cannot be Avoided, although they be betwixt two Noble Persons, as for Example, two Dukes, about the Preheminence of Place, none knowing which of them had the First Place, and neither Yielding, must needs Fight to Decide it; but such Cases are not often put to the Trial, or ought not to be, for Heraulds are for that purpose Judges. But these two Noble Persons which you mentioned in your last Letter, whatsoever their Quarrel was, the one is Kill'd, the other Banished; and now to speak of such Quarrels as generally cause Duels between Private Persons, they are either about Words, or Women, or Hawks, or Dogs, or Whores, or about Cards or Dice, or such Frivolous, Idle, or Base Causes; I do not say All Quarrels, but Most, for some are more Honourable, but of all Sorts or Causes of Quarrels, Drunken Quarrels are the most Sensless; As for the Manner or Fashion of Fighting, Duels in my opinion are not Proper, for in this Age in most Nations they Fight Private Duels, somewhat after the manner of a Publick Battel, as three against three, or at least two against two, also they Fight with Pistols and Swords, with their Doublets on, which serves instead of an Armour, and for the most part a Horse-back; first, they shoot off their Pistols at each other, and then they come to the Sword, if they be not shot Dead before their time comes to Fight, for Shooting is not a direct Fighting, because they must stand at some Distance to take Aim, which in my opinion appears Cowardly, to Pelt at each other, as if they were Afraid to come near each other; besides, a Child may have so much Skill & Courage as to shoot off a Pistol, and may chance to Kill a Man, but a Child cannot tell how to use a Sword, or manage a Horse; also a Peasant or such mean bred Persons, can shoot off Pistols, or Carbines, or Muskets, but they have no skill to use a Sword, nor know not how to manage an Horse, unless a Cart-Horse, & that better in a Cart than when astride: 'Tis true, Peasants or Common Souldiers will fight with Force and Fury like as Beasts, and Kill their Enemy with mere Strength, but not with pure Valour, for they fight as in an Uproar, and will knock one another down with their Staves, or But-ends of their Muskets, which is more a Club or Clown-fighting; and if they have Swords, they fight with the Pummel, not with the Point, for they know not how to use it, neither is it fit they should, wherefore the Gentlemen are too Strong for them, for the Gentleman's point of his Sword hath the Advantage of the Clown's Club; and the onely Grief to Gallant, Valiant Gentlemen in the day of Battel or Duel, is, the fear they should be Kill'd with a Bullet, against which they can shew no Active Valour or Well-bred Skill. The last Observation concerning fighting Duels in this Age, is, in choosing of Seconds, and the right Use of Seconds in all Ages that I have heard of, unless these Later, is, to be Overseers, Witnesses and Judges, wherefore they ought to be Upright, Honest, Judicious, and Skilful men, and Worthy, and Honourable Persons, for they are to Judge whether their Quarrel requires Blood, and may not be pass'd over without Dishonour; also they are to see that each man may be Equally Armed, and that there be no Untimely Advantages taken of each other; also they are to Help or Assist them when they are Wounded, as to Bind up their Wounds, and they are to witness to the World how they Fought; But in this Age, the Seconds are so far from being Judges, Overseers, Witnesses, or Helpful Friends, as they become Duellers themselves, Fighting for Company, not for Injury or Wrong done to each other, and for Fashions sake, which is an Unjust, Irrational, Inhuman, and Wicked Fashion or Practice; neither is it Manly or Noble, but Base and Beastly, as to Fight without Reason or Injury; where-fore Pistols and Fighting Seconds ought not to be. But, Madam, if any should read this Letter besides your self, I should be found fault with, it being not Fit, nor Proper for a Woman to Discourse or Write of Duels or Wars, nor of Horses or Swords, or the like, but pray, if you hear any say so, tell him, that I have a greater Privilege than other Women in this Discourse, for my Husband hath been a General of an Army of 30000 men, and hath fought Battels; also he is Master of those two Arts, the Use of the Sword, and the Manage of the Horse, as there is not any man, nor hath never been, so well Known, Skilful, and Practised, as he, so that he is the best Horseman and Swordman in the World; also two of my three Brothers were Souldiers, or Commanders in War, and well Experienced in that Profession, and my Father was a Swordman, who was Banished for a time, for Killing a Gentleman in a Duel of Honour.[1] Thus have I been Born, Bred, Lived, and Married, all with Sword-men, and to my greater Honour, all Valiant men; and so leaving this Discourse, I rest,

Madam,
Your faithful Fr. and S.

---

1   There may be some irony here, for Cavendish's mother and brother both suffered as a result of the Cavendish's father's duel. The mother was not allowed to marry the father until after the boy had been born out of wedlock. The boy was not allowed to inherit.

LETTER 69

Madam,

You were pleased to desire my Opinion of the Lord Bs. Works; truly it seems by his Writings, that he was Learned, Eloquent, Witty, and Wise, fit for State-Counsel and Advice, to Plead Causes, Decide Controversies, and the like, and his Works or Writings have been very Propagating and Manuring other mens Brains; the truth is, his Works have proved like as some sorts of Meats, which through Time, or mixture of some Flatuous, or Humid Substance, Corrupt, and Breed Magots or Worms; so his Writings have produced several other Books. The same have Homer's Works, although they were of another Sort than his. But you may say, I write more of the Transmigration than of the first Formation or Principle, more of the Effects than the Cause; I confess my Pen hath Wandred from your Question, and Asks your Pardon for my Transgression, and with all Passionate Love, I subscribe myself,

Madam,
        Your Ladiships most Humble and faithful Servant.

LETTER 70

Madam,

To give you an Account, as you desire, of Mrs. H.O. who, you say, is Reported to be such a Wit; all I can say, is, that I do not perceive a Super-fluity; her Tongue in my Hearing ran as other Women's usually doth, but a Friend of her's, who lives in the same House she doth, did tell me, that to some men she doth Railly and Sport with Words, for all her Discourse, or most part of it, is to Men, and to some she doth repeat several Places and Speeches out of Romances, and several Speeches and Parts of Playes, or Passionate Speeches, and if it be concerning Love, then she turns up the black of her Eyes and Whines, and lifts up her Hands after the French Mode; also she is ready and quick in giving Sharp Replyes, for which she is highly Applauded by the Court Gallants which gather about her, and whatsoever she sayes, they Cry out, I faith that is well said, and then Laugh and Railly with her; then she is Gay and Merry in Sportive Harmless Abuses, and Dances Much, although not Well, but speaks French like a Native; then she is very Learn'd in the Male and Female words, as the Learn'd term them, to wit, the Gendres of Words. As for Court-Servants she hath had Many, but now she is wholly Ingross'd by One. This is as much as I have Heard of her, and more than I would have Repeated, had it not been to You, And thus leaving her and her Wit, I rest,

Madam,
Your very Loving Friend and Servant

LETTER 71

Madam,
The five Ladyes which you Desire to have a Relation of, I cannot of my own Knowledge give you an Account of, for I have but little Acquaintance with them, but I can tell you what Report sayes; As for the Eldest, 'tis said, she wants not Experience, though her Experience comes more through Misfortune than Time, for she is not Old; also that she hath a good Judgment, but makes no Good Use of it, for she is oftner Ruled by others Perswasion than her own Judgement; neither doth she want Wit, but can Speak Well, and Promise Fair, though her Deeds and Words be not Answerable, nor her Performance to her Promises, for she will Speak better than Do, and Promise more than Perform; she is very Civil and Humble to all Persons, to gain their Applause, but she makes no Difference between the Noblest and Meanest, the Worthy and Unworthy, the Honest and False, but rather of the Two she Naturally Affects those that are Meanest, either for Birth, Breeding, or Merit, but to some Particulars she is very Partial, even so Partial as to do Unjust Actions for their Sakes or by their Perswasions. Her Confidents are such as have been False, but she believes they are so Honest now, as only fit for Trust, although in all her Affairs she hath had Ill Success, for all her most Secret Intentions are made Known before they have been put into Action; but Time may make her Wiser. As for the Second Lady, she seems at the first Acquaintance to be of a very Good and Generous Nature, but some time Discovers her to be rather of an Easie, Facil, than a Pure, Good or Generous Nature, a Foolish Kindness, and a Childish Liberality, that with Flattery is Ruled, Governed and Perswaded, she Loves and Gives but knows not Why, nor Wherefore; also she is Amorous, and at this time so in Love, as it is Reported she will Marry a Person, that is so Mean, and far below her in Birth, as the Marriage will not onely Disgrace the Family from whence she Sprung, but her Posterity that may live after her; neither hath her Beloved Person nor Parts, Wealth nor Fame. Concerning the Third Lady, she is Proud and Ambitious, and seems rather Obstinate than Facil, and if her Fortune were but Answerable to her Birth, she in my Opinion would Deceive the Belief of many in Doing those things

that might be Worthy a Person of her Quality and Dignity. The Fourth Lady is Simple, God know's, most of her Time is Imployed in Dancing and Eating, and in Foolish, Childish Sports and Pastimes; She is as Inconstant as her Sex can be; she is also Amorous, and would have Love-Servants, if she were not afraid of those that have some Power and Authority over her, which Restrain her, but 'tis believed she will break thorough all Restraints. As for her Estate, she only thinks of the Present, but never Considers the Future, which makes her Necessitated, as she will in time be a Begger. The Fifth Ladyes Time is only spent in Giving and Receiving Visits, in Balling, Dancing, and the like, but I hear nothing else of her. Thus, Madam, have I written what is Reported by those that are well Acquainted, as also by their Domesticks and Followers, not that I inquire into the Humours, Natures or Affairs of those Persons I have no Relation to, but I cannot but hear of many Actions and Persons and Passages in the World, unless I should stop my Hearing; but in this Letter I have done only my Duty, in telling you what I Hear of what you Desire to Know, and as long as I live, I shall be Obedient to all your Commands, and Industrious to Satisfie all your Desires, and Rest,

> Madam,
> Your faithful Friend and Servant.

LETTER 72

Madam,
You were pleased the last time you writ, to send me a Poem of your own making or Composing, and to desire my Opinion of it, which Opinion, were you not such a Friend as not to be Exceptious, I would not Declare, for though I will not Dissemble, as to speak against my Conscience, yet I may Conceal or Bury my Thoughts, Opinion, or Judgment in Silence; but I know your Humour is, that I should Speak or Write freely my Thoughts, and according to your Desires, give me leave to tell you, the Poem is good in that kind, but I do not like such kind of Poems, which are onely Complements and Gratulations put into Verses, in which Poems is seldom much Wit or Fancy, onely Flattery, Rime, and Number; wherefore give me leave to Perswade you to alter the Subject of your Poem, and to take such a Subject as hath Ground and Room for Wit and Fancy to move on; also you desire my Opinion of G.Vs.[1] Poems, I cannot Praise them,

---

1   One might suspect that G.V. refers to George Villiers, second duke of Buckingham. Buckingham wrote in the style of Pindar to praise his father-in-law, the Parliamentarian Fairfax, but that poem probably was composed in 1671.

because the Wit & Expressions are Stoln out of several Excellent Poets, only he turns their Fancies and Expressions to other Subjects, so as he only Varies other mens Wits, but Produces none of his Own, and such Writers may rather be nam'd Translators than Authors; Indeed, most Writings now a dayes, not onely Verse, but Prose, are but Variations, and not Creations. But leaving Wit-stealers, I return to your Poem, which is not Theft, but an Ill-chosen Subject, which I desire you to Alter. Thus Professing, as also Declaring my Friendship, in giving a Free and Plain Judgment, I rest,

> Madam,
> Your most faithful Friend and Servant.

LETTER 73

Madam,
I was reading to day some several Satyrs of several Famous Poets, wherein I find, that they Praise Themselves, and Dispraise all Others, which expresses a great Self-dotage, and a very Ill Nature; besides, they seem more Covetous than Generous, to desire All the Praise, and to give their Neighbour not Any; In truth, Writers should never speak of themselves, but in Praefatory Epistles, or in a History of their own Lives, wherein they may freely declare their own Acts and Opinions. But, Madam, I wish that all Writers would use their Pens as your Noble Lord and Husband orders his Discourse in Speech, to speak the Best of all men, and to Bury their Faults in Silence, which would make Virtue an Emulation, and Faults such a Novelty, as men would be Asham'd to Commit them, whereas declaring Former Faults, causes Precedent Faults no Strangers, nay, it causeth Precedent Faults to be more Confident and Active; But, Madam, you are so Innocent and Harmless, as you are not acquainted with the Faults of others, for which I am,

> Madam,
> Your most humble Servant, and faithful Friend.

LETTER 74

Madam,
Yesterday a Consort of Learning and Wit came to Visit me, but they became at last to be a Discord; This Consort was Natural Philosophers, Theological Scholars, and Poets, and their Discourse was their Musick, the

Philosophers were the Bass, the Theologers the Tenor, and the Poets the Treble, all which made an Harmony wherein was Variety and Delight, but the Poets that love Change of Place, Company, and Pastime, went away, and left the Philosophers and Theologers, who began a Serious Discourse, which was Dull and somewhat Tedious, for it was concerning the Soul, as also the Immortality of the Soul; some of the Theologers said, the Souls of Men were part of the Spirit of God, others, the Souls of men were the Breath of God, others, they were a Light proceeding from God, and all these Concluded that the Souls were an Immaterial or Incorporeal Form, but the Natural Philosophers said, that Mens Souls or any such Soul was an Essence, which was the Purest Matter, or Quintessence In and Of Nature, but the Theologers would not allow that Opinion, and said, the Natural Philosophers were Atheists, whereupon the Natural Philosophers said, that the Theologers were Ignorant, and full of Fallacy and Sophistry, for said they, How can No Matter have a Form or a Being? and if Souls are the Spirit of God, they cannot possibly be Evil, and if they be the Breath of God, they cannot be Corruptible, if so, then the Souls of Men cannot be subject to Sin, and if not subject to Sin, in Justice they were not subject to Punishment, and if the Souls of all Men were produced from God, as the Beams of Light from the Sun, although the Beams might be Obscured with Dark Clouds or Gross Vapours, yet they did not Lose any of their Purity or Propriety, nay, though the Sun Beams were Capable to Lose their Purity or Propriety, yet the Beams proceeding from God could not, for whatsoever Proceeds Immediately from God, can neither be Alterable nor Impure; at last the Theologers and Philosophers became so Violent and Loud, as I did fear they would have Fought, if they had had any other Wounding Weapons than their Tongues, but Heaven be praised, they had no Killing Swords, and so they did no harm to each other, but after the Violence of their Dispute was past, I ventur'd to speak, saying, Noble Gentlemen, you have Discoursed more Learnedly than Knowingly, and more Vainly than Wisely, for Solomon says, that not any thing is throughly Known, and that all is Vanity under the Sun, as well that which hath been, as what is, and shall be, and yet his Wisdom proceeded from Gods particular Gift; wherefore leave the Foolish Custom of Disputing, and bring in a Devout Custom of Praying, leaving your Souls to Gods disposing, without troubling them with Idle Arguments; and hearing me talk Simply, they laught at my Innocency, and in their Mirth became Good Friends and Sociable Companions, and after some time they took their leave, and left me to relate their Discourse in a Letter to your Ladiship. So leaving your Ladiship to your own Contemplations, I remain,

Madam,
Your faithful Friend and humble Servant.

LETTER 75

Madam,
It is seldom known that a Perfect and Famous Poet or Philosopher was ever very Cruel, David and Solomon were the most Bloody, but they were Kings, and it seems Reason of State was too forcible for Good Nature, and there is no Rule but hath some Exception. But had I Children I would endeavor with all the Rational Arguments & Witty Discourses I were Capable of, to perswade them to delight in Poetry and Philosophy, that they might be Civil, Generous, and Just, which would be a Greater and more Lasting Honour to them than Wealth or Titles; besides the Pleasure of Thoughts and Tranquility of Mind would be a Heaven upon Earth, all which Silent Contemplation brings them unto, for Contemplation brings Consideration, Consideration brings Judgment, Judgment brings Reason, Reason brings Truth, Truth brings Peace; also Consideration brings Conception, Conception brings Fancy, Fancy brings Wit, and Wit brings Delight. But you will say, Nature hath not made all Mankind Capable of Good Instruction, 'tis true, but give me leave to say, that I believe there are more Faults in Educators than in Nature; but, Madam, I have no Children, therefore no Tutoress, and if I had Children, 'tis likely I should have done as most Parents do, which is, to Breed them up in Vanity and not in Virtue; but, Madam, you have Children, which I am confident will be Sweetly Disposed, like your Self, for you Breed them Gently, rather with Reason than with Rods, wherein you do Wisely and Kindly, and I wish all Parents and Tutors may take an Example from you, who are a Lady of such Perfection, as I account my Self Honoured to be,

Madam,
Your Humble and Devoted Servant.

LETTER 76

Madam,

Since I last writ to you, I have been to hear Mrs. P.N. Preach, for now she is, as I did believe she would be, *viz.* a Preaching Sister. There were a great many Holy Sisters and Holy Brethren met together, where many took their turns to Preach, for as they are for Liberty of Conscience, so they are for Liberty of Preaching, but there were more Sermons than Learning, and more Words than Reason, Mrs. P.N. began, but her Sermon I do not well remember, and after she had Sighed and Winded out her Devotion, a Holy Brother stood up and Preached thus, as I shall briefly relate to you.

> *Dearly beloved Brethren and Sisters, We are gathered together in the Lord with Purity of Spirit to Preach his Word amongst us, We are the Chosen and Elect Children of the Lord who have Glorified Spirits and Sanctified Souls, we have the Spirit of God in us, which Inspires us to Pray and to Preach, as also to Call upon his Name and to Remember him of his Promise to Unite and Gather us together into his New Jerusalem, separating us from Reprobates, that we may not be Defiled with their Presence, for you Dear Brethren Know by the Spirit, that they are not the Children of the Lord but Sathans Children, they are the Children of Darkness, we the Children of Light, we are Glorified and Sanctified by Supernatural Grace, we are a Peculiar People, and the Holy Prophets of the Lord, to Fore-see, Fore-tell and Declare his Will and Pleasure, also we are to Incourage and Comfort the Saints in Afflictions and Times of Tribulation and Consolation, and to Help them to Present their Sanctified Sighs, Tears and Groans unto the Lord; but the Spirit moveth me to Pray and to leave off Preaching, wherefore let us Pray unto the Lord.*

So after the Holy Brother had done his Prayer, Mr. N.N. who was there, pull'd off his Peruick, and put on a Night-Cap, wherein he appeared so like a Holy Brother as they took him for one of their Sect, and he Preached this following Sermon.

> *Dearly beloved Brethren, We are here met in a Congregation together, some to Teach, others to Learn; but neither the Teaching nor Learning can be any other way but Natural and according to Human Capacitie, for we cannot be Coelestial whilst we are Terrestrial, neither can we be Glorified whilst we are Mortal and subject to Death,*

nor yet can we arrive to the Purity of Saints or Angels, whilst we are subject to Natural Imperfections both in Body and Mind, but there are some Men that Believe they are, or at least may be so Pure in Spirit by Saving Grace, as to be Sanctified, and to be so much fill'd with the Holy Ghost as to have Spiritual Visions, and ordinarily to have Conversation with God, believing God to be a Common Companion to their Idle Imaginations. But this Opinion proceeds from an Extraordinary Self-Love, Self-Pride, and Self-Ambition, as to believe they are the only fit Companions for God himself, and that not any of God's Creatures are or were Worthy to be Favoured, but They, much less to be made of Gods Privy Counsel, as they believe they are, as to Know his Will and Pleasure, his Decrees and Destinies, which indeed are not to be Known, for the Creator is too Mighty for a Creature to Comprehend him, Wherefore let us Humbly Pray to What we can-not Conceive.

But before he had quite Ended his Sermon, the Holy flock began to Bustle, and at last Went quite out of the Room, so that he might have Pray'd by Himself, had not I and two or three Ladies more that were of my Company, Stayed, and when he had done his short Prayer, He told me and the other Ladyes, that he had Done that which the Great Counsel of State could not Do, for he had by one short Discourse Dispersed a Company of Sectaries without Noise or Disturbance, but at last we dispersed our selves to our own Houses, although Mr. N.N. would have given us a Ball after a Sermon, but I was so tyred with the One, as I was not fit for the Other, for we were from Morning till Evening to hear them Preach; yet as Tyred and Weary as I am I could not choose but Repeat these two of their shortest Sermons which I heard, and so I subscribe myself,

> Madam,
> Your faithful Friend and Servant.

LETTER 77

Madam,
You were pleased to desire me to Read the Romance of A. as also, the Romance of C. which I have obeyed in reading the Romance of A; but as yet I have not read any part of C. and to give you an Account of my Perusal, I think there is more Love than Reason in it, and more Wit than Truth or Probability of Truth; and certainly it is deplorable, that so much

Wit and Eloquence should be wasted on Amorous Love, as also to bring all Scholastical, as Theological, Physical, Logistical and the like Arguments, Disputes and Discourses, into the Theme of Amorous Love, which Love is between Appetite or Desire and Fruition of Different Sexes of Men and Women; but I perceive that Romance-Writers endeavour to make all their Romance-Readers believe that the Gods, Nature, Fates, Destinies and Fortune do imploy or busie themselves only in the affairs of Amorous Lovers, which is a very low Imployment or Concern. Also I perceive that Romance-Lovers are very Rheumatick, for if all the Tears Romances express Lovers to shed, were Gathered or United, it would cause a second Deluge of the World; it seems Amorous Love is Composed more of Water than Fire, and more of Desire than Fruition. But leaving Amorous Lovers to more Folly than Discretion, to Lose more Time than to Gain Love, and wishing them Sound Lungs for Sighs, and Moist Eyes for Tears, I rest,

Madam,
Your faithful Friend and Servant.

LETTER 78

Madam,
In your last Letter you expressed that you had Presented C. with a Book of Gs. Writing, I wonder you would Present that Book to C. by reason that he is a Gallant for Pleasure, and not a Stoick for Study; also you express'd you sent one to D. the Student, let me tell you, Madam, I dare swear he will never read it Half out, not for the Bigness of the Volume, but for the Newness of the Style and Age, for most Students despise all New Works, and only delight in Old Worm-eaten Records; the truth is, few Books are read Throughout the First Age, it is well if at the Fourth Age the End be arrived at, especially in the same Nation where the Author is a Native, for as our Saviour sayes, A man is not Esteemed of in his Own Country, and yet in another place he sayes, A man is Known by his Works; wherefore the best way for a man that would have his Writing Known and Esteemed of in his Life time, is to send them to Travel into Forein Nations, for at Home they will find but little Applause, no not Romances, which the World Dotes on, for Distance of Place is next to Distance of Time, at least resembles it. But if any will present their Works to Persons of their Own Nation, they must present them to such as are Known to Delight in such Subjects their Books treat of, and then perchance they may read a leaf

or two, and by that Censure all the Book; But fearing you should Censure me for writing so Long a Letter, I rest,

> Madam,
> Your faithful Friend and Servant.

LETTER 79

Madam,
I Was yesterday presented with a Book Translated out of French into English, wherein I find the Author of the Book Condemns those that set their Images before their Books,[1] or that suffer their Friends to give their Opinions of their Books in Epistles, or that do write many, or some, or few Epistles before their Books, whereas himself writes so Long an Epistle, in finding Fault with Others, and civilly Applauding Himself, in not having his Picture or his Friends Applauses, as that Epistle or Preface is as Long, if not More, than many Short Epistles, and as Vain-glorious as Many Friends Praises. But I am so far from that Noble Persons Opinion or Modesty, that I wish, whereas I have One Friend to Praise my Works, although Partially, I had a Thousand, or rather Ten thousand Millions, nay, that their number were Infinite, that the Issue of my Brain, Fame, and Name, might live to Eternity if it were possible; neither do I think or believe it a Sin to Wish it, by reason it proceeds from Pure Self-love, which is the Root or Foundation of the Love of God and all Moral Virtues, I do not mean Corrupted Self-love, but as I said, Pure Self-love, by which God and Nature did Make, and doth Order the whole World, or Infinite Matter. But, Madam, give me leave to say, that this Age doth Corrupt all Wit and Wisdom with Sophistry, and because they cannot write Beyond the Antients, they will endeavour to Disgrace them, although most Writers Steal from them. But for this French Author, setting aside his Epistle, his Book is full of Wit and Reason, as it is rendred by the Translator, and wishing all Writers could fill their Books with Wit and Reason, I rest,

> Madam,
> Your faithful Friend and Servant.

---

1   There are three portraits of Cavendish that often serve as frontispieces for her books, but particular portraits do not attach to particular books with the exception of *Nature's Pictures*. The first edition of *Nature's Pictures* is usually found with a frontispiece that is connected to prefatory poems composed by Cavendish. Various portraits seem to have been included in gift copies but not in copies sold to the public.

LETTER 80

Madam,

By Relation, Reading, and Observation, I find that every Age is not alike
for Humour, Judgement and Wit, although alike for Kind, Life and Death;
for some Ages are so Heroick, as all their Thoughts are of War, and all their
Actions Fighting; in other Ages all their Thoughts are Considering, and
their Actions Experiments; in other Ages all their Thoughts are Super-
stitious, and their Actions ceremonies; in other Ages all their Thoughts are
Amorous, and their Actions Adulteries; and so in many other things, as
Humors, Passions, Appetites, Customs, as also in Diets, Accoustrements,
Behaviour, Discourse, and the like; all which I have seriously Consider'd,
what should be the Cause that men being of One and the same Kind, *viz.*
Mankind, should Differ so much in several Ages in the Course of their Life;
But I cannot find any more Reason for it, than for several Diseases in sev-
eral Ages, as for Example, a Disease, namely, the Sweating Disease, that was
Predominant in England, and after in Germany, and many other Diseases
which are Predominant in One Age and not in Another, which certainly is
produced from an Influence from the Planets. But this is to be observed, that
Evils may proceed from the Planets, but what is Good both for Body and
Mind proceeds from a Higher, Celestial Power. And as for this Age we
live in now, 'tis Prodigal to their Enemies, and Ungrateful to their Friends;
but, Madam, though this Age be so Infected in the Generality, yet some
Particulars escape this Infection, for You and I are as Constant in Friendship
as the Light to the Sun, which is the Happiness of

Madam,
Your Humble Servant.

LETTER 81

Madam,

In your last Letter you desired me to write some Letters of Complement, as
also some Panegyricks, but I must intreat you to Excuse me, for my Style
in Writing is too Plain and Simple for such Courtly Words; besides, give me
leave to inform you, that I am a Servant to Truth and not to Flattery;
although I confess, I rather Lose than Gain in my Mistress's Service, for she
is Poor and Naked, and hath not those means to Advance her Servants as
Flattery hath, who gives Plenty of Words, and is Prodigal of Praise, and is
Clothed in a Flourishing Style, Imbroydered with Oratory; but my Mistress,

Truth, hath no need of such Adornings, neither doth she give many Words, and seldom any Praise, so as her Servants have not any thing to live on or by, but mere Honesty, which rather Starves than Feeds any Creature; yet howsoever, I being bred in her Service from my Youth, will never Quit her till Death takes me away; and if I can Serve you by Serving her, Command me, and I shall Honestly Obey you, and so rest,

> Madam,
> Your faithful Fr. and S.

LETTER 82

Madam,

In your last Letter you Condemn me for living a Country Life, saying, I Bury my self whilst I Live, and you wonder, that knowing I love Glory, I should live so Solitary a Life as I do; I confess, Madam, both the Manner of my Life and my Ambitious Nature, If a Solitary Life be not to Live in Metropolitan City, spred broad with Vanity, and almost smother'd with Crowds of Creditors for Debts; and as I Confess my Solitude, so I Confess my Glory, which is to Despise such Vanities, as will be rather a Reproach to my Life, than a Fame to after Ages, and I should Weep my self into Water, if I could have no other Fame than Rich Coaches, Lackies, and what State and Ceremony could produce, for my Ambition flies higher, as to Worth and Merit, not State and Vanity; I would be Known to the World by my Wit, not by my Folly, and I would have my Actions so Wise and Just, as I might neither be Asham'd nor Afrai'd to Hear of my self. But, Madam, as you Condemn My Life, so I Condemn Yours, for the Nobles that live in a Metropolitan City, live but as Citizens, and Citizens that live in the Country, live like Noble men, with less Expences and more Liberty, having large Extension of Lands, and not Imprisoned in One House, and their Recreations are more Various and Noble, neither do they spend their Time in Idle Visiting, but Prudent Overseeing; In short, Madam, there is so much Difference in each sort of Life, as the One is like Heaven, full of Peace and Blessedness, the Other full of Trouble and Vice; and so living in the sweet Air of Content, I rest,

> Madam,
> Your faithful Friend and Servant.

LETTER 83

Madam,

In your last Letter you Chid me for Loving too Earnestly, saying, Extreme Love did Consume my Body and Torment my Mind, and that whosoever Love to a High Degree are Fools; If so, I Confess, Madam, I am as much a Fool as ever Nature made, for where I set my Love, it is Fix'd like Eternity, and is as Full as Infinite; My Love is not Fix'd Suddenly, for it takes Experience and Consideration to help to Place it, both which have been my Guides and Directors to Love you, which makes me Love you Much, and shall make me Love you Long, if Souls Die not, and so I shall alwayes, and in all occasions be,

> Madam,
> Your Constant Friend and Humble Servant.

LETTER 84

Madam,

Now we be both Return'd into our Native Country, let us Meet to Rejoyce together, for though our Husbands have Lost much, yet the Broken parts of their Estates they have Recover'd by the Just Laws of this Kingdom, will afford us some Recreation, Pastime, and Harmless Sports. As for the Place of our Meeting, if I may Advise, it shall be N. whose Owner is M.N.[1] a Person that hath Lost the Most of any Subject, yet he is the Best Contented, and so the Happiest, for he never Troubles himself for any Worldly Wealth, especially when he cannot tell Honestly which way to Repair his Estate; And though he be Wisely Prudent, yet he is not Basely Miserable, as to be Miserably Sparing, but will Entertain us Civilly, Friendly, Generously, Pleasantly, Delightfully. So expecting when you will appoint the Time, I rest,

> Madam,
> Your faithful Fr. and S.

---

1   M.N. clearly is the Marquis of Newcastle, husband to Cavendish. N. is Nottinghamshire, where the two lived at Welbeck Abbey. See letter 46 and note.

LETTER 85

Madam,

In your last Letter you did friendly Chide me for my Passionate Anger, and for some Words I did speak in that Angry Passion, I Confess my Error, but yet you must Know that my Passion proceeded from Extreme Natural and Honest Love, as to be Angry in Mind, and Bitter and Sharp in Words, to and of those, I know by Experience and Practice to be Envious, Spitefull, Malicious, and Ungratefull to those I do and ought dearly to Love, and this made me Speak that which Discretion perchance did not Allow or Approve of, although Honesty could not Forbid it; but had it been in my Own particular Cause or Person, I should neither have been Angry nor Bitter, neither in Thoughts nor Words, for I can easily pass over all Hate or Anger, either in Words or Actions to my Self, so they be neither Contumelious, nor Impairably Dishonourable, the First can proceed from none but my Superiors, the Other from none but Bestial Ruffians; As for my Superiours, I count none my Superiours, but those that Surpass me in Virtue, Grace, Wisdome, and Excellency of Mind, except my Natural Parents; and as for Rude Ruffians, I am of such Quality, as not to Keep such Company, nor to be Unattended by Servants that Wait upon me, or near my Call. But I Confess my Indiscretion, for Violent Passion doth neither gain Justice, Right, nor Truth, of Malice, Wrong, and Falshood, Yet I am obliged to you for your Love, for you have shew'd more True Friendship in your Reproof, than Feigned Friends do in their Flattery, for which I am,

Madam,
Your Faithfull and most Humble Servant.

LETTER 86

Madam,

I Have Read Rs. Book, which you were pleased to send me, and it is written Learnedly, Eloquently, Wittily, and Christianly, for all which the Author is to be Applauded and Admired, concerning the Truth, Method, and Ingenuity of the Work, and had he been a Divine by Order and Profession, the Subject of his Book, which is, concerning the Scripture, had been most Applaudable, but being a Lay-man and not a Consecrated Church-man, the Scripture was not a fit Theme for his Pen to work upon, at least not in my Opinion, for although I Keep strictly to the Church of England, yet I think it not fit for a Lay-man to busie his Pen concerning the Scripture; for it belongs only to Church-men, to Study, Interpret, Expound, Teach and Preach the Scripture, and its an Usurpation for Lay-men to meddle in Church-mens Profession, unless it be granted that a Lay-man have more Wit, Reason, Learning and Inspiration than all the Church-men have. But truly, Madam, the Book is an Excellent Book in that Kind, Only give me leave to tell you, that to Defend Scripture is partly to express Faults in Scripture; and to Dispute upon the Obscurities in Scripture is to Puzzle the Truth in Scripture. But leaving Scripture to the Church-men, and the Author to Fame, I rest,

Madam,
Your faithful Friend and Servant.

LETTER 87

Madam,
I Am Sorry Mrs. D. is so Despairingly Melancholy as not to be Comforted, and I am the more Sorry that the Ground of her Despair is the Bible and Ignorant Interpreters, such as rather Confound the Cleer Expressions therein, than Clear the Dark and Mystical. But many Pious persons have fall'n into the same Distemper, through want of Deep Capacities, Cleer Understandings, and Sound Judgments, to Interprete the Scripture, or to Conceive the Spiritual Inspections and Elevations of the Purity of Christian Religion, and all the several Opinions therein. The Church of England is the Purest, but yet it hath suffer'd the Scripture to be Read too Commonly, which hath caused much Disturbance, not only to Particular Persons, but in the Church it self, and hath lost much of the Dignity belonging to Church-men, nay, it hath so Discomposed the Church-Government, as it is a wonder it should settle in its Centre again. But the Church-men say, they give Lay-men Leave for to Read the Scripture, but not to Interprete it, but the Leave of the First gives Leave to the Latter. But, Madam, these Causes are not for our Sex to Discourse of, wherefore we will rather Pray for our Afflicted Friend Mrs. D. and so taking my leave of you, I rest,

Madam,
Your faithful Friend and Servant.

LETTER 88

Madam,

I Do not Wonder that the War in E. against O. hath no Better Success, since there are such Petty Commanders and Mean Governors, and I Fear the Warring designs of G. will have no Better fortune, because the Generals, which are to Command in Chief, are not much Better than those that are to be Commanded, neither for Skill, Conduct, Fame, Title, Friends, Wealth nor Power, in all which a General ought to Surpass those he Commands, for they may be Good Souldiers for a Troop, Regiment or Brigade, which are not Skilfull or Fit for a General, for to be a Good General, doth not only require Skill and Courage, but Wise Conduct, and Wisdome is not found in every Souldiers brain; besides, a General must be a man of Note, for an Inferiour Person will hardly be Obeyed, for if he be not a man of Fame, Title, Worth and Merit, every Under Commander will think himself as Good and fit to be a General as he, and will scorn to be Commanded by his Equal; Wherefore Superiors are only fit to be Commanders and Governours: Besides, a General or Governour must be full of Generosity, free from Covetousness, which Generosity seldom Cohabit's with Poverty or Inferiour Persons; also they must be Just, both to Punish and Reward, Resolute to execute the one, and Forward to perform the other. But Officers, Governours and Commanders are for the most part chosen by the means of Bribes, Faction or Favour, and not for Fitness, Worth and Merit, which Causes so many Disorders, Complaints and Rebellions, for few Nations live long in Peace, and most part of the World, at least all Europe is at this time fill'd with bloody War, and most Nations are forced to War with each other to Keep their Natives from Civil Dissentions. But War is not a Subject proper for our Sex to discourse of,[1] although in the Ruines of War we suffer Equally with Men; Wherefore leaving this Discourse of War I Conclude with Peace, for I am,

Madam,
Your faithful Friend and humble Servant.

---

1   In her biography of her husband (1667), Cavendish goes into the details of his campaigns during the Civil Wars. She sometimes casts women as warriors in her plays and makes them military commanders in her fiction (e.g., in "Assaulted and Pursued Chastity" from *Nature's Pictures*). See the contextual material in *Bell in Campo and The Sociable Companions*, ed. Alexandra G. Bennet (Peterborough, ON: Broadview Press, 2002).

LETTER 89

Madam,

I Am Sorry to hear Mrs. C.L. is married to one She Dislikes so much, as to profess she cannot Love her Husband, and to Complain of her Parents, for forcing her with Threats of Curses to that Match, but it is to be hoped, that Love will both begin and increase by Acquaintance and Society, and his Kindness to her, for he is reported to be a very Honest Good natured man, and then she will give her Parents Thanks, for it is to be observed, that Hot Amorous Lovers when they are Married, their Affections grow Cooler, and at last so Cold as to Dye Insensible, so as the Marriage-bed proves the Grave of Love, I mean of fond Amorous Love, for certainly Amorous Lovers have Poetical Imaginations of each other, and Fancy each other not onely Beyond what they are, but what is not in Nature to be, but such Matrimonial Acquaintance proves their Love was built on Fancy, and not on Reality, they Married Mortal Creatures, not Gods or Goddesses, nor such Worthy or Constant Damosels as Romances feign, so as their Love Vanishes as Poetical Airy Castles, or Inchanted Towers, and not any Love Remains, but if there doth, it is but as a Thatch'd Cottage, a Plain, Homely Love, whereas they that Marry Discreetly, and not Fondly, their Love is like Poor Beginners, who have Nothing or very Little to live on, but being Honest and Industrious, get something, and being Prudent and Thrifty, in time become Rich, nay, many times so Rich, as to Build stately Palaces, and have Respect and Honour from all that know them; so in those Marriages where Discretion joyns hands, Honesty begets Love, and thrifty Temperance makes Constancy, which builds Happiness and Peace for their Lives to live in, and all that Know or Hear of them, Honour and Respect them for their Worth and Merit, for their Wisdom and True Love. But as Time joynes Honest minds and Temperate persons with Love, so Time separates Vain Imaginations and Amorous persons with Dislike, and sometimes with Hate; and so leaving C.L. to Time, Reality, Temperance, Discretion, and Honesty, I rest,

Madam,
Your faithful Fr. and S.

LETTER 90

Madam,

I Am sorry the Plague is much in the City you are in, as I hear, and fear your Stay will Indanger your Life, for the Plague is so Spreading and Penetrating a Disease, as it is a Malignant Contagion, and Dilates it self throughout a City, nay, many times, from City to City, all over a Kingdom, and enters into every Particular House, and doth Arrest almost every Particular Person with Death, at least, layes grievous Sores upon them; Indeed Great Plagues are Death's Harvest, where he Reaps down Lives like Ears of Corn; wherefore, Madam, let me perswade you to Remove, for certainly Life is so Pretious, as it ought not to be Ventured, where there is no Honour to be Gain'd in the Hazard, for Death seems Terrible, I am sure it doth to Me, there is nothing I Dread more than Death, I do not mean the Strokes of Death, nor the Pains, but the Oblivion in Death, I fear not Death's Dart so much as Death's Dungeon, for I could willingly part with my Present Life, to have it Redoubled in after Memory, and would willingly Die in my Self, so I might Live in my Friends; Such a Life have I with you, and you with me, our Persons being at a Distance, we live to each other no otherwise than if we were Dead, for Absence is a Present Death, as Memory is a Future Life; and so many Friends as Remember me, so many Lives I have, indeed so many Brains as Remember me, so many Lives I have, whether they be Friends or Foes, onely in my Friends Brains I am Better Entertained; And this is the Reason I Retire so much from the Sight of the World, for the Love of Life and Fear of Death: for since Nature hath made our Bodily Lives so short, that if we should Live the full Period, it were but like a Flash of Lightning, that Continues not, and for the most part leaves black Oblivion behind it; and since Nature Rules the Bodily Life, and we cannot live Alwayes, nor the Bounds of Nature be Inlarged, I am industrious to Gain so much of Nature's Favour, as to enable me to do some Work, wherein I may leave my Idea, or Live in an Idea, or my Idea may Live in Many Brains, for then I shall Live as Nature Lives amongst her Creatures, which onely Lives in her Works, and is not otherwise Known but by her Works, we cannot say, she lives Personally amongst her Works, but Spiritually within her Works; and naturally I am so Ambitious, as I am restless to Live, as Nature doth, in all Ages, and in every Brain, but though I cannot hope to do so, yet it shall be no Neglect in me; And as I desire to Live in every Age, and in every Brain, so I desire to Live in every Heart, especially in your Ladiships, wherein I believe I do already, and wish I may live Long. Wherefore for my own sake, as well as yours, let me intreat you to Remove out of that Plaguy City, for if you Die, all those Friends you Leave, or Think of, or Remember, partly Die with you, nay, some perchance for Ever, if they were Personally Dead before, and onely Live in your Memory; Wherefore, as you are a Noble Lady, have a Care of your Friends, and go out of that City as Soon as you can, in which you will Oblige all those you Favour, or that Love you, amongst which there is none more Truly, Faithfully, and Fervently, your Friend and Servant, than,

Madam,
I, M.N.[1]

LETTER 91

Madam,
In your last Letter you say, that the Lady G.P. carried a Letter she received from Mrs. O.B. from Company to Company to Jest at, because it was not Indited after the Courtly Phrase, but after the Old manner and way, beginning thus, After my hearty Commendation, hoping you are in good Health, as I am at the writing hereof; this is to let you understand, etc. But I know not why any body should Jest at it, for 'tis Friendly to send their Commendations, and to wish them Good Health, and certainly Friendly and Kind Expressions are to be Prefer'd before Courtly Complements, the First sounds like Real Truth, the Other may be demonstrated to be Feigning, for all Complements Exceed the Truth; 'Tis true, the Style of Letters alters and changes as the Fashion of Clothes doth, but Fashions are not alwayes changed for more Commodious or Becoming, but for the sake of Variety, for an Old Fashion may be more Useful and Graceful than a Modern Fashion: But I believe the Lady G.P. carried Mrs. O.Bs. Letter about with her for a Pretence to visit Company, like as Gossips do Cakes and other Junkets to their Neighbours, the Junkets increasing the Company, and the Company the Junkets, so the Lady G.P. out of a Luxury to Talk and Company, like as other Gossips out of a Luxury to Talking and Eating, carried the Letter, to shew her several Acquaintance Sport, to get other Acquaintance, and if she had not had that Letter, 'tis likely she would have found some other Pretence rather than have stayed at Home. Indeed, one may say, that in this Age there is a malignant Contagion of Gossiping, for not onely one Woman Infects another, but the Women Infect the Men, and then one Man Infects another, nay, it Spreads so much, as it takes

---

1   Margaret Newcastle (*i.e.*, Cavendish).

hold even on Young Children, so strong and Infectious is this Malignity; but if any will Avoid it, they must every Morning Anoint the Soles of their Feet with the Oyl of Slackness, and Bath every Limb in a Bath of Rest, then they must put into their Ears some Drops of Quiet, to Strengthen the Brain against Vaporous Noise, and Stop their Ears with a little Wool of Deafness, to keep out the Wind of Idle Discourse, also they must Wash their Eyes with the Water of Obscurity, lest the glaring light of Vanity should Weaken them, and they must take some Electuary of Contemplation, which is very Soverain to Comfort the Spirits, and they must drink Cooling Julips of Discretion, which are good against the Fever of Company, and if they take some Jelly of Restraint, they will find it to be an Excellent Remedy against this Malignity, onely they must take great care lest they be too Relaxing to Perswasion, but rather so Restringent as to be Obstinate from entring into a Concourse; for there is nothing more Dangerous in all Malignant Diseases, than Throngs or Crowds of People; and this is the best Preparative against the Plague of Gossiping. But for fear with writing too Long a Letter I should fall into that Disease, I take my leave, and rest,

Madam,
        Your very faithful Friend and Servant.

LETTER 92

Madam,
In your last Letter you were pleased to tell me, that Sir A.M. was to Visit you, and hearing that the Lady B.V. was come to See you, he started from the Place he sate, and went away as in Hast, in my Opinion it was Strange he should do so, since he professes to Love her so much, as the Extremity makes him Unhappy, for though some may Run away through Fear, yet not for Love, for whatsoever is Loved or Beloved, is Sought after, & what men are Afraid of, they Fly from, and what they Love, they Fly to; so that Love Pursues, and Hate or Fear is as it were Pursued; but perchance he is a Despairing Lover, and Despair is beyond all other Passions; besides, Despair proceeds from Fear, for Fear is the Father that begets Despair; or perchance he was afraid that his Presence in her Company might Injure her Reputation, being Known to be her Lover; or he might fear his Presence might Displease her, and Lovers had rather Grieve Themselves, than Injure or Anger their Beloved; or else he was afraid that the Sight of her would Increase his Torments, or Tormenting Love: But howsoever, certainly Fear was the cause of his sudden Departure, and 'tis to be feared, that his Love is mixt with

an Unlawful Desire, that he was afraid to See her whom he had no Hopes to Injoy. But leaving Sr. A.M. to Despair, and her to her Chast Virtue, I rest,

Madam,
Your very faithful Friend and Servant.

LETTER 93

Madam,

You were pleased in your last Letter to express to me the Reason of the Lady D.Ss. and the Lady E.Ks. Melancholy, which was for Want of Children; I can not Blame the Lady D.S. by reason her Husband is the Last of his Family unless he have Children, but the Lady E.Ks. Husband being a Widdower when he Married her, and having Sons to Inherit his Estate, and to Keep up his Family, I Know no Reason why she should be troubled for having no Children, for though it be the part of every Good Wife to desire Children to Keep alive the Memory of their Husbands Name and Family by Posterity, yet a Woman hath no such Reason to desire Children for her Own Sake, for first her Name is Lost as to her Particular, in her Marrying, for she quits her Own, and is Named as her Husband;[1] also her Family, for neither Name nor Estate goes to her Family according to the Laws and Customes of this Countrey; Also she Hazards her Life by Bringing them into the World, and hath the greatest share of Trouble in Bringing them up;[2] neither can Women assure themselves of Comfort or Happiness by them, when they are grown to be Men, for their Name only lives in Sons, who Continue the Line of Succession, whereas Daughters are but Branches which by Marriage are Broken off from the Root from whence they Sprang, & Ingrafted into the Stock of an other Family, so that Daughters are to be accounted but as Moveable Goods or Furnitures that wear out; and though sometimes they carry the Lands with them, for want of Heir-males, yet the Name is not Kept nor the Line Continued with them, for these are buried in the Grave of the Males, for the Line, Name and Life of a Family ends with the Male issue;[3] But many times Married

---

1   Cavendish was childless but her husband had several children by a previous marriage. For a time, she received fertility treatments from the premier court physician of the time, Dr. Theodore Mayerne.

2   In *The Convent of Pleasure* (printed in *Plays Never Before Printed* [London, 1668]), Cavendish describes the problems caused to women by bearing and bringing up children.

3   While what Cavendish says is generally true, she must have been aware that her husband was especially proud of the title that he was able to derive from his mother, earl of Ogle. In like manner, her brother, John baron Lucas of Shenfield, was able to pass his title on to a daughter.

Women desire Children, as Maids do Husbands, more for Honour than for Comfort or Happiness, thinking it a Disgrace to live Old Maids, and so likewise to be Barren, for in the Jews time it was some Disgrace to be Barren, so that for the most part Maids and Wives desire Husbands and Children upon any Condition, rather than to live Maids or Barren: But I am not of their minds, for I think a Bad Husband is far worse than No Husband, and to have Unnatural Children is more Unhappy than to have No Children, and where One Husband proves Good, as Loving and Prudent, a Thousand prove Bad, as Cross and Spendthrifts, and where One Child proves Good, as Dutifull and Wise, a Thousand prove Disobedient and Fools, as to do Actions both to the Dishonour and Ruine of their Familyes. Besides, I have observed, that Breeding Women, especially those that have been married some time, and have had No Children, are in their Behaviour like New-married Wives, whose Actions of Behaviour and Speech are so Formal and Constrain'd, and so Different from their Natural way, as it is Ridiculous; for New Married Wives will so Bridle their Behaviour with Constraint, or Hang down their Heads so Simply, not so much out of True modesty, as a Forced Shamefulness; and to their Husbands they are so Coyly Amorous, or so Amorously Fond and so Troublesome Kind, as it would make the Spectators Sick, like Fulsome Meat to the Stomach; and if New-married Men were not Wise men, it might make them Ill Husbands, at least to Dislike a Married Life, because they cannot Leave their Fond or Amorous Wives so Readily or Easily as a Mistress; but in Truth that Humour doth not last Long, for after a month or two they are like Surfeited Bodyes, that like any Meat Better than what they were so Fond of, so that in time they think their Husbands Worse Company than any other men. Also Women at the Breeding of the First Children make so many Sick Faces, although oftentimes the Sickness is only in their Faces, not but that some are Really Sick, but not every Breeding Women; Likewise they have such Feigned Coughs, and fetch their Breath Short, with such Feigning Laziness, and so many Unnecessary Complaints, as it would Weary the most Patient Husband to hear or see them: besides, they are so Expensive in their Longings and Perpetual Eating of several Costly Meats, as it would Undo a man that hath but an Indifferent Estate; but to add to their Charge, if they have not what they Please for Child-bed Linnen, Mantels, and a Lying-in Bed, with Suitable Furniture for their Lying-Chamber, they will be so Fretfull and Discontented, as it will indanger their Miscarrying; Again to redouble the Charge, there must be Gossiping, not only with Costly Banquets at the Christening and Churching, but they have Gossiping all the time of their Lying-in, for then there is a more set or formal Gossiping than at other ordinary times. But I fear, that if this Letter come to the view of our Sex besides your self, they will throw more Spitefull or Angry Words out of their mouths against me, than the Unbeleeving Jews did hard Stones out of their hands at Saint Stephan; but the best is, they cannot Kill me with their Reproaches, I speak but the Truth of what I have observed amongst many of our Sex; Wherefore, Pray Madam, help to Defend me, as being my Friend, and I yours, for I shall Continue as long as I live,

Madam,
Your Ladyship's most Faithfull and Humble Servant.

LETTER 94

Madam,
It is to be observed, that Absence Cools Affections, and Presence Heats them, and Long Presence Burns them up, like as the Sun the Creatures of the Earth, which are Cold in his Absence, Warmed with his Presence, and Burnt with his Continuance; But some Affections live alwayes, as at the Poles, Frozen, and as in a Twy-light, wherein they can never be Seen Perfectly, and the Natures of such men for the most part are like Bears, Dull and Ravenous, which shews, that Bears are of Cold Constitutions, living alwayes in the Coldest Climates, for Cold Congeals the Spirits, Thickens the Skin, Stupifies the Senses, but Sharpen's the Hungry Appetite; and Different Extremes for the most part meet in Like Effects, for Extreme Heat Exhales or Exhausts the Spirits, Dimm's or Weakens the Senses, Hardens the Skin, and Quickens the Appetite of Drought, and Burning and Freezing is Equally Painfull, and the Pains are somewhat Alike, as both Peircing and Pricking, as if Cold and Heat were Sharply pointed; but a Hot Love is better than a Cold one, although a Cold Love is likelier to last Longer, like those that live in Hot Countries, who are not half so Long-Lived as those that live in Cold, the reason is, that the Spirits Exhaling out of the Body, carry out Life with them, whereas the Spirits being onely Congeal'd, Remain still within the Body, and Life keeps in, and lives with them, for Spirits are Life. But leaving Hot and Cold Love, which is Lukewarm, I rest,

Madam,
Your faithful Friend and Servant.

LETTER 95

Madam,

In your last Letter you were pleased to let me know, how Bravely the Lady F.O. lives, both for Rich Clothing, Costly Houshold-furniture, and Great Equipage; truly, for those that have a sufficient Estate to Maintain it, and a Noble Title to Countenance it, 'tis very Commendable and Honourable to live in Grandeur, otherwise it is Prodigal, Vain, Base, and Foolish: Prodigal, to live Beyond their Means or Wealth; Vain, to make a Fluttering shew with the Wast of their Estate; Base, to Usurp the Grandeur of Noble and Princely Titles; and Foolish, to make Enemies through Envy to their Vanity, to Triumph on them in their Poverty, which Poverty must of Necessity follow their Unnecessary Wast, if they have not a Staple-stock, so that they of Necessity must Break and Become Bankrupts, in which Condition they will be Despised, and so much the more as they were Envyed for their Vain Bravery, and Hated for their Base Usurped Grandeur, the more they are Scorned in their Poverty, and Laugh'd at in their Misery. Indeed, it is a Ridiculous Sight to see any live Above their Wealth or Dignity; 'tis like mercenary Stage-players, that Act the parts of Princes, but none of the Spectators give them the Respect and Honour due to Great Princes, knowing they are but Poor Players and Mean Persons; but true Noble Persons indeed, as they will not Quit any thing that belongs to their Dignities, so they will not Usurp any thing that belongs not to their Titles, and when such Persons chance to fall into Misery, yet they fall not into Scorn, but Pity and Compassion will wait upon them, or meet them with Respect; but in all Conditions, Degrees, and Dignities, it is better to Live Wisely than Bravely, and to Live Wisely, is, to Spend Moderately, to Live Plentifully, Easily, Peaceably, Pleasantly, and so Happily; to Spend Moderately, is, to keep within the Bounds of their Estate, not to go beyond the Limits of their Comings in; to Live Plentifully, is, to spend nothing Vainly, nor to spare nothing Useful, or Proper for their Quality; to Live Peaceably, is, to live Privately, free from troublesome Company, as Idle Visitors, and Trencher-Guests, who Censure every Word or Act to the Worst Intent and Sense, and Slander every one that is Better than themselves; to Live Easily, is, to have their Family in Order and Obedience, and all their Affairs to be done Methodically; to Live Pleasantly, is, to have such Delights as this Estate will Afford them, and such Pastimes as are Agreeable to their Humours, and the Company of Sociable and Conversable Friends; also to Banish all Perturbed Passions, and Extravagant Appetites, all which is to Live Wisely, as your Ladiship doth; But whether the Lady F.O. Live Wisely, I will leave to your Ladiships Judgment, who dwells Near her, and I at a Greater Distance, although not from your Ladiship, for my Thoughts and Affections are alwayes with you, so as you are Attended and Waited on by the Soul of,

Madam,
    Your faithful Friend and humble Servant.

LETTER 96

Madam,

I Wonder that Sir F.E. should turn his Back to his Enemy, as you say you heard he did, when heretofore he Out-faced his Enemies; wherefore, surely he either thought those Enemies he Turn'd from, their Cause to be Juster, or he had some Burden upon his Conscience that was Unrepented of, and knowing in himself, he was not fit to Die at that present, endeavoured to Preserve his Life by a Flight; or else he thought he might do some Greater Service if he Preserv'd his Life, whereas in that Fight he should Die Unprofitably; or else it was a Panick Fear, that may seize sometimes on Men of Great Courage, although True, Sober, Valiant Men are Seldom, if Ever, Seized with that Fear, by reason they never Venture their Lives but for Honour, and Honour forbids a Masker'd Flight, though not a Noble Retreat, for it is as Commendable to make a Wise and Honourable Retreat, as to Fight a Just Quarrel. But I have observed, that as some are Wise, Honest, and Valiant, or rather Couragious by Fits, so some are Couragious and Cowardly in several Causes or Cases; as for Example, Some have Courage to venture Hanging for Robbing or Stealing, yet are afraid of a Cudgel, to Fight although but at Cuffs; others have Courage to Betray a Friend, but dare not Assist or Conceal a Persecuted Friend, others have Courage to Commit Treason, yet dare not Fight an Enemy, and many the like; also some are very Couragious in a Passion, and mere Cowards when their Passion is over; also Fear makes some Stout and Couragious, and others Cowards, and so doth Drink, and the like; also Covetousness of Wealth makes more Couragious than any Thing or Cause else, for an Army of Souldiers, if they know they shall be Inriched by the Victory, will Fight with-out all Fear, nay, so as to Die Every man; but Propose to them Honour, or their Countries Safety, or their Kings Right, and they for the most part will Run away, unless they be sure to be Hang'd for it, and then perchance they may Fight for Life, rather than Run away to be sure to Die, for by Staying there is some Hopes, whereas by Running away there is none; but if they fear not to be Catch'd, they Fly. But the Commanders that

Fight more for Honour than Spoil, most commonly Stick to the Fight, fearing a Disgrace more than Death, and loving Fame more than Life. But the truth is, that generally there are more Cowards than Valiant Men, and more that have Courage to be Knaves, than to be Honest Men, for it requires both Wisdom and Valour to be Truly Honest, and Uprightly Just, but few have that Noble and Prudent Breeding, as to Know what is Truly Just, Honest and Valiant, insomuch as many Commit Errours and Crimes, and so are Disgraced, merely through Ignorance, whereas did they Know and rightly Understand the Grounds or Principles of Honesty and Honour, they would not hazard Infamy; But there are more that have not Breeding according to their Natures, than Natures according to their Breeding, for alas, the World wants Good Instructors, which is the cause of the Follies, Errours, Faults, and Crimes in Men and their Actions. But leaving the Generality, I am sorry for the Disgrace of Sir F.E. although it may be hoped, he may Recover himself out of this Reproach, by some Eminent, Honourable, and Valiant Action, which will be a Grave to Bury this Disgrace, for there are wayes and means for men to Recover a Lost Honour, but none for Women, for if once they Lose their Honour, it is Lost for Ever without Redemption, wherefore every one is to regard their own Actions. But lest I should Commit an Errour or Fault, in tyring you with so Long a Letter, I rest,

Madam,
Your faithful Friend and Servant.

LETTER 97

Madam,
The Lady G.R. and the Lady A.N. in a Visiting meeting, fell into a Discourse of Great Princes and Noble Persons, where the Lady G.R. said, that Great Princes and Noble Persons should or ought to have a Grandeur in their Behaviours, Habits, Discourses, Attendance, Life and Renown, as to their Persons, Garments, Speech, Ceremony, Actions and Fame, according to their Titles, Births and Fortunes; Nay, said the Lady A.N. not according to Fortune, for Misfortune or Ill Fortune Knocks Grandeur down, and makes it lye as Dead, also Age doth Lessen it: The Lady G.R. said, that True Grandeur did ride in Triumph upon Misfortunes back, for though Ill Fortune might Degrade Noble Persons of Wealth, and Poverty Degrade them of Ceremony, yet the Right Grandeur of True Noble Persons would appear through Raggs, and their Low Condition

like as the Sun, which though it could not shine Cleer and Bright through Thick, Black Clouds, yet it made Day in that Hemisphere it moved in, for a Dark Day is not Night; so, although Ill Fortune may Darken the Grandeur of Noble Persons, yet it cannot Benight it; and as for Age, said she, it is so far from Lessening Grandeur as it gives it Addition, for true Noble and Heroick Persons, their very Shadows do appear with a Majestical Grandeur, and their Fame sounds with a Solemn Renown, both to beget Respect, Reverence and Honour in the Eyes, Ears and Minds of all persons, in despite of Fortune or Time, for Grandeur, said she, lives both in the Ashes and Fame of Noble, Worthy, and Gallant Persons. But leaving their Discourse together with their Visit, I rest,

Madam,
Your faithful Friend and Servant.

LETTER 98

Madam,
I Received your Letter, which is Written in so Eloquent a Style, expressing such High Praises, that, were I apt to be Self-conceited, I should have become so Proud upon reading it, as I should have Denied my self, thinking my self not to be the Same I am; nay, so far I was already to this Pride and Self-denial, that I had a Better Opinion of my self, whilst I was Reading your Letter than Usually I have; But with returning thoughts I found my self the Same I am, and that your Praise did proceed meerly from your Civil Respect and Great Affection, and not from any Merit in me to Deserve it. Wherefore my Obligations are so much the More, as I do Less merit them, which Obligations shall always be acknowledged by,

Madam,
Your most Humble and Faithfull Servant.

LETTER 99

Madam,
I Hear there are many Noble Lords with their Ladies gone into F. which shews that in this Age there are many Kind Husbands, for usually when Husbands Travel, they leave their Wives behind, at least, think them to be a Trouble on their Journies, and counting their Trouble to be more, than the Pleasure of their Companyes, they are left at Home. But I believe, this

Mode-Travelling is only in this, and not in other Nations, for our Countrey-men make Kinder Husbands than men of other Nations. But since our Wars some are Necessitated and Forc'd to Travel into Forein Countreys, being Banish'd out of their Native Countrey, and the Wives of Banished men are forced to Travel to and from their Husbands, to seek for Means and Subsistence, to Maintain or Relieve their Necessitated lives, wanting Meat to feed on, and Cloaths to cover them; Yet be there not so many in this Banished Condition for Number as for Worth, for they are most persons of great Qualities or Dignities, and had great Estates, living formerly in great Splendor and Plenty, and now in low Despised Poverty and cold Charity, which makes their Conditions or Fortunes so much the more Sad and Lamentable, onely their Souls and Spirits are not according to their Fortunes, for their noble Souls and Heroick Spirits yield not to Fortunes Slavery, but they as Conquerors ride Triumphing on proud Fortun's back, spurring her sides with Scorn, for though Fortune may Starve or Inslave their Bodyes, yet she cannot Conquer their Minds. But in this Age there are more Women that Travel for Fashions sake, than out of Want, more that Travel for Breeding than for Bread, for Company than for Necessity, they spend more in Unnecessary Travels to see strange Nations and Men, than others can get, that Travel to their own Native Countrey and neer Relations, for these Travel not for Observation but Subsistence, they make not their Journies Frolicks of Mirth, but Weeping Departures, their Minds Swim in Troubled Tears, and are Blown with Sighs in their Bodily Barks, whilst they are Swimming on the dangerous Sea in Barks or Ships of Wood blown by blustring Winds; they venture not life for Sport and Fashion, but for Love and Charity; Indeed whereas other Women, either for Observation or Fashion, may with their Fathers, Husbands or Sons Travel all the World over, those Women must for necessity Travel as they can, having no Choice; And so leaving our Sex either at home or abroad in their own Native or Forein Countries, I rest,

> Madam,
> Your faithful Friend and Servant.

LETTER 100

Madam,

I Wonder at that which your Letter did Mention, that Sir C.K. should not Help his Friend, Sir O.R. in Distress, wherefore the Distress of O.R. doth prove, that Sir C.K. was never a True Friend to him, but only a

Seeming, as a Professing not an Acting Friend, for though Love lives in the Heart, yet the part of True Friendship Dwells or is onely made Known by the Action; But I have observed, that there's more that are Unkind to their Friends, even their Natural Friends, than Revengefull to their Enemies, and though both are Bad, yet the not doing Good or Timely Service to a Friend, is Worse than to do Hurt to an Enemy; for Preservation may Constrain them to the One, at least it is but quid for quo, as to Revenge an Injury, but nothing but a Treacherous Nature can make or Hinder them from doing a Service for a Friend, if they be able thereto; for it is Inhuman not to do a Timely Courtesie to a Stranger, nay, to an Enemy in Distress, for a Noble Person will not take Advantage of his Enemy, but rather Help him in Distress, although he takes Revenge when he is in an able Condition to Help himself. But not to Help a Friend in Distress, is a Nature worse than Devils, for sure one Devil will Assist another, if it be but for Acquaintance: But there are many sorts of Friends, if I may call them so, for some Friendships are Made in Adversity, which are for the most part Broken in Prosperity, either through Envy or Pride; and some Friendships are Made in Prosperity, and are Lost in Adversity, either by Scorn or Fear; some Friendships are Made by Mirth, which are for the most part Lost in Mourning, either for the Shunning of Melancholy or Sad Objects, or for the Love to Mirth, or for the Desire of Forgetfulness; some Friendships are Made by Luxury, which are Broken in Sickness; some Friendships are Made in Dangers, as to help each other, which are Lost in Security, and some are Made in Security, which are Lost in Danger, for to avoid the Dangers of each other; some Friendships are Made in Amours, and are Lost by Satiety; some Friendships are Made by Faction and Combination, and are Broken by Separation, and many the like Friendships, which are Made and Broken; but True, Undissolving Friendships are made by Faith, Love, Trust, Gratitude, Fortitude, and Honour, for they are alwayes Valiant for their Friends Safety, Industrious in their Friends Necessity, Careful for their Friends Security, Secret in their Friends Trust, Faithful in their Friends Service, Dispatchful in their Friends Affairs, Pleading in their Friends Sutes, Speaking in their Friends Behalf, Fighting in their Friends Quarrels, Dying in their Friends Causes, nay, ready to indure Torments for their Friends Ease, or Troubles for their Friends Peace, and there can be no Bar between True Friends, from Doing or Endeavouring Good for and to each others Good; Such a Friendship, Madam, is betwixt You and Me, and True Friends have an Undoubted

Belief of each others Love and Fidelity, wherefore it is but civil Ceremony to tell you, I am,

Madam,
Your faithful Friend and humble Servant.

LETTER 101

Madam,

In your last Letter you mentioned that Sir S.P. had lost 500 l. at Tennis, and 2000. at Cards and Dice, and was now Resolv'd to Play no more at those Games, but at Chess; (though Fox and Geese were a better Game for him in my Opinion) for although he may Lose as great Sums at Chess, yet not so Quickly as at Dice, Cards, or Tennis, for the Game at Chess takes time to Consider before he parts from his mony, besides, it requires a Good Judgment, which Sir S.P. did not prove to have by his former Adventures, wherein he had such Losses; Indeed, Wise men will Venture as little on Fortune as they can, by reason she never gives Assurance, and is too Inconstant to be Trusted without Bonds or Engagements of Friends or Lands, but I know none she hath, for she never keeps Friendship with any One, nor Dwells Constantly in any Place, so as she can neither be Sued, Arrested, nor Imprisoned; wherefore Prudent men will not Trust her, unless upon Necessity; But, certainly it is through a Covetous Humour, that causes men to Venture so much at Play; like as greedy Merchants, that will Venture their Whole Stock upon the Uncertain Winds, and Raging, Rough Seas, in hope of a Rich Return; and I fear Sir S.P. hath Lost his Stock in the Adventure, as many Merchants do, and so will become a Bankrupt. But to prove Gaming is out of Covetousness, and not for Pastime or Exercise, is, that Tennis is too Violent a Motion for Wholsome Exercise, for those that Play much at Tennis, impair their Health and Strength, by Wasting their Vital Spirits through much Sweating, and Weaken their Nerves by Overstraining them; neither can Tennis be a Pastime, for it is too Laborious for Pastime, which is onely a Recreation, and there can be no Recreation in Sweaty Labour, for it is laid as a Curse upon men, that they shall Live by the Sweat of their Brows, but those that Lose, shall Want, and become Poor by the Sweat of their Brows; wherefore Recreation which is Pleasure and Delight, Lives in Ease and Plenty; And thus it is through a Covetous Humour, that men Play at Cards and Dice, and not for Pastime nor Exercise, for as Tennis hath too Much Motion for Exercise, so Playing at Cards and Dice hath too Little, insomuch that when Gamesters rise from Play, their Limbs are Stiff, Numb, and Insensible, for want of Use, the truth is, they fall asleep through Laziness, having no Imployment; Neither can I perceive it to be a Recreation, by reason Cards and Chess require more Study than Arithmetick, or Logick, or any other Science that sets the Brain awork, and there is as little Recreation in the Labour of the Mind, as in the Labour of the Body, in the Labour of the Thoughts, as in the Labour of the Limbs; besides, their Stakes are Attended and Watch'd with as many Fears as Hopes, and both are Troubles of the Mind, for Hopes are built on Doubts; and for the Increase of their Wealth, Gamesters are like Chimists, that Seek the Philosophers Stone, in which Search they all become Bankrupts, Losing more Gold than they Get, in so much that when they Dye, they leave no Wealth behind them, only their Folly, which they leave at their Death, for Death will not be troubled therewith; But of Worldly Riches they are as Poor as Lazarus, yet whether they shall Lye in Abrahams bosome, I Know not. And as Gamesters are like Lazarus for the matter of Poverty, so Drunkards are like Dives for the matter of Drought, they are alwayes Dry, for much Strong Liquor causes Heat, and Heat causes Drought, so as they Drink themselves Dry, and many times in a Fevorish Distemper desire a Drop of Water to Cool their Parched Tongues, having Scalding Heat within them, so that their Wine, or Feavour which Wine causes, proves to their Bodies as Hell-fire, and a furious Madness in their Minds; only there is this Difference, that in Hell-fire, its said, the Body never Decayes or Dies, but in the Fire of Wine the Body doth Wast by degrees, or is suddenly Burnt up in Feavours, and so Dies; Also Drunkards have the Fate of Gamesters and Chymists, which is to be Poor, for as Chymists are Impoverish'd by a Wasting Fire, so Drunkards are Impoverish'd by Inflaming Wine; also Drunkards are Guilty of Covetousness, not so much of Wealth as of Drink, but they are as Insatiable for Drink as the others for Gold; and Whoremasters may come amongst them for Covetousness and Poverty, for should they neither Covet Gold nor Drink, yet they Covet other Men's Wives, Daughters, Sisters, Aunts, Neeces and Maid-Servants, and Impoverish their Estates, either by presenting the Coy with Gifts, as Bribes to Tempt them, or Maintain them for their Use; also they are as Short-lived as Drunkards, or as Diseased, & as full of Aches, Pains and Weakness. Thus some Toss away their Estates & Lives with a Ball, others Throw away their Estates and Lives with a Dice, some Shuffle away their Estates and Lives with a pack of Cards, others Spue out their Estates and Lives with Wine, others Kiss away their Estates and Lives with Mistresses, and so with the Pot and the Rot, the Ball, the Card and the Dice, men Busie the whole Time of their Life, or rather Waste the whole Time of their Life, together with their Life; And not in any one of these Actions is Honour, nor, as I can perceive, Pleasure; for their can be no Pleasure in Fear of Losing, nor in Sick-spuing, nor in Painfull Rotting, nor is there any Honour in these Actions, for it is not Honourable to beat a Ball, but to beat an Enemy, nor to deal out Cards, but to lead out Souldiers, neither is it Honourable to be Dead-drunk in a Tavern, but to be Wounded in the Field of War, for a Drunken Quarrel is not an Honourable Fight, the Fury in a Tavern is not the Valour in a Field; to be Inclosed in a Mistresses soft Armes is not to lye on the hard Ground open to all the Injuries of the Elements; neither shall men get an Eternal Fame, for Drinking, Gaming and Whoring, but they sooner may get an Eternal Infamy, although most are so Happy as to Dye in Oblivion, wherein let them rest; But if I Write my Letter much Longer, it may become as Troublesome as a Drunken Quarrelling, or Wrangling Gamester, or an Impatient Adulterer, or an Impertinent Woman, of which last you may think me to be Guilty by this Letter, wherein are more Words than Wit, more Truth than Reason, Wherefore I'le Write no more, only give me leave to subscribe my self,

        Madam,
           Your very faithful Friend and Servant.

LETTER 102

Madam,
I Was to Visit the Lady C.H. at her Country-House, but the House is too Good and Fine an House for the Situation, for the Air all about is Thick and Foggy, the Ground Deep and Miry in some places, and Mountainous and Rocky in others, also it is so Cold, as no Fruits will Ripen or Increase there; The truth is, she lives as if it were at the Poles, yet she is Merry and Gay, which shews that a Sun-shining Mind is not Dull'd with Cloudy Dayes, no more than a Cloudy Mind, or Sad and Melancholy Humour is pleased with Sun-shining dayes, but that every Place is Pleasant to a Chearful Mind and Lively Thoughts, which makes the Life Happy, for True Happiness Lives Within the Mind or Soul, not Without it, and whosoever build their Happiness Without it, shall Miss it when they Seek it, nay, those Buildings are like Airy Castles, which Vanish to nothing, or rather like Unwholsom, or Ill Vapor; or as a Snuff of a Candle, that goes

out, and leaves an Ill Savour behind it; so those that place their Happiness Without them, as on the Opinion of Men, or the Vanities of the World, shall have nothing but Loss, Trouble, and Vexation, instead of Peace, Rest, and Content; And the Difference betwixt a Wise man and a Fool is, that a Wise man carries his Happiness still Within him, and a Fool is always Seeking it Without him, & seldom or never Meets it, the other never Seeks it, for he always hath it; a Wise man doth like an Expert Chymist, that can Extract Cordials out of Poison, but a Fool Converts Cordials into Poison by wrong Application; But leaving the Fool to his Sick Mind, and Erroneous Practice, and the Wise man to his Healthful Mind and Experienced Prudence, I rest,

Madam,
Your faithful Fr. and S.

LETTER 103

Madam,
Since it is your Pleasure we should Write to each other, as if we were Personally Conversing, as Discoursing of what we Think, Say, or Act, and of the several Imployments of our Time, I must tell you, I was Invited to be a Gossip, to Name the Lady B.Rs. Child, of which she Lyes in, and at the Christening there were many Ladies and Gentlewomen, and being most Married Women, as is Usual at such Gossiping Meetings, their Discourse was most of Labours and Child-beds, Children and Nurses, and Houshold Servants, and of Preserving, and such like Discourses as Married Women and Mistresses of Families usually have; at last they fell into a Discourse of Husbands, Complaining of Ill Husbands, and so from Husbands in General, to their own Particular Husbands, where one Lady said, that her Husband was the Simplest man that ever Nature made; another Lady said, her Husband was become a Beggar with Gaming; another, that her Husband was the greatest Whoremaster in the City, and Corrupted all her Maids, for if they came Maids into her service, they went away none; another Lady said, her Husband got Children, and then Grumbled at the Charge of Keeping, and Bringing them up; another said, that her Husband had so many Faults, as it was an endless work to Relate them, for his Faults did Surpass all Account; at last, when they had Railed a Long time, I, to Express the Nature of our Sex, (which is, that we cannot Restrain our Tongues from Speaking, although it be on such Themes as we Understand not, or of such Subjects or Causes as we have nothing to do with, and which do not

Concern us) did most Foolishly Speak to the Ladies, saying, I wonder'd to hear them Rail at their Husbands, and Publickly Dispraise them, for if they had Faults, it was the Wives Duty to Wink at them, at least not to Divulge them, and if their Husbands would Speak of them, and Tell their Faults, it was likely they would Equal their Husbands Faults, if not Surpass them; but the Ladies being before Heated with Wine, and then at my Words, with Anger fell into such a Fury with me, as they fell upon me, not with Blows, but with Words, and their Tongues as their Swords, did endeavour to Wound me; wherefore I perceiving my own Folly of Unnecessary Speaking, and being Sorry for the Indiscretion, became as Silent as if I had been Dead, onely I did Move to shew I was Alive, for I took a Silent Leave, as with a Curtsie, and came away; and it hath so Frighted me; as I shall not hastily go to a Gossiping meeting again, like as those that become Cowards at the Roaring Noise of Cannons, so I, at the Scolding Voices of Women; but well may One Woman be Afraid of Many Women, whenas One Man will be Afraid of another Man; and so leaving you to Rejoyce, as I know you will, at my safe Deliverance or Escape, I rest,

Madam,
Your faithful Friend and Servant.

LETTER 104

Madam,
I Do not wonder that Mrs. S.P. should Report, she was the Cause, or the Maker of the Match betwixt your Noble Husband and You, although she Knew nothing of your Affections, or Intentions of Marriage, until the very Day you were Contracted; but she is rather to be Pardoned, because she is Poor and Inferiour to so Great a Person as your Ladiship, and a Lie in that Case, and Brag of that Honour, may Advantage her very much, as I believe it hath done, for others Hearing, and Believing what she Reports, because she was an Attendant and Follower of your Ladiship, it makes all the Young Men and Women Flock to her, to get them Husbands and Wives, thinking her a Fortunate and Powerful Woman, that could bring such Great Persons as you and your Noble Husband, to Meet, Love, and Marry; wherefore Persons of a Lower Degree perhaps she may Dispose of as she Pleases, and by Making of Matches, Gain on both sides, for Women do Fee her to get them Husbands, and Men to get them Rich Wives, so as she is become the Huckster or Broker of Males and Females, and no doubt but she Cozens them sometimes, so

that they do not alwayes find their Markets or Wares so Rich or Good as she Pretends they are. Indeed she is a Matrimonial Bawd, and I know not whether she doth as I.have heard of other Bawds, who many times gives Broken Maids for Pure Virgins, but if she deals Honestly, one may wish her to Thrive by her Trade, for Marriage is Honest, and the Procurers may be so too, if they give True Informations of and to each Person, otherwise they are but Cheats, and Bribes are great Temptations to Poverty; but Love, Beauty, Wit, Honour, Title, and Wealth, need no Procurers, every One is sufficient to Match it Self, wherefore your Ladiship and your Noble Husband, who had all those, had no Use of any other but your selves, to joyn your Affections, which Produced a Marriage, and certainly your Marriage was Designed by Nature, and Decreed in Heaven, to which Divine Angels were Witnesses, and the Invisible Bridal Guests, to Bless, and Rejoyce at your Union and Nuptials, which makes you both so Happy, which is the Joy of,

> Madam,
> Your faithful Fr. and S.

LETTER 105

Madam,
Here were some Ladies to Visit me, amongst the rest, there was one so very Fair, as I never Saw the like, but let me tell you, that was all which was to be Admired in her; and Mrs. F.W. who you know is a Salt Speaker, said, that her Wit was like her Complexion, Weak and Faint, Repeating the old Proverb, Fair and Foolish, and then she Sung a line of an old Song, Oh the Lovely Brown, as 'tis, how it Shames the Lilies! I told her, she Spoke out of Envy, she said, No, for Fair Women were seldom Handsom, I said, that the Usual Saying was, that Black men Liked and Loved Fair women best, she answer'd, that then Black men were as Foolish as Fair women. Thus you may know how one Woman is Apt to Dispraise another, for had she been either Brown or Black, although very well Favoured, yet it was likely she would have said somewhat to her Prejudice, for our Sex Loves or Approves not any Other which is Eminent, either for Wit, Beauty, Favour, Behaviour, or Virtue; But leaving Mrs. T.W. to her Envy, Opinion, or Fancy, and the Beauty of Mrs. E.D. to Admiration, I rest,

> Madam,
> Your faithful Fr. and S.

LETTER 106

Madam,

I Know not whether I shall give you Thanks for the Present of Fruits you sent me; By which Present, give me Leave to Tell you, you did Tempt me to Eat a Forbidden fruit, as the Serpent in Paradise did our great Grandmother Eve, for though I was not Forbidden to Eat of that Fruit by God, yet Nature did Forbid me, saying, I should be cast from Health into Sickness, and be Condemned to the Painfull labour of Physick; but it hath given me Knowledge as to Know and Perceive my own Weakness, both for Constitution of Body, and Reason of Mind, that it could not Govern my Appetite with Temperance, and I must have suffer'd the Torments of a Hot burning Feaver, had not Letting Blood Saved and Redeemed me there from. Thus, Madam, your Kind Friendship hath been a Devil to me, only you wanted a Devils Design, which is a Desire Hurtfull to Deceive, and you wanted the Malice, though not the Evil Effect. But some may think, this is a strange Style, or Conversation of Friendship, as to call my Friend a Devil, but my Friend being of a Divine Nature and a God-like Wisdome, knows that an Evill Effect may Proceed from a Good Intention as her Present shews; also she Knows that I her Friend Love and Honour her Intention, though I Rail and Exclame against the Effect, so that in the Effect and Intention of Friendship, we are as Intire and Loving Friends as ever we were, neither do true Friends take Exceptions at Words, knowing their Souls are so United, as not to be Divided neither in Life nor Death; But, pray Madam, if you send me any more Fruit, send me Good Advice with it, as to Advise me not to Eat so much as to make my self Sick; Howsoever, I will leave it to your Better Judgment, and rest,

> Madam,
> Your faithfull Friend and Servant.

LETTER 107

Madam,

I Am Sorry to hear that Mr. C.D. is Dead, and for Mr. E.A. and R.G. who you say, were very Busie, or rather Troublesome to Him in his Sickness, in perswading him to make his Will and Settle his Estate, I must Confess, I wonder they would Intrude themselves into any man's Private Affairs unless they were Desired, or had any Interest therein, for though an Honourable Person will not Deny his Assistance where he can do a

Worthy Service and is Desired thereto, yet he will not Press his Service, for that were to disserve; But to be forwardly Officious and Busie in a Dying man's Affairs, as in Making, or Causing of Making Wills, or in Advising and Counselling a Sick man in matters Concerning his Estate, or about Debts, Legacies, Annuities or the like, not being Invited or Desired thereunto by the Sick Person, it looks rather with a Covetous Face than a Friendly Heart, for though the Intention may be Honest without Self-ends, yet the Appearance is not so, for it Appears, as if he had a Desire, or did Hope, that the Sick man might make him his Executor or Administrator, at least to leave him a Legacy for his Care, Acquaintance and Friendship; but the World is so Covetous and Greedy after Dead-men's Shoos, as the Saying is, that if any man have an Estate to leave behind him, when he is Sick or Dying, all his Friends and Acquaintance flock about him like a Company of Carrion-Crows, to a Dead Body, and all to Devour that Wealth he leaves, when as a Poor man may be Sick and Dye, and none Come neer to Help him; Thus we may perceive by the Course of the World, that it is not Charity to the Sick, nor Love to the Man, that brings Visitors or hath profered Service, but Love to the Wealth. But if all were of my Humour, the Rich should have the Fewest Visitors, for I, for fear any should Imagine me one of these Human or rather Inhuman Vultures, should never Visit the Sick, unless they were so Poor as they wanted Relief. Wherefore, good Madam, have a Care of your Health, if you desire my Company, lest when you are Sick, I should not Visit you, yet if I should, I would not bring Lawyers or Notaries to Trouble you, but I would bring you the most Experienced and Famous Physician I could get, to Cure you, for as long as Life lasts, no Indeavour ought to be Wanting, it being the part of a Friend to Regard the Life, not to Search into the Estate, and when a Friend is Dead, to Execute to the utmost of their Power their Friends Desires, and to Obey Punctually all their Commands they laid upon them whilst they Lived, and not to let them be Buried untill they were sure they are past Reviving, nor to be laid upon the Cold Ground, untill their Bodies are Colder than the Earth they are laid on; but, Madam, you are likelier to Live to do this Friendly Office for me, than I for you, by reason you are Healthfull, and I am Sickly, and Sickness is Death's Serjeant to Arrest Life, and the Grave is the Prison: Yet whilst I Live, I shall always prove my self to be,

Madam,
    Your Ladiships faithful Friend and Servant.

Madam,

You were pleased to tell me in your last Letter, that the Lady F.L. is so Jealous of her Husband, as the Humour of Jealousie drives her sometimes into a Passionate Fury, or Furious Passion, insomuch as not only to Exclame and Rail on those Ladies he doth Visit, but on her Husband, which is neither Seemly, nor Decent, for Wives should Submit to their Husbands Follies, and Wink at their Crimes, if they cannot Reform them, neither is the way of Reformation by Railing and Exclamations, but by Gentle Perswasions, Meek Submissions, and Subtil Insinuations; but say these will not Reform them; therefore shall a Wife Double her Injuries, as first, to be Injured by her Husbands Inconstancy, and then by her Own Grief, Rage, and Fury? This were to make his Crimes her Tormentors, which would neither let the Mind, Thoughts, or Body, live in Rest or Peace; and why should a Wife Grieve for her Husbands Inconstancy, since she receives no Dishonour from it? nay, if it be for the Loss of her Husbands Affection, she is but a Simple Woman that will Trouble her self for him that Loves her not, or for him that Prefers another Woman in his Affection before her; neither ought she to Wrong her self by doing Indiscreet, Dishonest, or Dishonourable Actions, to Revenge her Wrongs, but rather to Strive and Endeavour to make her self appear more Virtuous; but for the most part Women are more Jealous through Envy to their own Sex, than Love to their Husbands, for every Woman would be the Chief for Wit, Beauty, and such like Attractives, and for my part, I wonder Men should desire Variety, since all Women are alike, for a Man can have but a Woman; as for Beauty, it is onely to Look on, and Wit to Listen to, but not Amorously to Enjoy; But if all Wives were as some, Husbands might freely take their Liberties, and their Wives would never Frown for it; and for the most part Careless Wives have the Chastest Husbands, I mean Careless, as Free from Jealousie. But leaving the Lady F.L. to Time, Custom, and Discretion, to Abate her Jealousie, I rest,

> Madam,
> Your faithful Friend and Servant.

Madam,

In your last Letter you were pleased to tell me, that you shew'd the Admirable Works of A.B. to L.C. and he did not Admire them, which was a sign he did not Understand them; Certainly, so little Understanding is in the World, that if the World of Mankind were Divided into Four Parts, Three Parts and a Half of the Four are Ignorant Dolts, which is the Reason that Rare Qualities, Learned Sciences, Curious Arts, and Divine Fancies are no more Esteemed or Admired; for if Understanding were General, Men would Run, Seek, and Sue, to see any One Person that had the Ingenuity to Invent Arts, or Find out New Sciences, or that had the Gift of Poetry, or the Deep Conceptions of Philosophy; but for the most, these enter not into their Capacity, and being not to their Capacity, it cannot be to their Pleasure or Delight, and so not to their Esteem; as for Proof, let the most Rare Poems, or some Deep Philosophy be Read to Several men, and tell them of some New Science, or shew them some Curious or Profitable Arts, and you shall find they will Express they are Weary of them, by their Yawning, Humming, Hauking, and Spitting, or sit as if they were Statues, without Life or Sense, as not being Sensible of them; but read to them something that they Understand, by their Brutish Nature, as Ribbaldry, a Wanton Song or Scene, or the like, although there be neither Wit nor Sense in it, and you shall hear them Loud with Laughter or Commendations, Swear all the Oaths they never heard Better, and Cry up the Author for a mighty Wit; or shew them any Vain or Useless Art, and they will Admire it, if it be but a Glass-ring, and will Wonder how it came to be Invented, and Admire the Inventor for a Person of an Ingenious Brain; but if it be an Art that is Rare or Profitable, they will Slight it, and cast their heads Aside, not out of Envy, but Ignorance; wherefore, Madam, those that are well Qualified and Witty, are Admired but by a Few, which is by the Wise and Knowing, and those Few are Worth all the rest; for the Wise and Knowing, indeed, are all the World of Mankind, the rest are but Mongrels, as Sensual Persons, viz. half Men, and half Beasts, or Dull, Ignorant Persons, as half Men, and half Stones or Blocks, nay, for the most part they are Three parts Beasts or Stones, and One part Men. Thus amongst all Nature's Works True Men are the Scarcest, being the Rarest, as the most Excellent Works in Nature. This is the reason that the most Excellent Works of Nature are not Admired by the General Bulk, so as it is no wonder that L.C. did not Esteem and Praise the Works of A.B. But, Madam, you have not onely Seen and Read them, but Approved and Praised them, which is a Sufficient Reward to his Ingenious Wit, and an Honour to his Person, as also an Honour to all those you think Worthy to Favour, of which I am One, although least Worthy, but I will endeavour to make my self such a one, as you may not be Ashamed to Acknowledge me,

Madam,
Your faithful and humble Servant.

LETTER 110

Madam,

I Am Glad to hear the Lady U.S. and her Husband live so Happily, as only to Themselves, and Love so well One Another, as seldome to be Sunder'd by Each others Absence, and I am Glad that She and He are so Wise as not to be perswaded from a Loving and Agreeable Course of Life. But I perceive by your Letter, that their Neighbours and Acquaintance Indeavour by their Little and Petty Flouts, Jeeres, and the like, to Disunite them, saying, the Husband was Gentleman-Usher to his Wife, and it was out of Fashion for a Husband to go abroad with his Wife, and her Husband had greater Wealth than Birth, and was a Plain man and no Gallant, and that a man of Humble Birth and Plain Breeding was Despised and Scorned amongst Men of Title, and she had Lost the Place of her Birth by Marriage; But I will Answer in her Behalf, as being my Friend, that as she had better keep to an Old Fashion, which is Becoming, Easie and Commodious, than follow a New, Vain and Mis-becoming Fashion, so 'tis more Seemly, Gracefull and Becoming, for a Wife to have her Husband alwayes with her, to be a Witness of her Honest Actions, than to give a Suspicion both to her Husband and the World, as if she desired to be Absent from him and out of his Sight, that she might take more Liberty to be Wanton; for none can Imagine, a Wife will Abuse her Husband before his Face, as in his Sight, unless her Husband were Mad, or Drunk, or an Idiot, as a Natural Fool, and she not only a Whore, but an Impudent Whore; and for his Wealth being Greater than his Birth, it shews, her Parents and Friends were Wise to Marry her to Plenty, for with Poverty lives for the most part Discontent, and it shews, she was Dutifull and Obedient to Accept of her Parents Choice rather than her Own; and shews her self to be Wise, preferring Honesty before Vanity, a Plain-Behavior'd man before a Fantastical Flatterer; and as for Birth, what Title he wants by Fortune, Favour and Time, Nature hath given him the Title of Merit, which is far beyond the Titles that Kings and Time give, for Outward Titles are far Inferiour to Inward Worth and Merit; and as for Place, Virtue and Merit take the First and Best Place in Fame's Palace, though not at Gossipping-Meetings, Vain Shews, and Expensive & Luxurious Feastings; and for that they say, no Respect will be given to her Husband by or from men of Title, Place and Authority, Solomon sayes, that the Husband of a Virtuous and Chast Wife sits in the Gates amongst the Elders with Honour, so that his Merit and her Virtue and Chastity will not onely keep him from Scorn, but give him Honour, Esteem and Respect, were he as Poor of Wealth, as Low in Birth; but having Wealth, had he neither Inward Worth nor Outward Title, he would be Respected, for all Bow down and Adore the Golden Calf or Image, and as Naturally Mankind loves Gold and such like Wealth, so Naturally they Love Mischief, wherefore it is out of Envy, that the Lady U.Ss. Neighbours and Acquaintance Dispraise or Undervalue her Husband, and his Birth and Breeding, and Laugh at their United Associating, and not out of Love, for true Love Commends true Worth, and Honest Unity: But as Women Envy Women for Beauty, Bravery, Courtships and Place, So Men Envy Men for Power, Authority, Honour and Offices. Wherefore leaving the Generality to Envy and Spite, and the Lady U.S. and her Husband to Love and Happiness, I rest,

Madam,
Your faithful Friend and Servant.

LETTER III

Madam,
Th' other Day the Lord N.N. arguing with others that were in Company, said, he was of an Opinion that all the Stars were Suns, and that Every one of those Suns had such Planets above and below them, like as the Sun hath that gives this Earth light; others said, that then those Planets would be Seen, he Answered, they could not be Seen, for those Suns we call Fixt Stars were at such a Distance as they appear but like Stars, and their Planets having but Reflected Lights from those Suns could not be perceived, by reason Reflected Lights are Faint and Dim in Comparison of Inherent Lights; also he was of an Opinion, that there were Many Worlds, and that those Worlds were Unalterable and Unchangeable, and therefore Eternal; Also he said, the several Kinds and Sorts of Creatures in those Worlds, as Animals, Vegetables, Minerals, and Elements were Eternal; but the Particulars of every Kind or Sort were Transmigrable or Transformable; whereupon others in the Company said, it could not be that those Worlds were Eternal, for if they were, then they had no Beginning, and that could not be, by reason the World seem'd to be Composed, Made and Ordered by some Infinite Wisdome, causing such Method and Measures, Proportions,

Distinctions, Order, Exactness, Rule, Degrees and Decrees, all which could not be without Design, and by Chance; N.N. said, that if the World was Eternal, it was not made by Chance, for Chance proceeded from some Alteration, or Change of some Motions, and not from Eternity, for Eternity was not Subject to Chance, although Chance might be Subject to Eternity, and to prove the World and Worlds were Eternal, he said, the Fundamental Frame, Parts, Motions, and Form, were not Subject to Change, for they Continue One and the Same without any Alteration. Thus, Madam, the Sages Discoursed, but they perceiving I was very Attentive to their Discourse, they ask'd my Opinion, I answered, they had left no Room for another Opinion, for the World was Eternal or not Eternal, and they had given their Opinions of either side; then they desired me to be a Judg between their Opinions, I said, such an Ignorant Woman as I will be a very unfit Judge, and though you be both Learned, and Witty Men, yet you cannot Resolve the Question, it being impossible for a Small Part to Understand or Conceive the Whole, and since neither you, nor all Man-kind, were they joyn'd into one Soul, Body, or Brain, can possibly know whether the World had a Beginning or No Beginning, or if it had, When it was Made, nor of What it was Made, nor for What it was Made, nor what Power Made it, nor what the Power is that Made it, nor whether it shall Last or Dissolve; wherefore said I, the best is to leave this Discourse, and Discourse of some other Subject that is more Sociable, as being more Conceivable: Then they Laugh'd, and said they would Discourse of Women, I said, I did believe they would find that Women were as Difficult to be Known and Understood as the Universe, but yet I thought they would find them more Sociable, at which Expression they made them-selves very merry; but being my near Relative Friends, I took their Mirth in good part, as I hope you will do this Long Letter, Knowing the Length of my Letter is to Express my Obedience to your Commands, in which I shall prove my self,

> Madam,
> Your Faithful Servant.

LETTER 112

Madam,
You writ in your last Letter, that I had given our Sex Courage and Confidence to Write, and to Divulge what they Writ in Print; but give me leave humbly to tell you, that it is no Commendation to give them

Courage and Confidence, if I cannot give them Wit. But, Madam, I observe, our Sex is more apt to Read than to Write, and most commonly when any of our Sex doth Write, they Write some Devotions, or Romances, or Receits of Medicines, for Cookery or Confectioners, or Complemental Letters, or a Copy or two of Verses, all which seems rather as Briefs than Volumes, which Express our Brief Wit in our Short Works, and to Express my self according to the Wit of our Sex, I will end this Letter, onely give me leave to subscribe my self, as truly I am,

Madam,
Your Ladiships faithful Servant.

LETTER 113

Madam,

In your last Letter you were pleased to tell me, you were invited to a Meeting, where many Ladies and Gentlemen were, and amongst their several Discourses, the Lady M.L. spoke of me, saying, I liv'd a Dull, Unprofitable, Unhappy Life, Imploying my time onely in Building Castles in the Air.[1] Indeed, if I were of her Ladiships Humour, I should be Unhappy, but as I am, I would not change the Course of my Life with her Ladiship, might I have the years of Methusalem to boot; and as for the Minds Architecture, as Castles in the Air, or Airy Castles, which are Poetical Conceptions, and Solitary Contemplations, which produce Poems, Songs, Playes, Masks, Elegies, Epigrams, Anagrams, and the like, they will be more lasting than Castles of Wood, Brick, or Stone, and their Architecture, if well Designed and Built, will be more Famous, and their Fame spread farther than those of Stone, *viz.* to the View and Prospect of divers Nations, if Translated into divers Languages, whereas Castles of Timber, Brick, or Stone, cannot be Removed nor Translated, if Built upon the Ground; neither is the Minds Architecture and Castles subject to Ruin, as Castles of Stone, which are subject to Time, Accidents, and the Rage of Wars, by which they are Destroyed, or Moulder to Dust, and are Buried in Oblivion, whenas Poetical Castles are set in Fames Palace; neither doth the Building of Poetical Castles Impoverish and Ruin the Builder's Families, as Corporeal Castles of Timber, Brick, or Stone, for the most part do, Wasting their Worldly Wealth so much, as they leave nothing for their Posterity, but

---

1 M.L. are the initials of Cavendish before she married, Margaret Lucas. Cavendish was reported to have been told by Bishop John Wilkins that she built castles in the air. There is some irony in the association of an alter ego with the Bishop.

leave them to Poverty, which Poverty forces them many times to Act Dishonourably, so that what Fame they get by building Brave and Sumptuous Castles, Houses, Tombes, and the like, they lose by their Childrens Base, Sharking, Cheating, Robbing, and Wicked Actions; and so instead of Fame get Infamy; at best, those Builders are accounted by Vain and Prodigal, whenas the Architecture of the Mind, which she names Castles in the Air, give a Reputation, not only to the Building, but to the Builder's Temporal Posterity; neither doth the Builder need any other Monument or Tomb, than his Own Airy Works, which, if Curiously Composed, and Adorned with Fancies, Similitudes, Metaphors, and the like, and Carefully Written and Printed, are more Glorious, Stately, and Durable, than Tombes or Monuments of Marble, Costly Gilt, and Carved, nay, more Lasting than the Tomb of Mausolus; for Homer's Works Live, and are Publick to the View, whereas that Famous Monument is Consumed, and onely Mentioned there was such a thing, and yet it was one of the Corporeal Wonders of the World; the like of the great Colossus; and what is become of the Egyptian Pyramids? By this we see that Poetical Castles are both Profitable and Lasting, and will be Remembred when the Lady M.L. is Forgotten; but as much as she Slights Poetical Castles, she would be well Pleased to have an Epigram made in her Commendation, and she will Crowd hard, & Sit so Long in a Masking Room upon a Scaffold, as to be Incommoded in her Seat, and Benumb'd with Sitting to see a Mask, and she will be at the Charge to give Mony to See a Play, and will sit two or three hours as a Spectator, and Weep, or Laugh, as the Poet pleases to have her; also she will be as Amorous as any Lover the Poet can make. Indeed, the Poet doth make her an Amorous Lover, his Wit moves her Mind to Love and Courtships, or Loving Courtships; but though she Delights in the Poets Works, yet she Dislikes the Poets Life, and wants a Poets Wit to build Poetical Castles; and so leaving her to her Little Wit, and Many Words, to her Gossiping-Life and her Light Heels,[1] I rest,

Madam,
Your faithful Friend and Servant.

LETTER 114

Madam,
In your last you Express'd, that the Lord G.P. was totally Govern'd by one of his Chief men, which shews the Man is the Master, and the Master the

---

1 Loose morals.

Servant; But there are different Governings; for Subjects are Govern'd by Laws; Children, by Natural Love and Fear; Servants by Profit, and Slaves by Force, but Few are Govern'd by Reason, and as Few by Honour; also Many are Govern'd by Flattery and Partiality, and More by Luxury, for the Sensual Appetites of the Body have a more Forcible Power for the most part, than Reason and Temperance hath in the Soul, and the Noble Passions or Virtues of the Soul, are made Slaves to the Base Appetites of the Body, sometimes by Force, but oftener by an Insinuating Perswasion, and Pleasing Temptation, like as the Lord G.P. is Ruled by his Flattering and Insinuating Servant, whereas the Appetites should be but as Servants to be Govern'd, not Masters to Rule, and although they ought to be Attended in their Sicknesses, Cherish'd and Nourish'd in their Weakness, Imployed in their Healthful Strength, yet they must be Corrected in their Extravagancies, and Punished for their Disorders; But a Man of Honour, a Gentleman, ought to be Free from them, as to have his Mind Free from the Slavery of the Bodily Senses, or Sensual Appetites, as also from Outward Accidents, Fortunes, or Objects, which is to have his Judgment, Understanding, Opinion, Justice, Prudence, Fortitude, Temperance, and the like, Free from Partiality, and Inticing Perswasions; and to let Reason, Honour, and Honesty be Judges, to Decide and Determine all Causes concerning the Actions of Life, for though Outward Causes or Things must be made Judges or Governours of Reason, Honour, and Honesty, yet Reason, Honour, and Honesty, must be Rulers & Governours of Outward Causes and Things, which if they cannot Rule, they may Condemn them, and if they cannot Punish them, they may chuse to Imploy them. Thus men may be Masters and Princes of themselves, for it is Unfit, nay Base, for a man of Honour, a Gentleman, either to be Led like a Slave, or to be Driven like a Beast; But a man of Honour, a Gentleman, ought not to Refuse to be Informed or Guided by Light and Truth, for which, Praise and Commendation, Love and Respect will follow him, as his Lackies, and Attend and Wait upon him; which Guides and Attendants I wish all men, and rest,

Madam,
Your faithful Friend and Servant.

Madam,

The News here is, that there are many Towns and multitudes of People Drown'd in H.[1] I cannot wonder at it, by reason they live Below Water, like Fishes, onely they do not Swim, so that one may say they are Housed-Fishes, or Fishes in Sluces; indeed, they are Incircled, or Wall'd in with Water, and for my part, I think it should be more secure to live in a Floating Boat, or Ship, Upon the Water, as Rivers, or Seas, than in a Fix'd House Under the Water, for the Water in most Places is Above their Houses; But, though they live like Fishes, for the Manner, or Matter of Water, yet they are not of the Temper of Fishes, for the Matter, or Manner of Nature, for, as for Industry, they are like Ants or Pismires, Prudently Provident, although not absolutely like them in their Government, for their Government is betwixt a Republick and Aristocracy. But by their Government and Industry, they do not appear to be Cold and Stupid, but Hot and Active, they neither want Courage nor Strength, Policy nor Industry, Wealth nor Jolity; they are as Happy, as yet, to all Outward Appearance, as any Nation, nay Happier than most Nations are, for now they live in Peace, only wanting Champain, or Firm Ground. Their Ships bring them in all Commodities, that are either Useful, Profitable, or Delightful. And as for their Wit, I do not know whether it be so Sharp and Quick as in Drier Climats, yet they seem by their Government, to have as Sound Judgments, and Clear Understanding, as any other Nation: Indeed, they seem to have the Subtilty of the Serpent, the Craft of the Fox, the Strength of the Lion, the Prudence of the Ant, the Sight of the Eagle, and the Wisdom of Rational Men; wherefore I observe, that Men are not according to the Temper of Climates they are Born and Bred in, but according to the Pleasure of Natures Will in Creating, or according to Fortune, Chance, or Breeding, Informing, Conforming, Reforming, Ordering or Disposing. But, Madam, I am not a fit Judg of Nations, People, nor Numbers, being of the Female Sex, who are seldom made Judges, for want of Judgement, and being Retired much to my own Thoughts, I want those Observations that Travelling and Commercing Persons have, or may have, although most Persons of either Sex are forward to give their Opinions, whether Wise or Foolish, and are apt to Censure, whether Truly or Falsly, Generously or Maliciously.

---

1 H is Holland, where Cavendish lived before the Restoration. The subject matter indicates that portions of *Sociable Letters* were composed before 1660.

But, Madam, lest you should Censure me to be a Tedious Writer, I take my leave, and rest,

> Madam,
> Your Ladiships faithful Friend and Servant.

LETTER 116

Madam,

Here was the Lord W.N.[1] to Visit me, whose Discourse, as you say, is like as a pair of Billows to a Spark of Fire in a Chimney, where are Coals or Wood, for as this Spark would sooner Go out than Inkindle the Fuel, if it were not Blown, so his Discourse doth set the Hearers Brain on a light Flame, which Heats the Wit, and Inlightens the Understanding; the truth is, Great Wits might be Thought, or Seem Fools, if they had not Wit to Discourse, but the Greatest Wits that are, or ever were, cannot Discourse Wittily, unless they either Imagine, or else have a Real Witty Opposite to Discourse Wittily to; like as those that can Skilfully Fence, cannot Fence, unless they have an Opposite to Fence with; or like as those that can Skilfully Play at Tennis, cannot Play, unless they have a Skilful Opposite; they may Toss the Ball, but not Play a Game. The same is in Conversation and Discourse; there is None can Discourse Well, Wisely, or Wittily, but with Wise, and Witty Opposites, otherwise their Discourse will be Extravagant, and as it were, out of Time or Season: But the Lord W.Ns. Wit is a Well-season'd Wit, both for Reason, Time, and Company, to which I leave him, and rest,

> Madam,
> Your faithful Friend and Servant.

LETTER 117

Madam,

Th' other day, at Mrs. D.Us. house, I heard Harmonious, and Melodious Musick, both Instruments and Voices, but in my Opinion, there is no Musick so Sweet, and Powerful as Oratory, for Sweet Words are better than a Sweet Sound, and when they are Joyned together, it Ravishes the Soul; wherefore Lyrick Poetry hath Advantage of all other Poetry, because

---

1   Doubtless William Newcastle, husband to Cavendish.

both Sound and Sense are Harmonious, wherefore the Antients had both their Heroick Poems, and Comedies, and Tragedies, in Verse, and Tunes set to them, and Sung, both in their Theatres of War and Peace, as in the Fields and Stages, the One rais'd up their Spirits to Action, the Other caused more Attention. But, perchance you will say, that Oratory is Elegant Prose, and not Elegant Verse. Certainly, there is as much Oratory in Elegant Verse, as in Elegant Prose, for as Oratory, which perchance some think onely Eloquent Prose, moves Passion, and makes all the Auditory to be of the Oratours Opinion; so do Eloquent Verses: for who moves Passions, as Love, Hate, Anger, Grief, Pity, Piety, and the like, more than Poets? or who can Perswade more Powerfully than Poets? for so great a Power have Poets in their Poetry, as to make the Minds of Men to believe Feignings for Realities, and can there be better Orations, Arguments, and Disputations, than in Homer, Virgil, and many other Poets Works? But Oratory in Prose and Verse, is both to Move the Mind, and to Stir up the Spirits, as also to Quiet the Mind, and to Allay the Spirits, onely this Advantage Poets have over Oratours, that there is no Good, or Excellent Poet, but he Naturally is an Oratour, whereas there have been, and may be, very Good Oratours, which are no Good Poets; yet howsoever, both Eloquent Prose and Verse are Harmonious and Delightful both to the Ears and Mind. And so leaving those Gifts to Natures, Favorites, and Times Practice, I rest,

> Madam,
> Your faithfull Friend and Servant.

LETTER 118

Madam,

I Do not Wonder, that some Persons which seem so Kind, as to be, as it were, ready to deliver their Lives for the Sake of some others, they never Saw, nor Knew, before their Kind Meeting, yet the Next time of Meeting, strive to Affront those to whom they Made or Profess'd such Services, Love, and Adventures, and if they should not endeavour to Affront them, yet will Look upon them, or Pass by them, as if they had never Seen, or Spoken to them; Neither do I wonder, that Others in Great Authority and Power, will Advance Some Persons, when they have but a New Acquaintance, or rather, a Sight of them, to Place and Office, and before they are Setled in their Offices, Displace them again, without any Reason, or Knowledge, either of Advancing or Displacing. Nor do I wonder, Others will be so in Love for two or three Dayes, as they almost Sigh out their Breath of Life, for their

Wished Desires, and a Day or two after, Reproach, or Laugh at those they were so much in Love with, as they Desired their Favour more than Heaven; All this, I say, I do not Wonder at, Observing and Perceiving the Inconstant Natures of Mankind; But I wonder to Perceive or Find any one to be Constant Seven Years, or One Year, much more, to be Constant their Whole Life time; for Constancy is as Seldom or Rarely Seen, as a Blazing Star; Indeed, Constancy in this World is somewhat like a Blazing Star, it Lasts for a time, and then Goes out, for it is not as the Fix'd Stars, but rather as the Wandring Planets; though truly I am constantly Fix'd to be,

> Madam,
> Your faithful Friend and Servant.

LETTER 119

Madam,

I Give you many Thanks for your Counsel, and Advice concerning my Health, for certainly an Over-studious Mind doth Wast the Body, which is the Cause, for the most part, that Painful Students are Lean, for the Mind Feeds as much upon the Body, as the Body upon Meat; But truly, I am sometimes in a Dispute with my self, whether it be better to live a Long and Idle, than a Short, but Profitable Life, that is, to Imploy a Little time Well, or to Wast a Great Deal of Time to no Purpose; and I Conclude, that a Little Good is better than Nothing, or better than a Sum of Evil; for 'tis better through Industry to Leave a Little to After Age, than Die so Poor as to Leave Nothing, no not so much as After Ages may say, there Liv'd such a one in Former Ages, than to Die, and be quite Forgotten; and therefore should I live out the Course of Nature, or could live so Long as Methusalem, when the Time were Past, it would seem as Nothing, and perchance I should be as Unwilling to Die then, as if I Died in my Youth, so that a Long, and a Short time of Life, is as one and the same; 'Tis true, Death is Terrible to Think of, but in Death no Terrour Remains; so as it is Life that is Painful both to the Body and Mind, and not Death, for the Mind in Life is Fearful, and the Body is seldom at Ease. But howsoever, I will endeavour, Madam, so to Divide the time of my Bodily Life, as to Imploy part of my Time for Health, and part for Fame, and all for Gods Favour, and when I Die, I will Bequeath my Soul to Heaven, my Fame to Time, and my Body to Earth, there to be Dissolved and Transformed as Nature Pleases, for to her it belongs. I do not much Care, nor Trouble my Thoughts to think where I shall be Buried, when Dead, or into what part of the Earth I shall be Thrown; but if I could have my Wish, I Would my Dust might be Inurned, and mix'd with the Dust of those I Love Best, although I think they would not Remain Long together, for I did observe, that in this last War the Urns of the Dead were Digged up, their Dust Dispersed, and their Bones Thrown about,[1] and I suppose that in all Civil or Home-wars such Inhuman Acts are Committed; wherefore it is but a Folly to be Troubled and Concerned, where they shall be Buried, or for their Graves, or to Bestow much Cost on their Tombes, since not only Time, but Wars will Ruin them. But, Madam, lest I should make you Melancholy with Discoursing of so sad Subjects as Death and Graves, Bones and Dust, I leave you to Livelier and Pleasanter Thoughts and Conversation, and rest,

Madam,
Your faithful Friend and Servant.

LETTER 120

Madam,
You were pleased to tell me in your last Letter, that Many have desired your Charity, which have been Ruined by these last Civil Wars, and that they, who before this time were able to Relieve many with their Wealth, now do Want Relief themselves; by which we may know, that neither Riches nor Peace is Permanent; and many are not only Ruin'd in their Estates, and Banished their Native Country, but Forsaken of their Friends, which is a terrible Misery; but Misery and Friends seldom keep together, and it is to be observed, that a Civil War doth not only Abolish Laws, Dissolve Government, and Destroy the Plenty of a Kingdom, but it doth Unknit the Knot of Friendship, and Dissolve Natural Affections, for in Civil War, Brothers against Brothers, Fathers against Sons, and Sons against Fathers, become Enemies, and Spill each others Blood, Triumphing on their Graves; for when a Kingdom is Inflamed with Civil War, the Minds of all the People are in a Fever of Fury, or a Furious Fever of Cruelty, which, by nothing but Letting Blood by the Surgeon of War, can be Cured, and that not a Little, but Most must Bleed, ere there will be a Perfect Cure; It is the Plague of the Mind, as well as the Plague of the Body, for the Minds of Men are Infected with Covetous Desires, Ambitious Designs, Treacherous Plots, and Murderous Intentions, and so General it is, that Few Minds escape the

---

1 Parliamentary soldiers desecrated her family's tombs in Colchester during the Civil Wars. See letter 187.

Infection, which shews, it proceeds from the Malignity of the Air, or the Influence of some Raging Planet, and if so, it proceeds from a Natural Cause, although it be an Unnatural War; or else it proceeds from Unwise Government, where many Errours gather into a Mass, or Tumor of Evil, which Rises into Blisters of Discontents, and then Breaks out into Civil War; or else Heaven sends it to Punish the Sins of the People. Besides, it is to be observed, that Vices Increase in a Civil War, by reason Civil Government is in Disorder, Civil Magistrates Corrupted, Civil Laws Abolished, Civil Manners, and Decent Customs Banished, and in their Places is Rapine, Robbing, Stabbing, Treachery, and Falshood, all the Evil Passions and Debauch'd Appetites are let Loose, to take their Liberty; But this is so commonly Known to those that have seen a Civil War, as I should not have needed to Mention it, although those that have Liv'd alwayes in Peace will not Believe it, but I have Suffered so much in it, as the Loss of some of my Nearest, and Dearest Friends, and the Ruin of those that did Remain, that I may desire to Forget it. Wherefore leaving this sad Discourse, I rest,

> Madam,
> Your faithful Friend and Servant.

LETTER 121

Madam,

In your last Letter you were pleased to tell me, that the Lady E.E. and the Lady A.A. are alwayes Quarrelling with each other, when they Meet, and Rail on each other, when they are Asunder, and their Husbands in the Behalf of their Wives do the like; But I Wonder they should do so, whenas they are both in an Unfortunate Condition, as being both Wives to Banished Men; and to make their Condition more Unhappy, their Banishment is Joyn'd with Poverty, which is a Double, nay, to Live in Wars with Companions in the same Condition, a Treble Misery. Neither is it Usual, for though Acquaintance, Neighbours, and Friends, be apt to Quarrel, Rail, and Hate one another, in times of Prosperity, through Envy and Pride, yet in Adversity Men are apt to Unite in Loving and Agreeable Societies; But they have this Excuse, that their Misfortunes make them Froward; and truly, great Misfortunes make us apt to Quarrel with our selves, for Patience and Misery seldom Dwell together. But leaving the two Ladies to Agree, I rest,

> Madam,
> Your faithful Fr. and S.

LETTER 122

Madam,

I Cannot Blame you, if you cannot Entertain those of your own Sex in Conversation, as to Please them with such Discourse as is according to their Humours and Capacities, for if your Discourse be according to your own Capacity and Wit, you must Discourse to your self, for such Discourse is beyond their Understanding; but if you will Entertain them with Conversation, you must Descend from your own Height, and Discourse with them on Even Ground, which is, you must Speak as Foolishly as they do: the Question only will be, whether you can do so, or not? Another Help there is, as I have heard from one of our Sex, who had a Good Wit, and Loved not Gossiping, when she had any Female Visitors, she, after a little time, would fall to Brag of her self, and tell what Fine things she would have, or had, whereat they became Inwardly Spiteful or Angry, and then would soon take their Leaves and be Gone; But whether you will use this Remedy or not, I cannot tell, for I believe it is against your Nature; yet you must either use this Remedy, or else you must learn to Gossip, and to Entertain Gossips, although I believe you will be but a Dull, Untoward Scholar to Learn; But the best Tutoress I know of, if you will Learn, is, Mrs. T.W. and if you cannot Civilly Deny Visitors, you must use the Lady M.Ns.[1] Bragging Medicine, or Mrs. T.Ws. Instructions, to which Instruction or Medicine I leave you, and rest,

> Madam,
> Your faithful Friend and Servant.

LETTER 123

Madam,

I Wonder how that Person you mention in your Letter, could either have the Conscience, or Confidence to Dispraise Shakespear's Playes,[2] as to say they were made up onely with Clowns, Fools, Watchmen, and the like; But to Answer that Person, though Shakespear's Wit will Answer for himself, I say, that it seems by his Judging, or Censuring, he Understands not

---

1   Margaret Newcastle (i.e., Margaret Cavendish).

2   Although *The Riverside Shakespeare* questions the wisdom of Cavendish in publishing much of what she wrote, it credits her with being "the first to give a general prose assessment of Shakespeare as a dramatist" (*The Riverside Shakespeare*, ed. G. Blakemore Evans [Boston: Houghton Mifflin Co., 1974] 1847).

Playes, or Wit; for to Express Properly, Rightly, Usually, and Naturally, a Clown's, or Fool's Humour, Expressions, Phrases, Garbs, Manners, Actions, Words, and Course of Life, is as Witty, Wise, Judicious, Ingenious, and Observing, as to Write and Express the Expressions, Phrases, Garbs, Manners, Actions, Words, and Course of Life, of Kings and Princes; and to Express Naturally, to the Life, a Mean Country Wench, as a Great Lady, a Courtesan, as a Chast Woman, a Mad man, as a Man in his right Reason and Senses, a Drunkard, as a Sober man, a Knave, as an Honest man, and so a Clown, as a Well-bred man, and a Fool, as a Wise man; nay, it Expresses and Declares a Greater Wit, to Express, and Deliver to Posterity, the Extravagancies of Madness, the Subtilty of Knaves, the Ignorance of Clowns, and the Simplicity of Naturals, or the Craft of Feigned Fools, than to Express Regularities, Plain Honesty, Courtly Garbs, or Sensible Discourses, for 'tis harder to Express Nonsense than Sense, and Ordinary Conversations, than that which is Unusual; and 'tis Harder, and Requires more Wit to Express a Jester, than a Grave Statesman; yet Shakespear did not want Wit, to Express to the Life all Sorts of Persons, of what Quality, Profession, Degree, Breeding, or Birth soever; nor did he want Wit to Express the Divers, and Different Humours, or Natures, or Several Passions in Mankind; and so Well he hath Express'd in his Playes all Sorts of Persons, as one would think he had been Transformed into every one of those persons he hath Described; and as sometimes one would think he was Really himself the Clown or Jester he Feigns, so one would think, he was also the King, and Privy Counsellor; also as one would think he were Really the Coward he Feigns, so one would think he were the most Valiant, and Experienced Souldier; Who would not think he had been such a man as his Sir John Falstaff? and who would not think he had been Harry the Fifth? & certainly Julius Caesar, Augustus Caesar, and Antonius, did never Really Act their parts Better, if so Well, as he hath Described them, and I believe that Antonius and Brutus did not Speak Better to the People, than he hath Feign'd them; nay, one would think that he had been Metamorphosed from a Man to a Woman, for who could Describe Cleopatra Better than he hath done, and many other Females of his own Creating, as Nan Page, Mrs. Page, Mrs. Ford, the Doctors Maid, Bettrice, Mrs. Quickly, Doll Tearsheet, and others, too many to Relate? and in his Tragick Vein, he Presents Passions so Naturally, and Misfortunes so Probably, as he Peirces the Souls of his Readers with such a True Sense and Feeling thereof, that it Forces Tears through their Eyes, and almost Perswades them, they are Really Actors, or at least Present at those Tragedies. Who would not Swear he had been a Noble Lover, that could

Woo so well? and there is not any person he hath Described in his Book, but his Readers might think they were Well acquainted with them; indeed Shakespear had a Clear Judgment, a Quick Wit, a Spreading Fancy, a Subtil Observation, a Deep Apprehension, and a most Eloquent Elocution; truly, he was a Natural Orator, as well as a Natural Poet, and he was not an Orator to Speak Well only on some Subjects, as Lawyers, who can make Eloquent Orations at the Bar, and Plead Subtilly and Wittily in Law-Cases, or Divines, that can Preach Eloquent Sermons, or Dispute Subtilly and Wittily in Theology, but take them from that, and put them to other Subjects, and they will be to seek; but Shakespear's Wit and Eloquence was General, for, and upon all Subjects, he rather wanted Subjects for his Wit and Eloquence to Work on, for which he was Forced to take Some of his Plots out of History, where he only took the Bare Designs, the Wit and Language being all his Own; and so much he had above others, that those, who Writ after him, were Forced to Borrow of him, or rather to Steal from him; I could mention Divers Places, that others of our Famous Poets have Borrow'd, or Stoln, but lest I should Discover the Persons, I will not Mention the Places, or Parts, but leave it to those that Read his Playes, and others, to find them out. I should not have needed to Write this to you, for his Works would have Declared the same Truth: But I believe, those that Dispraised his Playes, Dispraised them more out of Envy, than Simplicity or Ignorance, for those that could Read his Playes, could not be so Foolish to Condemn them, only the Excellency of them caused an Envy to them. By this we may perceive, Envy doth not Leave a man in the Grave, it Follows him after Death, unless a man be Buried in Oblivion, but if he Leave any thing to be Remembred, Envy and Malice will be still throwing Aspersion upon it, or striving to Pull it down by Detraction. But leaving Shakespear's Works to their own Defence, and his Detractors to their Envy, and you to your better Imployments, than Reading my Letter, I rest,

Madam,
  Your faithful Friend and humble Servant.

LETTER 124

Madam,
Though I am not Acquainted with my Neighbours, yet I Hear of them sometimes, and I Know some by Sight, going sometimes Abroad; But one of them is Notedly Jealous of her Husband, the rest, if they be Jealous, 'tis not so Publickly Known as this Lady is; whether it be only her

Humour, or her Husband's Inconstancy, or both, I know not; she is a Proper, Handsom Woman, and, if the Humours and Conditions of her Mind be Answerable to the Beauty of her Person, her Husband hath no Reason to Seek Abroad, having such a Wife, neither hath she reason to have such an Ill Opinion of her self, as to believe her Husband should be Weary of her, especially so soon after Marriage, for she hath not been Married above two Years, though perchance some may account, or think Two Years Twenty Years in Marriage; But this Lady is so Jealous, that she believes her Husband makes Love to the Greatest Beauties in the City, and that they Receive her Husbands Addresses; Amongst the rest of those, was one of my Waiting-maids, who indeed is very Handsom, and I believe, as Honest, as Handsom; but to tell you, there is an Unfortunate Window, and a Door, (I can only say, they are so to the Wife) this Window looks out of her House into our Garden, and the Door Belongs to our Garden, but Opens into this Man's Garden, which Door is Nailed close up,[1] but out of the Window her Husband, it seems, would Look sometimes, and Spie if he could see my Maids Walking, who many times in the Morning did Walk there for their Health; also in the Door was a little Hole, as they tell me, for I had not Observed it, which Hole he would fill full of Flowers, which they did use to Pull out, not knowing who put them there; but his Wife hearing of it, was in an Extraordinary Passion, as it seem'd, with her Husband, and such a Falling out they had, as they were upon Parting, whereupon she sent a Divine to my Husband, to Complain of her Husband, my Maid, and the Door, Desiring, the Hole of the Door should be Stop'd up; My Husband said, if there were any such Hole, he would give order it should be Stop'd, and if that would not Satisfie her, the Door should be Taken away, and the Passage Wall'd up, and as for his Wife's Maids, he could not say any thing, for he never medled with them, but would tell his Wife; so the Hole of the Door being Closed, she was Indifferently well Satisfied with that, although not with her Husband, for he and she, it was said, Liv'd as Enemies, not as Friends in Matrimony; But she hearing other Reports, (for when her Humour was Known, her Neighbours took delight to Vex her, it being the Nature of Mankind to Add Discontent upon Discontent, and Affliction on Affliction, being never better Pleas'd than when Doing, or Speaking Ill, to some or others Disadvantage) after some Six Weeks, sent a Letter to my Husband, wherein, after some Complements, she made great Complaints of her

---

1   The events related took place when the Cavendishes were renting the house of the Dutch painter, Peter Paul Rubens. That house, in Antwerp, is currently a museum. See Grant, 139.

Husband, and Named which of my Maids she was Jealous of, saying, she had received Presents from her Husband, as Sweet-meats, and Linnen, and a great many words of I know not what, neither can I remember them, though I heard the Letter read, for being in another Language, I could not read it my self, but my Husband did read it to me; and when he had read it, Now, says he, what say you to this Letter? Truly, said I, I am of the Opinion, she would be Courted by some other than her Husband, since he leaves Courting of her, and Addresses himself to others; next, I am of the Opinion, she would have all her Neighbours Wives, or at least some, and my self particularly, as Jealous as her self, otherwise she would never have Written to you, but to me, especially in a Case concerning the Women in my House, and if I were of her Jealous Humour, I should Write to her Husband, how his Wife Writ a Letter to my Husband, Aggravating, (for Jealousie is alwayes Adding and Aggravating) that you two held a Correspondence by Letters, and for any thing I knew, had Private Meetings, but being not Jealous, I Approve of her choice of Writing to you, wherefore send for her she Accuses, and Examin her. Truly, not I, said my Husband, I am no Confessor, though I believe Confessors take great Pleasure in Young Maids Confessions, so my Husband caused me to Examin my Maid, whether she had received any Presents from C.K. she said, she never received any from him in her Life, nor had she any Acquaintance with him, but by Sight, as she had of most of the Town, seeing them in the Streets; but, said she, I believe these Sweet-meats, and Linnen she mentions in her Letter, is a Handkerchief with Sweet-meats, for the Weather being Hot, we usually have our Chamber Windows open, until we go to Bed, and my Chamber-fellow and I, as we were Undressing us one Night, there was flung into the Window a Lawn, Buttoned Handkerchief, tied up on two or three knots, with Sweet-meats in them; at the first we were Affrighted, to see a white Bulk come Flying, as we thought, into the Chamber, and Falling with a Noise upon the Ground; but at last we took it up, and found it was a Handkerchief full of Sweet-meats; at first, we Resolv'd to fling it back, but then we Consider'd, we had best Call out of the Window, and Ask who it was that flung them in, so we Call'd, but No body would Answer, and then we thought, that if we flung them out again, they would be taken up by some Stranger; and you were will-ing, said I, to Keep, and Eat them, you made so many Doubts? Indeed, Madam, said she, we did Eat them soon after, but we knew not what to do with the Handkerchief, not knowing the Owner, yet we were Resolved to Ask of all our Acquaintance, if any would Own the

Handkerchief; and making Inquiry for the Owner, one of our Acquaintance told us, a Fortnight after, it was C.Ks. which when we Knew, we Durst not Send it to him, for Fear of his Wife, neither Durst we Give, or Fling it away, lest he should Desire it again, and this, upon the Salvation of my Soul, said she, is all the Linnen, or Sweet-meats we ever had of him; neither did we know they were his, until a Fortnight after. Now, if she should have been Judged by the Letter, without any Examination, she might have been Condemned for a Criminal, whereas her own Confession, and other Witnesses, set her Free; but Jealousie and Suspicion, for the most part, are False Accusers, and Cruel Judges. By this we see how Unquiet and Restless some Married Persons are, being alwayes Tortured with their own Thoughts, and their Minds are Rack'd on the Wheels of Suspicion. But my Husband sent for the Divine that formerly came from her, and told him of her Letter, and of my Maids Confession, and that she had no Cause to be Jealous of her, for she was very Virtuous, neither had she any Acquaintance with her Husband. So the Divine went between, and between, not to bring Unlawful Lovers together, for he was a very Worthy, and Wise man, but to Pacifie a Disquiet Mind, and to make Love and Unity between an Husband and his Wife. And so leaving them to Agree, I rest,

> Madam,
>   Your faithful Friend and Servant.

LETTER 125

Madam,
I Cannot Blame you, if you were in a Passion, as in your Letter you Express you were, for there is nothing so apt to Inkindle an Anger in my Mind, or to Inflame my Spirits, than to receive a Contumely from my Superiours, or a Rude Boldness from my Inferiours, unless Cold Discretion, and Fluent Prudence could Quench those Flaming Spirits into an Unactive, and Dead Patience; When I say Superiours, I mean, Superiours for Outward Title, and not for Inward Worth. But you must Consider, Madam, that Bold Rudeness, or Negligent Contumely, proceeds from Ignorance or Envy, as either Ignorant of Civil Manners, being a Kin to the Brutes; or Envious, having no Worth or Merit in themselves, and if you call your Reason to Counsel, and your Judgment to Decide the Cause, those would let them pass, as Inconsiderable, and not to be Regarded; for Reason and Judgment will never regard the Braying of an Ass, the Barking

of a Dog, the Buzzing of a Flie, an Idle Drone, the Speech of a Fool, the Follies of a Knave, nor the Envy of the Base; But, Madam, your Worth and Merit is so Transcendent, as the Tongue of Malice, nor the Eye of Envy, can never Reach to, no more than the Blind can See the Light of the Sun, or the Dumb Teach the Truth of Knowledg; and I am Happy in Knowing that I am,

> Madam,
> Your Humble and Devoted Servant.

LETTER 126

Madam,

In your last Letter you were Pleased to tell me, that the Works of W.T. were so much Admired, as many were Desirous to See the Author, and Hear him Speak, but after they had Seen, and Heard him, they did not Admire his Works so much as they did before, so as it seems, they did Esteem the Works the Less for the Author, and not the Author the More for his Works; which in my Opinion is Unjust, and a sign they either have not Read the Scripture, or not Believed what there is Written, *viz*. That a Man is Known by his Works; and we Admire the Creator Through and By his Works; but the Foolish part of the World, which is the Most part, thinks that a Man's Learning, or Wit, or Ingenuity, is Printed in his Face, and Expects he should Speak beyond the Invention of Words, and such high Raptures as they could not Understand. Indeed, so Foolish are Most, especially Women, as when they see a Famous, Learned Man, or Witty Poet, or the like, they will streight say, Lord! Is this the Learned Man that is so Famous, that Writ such and such Books? how Simply he Looks; or, Is this the Famous Poet that Writ such Poems, Scenes, and Songs? how Sneakingly he Appears, says another, I heard no Wit from him, but he Spoke as other men Ordinarily do: But all such Famous Men, if they would not have their Works the Less Esteemed for their Presence and Ordinary Conversation, and would be Admired by the Most, which are the Ignorant, must put on a Constrain'd Garb, and Speak some Gibbrigge that sounds not like a Perfect Language, or some wayes they must Speak that they Understand not, and then they shall be Admired, both for their Conversation and Contemplation, which are their Works; or they must Incloister themselves from the View of the World; for the World of Mankind is apt to Despise that which they Know, or have Seen, and only Admire that which they Understand not. But I have Spoken of this Subject in an Epistle before my Book of Playes; wherefore I shall not Trouble you with any more Discourse thereon, but rest,

Madam,
Your very Faithful Friend and Servant.

LETTER 127

Madam,
I May not Discommend the Old Historical, or Heroick Poets, for if I should, I should be Condemned for a Fool, as not having neither Judgment nor Understanding, yet I may say, my Reason believes they Writ Unreasonably, not only of their Feigned Gods, but of their Feigned Fights, and of their Feigned Fortunes or Successes; The truth is, they are for the most part Romances, containing more Lies than Truth, more Impossibilities than Probabilities, for though Feigning is the Ground of Poetry, yet, methinks, such kind of Poetry should not have such kind of Feignings, for to Reason it can neither be Pleasant nor Profitable, for Reason takes Delight in Probabilities, not in Impossibilities, for though the Ground or Subject of an Heroical Story, or Poem, may be Feigning, yet the several Actions should be Natural, not beyond the Power of Men, nor Unusual to their Practice; neither can it be Profitable, for what cannot be Practised, cannot be Imitated; the Way of Writing may be Imitated, but not the Actions; for what One man can Disorder, or Rout an Army, with his Single Strength or Courage? nay, what One man can Disorder, or Rout a Brigade, nay, a Company of an Hundred? The truth is, a Hundred to One is too great Odds to Encounter, and too Many for One man to Overcome; neither can I believe, a Hundred men should be so Afraid of One man, were he as Big, and as Strong as Goliah, so as to Run away, unless they did apprehend he had Followers; but yet when I remember the Story of Sampson, I Dare not say, it Cannot be, but I Dare say, it cannot be without a Miracle, wherefore most of the Heroick Poets make their chief Heroes to have the Assistance of particular Gods and Goddesses, so as to Impower them above the Effects of Nature; but of all the Heroick Poems I have read,[1] I like Sir W.Ds. as being Most, and Nearest to the Natures, Humours, Actions, Practice, Designs, Effects, Faculties, and Natural Powers, and Abilities of Men or Human Life, containing no Impossibilities or Improbabilities: Indeed, such an Heroick Poem it is,

---

1   Probably Sir William Davenant's *Gondibert* (1651).

that there cannot be found any Fault therein, unless he seem'd to have too much Care or Pains taken in the Expression of his Descriptions, for the Language is like so Curious and Finely Ingraven a Seal, as one cannot readily see the Figure Ingraven therein, without a Magnifying glass, or like as many several Figures, so Curiously Cut, as to be all in the Compass of a Cherry-stone, wherein they cannot be Distinguished, without often Perusal, and Strict Examination, and Quick and Ready Sight; But had the Language been as Easie, as Fine, and had not those Choice Expressions been so Closely Compact; but were as Usual, as his Descriptions are Natural, certainly it had been a President for all Heroick Poems; indeed, his Language or Expressions of his Descriptions are like Gold that is too Pure and Fine to be Wrought, and wants some Allay to make it Proper and Fit for Use; The Truth is, very Spruce Language, or Extraordinary Choice Phrases, take off the Pleasure of the Reader, being rather Tedious than Delightful, whereas Extraordinary, and Courtly Expressions, and Choice, and Nice Phrases, are to be Highly Commended, in comparison of Clownish, and Rude Expressions or Phrases, such as are in Homer, I know not whether they be so in the Original, surely in the Translation they are in many Places, where not onely the Men Speak Rude and Clownish, but he makes the Gods to Speak so too. Wherefore, for my part, I had rather read Sir W.Ds. Work ten times, than Homer twice, as he is Translated. But I'le leave off Judging of such Master-Poets as my Pupil-aged Wit cannot Understand, for should I live to Methusalem's Age, my Wit would be but a Novice, my Judgment an Ignorant Fool, and my Opinions Erroneous, for Women are neither fit to be Judges, Tutors, nor Disputers, neither are we fit to be Commanders, or Rulers, we are alwayes fitter to Learn than to Teach, and in a Condition rather to Obey than to Command, apter to Dispute than to Confute, to Prate than to Preach. And so leaving to write more for this time, I rest,

Madam,
Your faithful Friend and Servant.

LETTER 128

Madam,
I Should take it for a Favour, if you would be Pleased to send me that New-fashion'd Garment you mentioned in your last Letter, not that I think to make use of the Fashion, for I take more Pleasure to Devise a Fashion than to Follow it, but only to Satisfie my Curiosity, I would see

it, whether it be a Fashion for Use, or Ease, or Becoming, or for Grandeur; for Fashions of Use are for the several Seasons of the Year, as also for several Actions, for those Fashions that are Proper for Dancing, are not Proper for Riding; as for Example, Pumps are of no Use a Horseback, nor Boots, nor Spurs in a Galliard, or Courant, unless it were to Tear the Ladies Gown the man Dances withall, for he cannot well cut a Caper in a pair of Boots and Spurs, nor a Horseman Spur a Horse with a pair of Pumps, but Spurs would be as Hawks Bells in Dancing, especially if they were Gingling Spurs; yet men either Riding a Horseback, or Dancing on a Carpet, might wear Feathers in their Hats, for the Head is not Imployed so much in those Actions as the Heels, only a Feather is a Fashion of no Use, but merely for Grace and Becoming. Many other Fashions I could Repeat for Use, and Action, but it were too Tedious. As for the Fashions for the Seasons of the Year, In Winter, Sable Skins, or meaner Fur, to Wear about the Neck, and Muffs, are both Graceful and Useful, as to keep one from Cold; and for Summer, Fans, to Cool the Sultry Heat, and to Shadow the Face from the Sun, who seems to be an Enemy to Beauty, and strives to Burn it off, wherefore it may be thought Envious; Such, and many other several Fashions there are, according to the several Seasons of the Year. Besides, there are Fashions for Ease, which Religious persons Use, as only a Loose Garment, tied Loosly about their Wast, wherein is neither much Curiosity in Making, nor Labour in Dressing, nor Pain in Wearing, it is Quickly Put on, and as Quickly Pull'd off, a Garment fit for a Solitary, and Studious Life, wherein must be no Incumbrances on the Body, to Obstruct, or Hinder the Contemplations of the Mind; Also there be Fashions of Grandeur, which are more for Grace, and Becoming, than for Ease, or Use, as Gowns with Long Trains, Streight Bodies, Heavy Imbroyderies and Laces, Jewels in the Ears, and many the like, High Heel'd Shoes, Boot-hoses, Feathers, Roses, Hatbands, and many more, which are Requisite for Grace & Becoming. Again, there are Fashions to Distinguish Persons, as to know a Priest, a Lawyer, a Mayor and his Aldermen, a Constable, & many other several Professions and Officers; and thus there should also be Degrees to Distinguish the Nobles from the Commons, but the Commons have Incroch'd so much upon the Nobles Prerogative of Fashions, as all Fashions are Common amongst them: also there are Fashions for Times of Mirth, & Fashions for Times of Mourning, for Publick Meetings & Nuptials, as also for weeping Funerals; But Fashions for Grandeur are fit only for Courts, at Masks, Plays, Balls, & Triumphant Shews; Fashions of Cavalry are proper for the Field in time of War, as for Commanders or Generals; Fashions of Distinguishments are fit for Cities, as for Magistrates, Officers, Professions, Trades, & the like; Fashions of Ease are fittest for Cloisters, and a Private Country Life; and Fashions of Use are fit for all Sorts, Degrees, Professions or Qualities; But Fashions that are neither Useful, Easie, Proper, Becoming, nor Graceful, ought to be Banished, if any such there be. But, Madam, I shall Discourse so long of Fashions, as I shall Forget your Patience, and make you so Angry as to fling this Letter into the Fire, and so Burn all the Garmental Fashions in my Letter, where if all Fashions could be as Easily Consumed as my Letter, you would leave the world of Mankind Naked, unless they would Cloth themselves with Beasts Skins, or Figleaves, which would soon becom a Fashion too, if once worn; wherefore lest I should be stript of your Favour, I will leave the Repetition of Fashions, and rest,

Madam,
Your very faithful Friend and Servant.

LETTER 129

Madam,
You were pleased to tell me in your last Letter, that you had spent most of the Morning in Reading a New Work, which is highly Commended, *viz.* Paraphrases on the Life of some of the Holy Prophets and Kings: I cannot say, but it may be Pleasing to Read, but I doubt whether it will be Well to Write it; for whosoever doth Heighten the Sacred Scriptures, by Poetical Expressions, doth Translate it to the Nature of a Romance, for the Ground of a Romance is for the most part Truth, but upon those Truths are Feignings built; and certainly the Scripture and Feignings ought not to be Mix'd together, for so Holy a Truth ought not to be Express'd Fabulously; wherefore in my Opinion no Subject is so Unfit for Poetical Fancies, as the Scripture, for though Poetry is Divine, yet it ought not to Obstruct and Obscure the Truth of Sacred Historical Prose. 'Tis true, Divine Poetical Raptures, such as Davids Psalms, are Commendable and Admirable, being an Effect of a Devout Soul, and Zealous Spirit, which Flames into Poetical Raptures, and is Inspired with a Divine Influence, Delivering it self through Harmonious Numbers, Sympathetical Rithmes, Elegant Phrases, and Eloquent Language, all which is Presented to God from the Heart, as an Offering, or Sacrifice of Thanksgiving, or an Imploring of Mercy, or an Humble Acknowledgment of sins, and Promise of Amendment, which Sacred Poems are Express'd in a Tragick Vein concerning Sins, and in a

Comick Vein concerning Blessings, and Poets in their Morning Hymns are like the Larks that Begin the Day, and in their Evening Hymns like the Nightingals which Begin the Night. Thus Divine Poets are Heaven's Birds, that Sing to God, and their Divine Poems are their Brood, which are kept in the Cage of Memory, and Sing their Parents Notes to After Ages. But, Madam, perchance you will think I am very Peremptory, to give my Opinion of the Poets Work before I see it; but I give my Opinion only upon the Ground of his Work, which is the Scripture, saying, it ought not to be Paraphrased, besides, I give it from my Conscience, not from my Conceited Brain, and perchance I may alter my Opinion, upon more Rational Arguments from those that are more Learned and Knowing than my self, and if your Opinion Differs from mine, pray send it me in your next Letter, for I would willingly be of your Opinion, believing you cannot Err, nor I in Expressing my self,

Madam,
Your very Faithful Friend and Devoted Servant.

LETTER 130

Madam,
Here is the Lady V.R. in this City, who is so Strict to Chast Wedlock, and so Fearful of Dishonour or Scandal, as she will have no Usual Conversation with any Man, but those she is nearly Allyed to, or hath an Obligation to of Duty or Gratitude; Nay, she is not only Chast, but her Life and all her Actions are Devoted to Chast Wedlocks, the truth is, She lives as if she were an Incloister'd Nun, although a Wife, and her Husband is her only Confessor and Instructor, or rather her Saint, whom she Adores, and Worships, and Prayes to, to Pardon her Sins of Omission, (for of Sins of Commission she is not Guilty, unless to Omit be to Commit;) and the greatest Sin of Omission is the Neglect of her Health,[1] which he accounts as a Deadly Sin, and will hardly Pardon unless she Reform; but although she promises Amendment, as all Penitents do, yet as soon as she hath Promised, she Commits the same Sin again, so as the best part of her Life is, as it were, Spent in Promises, but not in Performance: And when she is Sick, she doth like the man that was in a Storm, who in the time of Danger promised the Blessed Virgin Mary, to Offer to her Altar a Candle as Big and as Long as the Mast of the Ship, if ever he came on the Shore; so the Lady V.R. when

---

1 Cavendish may parody her own tendency to neglect her health and to live in retirement. See letter 210 and note.

she is Sick, promises, if ever she Recover, she will Take the Air, and Use Exercises, but being Restored to Health, she Forgets her Promise, or only Looks out of a Window for Once or Twice, and Walks Two or Three turns in a Day in her Chamber, which is as little Exercise as she can do, the truth is, she Errs as much in living too much a Retired Life, as other Ladies in too Much and Often Gadding Abroad, wherein she loses as much Health, as they Time, if not Reputation; But leaving her to her Retired Life and Promising Words, I rest,

Madam,
Your faithful Friend and Servant.

LETTER 131

Madam,
You desired me to send you the Sixteen Books I Writ in my Childhood, methinks they sound like the Twelve Labours of Hercules, only that there are Four Labours more; but though mine were not so Profitable to the World, nor so Difficult to Achieve, nor so Dangerous in their Encounters, yet you will find my Works like Infinite Nature, that hath neither Beginning nor End, and as Confused as the Chaos, wherein is neither Method nor Order, but all Mix'd together without Separation, like Evening Light and Darkness, so in my Sixteen Books is Sense and No Sense, Knowledg and Ignorance Mingled together, so that you will not know what to make of it; or in a Lower Comparison, you will find every Book like a Frippery, or Brokers-shop, wherein is nothing but Remnants, Bits and Ends of Several things, or like Taylors Shreds, that are not fit for any Use; wherefore I cannot Imagine why you should Desire them, unless out of a Friendship, you will See, and Burn them before I Die, fearing I should Neglect the Sacrificing of them my self, for you are Pleased not only to send for One, but all the Sixteen. But, I suppose, you believe them to be so many several sheets of Paper folded into Quarters, or Half Quarters, as into little Baby-books, for it was in my Baby-years I Writ them, and it had been well they had been no Bigger than Baby-Books, but the least of these Books are two or the Quires of Paper; Neither can you Read them when you have them, unless you have the Art, or Gift to Read Unknown Letters, for the Letters are not only Unlegible, but each Letter stands so Cowardly from th' other, as all the Lines of your Sight cannot Draw, or Bring them into Words, nay, they will sooner be Torn in pieces; besides, it will Weary your Eye-sight to Move from Letter to Letter, it will be

almost as great a Journy for your Eyes, as it was for Coriat's Feet,[1] that Travelled a Foot to Mogorr,[2] I know not whether his Journy Lamed them, but certainly it Tired them: so will my Books do your Eyes, if they do not quite Blind them, I cannot say, in Reading them, but Endeavouring to Read Scribbles for Letters. Moreover, there are such huge Blots, as I may Similize them to Broad Seas, or Vast Mountains, which in a Similizing Line will Tire your Eyes to Spread to the Circumference, like as for the Feet to Walk to the Top of the Alps; Also there are Long, Hard Scratches, which will be as Bad for your Eyes, as Long, Stony Lanes would be to your Feet; wherefore let me perswade you as your Friend, not Desperately to Venture to Read them, since you can neither receive Profit nor Pleasure in the Labour; were there any Probability to Increase your Knowledge, or to Inrich your Understanding, you had some reason to Venture, but you will be so far from Increasing your Knowledge, as you will enter into a Vast Wilderness, and Intricate Labyrinth, wherein you will Lose your Patience, and be so far from Inriching your Understanding, as you will Impoverish your present Memory; and let me tell you, that my Sixteen Books will be as Tedious, Troublesome, and Dangerous, to your Understanding, as the Dry, Deep, Sandy, Barren Deserts of Arabia to Travellers, and so thick a Mist of Nonsense, and Clouds of Ignorance will fly in the face of your Understanding, that it will not only Blind it, but be apt to Smother it, not otherwise than the Clouds, or Hills of Sand, that Fly, and Blind, and sometimes Choak those that pass through those Deserts. But if no Perswasion will Alter you, but you are Resolved to See them, send me word in your next Letter, and I will send them to you, although much against the will of

Your faithful Friend and Servant.

LETTER 132

Madam,
The Lady S.K. Presents her Service to you; Truly she is not Well, although not so Sick, as Forced to keep her Bed; I know not how to Judg of her Disease, for she is both Lean and Fat, like as the Idol mentioned in the Holy Scripture, which was partly Clay, partly Stone, and

---

1   Thomas Coryate described his European travels, which he conducted mostly on foot, in *Coryats Crudities* (1611). A second set of travels took him through Asia Minor to the Great Mogul. Many jokes were made at his expense.

2   The Grand Mogul or emperor of Delhi.

partly Metal, onely, as I remember, its Feet and Legs were made of Clay,[1] whereas her Feet and Legs are all Bone, for they are so Wasted, as they have no Flesh on them, but her Hips, Body, and Breast are so Fleshy, and Fat, as one may think she had no Bones, by reason none can be Seen, or Felt; and her Arms, Hands, Neck, and Face are so Pale and Lean, that they appear White as Silver, and for want of Blood and Flesh, they are so Dry, as they are so Rough as Unpolished Stone, and with her Sickness she is become so Melancholy as she appears like a Dead Image, or Senseless Idol; but her Real Virtue, and Noble Soul, and Honourable Life, hath made her more Worthy of Human Worship, than the Signifying fore-mentioned Idol, or Image, his Idolatrous, Divine Worship, and she is more Worthy to be set up on an Altar of Fame, than such Idols on an Altar of Religion, and to have Praises, though not Prayers, Offer'd to her. Thus she may be Worshipped as a Goddess, without Superstitious Idolatry, and have Virtuous Devouts; but yet she desires she may have the best Doctors Advice for her Health, wherefore she Intreats you to send her the most Renowned Doctors of Physick that are in your City, she will not spare Cost, if they have Skill, but Pay them for their Advice; for Doctors sell their Knowledge, and Patients Buy Healths, and their Knowledge is a Staple-Commodity, for the more Knowledg Doctors of Physick sell, the more Knowledg they get for Experience of Diseases; and so all things come in more by Practice than by Study, and Health gains more by Temperance, Exercise, and Air, than by Physick; And so Adding my Prayers to her Temperance, the Doctors Skill, and Physick, I rest,

Madam,
Your faithful Friend and Servant.

LETTER 133

Madam,
You were pleased to tell me the Complaints of Mrs. W.A. concerning the Incivilities of Sir A.M. she is not to be Pitied, since it was her own Fault, to be in the Company of Uncivil Men, but certainly he was Drunk, or she Wanton, either in her Behaviour, or Discourse, or both, otherwise it is not Easily to be believed, that a Person of his Quality should be so Uncivil to a Person of her Quality, for Honourable Men are, or should be a Guard to Womens Honours, to Protect them Safely, and not to Betray them to

---

1   Ezekiel 37:3.

their Incivilities. Wherefore the Surest way for Women is not to Accompany any Man Singly, and Alone, but when there are more than they themselves, unless it be such Men as they have a near Relation to, as Husbands, Brothers, Fathers, Sons, Uncles, and the like; but Women are so far from Shunning Mens Companies, as they go from place to place to Meet them, and will Invite them to Cards, Dancing, or other Meetings, and they seem Dull, Melancholy and Indisposed, whenas they are not in the Company of Men, and for the most part, the Wilder the Men are, the better Pleased the Women are, at least they seem so. But, perchance Mrs. W.A. is Jealous of some other Women, for Jealousie is full of Complaints, and their Tongues are apt to speak Sharply of those they Love best, and that which makes me think so, is, that Mrs. W.A. hath been often in Sir A.Ms. Company, and never Complain'd, but seem'd best Pleased when he was with her; wherefore, when the Jealous Humour is Abated, she will perchance Repent of her Complaints, fearing he may Hear of them, and so be Angry, and come not near to Visit her, and then 'tis likely she will Praise him more, than she hath Complain'd, or Spoken against him, to Invite his Company again; for some Praises are rather to Intrap or to Allure, as Insinuating Praises, than Just Praises to Reward Merit; But leaving Mrs. W.A. to her Complaints, or her Complaints to Sir A.M. I rest,

Madam,
     Your faithful Friend and Servant.

LETTER 134

Madam,
You were pleased in your last Letter to tell me, that you had Heard of the Seven Wonders of the World, but you had onely Seen that which might be accounted the Eighth, which are those Books I sent you; But, Madam, it is a greater Wonder to me, that you would take the Pains to Peruse them, than it was that I should Write, or Wast so much Paper, for Girls are alwayes Busie to no Purpose, they will take delight to scratch a Coal upon a White Wall, or Ink with a Pen upon Paper, whenas they account it a Torment to be Taught a Fair Hand-writing, or the Art of Limning; and in my Opinion, there is no better Argument for Free Will, than to Observe how Opposite Constraint and Inforcement is to the Nature of Mankind; But when I Consider, that Mankind for the most part Will what is Worst, and most Hurtful for themselves, or their Kind, I then am apt to think Mankind are Predestinated so to do, otherwise it were

strange that Mankind should Wilfully Hurt themselves, when they have that which is call'd Reason, which Informs them, that that which they Will, is Hurtful for them, or to them. But as for my Books, you might think I have been bound to the Profession of a Scrivener, not to Write an Intelligible Hand, but to make Wast Paper, for they being paid for the most part by the Sheets, and not by the Letters, put as few Letters in a Sheet of Paper as subtilly they can, leaving a Large Space betwixt every Line, and they make their Letters as Big, and Broad as they may, as not to Mis-shape them, also with Large, and Long Flourishing Scratches; but my Paper Book is an Advantage to you, who pay nothing for the Writing, but your Sight, although Sight, indeed, is more worth than Pluto's Riches, for it is the most Curious, Glorious, and Pretious Jewel in Nature's Treasury; But, Madam, lest I should Doubly or Trebly Tire your Sight, as with my Books, and then with this Tedious Letter, I take my leave, and rest,

Madam,
    Your Ladiships most faithful Friend and Servant.

LETTER 135

Madam,

I Am not of the Opinion, that the Planets have an Influence or Power on the Fortunes, or any Outward Accidents of Men, as that such shall be Slaves, and such Kings, such be Rich, and such Poor, such be Kill'd in the Wars, and such Drown'd, or Killd with a Stone falling on their Heads; such be Burnt, such Hang'd, and such Escape those and the like Dangers; such Men and Women shall Love, and Marry, and such not, also how many Husbands such a Woman shall have, and such a one shall have None, and so for Men, Mistresses and Wives, for Advancement and Disgraces, Honours and Dignities, Offices and Authorities, and for all manner of Fortunes or Accidents, I say, I believe the Planets are not the Causes of these Outward Effects; but as I believe the Stars and Planets have an Influence upon the Bodies of men, as their Bodies have on the Planets and Elements, so they may have an Influence upon the Humours in the Body, as upon Phlegm, Choler, Melancholy, Blood, and the like, and they may Work Effects either for Health, Sickness, Pains, and Sores, Rheums, and the like. But I am in Dispute with my self, whether they also have an Influence, or Work several Effects upon the Minds of Men, as upon their Bodies; and when I Consider the various Inconstancies of

Mens Minds, and the Alterations and Changes which are in Mens Minds, I think they are Moved and Altered according to the Motions, and Influences, and Effects of each Planet, or Star. For if we do Observe, not only their Thoughts, Passions and Affections Vary and Alter Minutely, Hourly, Daily, Weekly, Monthly, and Yearly, but also their Capacities, Conceptions, Judgments, Understandings, Opinions, and Wit; for most have Deeper Capacities, Higher Conceptions, Sounder Judgments, Clearer Understandings, Probabler Opinions, and Quicker Wits, at some, than at other times, as at some times they may be thought Wise men, and at other times mere Fools, sometimes they will speak very Wittily, at other times mere Nonsense, or at least, Words without Wit, sometimes they will be able to give as Wise Counsel as Nestor, Ulysses, or Achitophel, at other times, they are neither able to give, nor to take Counsel; sometimes they Conceive, and Understand Readily and Clearly, whatsoever is Conceivable and Understandable by Mankind, at other times they are as if they had not Sense and Reason; The like for the Qualities, Passions, Affections, and Virtues of the Mind; as at some times they are very Valiant, at other times mere Cowards; sometimes Nobly Generous, other times Basely Covetous; sometimes Uprightly Just, other times Wrongfully Unjust; sometimes very Compassionate, other times very Cruel, or Uncharitable; sometimes so Angry, as to be so Furious that none dare Speak to them, at other times so Patient, as to suffer any one to Pull them by the Nose; sometimes they Love to Death, and sometimes they Hate to Death, one and the same thing; and this is Usual, and General amongst Mankind, which makes me lean to the Opinion, that the Stars and the Planets have an Influence upon the Minds of Men; but I am absolutely of the Opinion, that they have no Influence or Power on the Educations of Mankind, no more than they have on the Fortunes or Accidents of and to Mankind; for in those men that are Educated throughly Well, and Wisely, the Effects of Education are too Strong for the Effects of the Stars or Planets, so that some men may be Constantly Prudent, Just, Valiant, Generous, Understanding, Judicious, Witty, and Wise. Also the Effects of Education, and the Effects of the Planets, may be Crossing, and Opposing each other, and then the Strongest Effects bear away the Victory, whether to Good or Ill; and this is the reason of Long Debates, Doubts, and Considerations, ere some men come to Conclusions or Resolutions; and truly, I think the Senses have as great an Influence upon the Mind, as the Stars and Planets have, as Fair Objects, Melodious Sounds, Sweet Saviours, and Delicious Touches, have as great an Influence upon the Mind, and Cause as Various and Strong Effects, as the Stars and Planets do, or can. But leaving the Stars, Planets, Education, and the Senses to their Influences, I rest,

> Madam,
>> Your faithful Friend and Servant.

LETTER 136

Madam,

You were pleased in your last Letter to Desire me to send you my Opinion of the Lady S.Ks. Sickness or Weakness, but truly, I should not be so Presumptuous of my own Judgment, as to give my Opinion, if I were not Commanded, or Desired so to do by your Ladiship, who hath Power to Command both my Mind and Body, to their Utmost Endeavours to Serve and Obey you. As for the Lady S.K. I believe her Disease comes from the Obstruction of the Meseraick,[1] and Liver Veins, which being Stop'd, either by Clammy Humours, or Dryness, or Sharpness, cannot Draw or Suck a Sufficient Nourishment, to Spread or Dilate to the Extreme parts, for Clammy or Slimy Humours Choak the Veins, by Sticking in the Mouth or Orifice of them; and Sharpness, or Bitterness, Dries the Veins, and so Shrinks or Surfles them up, and Closes the Mouth of the Veins, so as they cannot readily Open themselves, to Draw or Suck in Sufficient Nourishment, by which the Extreme parts Famish, and the Body becomes Foul and Impure, and it makes an Overflow in the Body, causing it to Swell out Big, for want of Passage or Vent, or else it causes an Unnatural Heat, which Dries the Body into a Hectick Fever, Burning the Intrals, and Noble Vital parts with a Smothering Heat, which Dries those Parts, like as Neats-Tongues, Bacon, and Hung Beef is Dryed in Smothering Smoak; or it sets those Humours, Gather'd, and Heap'd up, on a Flame, like a Stack of Wet Hay, or a Chest full of Wet Linnen, wanting Vent to Breath out Vapor. Thus the Lady S.K's Body is Fat, and her Legs and Arms, Neck and Face, Lean, for those Parts that are next to the Mouth of the Veins, Nourish, and grow rather too Big, as having more than Nature requires, for the Inward Parts are Doubly Fed, having the Food, not only that Belongs, or is Sufficient for them, but also that which Belongs to the Extreme Parts, as the Legs, Feet, Arms, Hands, Neck, and Face, so that a Stoppage of the Veins causes the Body to Swell, or Puff Outward, like as when ones Lips are Closed, and Ascending Vapor, or Forced Wind, Fills

---

1   Mesentery, tissue connected to the digestive tract.

the Mouth, the Cheeks, and all the Face will Swell, and Puff out so much, as to be as Big as a Face and a Half; the same is with the Body, when the Mouths of the Sucking Veins are Stop'd; also it causes Vomitings, or Fluxes, for when the Veins are too Full of Wind, or Blood, or are Stop'd by Humour, or Dryness, the Body growing too full of Humour, Overflows, and so Forces out a Passage, either at one, or both Ends of the Body, for the Veins being Over-full, can no more receive any Liquor into them, than when a Stomack is Over-fill'd with Meat or Drink, but are Forced to Cast out whatsoever is Offer'd to them, so as the Veins become as an Over-charged Stomack, and when they are Stop'd, they are as if the Throat were Choak'd, or the Neck Strangled, and can receive Nothing, for not Any thing will Pass, which causes them to Cast back whatsoever is Offer'd to them, so that the Effect is as one, both of Over-full, and Empty, Stop'd Veins, only Over-full Veins cause the Body to be Swell'd, and Puff'd, all over the Extreme Parts, as well as the Inward, or next Adjoyning Parts, whereas the Empty, Dry Veins, cause only the Inward, and Joyning Parts to the Mouths of the Veins to be Swell'd, or Puff'd out; but for Casting out from them, or Resisting, they are alike. Thus, Madam, I have Obeyed your Commands, in Writing to you my Opinion; and Begging your Pardon for being so Tedious in Explaning and Declaring it, I rest,

> Madam,
> Your faithful Friend and Servant.

LETTER 137

Madam,

You were pleased to tell me in your Letter how much out of Countenance you were, being Surprised with a Visit you Expected not; Truly, Madam, I am very Sensible of your Pain, insomuch as methinks I Feel what you Suffered, for I my self have been, and am still, so Troubled with that Imperfection, (if it may be call'd one) that I have been often so out of Countenance, as I have not only Pitied my self, but others have Pitied me, which is a Condition I would not be in, and the Thoughts that Bashfulness leaves in the Mind, are as great an Affliction as the Mind can have for a Crimeless Defect, for 'tis no Crime to be Bashful, nor a Disgrace, neither to the Life, nor Soul, although it be a Disadvantage to the Person, for Bashfulness Works divers Effects upon the Body, and in the Mind;[1] As for

---

1 Cavendish describes her own shyness at the court of Henrietta Maria in "A True Relation" (*Nature's Pictures*, 374; *Paper Bodies*, 46).

the Mind, it Disturbs the Thoughts so much, as the Thoughts are all in a Confused Disorder, and not any one Thought moves Regularly, neither will they Suffer the Words to pass out of the Mouth, or if they do, they are Uttered without Sense, nay, sometimes in no Language, being but Pieces of Words, or Pieces of the Letters of Words; and others, quite contrary, will speak so Much, and Fast, as none can Understand what they Say, or would Say, Indeed, so Fast, as they make neither Stop, nor Distinction; Again, others will Speak so Shrill, and Loud, as it Deafens the Ears of the Hearers, and others so Soft and Low, as it cannot be Heard what they Say; and some when they are out of Countenance, will Laugh at every Word they Speak, or is Spoken to them, although the Subject be so Sad and Lamentable, as it is proper to be attended with Tears: And for the Body, when the Mind is Bashful, it hath Divers, and Several Misbecoming Motions, as in some their neather Lip will so Quiver, as it will Draw quite Awry, like as in a Convulsion, and in some, their Eyes will so Squint, as they can see nothing Perfectly, and some will Shake their Heads so much, as if they had the Shaking Palsie; and in some their Legs will so Tremble, as they can hardly bear up the Body from falling; and some, their whole Body will be as if they were in a Cold Fit of an Ague; and others, when they are out of Countenance, have such a Supressing of Spirits, as they are forced often to Humm, to raise them up; and others, when they are out of Countenance, will look so Pale, as if they were Departing with Life, and on the Contrary, others will be so Red, having a Torrent of Blushes Flow to their Face, that they will appear as if they were Drunk, and that it were the Spirits of Wine which made that Firy and Flaming Colour, and many other Misbecoming Countenances, and several Misbecoming Garbs, Postures, Motions, and Sensless Words, which are not to be Express'd. But howsoever, a Bashful Countenance Expresses a Sensible Mind, and a Modest Nature, and not a Guiltiness of Crimes, for those that are so Bold as to Commit a Crime, will not want Confidence to Out-face it. Wherefore, Madam, let not your Bashful Behaviour be a Disturbance to your Harmless Thoughts, and Virtuous Life, to which Thought and Life, I leave you, and rest,

Madam,
Your faithful Friend and Servant.

LETTER 138

Madam,

You did once, before your last Letter, Desire me to give my Opinion concerning the Influence of the Stars, I did so, and now you Desire my Opinion again, which if I do, I may chance to Contradict my self; But truly, I believe the Planets, or Stars, have no more Influence upon the Bodies, Minds, and Natures of Men, than one Creature hath upon another, or several Creatures upon one, or one upon more; for though the Bodies, Humours, Constitutions, and Minds of Men are subject to Alterations and Changes, yet it is from their Principal Natures, as from the Nature of Mankind, and we see by Experience and Observation, that the Planets have not Power over Laws, Customs, and Education, which are more Firmly Setled, than to be Altered by the Various Effects of the Stars and Planets, which Laws, Customs, and Educations, have Power over the Appetites, Passions, and Constitutions of Men. But we may observe, that the Effects of the Planets Vary Perpetually, for if they were Constant in their Effects, there would be no Change or Alteration, and if they had an Absolute Power over the rest of Nature's Works, as many think, or as others say, onely over Mankind, their Cross Effects or Influences would make such a Confusion, as it would make an Utter Destruction of that they have Power of, which would Cross and Hinder Natures Methodical Proceedings, and certain Rules and Decrees, by which she Governs, unless you will say, the Stars, or Planets, are the Fates and Destinies to all Mankind, if so, there needs no Education, Laws, or Justice; but the Stars and Planets are too Inconstant and Changing to Decree and Destinate any thing, for there is no Assurance or Certainty in the Effects or Influence of the Stars and Planets, there is more Assurance in the Educations, and Customs of Men,[1] and Custom and Education hath Stronger Effects, for Custom and Education can Alter the Unaptness in Natural Capacities and Understanding, the Dull Dispositions, Froward, or Evil Passions of the Mind; also it oftentimes Tempers the Irregular Humours of the Body, and can Restrain the Unsatiable Appetites of the Body and Senses, and Long Custom Alters the Nature of Men: Besides, Healthful and Strong Constitutions will become Sick and Faint with Debaucheries and Irregularities, and Sick and Weak Constitutions will grow Healthful and Strong with Temperance and Regularity; also Education makes a Man a Thief,

---

1   For her husband's similar views on the topics of custom and education, see *Ideology and Politics on the Eve of the Restoration*, 68–72.

and a Thief an Honest Man, and it is Fortune that makes Kings and Beggars, and not the Planets, for all that are Born at one point of Time, have not the same Fortune, as when a King is Born, or else there would be thousands of Kings, so many Children being Born at the same point of Time. Likewise all that were Born in such or such a point of Time, would be Poets, Natural Philosophers, and the like, whereas there are as Few of them as of Kings; also all that are Born in such a point of Time, would be Wise, Just, and Prudent men, according to the Influence of the Stars; but if so, I believe there would be more Wise, and Just men than there are, whereas now for One Wise man there are Millions of Fools; Besides, it would shew the Stars to have more Power, and greater Influence, to Produce Fools, Knaves, Slaves, and Beggars, than Wise, Just, Free, and Rich Noble men; and if the Planets had no Power over the Fortunes, nor over the Minds of Men, but over the Bodies of Men, then the Influence the Soul hath on the Body, would Contradict the Influence of the Planets, and the Planets Influence would Contradict the Influence of the Soul, so as by their Crossness the Body would be Perpetually Tortured, and the Mind Disquieted; and if the Planets had an Influence over the Soul and Body, then we would be Good and Bad, Wicked and Pious, Valiant and Cowards, Sick and Well, Hungry and Dry, or otherwise have no Appetite, according as the Planets please, or according to their Influences; also all men would be Good and Bad, Sick and Well, Wise and Fools, Valiant and Cowardly, just at one time, as the Sign or Influence is, so that all men under the Domination of such Stars or Planets, would be alike at one Minute, and if all Men should Like or Love one Woman, at one Minute and Time, or all Women one Man, that is, as many as See her or him, that Woman would have more Servants and Suters than she could Please or Answer, and the Man more Mistresses than the Great Turk. Also, if it were according to the Dominion of the Planets, thousands on Sudden would be Inspired with Poetical Raptures, and soon after be Dull, and Stupid Dolts whenas that Influence Changed: but I believe there is greater Influence from one Nation on another, according to Interest, Strength and Potency, and so from one Man to another, according to Interest, Power, and Authority, than the Stars and Planets have on Several Nations, and Several, and Particular Men, which Produces greater Effects, than the Planets Effects and Influences can do; not but that I believe the Planets can Work as Sudden Effects, nay, far Suddener and Immediate, as we see by the Effects of the Heat, and Light of the Sun; but I believe, that Beauty and Wit have a greater Influence upon the Passions of the Mind, and Senses, and Appetites of the Body, than the Stars; and why may not we think as well, that the Actions, especially the General Actions of men, might have as great an Influence or Power over the Stars and Planets, as the Stars and Planets are thought to have over Men? for I see no reason to the contrary, since they are Fellow Creatures, and not Gods. But surely, every several part and particle in Nature hath an Influence on each other, from which are produced several Effects, and Effects have Influence upon Effects, some on some, and some on others, or perchance they have all a Working Effect to each other, as many Grains of Corn are ground for one Loaf of Bread, many several Materials go to one House, many several Families to one Commonwealth, many several Nations, to one World, and many several Worlds to one Universe. Thus, Madam, I have Obeyed your second Command, concerning the Influences of the Stars and Planets, as I did your first, but in this Later Discourse, I seem to have no Belief that the Stars have an Influence over the Bodies or Minds, no more than the Bodies or Minds have over the Planets, and so over Fortune, Education, Laws, Custom, and the like, whereas in my Former Letter, I said, they had over the Body, and was apt to Believe they had also over the Mind; but since I Writ the Former Letter concerning this Subject, I have thought of it more than I had then, and Believe every Creature hath some Influence to each other. But I leave both Letters, and the Opinions and Arguments written therein, to your Better Judgment, and rest,

Madam,
Your faithful Friend and Servant.

LETTER 139

Madam,
I Am sorry to hear that Sir S.K. is so full of the Dropsie, as to be Dying, indeed the Dropsie is a Disease that Quenches out the Fire, or Flame of Life, as a Torch, Candle, or Lamp, having more Water than Radical Oyl, or Vital Heat, so that one may say, those that are full of the Dropsie, have a River, or Sea in their Body, they are Drown'd, not with Water Without, but Within them, it is an Inward Deluge; and a Dropsical Body is like Noah's Flood, wherein the Inward Parts are as the several Nations, and the Animal Spirits as the People Drown'd therein, but the Soul, as Noah, is Saved in the Ark of Heaven, and at the Day of Judgment is to be Restored to the Bodily World again. But leaving this Similizing, Dropsie proceeds from Divers Causes, as sometimes through a Dry, sometimes through an Hot, and sometimes through a Cold Cause, some Dropsie through a Wasting Cause, some

through an Obstructive, and some through a Superfluous Cause; In some the Effects may be Cured, by Altering, or Removing the Causes, in others, the Cause is Essential, not to be Removed, but by Death, and so not to be Cured in Life; but whatsoever the Cause be, whether Curable or Incurable, the best Remedy either to Prolong the Life of the Diseased Body, or to Cure those that are Curable, is to make Issues, which as Sluces, Drain the Water out of the Body, or so much as to keep it from Overflowing, or they are like Taps set to Barrels full of Liquor, which runs forth at the Tap-holes: But there must not only be One Sluce, or Tap-hole, but Two or Three, to Vent the Superfluity of the Water that Comes, or is Bred in the Body. 'Tis true, I have heard those that have Issues, say, they are somewhat Troublesome, but yet they are not so Troublesom as a Swell'd, Unwieldy Bulk, or Sick, and Indisposed Body. But by your Letter I perceive that Sir S.Ks. Body is so much Overflowed, as it cannot be Drained so soon as to Save his Life, but it will be Drowned, and Overwhelmed in the Whirlpool of Death. And so leaving his Soul to God, I rest,

> Madam,
> Your faithful Friend and Servant.

LETTER 140

Madam,

You writ in your last Letter, that the Lady G.D. takes Cooling Julips in the Morning, and Cordials when she goes to Bed, to Digest Crude Humours; but my Reason says, she is in an Errour, as for Example, Dry Wood and Wet Wood, or Sear Wood and Green Wood, although there should be put much Fire to the Green, or Wet Wood, it will not hastily Burn, nay, such Wood doth oftener put Out the Fire, than the Fire doth Inkindle the Wood, for the moist Vapors that Issue, or are Drawn forth by the Heat of the Fire, do Destroy that Heat that Drew those Vapors out, whereas on the other side, Dry, or Sear Wood, when Kindled, and all of a Firy Flame, fling but a little Water on it, and it will Quench out the Flaming Fire. The like are the Bodies of Mankind, they are easier Cooled, when Inflamed, Applying Cooling Liquors, as Julips, Ptisan, Barly Water, and the like, than to Heat them with Cordials, when they are full of Raw, Crude, and Waterish Humours; for Fevers, although Violent, if they Proceed from no other Cause but a Supernatural Heat, are Sooner, and Easier Cured, than Cold Palsies, and other Cold Diseases; wherefore it is better to take Hot things first, and Cooling after, than to take Hot things after Cooling, for Hot things after Cooling do rather make a Smothering Heat, than a Concocting, Digesting, or Expelling Heat, so as it only fills the Body full of Vapors, like as Wet, or Green Fuel fills a Room with Smoak, but a Healthful Body must neither be too Hot, nor too Cold, nor too Dry, nor too Moist. And so leaving the Lady D.G. to her Julips and Cordials, I rest,

Madam,
Your faithful Friend and Servant.

LETTER 141

Madam,

I Was sorry to hear you intended to return into E. for I know that nothing but Necessity could Force you thither, although your Native Country, having been so Unnaturally Bereaved of all your Maintenance, by the Covetous Purloyning of your Unnatural Countrymen, and left to Seek, in a Wandring Condition, Fortunes Favour, which is as Inconstant as they are Cruel, but I perceive by your staying that Journey, that Fortune, as Inconstant as she Usually is, yet hath had more Pity and Compassion of your Sufferings, than they who keep you from the Extremity of Misery they have Exposed you to; yet those who have your Estate,[1] cannot be much Happier, although you never have it again, for they cannot Enjoy it Long, the Longest Life being but Short, and there is an Old Saying, We cannot Carry our Worldly goods to the Grave; indeed Death hath no Use of them, nor Life so much Pleasure, as Trouble with them; the truth is, 'tis best to have no more than for Necessity, a Superfluity most commonly runs into Luxury, which causes Painful Diseases in the Body, Restless Desires in the Mind, and Hinders the Life from that Sweet Repose it would have in a Satisfactory Temperance, and in a Moderate Fortune; and surely, it is the Best, and Happiest Life, to be neither Oppress'd with Riches, nor Distress'd with Poverty, and if Heaven Bless us from the Misery of the one, we shall not have cause to Repine at the Loss of the other; thus, it is likely, those may Suffer more that have Robbed you of your great Estate, by their Griping, and Accusing Consciences, and Uncertain Possessions, than you,

---

1   Cavendish returned to England (the E. above) to try to claim a portion her husband's estates. Other wives of defeated Royalists were successful in such claims, but the request of Cavendish was refused because she had married after her husband's exile and because he was a "traitor" to the Parliamentary government.

that are Robbed of all, but what they could not get, as your Virtuous
Nature, your Honourable Mind, your Peaceable Thoughts, and Heavens
Protection, to which I leave you, and rest,

Madam,
Your faithful Friend and Servant.

LETTER 142

Madam,
It is to be Observed, that most Men and Women are so Busie to find out
other Mens, or Womens Faults, as they Forget their own, and when
they Perceive any Faults in others, they are so Joy'd, as their Tongues are
like Trumpets, to Sound out their Reproach; also they are Busie in the
Inquiry of others Misfortunes, but never Consider, the Same, or some
other Misfortunes may Light upon them; also they are Busie to Inquire of
every Particular Persons Private Affairs, as their Wealth, Ordering their
Families, their Pleasures, or their Discontents, nay, of every Person, or
Thing that Concerns them not; but these Busie Natures or Humours
Dwell with Idle Persons, as the most part of the Gentry, and not with
Laborious, nay, with the most Foolish of the Gentry, not with the Wisest
of them, for Wise men never Inquire into other mens Affairs that
Concern them not, nor Meddle with other mens Faults, if they Touch
them not; they Wish Well to All, but Regard Nothing but their own
Affairs; they let other men Suffer for their own Crimes, and will have a
care that they may not be guilty of Crimes to Suffer for; they will Inquire
how Provision is Sold, when they are to Buy, not what their Neighbours
Spend; they go not to Sessions or Assizes, to hear the Accusations or
Condemnations, unless they be Commanded or Call'd, nor do they
Inquire what Thieves are Hang'd, or how many, but are careful that no
Thief may Rob them; and if they be Country-Gentlemen, and not
Courtiers, they Inquire not what Masks, Balls, and Playes are at the
Court, but what Hawks and Hounds are in the Country, for their own
Sports and Exercises, and if they be Wise Courtiers (although not Wise
Men) they do not Inquire what Wakes and Fairs there are in the
Country, but what Offices, or Places they may Beg; neither do Wise
Citizens Inquire after Hawks and Hounds in the Country, nor what
Mode-Congies are at the Court, nor of the Courtiers Amours, but they
Inquire after their Merchandizes, and how they may Sell off their Wares,
and what Fairs to Send them to; indeed they will Inquire after a Courtier,

if he Ow them Mony; Neither do Wise Farmers Inquire after the Price of Sattin, but how the Market goes for Corn, nor do their Wives Inquire how Paint is Sold, but what Cheesemongers will Buy their Cheeses and Pots of Butter; wherefore, in my Opinion, Societies should be apart by themselves, like several Commonwealths, Courtiers should only Converse with Courtiers, or Courtly Persons, and Country Gentlemen with Country Gentlemen, Citizens with Citizens, Farmers with Farmers, and I think they do so, at least, are most pleased with the Conversation of their own likeness: Also Statesmen should only Converse with Statesmen, Learned men with Learned men, Wits with Wits, or else their Wit will be Lost; indeed, Societies should be Chosen, and not Mix'd, and every Society should Move in its own Sphere, for the truth is, in Mix'd Societies is Confusion of Tongues, of Wits, of Capacities, and the like. But lest I should make a Confusion of Words in this Letter, I take my leave of you, and rest,

Madam,
Your faithful Friend and Servant.

LETTER 143

Madam,
I Heard the Ship was Drown'd, wherein the man was that had the Charge and Care of my Playes, to carry them into E. to be Printed, I being then in A. which when I heard, I was extremely Troubled, and if I had not had the Original of them by me, truly I should have been much Afflicted, and accounted the Loss of my Twenty Playes, as the Loss of Twenty Lives, for in my Mind I should have Died Twenty Deaths, which would have been a great Torment, or I should have been near the Fate of those Playes, and almost Drown'd in Salt Tears, as they in the Salt Sea; but they are Destined to Live, and I hope, I in them, when my Body is Dead, and Turned to Dust; But I am so Prudent, and Careful of my Poor Labours, which are my Writing Works, as I alwayes keep the Copies of them safely with me, until they are Printed, and then I Commit the Originals to the Fire, like Parents which are willing to Die, whenas they are sure of their Childrens Lives, knowing when they are Old, and past Breeding, they are but Useless in this World: But howsoever their Paper Bodies are Consumed, like as the Roman Emperours, in Funeral Flames, I cannot say, an Eagle Flies out of them, or that they Turn into a Blazing Star,

although they make a great Blazing Light when they Burn; And so leaving them to your Approbation or Condemnation, I rest,

Madam,
Your faithful Friend and Servant.

LETTER 144

Madam,
You Express'd in your last Letter, that Sir O.B. told an Acquaintance of yours, he did not Understand my Philosophical and Physical Opinions, and I believe him, because he hath not a Philosophical Brain, and therefore cannot Understand Philosophical Reasons, but had he said, there was no Sense and Reason in those Opinions, I could not have Believed him, unless he would have Proved it, which I am Confident he Cannot: But it is impossible to Expect my Book should be Understood of every one that Reads it, for there is more Strength of Brain required to Understand it, than to Understand a Horn-book; besides, it is harder, because they are New Opinions, never Vented before; as for Example, if a man did make an Oration in such a Language which his Auditors never heard before, and because they do not Understand the Language, would they Condemn this Oration? that were not only Unjust, but Foolish, to Condemn what they cannot Judg of, as not Understanding it; or would they say, it cannot be Understood, because they never Learn'd that Language? If every one were of that Opinion, there would be no Languages Taught or Learned, but every one would keep to their Native Language; nay, all Languages would Cease, for they would not teach them their Children, because it would be a Lost Labour, & so they would Forget whatever they did Learn themselves, or else that Opinion could not hold; wherefore, whatsoever hath been Invented, may be Taught, and Learned by good Capacities. But this is only to Express how Simply People Judg, or Spitefully Censure, and I believe that the Opinions or Doctrines of former Natural Philosophers, were no more Understood at first, than if they had Written, or Spoken in Unknown Languages, till by Degrees their Language was Learned, that is, their Opinions were Understood by those that did make it their Employment to Study, and so to Understand them, but they had this Advantage, being Men, that they had liberty not only to Write their Opinions, but to Preach, Teach, and Instruct others to Understand them; Pythagoras imposed five years Silence to his Pupils, because he would not have their Speaking Hinder their Studying, or Obstruct their Under-

standing, and there is not any Famous Philosopher, that ever I heard of, which did not Teach and Explane his Own Opinions, besides Inscribing them either in Letters, Figures, Cifres, or the like. Wherefore I fear the Right Understanding of my Philosophical Opinions are likely to be Lost, for want of a Right Explanation, for they may be Interpreted not that way I Conceiv'd them, that is, not to my Sense or Meaning, for it is not Proper for my Sex to be a Publick Oratour, to Declare or Explane my Opinions in Schools, and if it were, yet I have neither Confidence nor Learning to Speak to an Assembly, nor in such Forms or Phrases, as Masters of Learning Use; Neither is it fit I should be a Private School Mistress, to Teach and Instruct Scholars, although concerning onely my Philosophical Opinions, nor do I believe I have so much Patience, being a Woman, for that Profession, as to Hammer, or Beat in Understanding into Dull Capacities, & Hard Brains; wherefore I must leave that Work of mine Unexplaned by Words, though I have Written it as Plain for Understanding, as the Nature, or Matter, or Subject, doth Afford, or give Way to; But I leave it to Heavens Protection, and Nature's Reward, as to Favour and Bless my Harmless Labours, and to Reward my Natural Studies with Right Understanding, and Due Commendations, that neither Spite nor Ignorance may Condemn them, but that Time may Keep, and Fame Divulge them, that they may Live to and in After Ages, so that this Work that Sir O.B. Understands not, may be Understood when Sir O.B. Lives not, and Live when Sir O.B. is Dead and Forgotten. But, Madam, lest I should Forget my self in writing so Long a Letter, as it may Trouble your Pastime to read it, I rest,

> Madam,
> Your Ladiships very faithful Friend and Servant.

LETTER 145

Madam,

I Am sorry, that when you were last in this City, I was forced through my being Sick, to deny my self the Honour of your Company, but I did it rather out of Respect to your self, than to my self, for your Company would have been some Recompense for the Absence of my Health; but though your Presence would have been as a Cordial to me, and might have Refreshed, and Nourished my Faint Spirits, yet I should have been to you as a Draught of Pudled Water, for Sickness is full of Trouble, and a Sick Body cannot have a Sociable Mind, nor Pleasing Discourses, your

Ears would have been fill'd with nothing but Complaints and Groans, your Eyes would have been Benighted in a Dark Chamber, wherein the Light was Shut out. Thus would you have been as in a Tomb, for a Sick Bodies Chamber is in a Degree of a Dead Bodies Grave, and their Groans as a Passing Bell, which would not have been Agreeable to your Ladiships Humour, who hath a Healthful Constitution, which makes your Mind like as the Spring, and your Thoughts like Nightingals, Singing with Pleasure and Delight therein. And thus, had I received your Charitable Visit, I should have been as a Dark Cloud to the Sun-shine of your Mirth; But since I am Recovered to Health, I shall come to that City you are in, to give your Ladiship Thanks for your Favours, and to Express how much I am Really,

Madam,
Your Ladiships most Humble Servant.

LETTER 146

Madam,
You were pleased in your last Letter to Request me to send you my Opinion of Virgil and Ovid, as which I thought was the better Poet; Truly, Madam, my Reason, Skill, or Understanding in Poetry and Poets, is not Sufficient to give a Judgment of two such Famous Poets, and their Poetry, for though I am a Poetess, yet I am but a Poetastress, or a Petty Poetess, but howsoever, I am a Legitimate Poetical Child of Nature, and though my Poems, which are the Body of the Poetical Soul, are not so Beautiful and Pleasing, as the rest of her Poetical Childrens Bodies are, yet I am nevertheless her Child, although but a Brownet. But you may say, you ask'd my Opinion of two Famous Poets, and I Talk of my self; Truly, Madam, I am forced to do so, in order to your Commands, at least to your Desires, for my Will is to Obey you, and first, to let you know, that though I am not a Learned, or Supreme Judg, yet I am an Inferiour Officer in the Poetical Court, and therefore not altogether Ignorant in Poetical Causes or Cases; But, Madam, I am in a Dispute with my self, as whether it be Warrantable for me, a Private Person, to give my Judgment in so Publick a Cause, for though those two Persons, if they were Living, might with an United Consent appoint me to be a Judg between them, yet a Third Person, as your Ladiship, cannot Properly make a Judg without their Knowledg and Consent, unless you were a Caesar, and had the Power to make what Judges, or Laws you pleased; But yet by reason you are my Caesar, to Rule,

Govern, and Command me, as you Please, I will Obey you, and as I hope, without Partiality, for I am neither of their Country, or their Kindred, nor have I taken Bribes from either, nor hope to have a Reward from any, but rather I fear a Censure for Punishment, howsoever, for your sake, I will Venture, and thus I give my Opinion, That Virgil was the Craftier, but Ovid the Wittier man, that Virgil was the better Flatterer, but Ovid the better Poet, that Virgil was the more Fortunate, and Ovid the more Unhappy. And to Prove Virgil's Craft, he Flattered the Emperour, and the most Noble Families in Rome; and as for his Flattery, he made the Ground of his Poems or Poetry, the Antiquity and Original of the Emperour, and the Noble Families of Rome, whether False or True, I leave to his own Belief and Knowledge, although Poetry, for the most part is Feigning, at least so Illustrated, that the End is False; yet howsoever he gain'd the Applause of Caesar, and all the Chief of the Romans, and one Great and Eminent Persons Praise, is the Foundation of a Hundred Inferiour Persons Commendations, Admirations, Estimations, and Fame or Renown; Again, to Prove his good Fortune, he was in the Emperours Favour so much, as to be Honoured with his Company, Privacies, Counsels, Affections, and Inriched with his Gifts, whereas Ovid was Banished from his Friends and Country, into an Unwholsom Air, although his Fault was not so Notorious as to be Visible, or Publickly Known, so as one may Judg, that Ovid's Banishment was through Caesar's Partial Envy to him for Virgil's sake, and not for any Crime, for he Banished Ovid, fearing he might Out-shine Virgil, his Flattering Favourite, and Deifier, at least, Glorifier; but Ovid was too Rich, and Nobly born, to be a Flatterer, at least, so Gross a one as Virgil, he rather thought to be Flattered, than to Flatter; neither had he an Insinuating Craft to get Applause and Wealth, for he was Open and Free, not Bound up to Subtilty; And for his Wit, 'tis said, that his Prose was only Dissolved Verse, and his Poetry was Brief, and yet Satisfactory, it was full of Fancy, yet Natural, Moral, and Human Descriptions, it was full of Variety, yet Compendious, so that his Poetry Express'd his Judgment, Under-standing, Learning, Wit, Eloquence, and Fancy; Neither did he spend his Reason, Judgment, Wit, and Fancy, on One Tedious Feigned Story, but on Hundreds of Stories, and Express'd himself in his Metamorphosis, as much a Moral, and Natural Philosopher, a Courtly Lover, an Heroick Souldier, a Valiant and Prudent Commander, a Politick States-man, a Just Governour and Ruler, a Wise and Magnificent Prince, a Faithful Citizen, a Navigator, Fortificator, Architect, Astronomer, and the like, as also a Learned Scholar, and had an Insight into Arts and Husbandry, as well as Virgil in his Georg-icks, nay far more, as having more Variety; neither was he so Palpable an

Imitator as Virgil was; the truth is, in my Opinion, Ovid was the far Wiser, Wittier, Ingenious, and Nobler Poet, and by his Poetry we may perceive, that though he was not one of Augustus Caesar's Favourits, yet he was Nature's Favourite, and was Beloved of all the Muses, and though Caesar took away his Right of Human Inheritance, and Native Soil, yet he could not take away his Natural Poetical Birth, for he had his Worthy Due in the place he was Banished to, having, as I have heard, Divine Honours given him after his Death, and great Respect and Love in his Life-time, by those People he Lived amongst, by which we may say, Happy Ovid, in an Unhappy Condition; And for Language, wherein Virgil is so Highly Praised, I cannot Perceive in the Translation, but that Ovid is fully as Copious, Significant, Sweet, Eloquent, and Illustrious, as Virgil, I cannot tell what it is in Latin. But to Conclude, had Ovid's Design been Favour, and his Poetry Flattery, fitted to the Genius, Humour, or Pride of those Times he Liv'd in, Virgil would have been Buried in his Fame; but it is to be Observed, that not only the Inferiours of the same Time, Follow, Imitate, or Believe, according to a Grand Superiour, but Following Ages do the like, so Powerful and Lasting is a Grand Superiour's Esteem, Favour, or Opinion. And thus, Madam, I have given Judgment, at least my Opinion, for Ovid, not but that I do Highly Admire and Reverence Virgil, but yet not so much as I do sweet Ovid, whose Fancy, Wit, and Language, is like his Birth, Soft, Gentle, and Noble, Rational, Observing, Understanding, and Judicious, Quick, Ingenious, and Delightful, Beautiful, Graceful, and Taking, or Moving, Heroick, Generous, and Magnificent, Eloquent, Elegant, and Fluent, Distinguishing, Similizing, Forming, Winding, Composing, Contriving and Uniting; to all which I leave his Poetry, and his Fame to Everlasting Life, or Memory, and rest,

Madam,
Your faithful Friend and Servant.

LETTER 147

Madam,
Th' other day Mr. H.Us. Daughter and Neece were here to Visit me, and I Endeavouring to Entertain them Kindly and Friendly, Talk'd so much, as they might easily believe, my Tongue was in a Perpetual Motion, especially being Strangers to me, not knowing my Solitary, Silent Humour, who Speak only much when I Entertain Strangers, which I do but seldom, so that my Talking is like Fits of a Quartan Ague, and as hard to

be Cured, for much Talking is a Disease, or a Natural Defect, or rather Effect in the Female Sex, and the Defects and Effects of Nature may be Obscured, but not Altered, so that it is very Improbable, if not Impossible, for a Woman to be Silent; indeed it is against the Nature of Women, so that a Silent Woman would be as a Monster in Nature; but howsoever, my Desire is rather to be a Monster for Silence, than a Natural in Talk; wherefore, lest I should Commit a Double Fault, in overmuch Writing of my overmuch Talking, I take my leave of you, and rest,

Madam,
Your faithful Fr. and S.

LETTER 148

Madam,
I Thank you for the Cup you sent me, but I cannot Guess whether it be Glass, Metal, or Stone, for it seems too Light to be Metal, too Thin to be Stone, and too Strong to be Glass, but I suppose it is of a Mix'd Nature, as many things are; as for Example, Feathers seem to be betwixt Hair and Wool, for the Quils seem to be somewhat like Soft Souls, being Hollow, and within them a Pith, somewhat like Brains, and the Small Sprigs of Feathers are like as Hair Growing thereupon, and Sprouting thereout, and the Downy part of Feathers which Grow towards the Bottom, or Root of the Quils, are of the Nature and Likeness of Wool; so the Scales of Fishes seem to be betwixt Sinews or Gristles, and Skin, for they are like Gristles in being Tough and Clammy, and like Skin in being Smooth, Slick, and Thinner than Sinews are; Also Horns of Beasts, Hoofs, and Claws, Bills of Fowls, and Nails of Men, are betwixt Bones and Gristles, as to be Harder than Gristles, and Softer than Bones. Also there are many several Creatures, which seem to be of a Mix'd Kind, as a Bat seems to be betwixt a Beast and a Bird, having a Body like a Mouse, and Wings like a Bird, and an Owl seems somewhat like a Cat, and hath the Nature of a Cat, to catch Mice, and many other Creatures could be brought for Examples, which would bee too Tedious for a Letter. But to return to your Present, which is now my Cup, I am so Pleased with it, as to my thinking my Drink is nothing so Tastable out of any other thing as out of that, for if I Drink out of any thing that is Metal, methinks my Drink tasts Brackish, as if it were mix'd with Mineral Waters, although it were Gold, and out of any thing made of Earth, methinks my Drink hath a Musty Tast, although out of Purceline; and out of Glass, it is so Cold in Winter

time, that it Deads my Tast so much, as if it had no Tast at all. But these Faults are found only since I have the Cup you sent me; wherefore by this you may see, a New Acquaintance is Preferr'd before an Old, like as Men that find so many Sweet Graces in a New Mistress, at least do think so, and so many Foul Faults in a Wife, as the Wife is cast By, and the Mistress only made Use of. But 'tis most Probable, I am so Pleas'd with the Cup because it was yours, and now it is mine, yet it is yours still, for whatsoever is mine, is yours, for I my self am so, as,

Madam,
Your very faithful Friend and Servant.

LETTER 149

Madam,
I Am sorry to hear, as by your last Letter, that Mrs. B.U. is so Sick; Truly, I do believe, she takes too many Cordial Waters; if there were a Mean betwixt her Diet and mine, I believe it would be better for us both, for as I Quench out my Spirits by Over-cooling and Moistening Drinks, as Water, and Clarified Whay, so she Burns up hers, with too Hot, and Dry Cordials, as Hot Waters; but the Fire of Life should neither be Burnt up, nor Quenched out, although Quenching is less Dangerous than Burning out, for if the Fuel of Life be Burnt to Ashes, there is no hopes of Reinkindling that Fire again, by reason those Ashes are Insipid, and yield no Nourishing Food, nor Oily Flame, but if it be only Quenched out, and the Fuel Remaining, 'tis probable it may be Inlightened again with a few live Coals, that is two or three Spoons full of Cordial Water, so as that which will Kill her, if she take too much of it, may in Extremity Cure me, if I take a little; the Fuel of Life are the Vital Parts, the Fire of Life are the Vital Spirits, the Fuel of the Vital Parts is Food, the Fuel of the Vital Spirits is Radical Moisture, which is an Oyly, or Balsamick Substance; when this Radical Moisture is too Thin, it Quenches the Spirits out, and when it is Consumed with Excessive Heat, as being Burnt up, or Evaporated, there is nothing for the Spirits to Feed on. Thus Radical Moisture is the Prolonging, or Decaying of Life, 'tis the Oyl to the Lamp of Life. But Mrs. B.U. Drinks not Cordials through an Appetite to those Strong Liquors, no more than I do Drink Tastless Water; But we being both Studious Persons, are Conceited, for all Students are Conceited more or less, especially concerning their Diets, for Contemplative Persons either Change oftener in the Course of their Diet, than Fantastical Persons in the Fashion of their Clothes, or be so Obstinate in one

particular Diet, as neither Sense nor Reason shall be able to Perswade them from it, nay, they will rather Die in their Obstinacy; But I hope Mrs. B.U. will be Ruled, and none hath such Power to Perswade her as your Ladiship, neither is any one so Able to Advise her; And so leaving her to your Ladiships Advice, and Heavens Protection, I rest,

> Madam,
> Your Ladiships faithful Friend and Servant.

LETTER 150

Madam,
My Thoughts, although not my Actions, have been so busily Imployed about Huswifry these three or four Dayes, as I could think of nothing else, for I hearing my Neighbours should say, my Waiting-Maids were Spoil'd with Idleness, having nothing to do, but to Dress, Curl, and Adorn themselves, and they Excusing themselves, laying the Blame upon me, that I did not set them to any Imployment, but whereas they were ready to Obey my Commands, I was so Slow in Commanding them, as I seldom took any Notice of them, or Spoke to them, and that the truth was, they oftener Heard of their Lady, than Heard, or Saw her themselves, I living so Studious a Life, as they did not See me above once a Week, nay, many times, not once in a Fortnight; wherefore, upon the Relation of these Complaints, I sent for the Governess of my House, and bid her give order to have Flax and Wheels Bought, for I, with my Maids, would sit and Spin. The Governess hearing me say so, Smiled, I ask'd her the Reason, she said, she Smil'd to think what Uneven Threads I would Spin, for, said she, though Nature hath made you a Spinster in Poetry, yet Education hath not made you a Spinster in Huswifry, and you will Spoil more Flax, than Get Cloth by your Spinning, as being an Art that requires Practice to Learn it; besides, said she, the Noise the Wheels make with Turning round, will be Offensive to your Hearing. I was very much Troubled to hear what she said, for I thought Spinning had been Easie, as not requiring much Skill to Draw, and Twist a Thread, nay, so Easie I thought it was, as I did imagine I should have Spun so Small, and Even a Thread, as to make Pure Fine Linnen Cloth, also, that my Maids and I should make so much, as I should not have needed to Buy any, either for Houshold Linnen, or Shifts. Then I bid her leave me, to Consider of some other Work; and when I was by my self alone, I call'd into my Mind several Sorts of Wrought Works, most of which, though I had Will, yet I had no Skill to Work, for which I did

Inwardly Complain of my Education, that my Mother did not Force me to Learn to Work with a Needle, though she found me alwayes Unapt thereto; at last I Pitch'd upon Making of Silk Flowers, for I did Remember, when I was a Girl, I saw my Sisters make Silk Flowers, and I had made some, although Ill-favour'dly; wherefore I sent for the Governess of my House again, and told her, that I would have her Buy several Coloured Silks, for I was Resolved to Imploy my Time in making Silk-Flowers; she told me, she would Obey my Commands, but, said she, Madam, neither You, nor any that Serves You, can do them so Well, as those who make it their Trade, neither can you make them so Cheap, as they will Sell them out of their Shops, wherefore you had better Buy those Toyes, if you Desire them, for it will be an Unprofitable Employment, to Wast Time, with a Double Expence of Mony. Then I told her I would Preserve, for it was Summer time, and the Fruit Fresh, and Ripe upon the Trees; she ask'd me for whom I would Preserve, for I seldom did Eat Sweet-meats my self, nor made Banquets for Strangers, unless I meant to Feed my Houshold Servants with them; besides, said she, you may keep half a score Servants with the Mony that is laid out in Sugar and Coals, which go to the Preserving only of a Few Sweet-meats, that are good for nothing, but to Breed Obstructions, and Rot the Teeth. All which when I heard, I conceived she spoke Reason; at last I considered, that I and my Maids had better be Idle, than to Employ Time Unprofitably, and to spend Mony Idely; and after I had Mused some time, I told her, how I heard my Neighbours Condemn'd me, for letting my Servants be Idle without Employment, and that my Maids said it was my Fault, for they were willing to be Employed in Huswifry; she said, my Neighbours would find Fault, where no Fault was, and my Maids would Complain more if they were kept to Work, than when they had liberty to Play; besides, said she, none can want Employment, as long as there are Books to be Read, and they will never Inrich your Fortunes by their Working, nor their Own, unless they made a Trade of Working, & then perchance they might get a poor Living, but not grow Rich by what they can do, whereas by Reading they will Inrich their Understandings, and Increase their Knowledges, and Quicken their Wit, all which may make their Life Happy, in being Content with any Fortune that not in their Power to Better, or in that, as to Manage a Plentiful Fortune Wisely, or to Indure a Low Fortune Patiently, and therefore they cannot Employ their Time better, than to Read, nor your Ladiship better than to Write, for any other Course of Life would be as Unpleasing, and Unnatural to you, as Writing is Delightful to you; besides, you are Naturally Addicted to Busie your time with Pen, Ink, and Paper; but, said I, not with Wit, for if Nature had given me as much Wit to Write, as Fortune hath given me Leisure, my Writing might have been for some Use, but now my Time and Paper is Unprofitably Wasted in Writing, as my Time and Flax would be in Spinning, but since I am fit for no other Employment but to Scratch Paper, leave me to that Employment, and let my Attending Maids have Books to read. Thus, Madam, for a time did I Trouble my Mind, and Busie my Thoughts to no Purpose, but was Forced to Return to my Writing-Work again, not knowing what else to do, and if I had been as Long Absent from my Lord as Penelope was from her Husband Ulysses, I could have never Employed my Time as she did, for her work only Employed her Hands, and Eyes, her Ears were left open to Loves Pleadings, and her Tongue was at liberty to give her Suters Answers, whereas my Work Employes all the Faculties and Powers of my Soul, Mind, and Spirits, as well as my Eyes and Hands, and my Thoughts are so Busie in my Brain, as they neither Regard, nor take Notice what Enters through the Ears; indeed those Passages are as Stop'd up, or Barr'd close, whereas had Penelope's Ears been so Barr'd, her Lovers Petitions, Sutes, and Pleadings, would have been kept without doors, like a Company of Beggars, they might have Knock'd, but not Entred, nor any of the Mind's Family would have ask'd them what they Desired;[1] neither would the Tongue, the Mind's Almner, have given them one word of Answer, and then it was likely her Amorous Lovers would have gone away, and not stay'd to Feed upon her Cost and Charge, as they did. But, Madam, give me leave to beg your Pardon for Writing so Long a Letter, though it is your Desire I should, I will Tire you no Longer, but Subscribe my self,

Madam,
Your faithful Friend and Servant.

LETTER 151

Madam,
You were pleased in your last Letter to tell me, that you did see the Lady C.C. and that her Face seems Young, although she be Old in Years; but, Madam, Youthful Appearance is like Green Moss on Aged Trees, and not as the Green of Springing Buds, or Flourishing Leaves; the truth is, some Bodies are Happy in being so Healthful, and of so Lasting a Constitution; for like as the Holly, Ivy, Bay, or Lawrel, last Green all their Time, not only in Summer, but also in Winter; so some Men and Women will

---

1 In *The World's Olio*, Cavendish suggests that Penelope encouraged the suitors.

appear Young in the Winter of their Age, with a Fresh, and Lively Colour, and so Smooth, and Free from Wrinkles, as if Time had no Power on them; But there are not many Bodies, or Faces, that can Boast they are too Strong for Time, and although they should be Victorious over Time for a Time, yet Time Ruins them all at Last. And so leaving the Lady C.C. to her Old Years, and Young Face, I rest,

Madam,
Your faithful Friend and Servant.

LETTER 152

Madam,
The Messenger you sent, is returning to you again, and with him I have sent some Babies, and other Toyes this City Affords, as a Token to your Daughter, I do not send them for Bribes, to Corrupt her from Edifying Learning, and Wise Instructions, for I would not have her Bred to Delight in Toyes, and Childish Pleasures, but I send them as Gifts, to Allure her to that which is most Profitable, and Happiest for her Life, for Children are sooner Perswaded by the Means of Tinsell-Toyes, and Flattering Words, to Listen to Wise Instruction, to Study Profitable Arts or Sciences, to Practice Good, Graceful Behaviours, and Civil Demeanours, than they can be Forced thereto, by Terrifying Threats, and Cruel Blows;[1] 'tis true, they may be Forced to the Outward Forms, or Actions of Learning, but not to the Understanding, Profit, Grace, or Becoming, for Force Breaks the Understanding, Destroyes all Ingenuity, for the Fear of Punishment Confuses the Brain, and Disquiets the Mind so much, as it makes them Incapable of Right Impressions, whereas the Hope of Rewards Delights the Mind, and Regulates the Motions in the Brain, and makes them so Smooth, as the least Impression of Learning Prints Fairly therein, and so Plainly, as to be Remembred in their Elder Years; also it makes their Thoughts and Actions Industrious, to Merit those Rewards, and their Endeavours will be the more Active, through a Covetous Desire to Increase those Rewards; so that those Toyes which are given to Children in their Childish Years, may be a Means to Teach them, when Grown to Elder Years, to Know, and Acknowledge, that all Toyes are Vanities, and that nothing is to be Prized, or Esteemed, but what is Useful, and Best,

---

1 Cavendish explains in *A True Relation* that her mother avoided cruelty in child rearing (*Nature's Pictures*, 370; *Paper Bodies*, 49).

either for their Present, or Future Life, as the Life of their Memory, or Renown. Thus, Madam, the Toyish Present is to a Good Design, and may prove to a Good End, which is the Wish of,

Madam,
Your faithful Friend and Servant.

LETTER 153

Madam,
Th' other day the Lady M.L.[1] was to Visit me, and by her sad Countenance I perceived she was full of Melancholy, ready to be Delivered of the Burden, as to Vent her Grief through her Mouth, but I Observing she could not Readily make her Complaints, did as a Midwife, Help them forth, by asking her what the Cause of her Sadness was; with that Tears Flowed forth her Eyes, as Ushers to her Complaints; said she, although I was a Joyful Bride, yet I am an Unhappy Wife, for on my Wedding day I Joyed, because I had Married such a man as had Proved himself to be Valiant, Generous, and Wise, all which I thought was a Greater Honour, to be the Wife of such a Worthy man, than if he had been Rich, Handsom, and Dignified with Title, although he did neither Want those, which was an Addition to my Joy; nor did I think my self Unhappy, that he Married me not through his Own Choice, but his Friends Perswasions, or that he did seem not to Love me, for I thought when Time had Proved my Virtue, Duty, and Obedience, Justice would have Perswaded him to have Loved me; neither did I think my self Unhappy, that he Endeavoured to make me a Servant, nay a Slave to his Mistress, because I thought he desired by this means to keep me from Jealousie, and to learn me Patience; neither did I think my self Unhappy, that he Tortured me, nay Threatned Death to me, to Force me to Serve his Concubines, because I took more Comfort in that my Resolution was so Strong, as neither Pain, nor Fear of Death could Alter it, and Gloried more in my Sufferings, than Grieved for my Pains, as that I would rather Die than do a Base Act, as to be a Bawd to my Husbands Whores; But my Unhappiness is, that my Husband will be Divorced from me, which Divorcement is far Worse than Death, or Bodily Pains in Life, for in the Grave I shall lie in Rest and Peace, and if I be not Remembred with Honour, yet I Die not in Disgrace; and for the Pains in Life, it Learns

---

1   Elsewhere M.L. is Margaret Lucas, Cavendish using her maiden name. The contents of this letter, however, do not match up with biographical fact as we know it.

me to Practise Moral Philosophy; but to be Divorced, is to Live in Disgrace and Scorn, which is Worse than any Pain, or Death, for he having got the Reputation of a Worthy Man, the World will think I am a very Unworthy Woman if he Forsakes me, and that he knows me to be guilty of some Notorious Faults, but that he will not Divulge them, for Fear of his Own Dishonour, or out of Respect to the Female Sex. Thus, by a Divorcement, I shall be left to the Censure, and Scandal of the World, whilst he will be thought a Wise man for Parting from me, as being not Honourable for him to Live with me; with that she Wept, as if her Eyes had been two Perpetual Springs, and mean'd to make a Deluge of their Tears, and with seeing her, my Eyes began to Drop too; at last I told her, I did verily believe her Husband did but Pretend a Divorce, only to Fright her to what he would have her, and intended not a Divorce to Grieve her, for though he was a man that did take a liberty of Variety of Women, knowing that Liberty could be no Dishonour to the Masculine Sex;[1] and though he loved a Wanton Mistress, yet certainly he was not so Unjust, or Unwise, as to Hate a Chast Wife, or to Part from a Virtuous Wife, for the sake of a Lewd Mistress, and therefore I thought she might take Comfort, and the best Remedy, at least, Cordial, for Grief, was Patience, for though her Husband was an Independent to Amour, yet he was an Orthodox to Honour, and Moral Honesty, only he wanted some Temperance, at which she Smil'd; by that I perceiv'd her Complaints and my Opinion had somewat Removed the Heavy Oppression of Melancholy, and after some time, she took her leave of me, giving me Thanks both for hearing her Discourse of her own Grief, and for Comforting her; and by this Relation you have as it were Received the same Visit, as also a Visit from me, so as we have been both with you, onely a Letter doth Carry us to you instead of a Coach. But now I think it is time to leave you, and rest,

Madam,
　　　Your very faithful Friend and Servant.

LETTER 154

Madam,
You writ in your last Letter, that Mrs. P.C. drinks New Milk every Morning Fasting, for Nourishment, and to Increase Natural Moisture;

1　In her fiction, Cavendish punishes men who are unfaithful. See in particular "The Matrimonial Agreement," *Nature's Pictures*, 201.

truly, I believe she had better Drink Cream, for as Milk hath Thin Whay in it, so it hath also Hard, Dry Curds in it, for Milk is Compounded by Nature, of three Substances, as Butter, Curd, and Whay, as the Oyly, Earthy, and Watery Part, whereas Cream hath only the Oily and Watery Part, for Thick Cream cannot be turned into a Hard Curd, which makes it so much the Better, for Dry Curd is of the Nature of Horn, as we may observe by such Cheeses as are made of Fleeted[1] Milk, which are Tough, Hard, and Insipid, whereas Cream-Cheeses are only Press'd Butter; indeed, it is not to be done, as to make a Cheese, or Cheese-Curd, only of Thick Cream, unless there be Water, or Thin Milk mix'd with it. 'Tis true, the Whay of Cream, which is Butter-milk, will Curdle, that is, when the Oily Part is taken out of it, and this is the reason that I say Cream is more Nourishing, and Moistening than Milk; but I may chance to Plead the Good Effects of Cream, and leave out the Evil, as I did once for Brown Bread, which was, that Brown Bread in Effect was much Cooler than White, my reason was, that the Flowry part being Boulted out, wherein lies the Strength, and so consequently the Heat, the Remainder, as the Branny part, was like Grains, which is the Insipid part of Barley, so that Brown Bread in Effect, is like Small Ale, and White Bread like Strong, and for this Reason I did eat Brown Bread, but my Weak Stomack soon grew Sick, for though my Reason found out the Cool Effect, yet it did not perceive, that the Grossness made it Hard of Digestion, until Experience Taught it: so some may Object, that Cream being Thicker than Milk, may not pass out of the Stomack so Easily, but surely, if the Milk Curdles in the Stomack, as certainly it most Usually doth, those Curds will not only be Harder to Digest, but Breed great Obstructions, whereas Cream, which is as Butter, will make the Body Soluble. Yet though I Argue for it, I Eat little of it, by reason the nature of Cream is Hot, and my Diet is for the most part Cooling; some may say, by reason Milk Nourishes Children, it may Nourish those that are Grown up to Years, but Experience tells us, that the Nature of Mankind, for the most part, Alters with Time, and that which is Natural to a Child, may be Unnatural to a Man; but perchance some have Childish Constitutions all their Life-time, and the truth is, that Diet is much according to the Constitution, for, that which will Agree with some, will Disagree with others, and for Milk, it better Agrees with Weak Constitutions than Strong, yet Womens Milk, and Asses Milk doth Agree better than any

---

1   What floats upon the surface.

other Milk, by reason those Milks are Thinner, and not so full of Curds. But leaving Mrs. P.C. to her Milk, I rest,

Madam,
Your very faithful Friend and Servant.

LETTER 155

Madam,
Two or three dayes since the Lady M.L. was to Visit me again, with a Countenance as Joyful, as formerly it was Sad, I told her I was very glad to see such an Alteration in her Face, which shew'd her Mind to be more Chearful than it was; she said, it was true, for she hoped she would be as Happy, as she thought she was Unhappy, for my Husband hath Confess'd said she, that his Unkindness to me was rather Seeming than Real, more to Prove my Virtue, than to Dislike my Person or Humour, and that if he were Unmarried, and Free to Choose any Woman through the World, he would Choose me for his Wife, and he sayes, he would not Part from me, were he sure to be the Master of the World, by being Perfid, or Divorced from me, and hereafter he would endeavour to be as Good a Husband as I am a Wife, and with this Joyful Relation, her Blood Flush'd into her Cheeks, which shew'd, that her Cold, Dark, Melancholy Thoughts were Dispersed, like as the Sun breaks through Dark, and Broken Clouds, which Clouds, when Joyned, Obscured his Light, and Abated his Heat; the truth is, her Joy was so much, as I may say it was Contagious and Infectious, for it Affected me with Joy, to See, and Observe her, and if all her Neighbours were the like Affected, she might do as the man, that call'd his Neighbours and Friends, to Rejoyce at the Finding his Lost Sheep; but her Husbands Affections were not so much Lost, as Hidden, or Obscured from her Knowledge; and truly, she deserves to be Loved, for her Virtue, Chastity, Love, and Honour, for there are but Few Women that make so good Wives as she, for many Wives Dislike their Husbands, not out of a Dislike to their Faults, but out of Love to Variety, and some Hate their Husbands through Hate to their Faults, making no Distinction between the Man and the Faults, nay, some Dislike their Husbands Virtues, and Good Qualities, through a Dislike to their Persons, and many Wives care not whether their Husbands Love or Hate them, Live From, or With them, nay, for the most part, they love their Husbands Absence better than their Presence, and will make Quarrels to Part; but the Lady M.L. is not of the number

of such Wives, for she Loves her Husband, which Love makes her Wink at her Husband's Faults, she is Patient with her Husband's Anger, Rejoyces at her Husband's Presence, is Proud of her Husband's Favours, Obedient to her Husband's Honest Commands, and had rather Die, or Indure Torment, than to Part, or be Divorced from him; All which every Good Wife ought to do. But leaving the Lady M.L. to her Virtue, Joy, and Happiness, I rest,

Madam,
Your faithful Friend and Servant.

LETTER 156

Madam,
I Am sorry to hear you are not Well, but if your Disease be only a Faint-tiredness, or Weakness, when you stand still any time, since you can Walk an hour together, and find no Weariness, but rather Ease, there is no Danger of Death, for to be Weary when you Stand still, so as to be near Fainting, and to find Rest and Ease by Walking, is a Natural Effect of a Natural Cause, the reason is, that when any one Stands still, the Nerves and Sinews are Stretch'd straight out at Length, but when one Walks or Moves, they have Liberty, as being Unbent, and Unstretch'd; as for Example, when Mankind Stands, their Legs, Thighs, Hams, and Back, are Straight, as one Straight Line, but when they Go, their Legs Tuck up, as first one Leg, then th' other, which Pulling, or Tucking up, Slackens all the Nerves and Sinews, from the Back Downwards, and that gives Ease; for 'tis not only Change that gives Ease, but the Slacking of the Nerves and Sinews, which are as if they were Stretch'd upon a Rack, when they are Drawn Straight out at Length by Standing, but it shews, your Sinews and Nerves are not very Tough and Strong, but rather Tender and Weak, being soon Weary in Standing Still, for the Nerves and Sinews are as Strings, or Cords, which Tie, or Knit the several Parts of the Body together, where some are Stronger, and Tougher, as not easily Stretch'd; like as Wyer, or Lute-strings, or Bow-strings, some are so Hard, as they will sooner Break than Stretch, others so Limber, as to Stretch into a Hairs Smallness, which makes them not so Firm nor Steady, but apt to Tremble and Shake, at the least Touch, or Motion of the Air, whenas those that are Hard and Tough, require some Strength to Stir them. The like is with the Nerves and Sinews, those that are Weak and Tender, when Stretch'd, are apt to Move, which is the reason

that many with Standing Long, will so Tremble and Shake, as to be ready to fall to the Ground, the Lower Parts of their Body being not able to bear them up, being as it were, Loose, or Untied, or Over-stretch'd; and this is the reason that when Soft and Delicate Persons take up a great Weight, or hold a Weight something above their Strength, their Arms, or Hands, or Bodies, will be as if they had the Shaking Palsie in them for an hour after, for the Weight did Over-stretch their Sinews and Nerves. But, Madam, I am Troubled with the same Tenderness, insomuch as it is Tiresom to my Life, and certainly the best Remedy will be to endeavour to Strengthen our Sinews and Nerves, only the Mischief will be, that what is good to Strengthen the Sinews and Nerves, is Hurtful, and apt to Obstruct the Liver, Splene, and Veins, so as the Remedy may prove worse than the Disease, for Gluttonous Meats are Good for the Sinews and Nerves, but Nought for Obstructions. But Physicians perchance can tell Remedies, for I that am none may be Mistaken in the Cause, and Ignorant of the Cure, wherefore I will leave you to the Advice of the Learned Practicers, and rest,

Madam,

Your faithful Friend and Servant.

LETTER 157

Madam,

Those that take Exceptions at my Philosophical Opinions, as for Example, when I say there is no such thing as First Matter, nor no such thing as First Power, are either Fools in Philosophy, or Malicious to Philosophy; As for Infinite Power, it is in God, and God hath no Beginning, nor his Power, as being Infinite and Eternal, wherefore there can be no First, or Beginning, either in Quantity or Quality; And as for Matter, or Substance, let it be as is Believed, that Matter, or Substance were made out of Nothing, that is, that God was the First Producer of the Matter that made the World, yet the Power that God Had, and Hath, to make the Matter, was Infinite and Eternal, and the Mattter being in the Infinite and Eternal Power, is also Infinite and Eternal, without Beginning or Ending, so as the Produced hath no more Beginning than the Producer; the like for the Form, Figure and Motion; but to answer every Idle Objection, or to Instruct every Shallow Understanding, were Infinitely Troublesome, and Tedious, if not Impossible; and there are not many that Read and Argue with a Deep Consideration, or Clear Understanding, for when they Argue, they Argue in a

Misty Understanding, which makes many Objections which Reason Stumbles at, and make so many Words, as they Confound Reason and Sense, and when they Read, or Hear any other Argue, or Discourse of Nature, they Read, or Hearken Superficially, rather Listening to the Sound, than Marking, Observing, or Considering the Sense and Reason, or the Ground and Composition; like as those that Barely View a Picture, but Understand nothing of the Art, yet will Censure the Painters Skill, and many times out of a Presumptuous Opinion of their own Understanding, do give a Midas Judgment,[1] Preferring, not only in their Opinion, but in their Commendation, Sign-Posts, or Sign-Pictures, before the Rarest, and most Curious Pieces, Drawn to the Life. But leaving them to their Dull Understanding, and Foolish Judgments, I rest,

Madam,
Your faithful Friend and Servant.

LETTER 158

Madam,
You were pleased to tell me in your last Letter, that the Lady D.M. and you were Fall'n out, about some Speeches she should Speak in your Dispraise, and those, when you were not by to Answer for your self. Truly, Madam, I cannot Imagine what Fault she could perceive in your Ladiship, to Dispraise you, unless Envy have power to make Virtue Vice, Beauty Deformity, and to turn the Graces into Furies; But, Madam, I have often Observed, that Women with Women seldom Agree, for our Sex is so Self-loving, as we cannot Indure a Competitor, much less a Superiour, especially for Beauty, Wit, and Worth; Birth, Title, and Wealth are somewhat Easier to Indure, yet neither so well, but that we are apt to look a Squint upon them that Surpass us therein, and therefore the less Acquaintance we have with each other, the better, unless they be Chosen by an Immaculate, and Pure Sympathy, and Honour Knit the Knot of Friendship, otherwise the more Acquaintance we have, the more Enemies we have; wherefore to Live Quietly, Peaceably, and Easily, is to be Strangers to our own Sex, and to Live Honourably, is to be Strangers to the Masculine Sex, for Masculine Acquaintance most commonly Causes Suspicion, and a Masculine Friendship never fails of an Aspersion;

---

1 Midas said that the music of Pan was superior to the music of Apollo and was subsequently provided with ass's ears.

wherefore a Retired Life is most Happy, as being most Free from Censure, Scandals, Disputes, and Effeminate Quarrels, I mean not Retired from those we have Relation to, as by Nature, Birth, Marriage, Breeding, Obligation, and the like, for that were to be Buried Quick, but to be Retired from those we call Strangers, such as we have no Relation to, or Obligation from; but our Sex is so far from Retirement, as they seek all Occasions, and let no Opportunity slip, by which they can go to Publick Meetings, or Private Visitings, or Home-Entertainments, they will Ruin their Friends, Fortunes, or Fame, rather than Miss, or Want Company. But if this Letter were not written to you, but to another Lady, it were Probable that Lady would become my Enemy upon this Subject, as speaking so much against our Sex; wherefore there is Male-Gossipping, and Male-Brabling as well as Female, and there are more Effeminate Men than Masculine Women, that is, there are few Women so Wise as Men should be, and many Men as Foolish as Women can be; But now you may think me like a Priest of a Parish, that Exclames against his Parishioners Faults, but never Mentions his own, or perhaps hath the same Faults, but thinks to Obscure them by speaking against them in other Persons; And therefore being already sensible of my Fault, in writing so Long a Letter to you, I do Beg your Pardon, only Subscribing my self,

Madam,
Your Ladiships faithful Friend and humble Servant.

LETTER 159

Madam,
You desire me to Explane that Chapter of Atomes, which is before my Book of Philosophical Opinions, but truly I cannot Explane it more Clearly than I have done, which is, that I thought this World could not be made out of Atomes, but if it was made by Atomes, they must be both the Architects and Materials, neither could they do that Work, unless every Atome was Animated with Life and Knowledg, for an Animated Substance is a Living, Knowing Substance, which Life and Knowledg is Sense and Reason; and thus every Atome must have a Body, which is a Substance, and that Substance Sense and Reason, and so Probably Passions and Appetites, as well as Wit and Ingenuity, to make Worlds, and Worlds of Creatures, as also Passions and Appetites that Sympathize and Antipathize, as not only to Create, but to Dissolve the Self-creating Figures, which Sympathy and Antipathy might cause the Continuation of the World, for if they did

alwayes Agree, there would be no Change, and if they did alwayes Disagree, there would be a Confusion. But I have written so much of Atomes, in my Book of Poems, as I cannot well write more of that Small, though Infinite Substance; wherefore leaving them to Better Judgments, Learning, and Rational Arguments than mine, I rest,

> Madam,
> Your faithful Friend and Servant.

LETTER 160

Madam,

You desire me to give my reason why much Cream is apt to make a Cake Heavy, I say, the same reason that much Butter makes Pye-crust Heavy, for it is much Moisture that causes such things to be Heavy, like as Dough is much Heavier than when it is throughly Baked, for the Fire Drying up the Moisture, causes it to be Light; also when the Sun Drinks up the Moisture of the Earth, it causes it to be Dusty, and Dust is Lighter than Water, and much Lighter than Dirt, which is Earth and Water mix'd together, for although Rarified Water is so Light as to Ascend, yet when Water is an United Body, it is Heavy, even so Heavy, as to Descend Weightily; Indeed Vapor one may say is the Dusty Part of Water; but leaving Dust and Water, I return to Cake and Pye-crust, Cream and Butter; the more Cakes and Pies are Baked, the Lighter they will be, and much Lighter, if the Flower be Dried before it is Mix'd, and by reason Cream and Butter are of a very Moist Nature, when there is much of them in Cakes, and such like Meats, it is not easily Dried up, which makes them require so much the more Baking and Working; but many Good Huswifes put the Fault in the Cream and Butter, when it is the Fault of the Oven, and many Impatient Huswives will have their Cake before it is Baked, they will not stay the time, their Appetites being Hotter than their Ovens; but there is an Old Saying, Too much Cost Spoils a Pudding, and in my Opinion, it is too much Hast that Spoils it, for Good Ingredients Well ordered, cannot be Amiss. But, Madam, having had no Practice, I cannot have much Skill in these Meats, and 'tis Probable my Cook can give better Reasons than I can, yet howsoever to Obey your Commands, I have given you my Opinion, and rest,

> Madam,
> Your faithful Friend and Servant.

LETTER 161

Madam,

You desire my Opinion whether there be a Vacuum or not, I have
written of it in my Former Books, as in my Poems, Olio, and
Philosophical Opinions, and cannot write More, nor Better of it, than I
have done there, unless I had more Learning, or Judgment, or Wit, or
Conceptions, or Understanding; but yet to Satisfie you, I'le send you the
same Opinion, or but little different, which is, that if there were no
Vacuum, but that all the Universe were full, only the Gross Bodies
Moved in the Thin Bodies, as is held by many they do, then the Places
of each Solid or Bulky Body must be fitted just to their Measures, and
their Places must be Supplied so, as when they Move, the Liquid, or
Rare Bodies must Contract and Dilate, according to the Motion of
those Bulky Bodies, to fill up their former Places, or following Places,
and to Contract, to make Room and Place for those Solid and Grosser
Bodies, otherwise there would be a Vacuum, or a Stoppage of all
Natural Motions. But I cannot conceive how the Thin or Rare Matter,
can Contract or Dilate, if there be no Vacuum, for to my Reason, there
must be a Space to Dilate, and Contract into, so as the Rare Parts must
be Porous to Contract, and there must be Empty Places, or Space to
Dilate, and if they say the Space or Place is the Place or Space where the
Solid Bodies were in, which they fill up as soon as they Moved out, yet
the Space or Place must be Empty before the Rare Bodies Enter, for
two Bodies cannot be in one Place at one Time, and if the Great, or
Solid Bodies, leave no Places or Spaces, but alwayes Move in Full
Matter, I cannot Imagine how they should Move if all Places be Full,
although they should move in Rare, or Thin Matter, for as I said, the
Thin Matter must be Porous to Contract and Dilate, to make Way, or
Fill up, for if there were not Pores, or Spongy, or Hollow Spaces and
Places, that which is Liquid and Rare would be as Firm as Brass or Glass,
nay more, for those, no doubt, are Porous, for if there were no Vacuum,
every part would be Press'd, and Joyn'd into a Firm Body or Substance,
nay surely there would be great Confusion amongst all the Works of
Nature. But why may not Dilatation and Contraction cause Vacuum to
be sometimes more, and sometimes less? But one would think there
were no Vacuum in Nature, because Nature is Forced, or seems to be
so, as to make Way for Life by Death, as if she had no Room, or Space

for Life, but what was caused by Death. But leaving these Empty and Filling Opinions, I rest,

Madam,
Your faithful Friend and Servant.

LETTER 162

Madam,
Remember, when we were very young Maids, one day we were Discoursing about Lovers, and we did injoyn each other to Confess who Profess'd to Love us, and whom we Loved, and I Confess'd I only was in Love with three Dead men, which were Dead long before my time, the one was Caesar, for his Valour, the second Ovid, for his Wit, and the third was our Countryman Shakespear, for his Comical and Tragical Humour; but soon after we both Married two Worthy men, and I will leave you to your own Husband, for you best know what he is; As for my Husband, I know him to have the Valour of Caesar, the Fancy, and Wit of Ovid, and the Tragical, especially Comical Art of Shakespear; in truth, he is as far beyond Shakespear for Comical Humour, as Shakespear beyond an Ordinary Poet in that way; also he is the Best Lyrick[1] Poet in this Age, nay in my Judgment, in any, for I have seen him make Twenty Songs upon one Theme or Subject, as Music, and not one Song like another; and for Comedies,[2] he Hits, or Meets, or Imitates the Humours of Men so Justly, as he seems to go even with Nature; Indeed he is such a Person, that I Glory more to be his Wife, than Livia to be Augustus's Wife, or had I been Titus's Wife, who was call'd the Delight of Mankind,[3] although I never heard he had any; for in my Opinion he is as Wise a man as Augustus, and of as Sweet a Nature as Titus, all which is my Happiness in any Condition of Worldly Fortune, in which Happiness I know you Rejoyce, and this Rejoyce proves us Inseparable Friends.[4]

---

1   Originally printed as "Heroick." Probably a revision by the author rather than a correction by the printer.

2   Ann Barton agrees about the value of the comedies. She writes that William's *The Variety* has "social implications more complex than *Everyman in His Humour*" (*Ben Jonson: Dramatist* [Cambridge: Cambridge University Press, 1984] 301).

3   Cavendish echoes Philemon Holland's translation of Suetonius (1606). Holland writes that Titus was "the delightful joy of all mankind."

4   There is no formal closing for this letter.

LETTER 163

Madam,

You were pleased to desire me to let my Steward receive five hundred Pounds for you here in this Town, but you must have a little Patience, for they will pay no Mony, although it be Due, until these Christmass Holy-dayes be past, I know not whether they are so Strict as to Receive none, methinks they should be apt to Take, for they are all busie in Entertainments, Eating, Drinking, and Feasting; but I observe some things which I wonder at, *viz.* that Mony should pass, or move so Slowly in Matters or Affairs of Right and Due, as Debts, Rewards, and Gratitudes, or concerning Honour, as Generosity, or for Heaven's sake, as Charity, whenas in Causes of Injustice and Wrong, as in Bribes, or Wars, or for Vice and Vanity, as for Unlawful Love, Gaming, Drinking, Gluttonous Feasting, Vain shews, and Superfluous Bravery, it runs about with that Swift Speed, that there is no Catching hold of, as to Stay it; but it seems to be the Minds of Men that hold it from going forth to Good and Noble Uses, and the Appetites of Men that make it run to Base, Wicked, Vain, and Foolish Imployments, so that we may perceive that the Appetites have more Power to do Evil, than the Mind hath Will to do Good. But, Madam, my Will hath a Mind to Serve you, although I have not Means, nor Power to do it, yet in what I can, your Ladiship shall alwayes find me,

Your most faithful Friend and Servant.

LETTER 164

Madam,

In your last Letter you writ, that your Imployment was to read the History of King Charles the First, written by S.A.[1] give me leave to tell you, Madam, you lose your time in reading that History, for it is only a number of Weekly Gazets Compiled into a History, wherein are more Falshoods than Truth, for he being Mean and Poor, had not Wealth nor Power to Inform himself Truly of every Particular Action, much less of their Designs; but you tell me, he mentions an Entertainment my Lord made the King,

---

1 S.A. is Sir William Sanderson, who wrote *A Compleat History of the Life and Raigne of King Charles* (London, 1658). According to the *DNB*, Sanderson relied heavily on newspaper accounts and was frequently inaccurate.

where he sayes it cost 5000 l.[1] or thereabout, Condemning another Writer of the same Subject, for saying it cost more; let me tell you, Madam, that neither of them was my Lords Steward, nor Treasurer, to know the Expences, but only what they have heard Reported; and therefore in this I cannot say S.A. writes False nor True, for it is a Mistake, for when the King went into Scotland to be Crown'd, in the Way he was pleased to take a Dinner at one of my Lords Houses, namely Welbeck, which cost between four and five thousand Pounds, and the next Summer following, as I heard my Lord say, the King sent him word, that he and the Queen would make a Progress into the Northern Parts, and Liking his former Entertainment, he Desired my Lord should do the like, which he Obey'd, for, whenas the King came with his Queen thither, my Lord, to shew his Love, Duty, and Loyalty, made them an Entertainment, as one Dinner, and a Banquet, that cost fifteen thousand Pounds Sterling, at his House at Bolesover, which is five Miles from the former House call'd Welbeck, which Entertainment it seems S.A. Mistook, setting down the first for the last, or for both; but this is not the only Mistake in his History, for there are many, and not only Gross Mistakes, but very False Relations, which I can Prove; as for Example, concerning the Wars in the Northern Parts, I know every Particular from the Chief Actor, which was my Lord, and he is a most True Speaker, as being both a Noble Person, and a Just, and Honest man, which all that know him must, if Conscience speaks, witness for him. But, Madam, you desire me to ask my Lord concerning his Army, *viz.* the Number, and by what Power he rais'd so many men, as also of the several Successes, and how many several Armies were against him, I desire you will pardon me, if I do not send you a Relation, by reason I intend to Write the History of my Lord's Life,[2] if I live, and he pleases to Inform me, as he hath promised he will, in which History I intend to Write all the Several Passages, and Particular Actions of the Wars in those Parts, where my Lord was the Chief for the King, as being General to Command all the Kingdom of that side, and I will Write it Truly, Honestly, and Uprightly,

---

1 The accounting put forth by Cavendish is supported by derisive remarks composed by Edward Hyde, earl of Clarendon. "Such excess of Feasting, as had scarce ever before been known in England, and would be still thought very prodigious, if the same Noble Person, had not, within a year or two afterwards, made the King and Queen a more stupendous Entertainment." *History of the Rebellion*, Vol. I (Quoted from A.S. Turberville, *A History of Welbeck Abbey and Its Owners* [London: Faber, 1938] 49). The two royal visits were capped with entertainments composed by Ben Jonson.

2 *The Life of William Cavendish, Duke of Newcastle* (1667) goes into great detail about William's part in the Civil Wars. It was taken to be accurate by such serious contemporary historians as John Rushworth.

without any Aggravation, or Feigned Illustration, for my Lord and I believe that the Chief Principle of Religion, Honour, and Honesty, is Speaking Truth, and Doing Justly in all our Actions, and I take Heaven to witness, that I have Observed in him, and Found in my self, not so much as an Inclination to do otherwise, but alwayes a Delight and Pleasure in Truth and Right; But, Madam, to return to speak of General Histories, they are for the most part mere Fables, and it is almost impossible they should be otherwise, unless every Particular Author do Write his own Story, nay, those may be False through Vain-glory and Self-partiality, unless they be such Noble and Worthy Persons, as make Justice, Honour, and Honesty, the Ground and Foundation of their Relations upon which they build their Story. And, Madam, by reason you desire some particular Passages and Affairs concerning my Lord's Actions, I shall be the more earnest with him to set some time apart to Declare them to me; in the mean time, I rest,

Madam,
Your faithful Friend and Servant.

LETTER 165

Madam,
As for our Husbands going into their Native Country in a Glorious Condition, as you were pleased to say in your last Letter you were in hope they should do, give me leave to tell you, I hope well of our going into our Native Country, but I doubt of the Glory, for our Noble Husbands Losses will Eclipse that Splendor, for we shall only find Ruins, meet with Opposers, and have Debts Attend upon us;[1] 'tis true, I believe we shall be in some better Condition in our Return than in our Banishment, but not very much, unless we be Restored to our Lands, and our Losses Repair'd, and our Debts Pay'd, all which I doubt, for it is probable that those Persons that were the First Honest Actors, will be the Last Honest Sufferers; Had our Masculine Friends been as Prudent as Honest, they would have done like to the Old Saying, To be at the Beginning of a Feast, and at the Later end of a War, but our Friends being at the Beginning of the War, will have none of the Feast. But setting aside our Losses, Crosses, and Misfortunes, our National Agreement will make you and me Happy, although they

---

1   As with James Howell, Cavendish presents us with a letter that appears to have been composed in the past but is really a product of the present. Certainly her husband expected that the Restoration would bring him compensation for losses. He was deeply disappointed in these expectations but was careful not to blame Charles II.

Restore not our Husbands to their Riches, for then we shall Enjoy each others Company, where we shall more Freely Converse by Words than we now do by Letters. In the mean time I shall Please my self with the Hopes of that Happiness, and rest,

Madam,
Your faithful Friend and Servant.

LETTER 166

Madam,

I Am sorry to hear that the Lady H.R. should have any Aspersion cast upon the Honour of her Chastity; truly, I do believe she doth not deserve it, but so full of Detraction the World is, that neither Maids, Wives, nor Widows, can Escape their Slandering Tongues, whether Old, Ill favour'd, Poor, or Diseased, much less those that are Young, Beautiful, Rich, and Healthful, nay, not Incloistered Women, which have Vowed Virginity, are free from Slanders, only I believe Sucking Females are not subject to be Mistrusted; and it is not only Men that Slander Women, but one Woman Slanders another, indeed, Women are the Chief Dishonourers of their own Sex, not so much by their Crimes, as by the Reproaches of each other, some through Envy, and some through Jealousie; but 'tis alwayes a certain Rule, that those that are Guilty, will never fail to Accuse the Innocent, thinking it Hides their Faults, or at least Lessens them, in having it thought that all other Women are as Bad as they themselves; some may say, then it is to no purpose to live a Strict Life, since a Cloister cannot secure them from Slandering Tongues; I answer, that Slanders must not Deterr Virtuous Women from a Reserved Behaviour and Course of Life, but these must Endeavour by their Actions and Sober Life, to prove Slanders to be Slanders; and say all Women were Slandered, and none did Escape, yet Heaven forbid that Virtuous Women should be thought Guilty, no, their Virtuous Life will Quit them, and Beget thoughts of Respect and Esteem in every Mind, even in their Enemies, for though Ill-natur'd Minds have Ill-spoken Tongues, yet they cannot Believe what they speak, if they have no Ground, nor Probability for their Belief. Wherefore Women should behave themselves so as to get a Good Belief, if they cannot get a Good Report, but if Women behave themselves so as to cause a Suspicion, they are Justly Served if they be Censured both in Words and Thoughts. And as Virtuous Women Suffer in Report through the Envy, and Jealousie, and the like, of their own Sex, so through the Base

Vain-glory of some Men, who think it an Honour to be thought Servants to Fair Ladies, especially if they be Eminent Persons, Professing in all Companies how much they are in Love with them, and going to every Place or Company they are in, where every Particular will Address himself to one he Pretends to be in Love with, and Scrape, and Complement only to her, whereupon the Company straight is apt to imagine she hath given him some Signs or Favours to Incourage his Hopes, for if he had no Hopes, he would Cease or Desist from his Courtships, and he is Pleased they should Think so, although he Knows the contrary; and when he is with his Companions, they will Jest and Sport with his Pretended Amorous Passions, and Name the Lady to him, where-upon he Shrugs, Sighs, and Lifts up his Eyes, Professing himself an Unfortunate Man, but he will Order these Actions so, as to make the Company Believe he is not in Despair. Besides, the very Joyning of a Mans & Womans Names begets in time a Suspicion, especially in those that are Strangers to the Lady, when perchance the Lady Hates that Man worse than Death, out of fear she might Suffer in her Reputation, through his Vain Folly; nay many times such Men will Pretend to be in Love with such or such a Lady, although they have no Acquaintance at all with her; and some are so Basely Wicked, as to Report they have Favours from such and such Ladies, when all is False they say; yet these are most Inferiour Persons, whereas those of the First Description are often amongst the Higher Sort. But then for a Virtuous Womans Comfort, the Reports, or Suspicions that are Raised by such Unworthy Persons, Vanish like the Steam or Breath upon a Glass, which leaves no Stain behind it; for the Base Humour of the Man is soon perceived, and then the Credulous Suspecters and Rash Reporters Condemn the Man, and Extoll the Woman, Scorn the Man, and Honour the Woman, the which Wipes away all Dusty Aspersions;[1] and so I hope will be the Aspersion of the Lady H.R. she is but Clouded for a time, but when those Vaporous Reports are Vanished, she will appear as Pure and Bright as ever she did. But my Concernment for her hath made me forget I was writing a Letter, which should be Brief, wherefore, I pray Pardon me, Dear Madam, and I will promise you the next shall be Shorter, yet my Friendship shall not, for I shall be to the end of my Life,

Madam,
Your Ladiships faithful Friend and Servant.

---

1   Compare views on the subject of aspersions as articulated by Milton's Adam and Eve in Book IX of *Paradise Lost*.

LETTER 167

Madam,

You may Chide me for my Idle, Vain Discourse, when you were last to Visit me, but though I may for Pastime speak Vainly of Vanities, yet I do not make them the Object, or Subject of my Thoughts, nor the Imployment of my Mind, nor do I suffer them to Dwell therein, they may Peep in sometimes, but they are straight Thrust out, as Cheating Deceivers; for should they Visit my Mind often, they would Cause such Troubles and Discontents, with Idle Desires, as my Life would be Unhappy; for though I am Ambitious, yet it is not for such Trifles as Worldly Wealth, Gay Shews, and Empty Titles, but for Inward Worth, Just Actions, and Outward Fame, for which my Endeavours shall never be wanting, as long as my Life doth last, not that I would refuse Fortunes Favours or Bounties, but I am not Covetous of them; the truth is, my Tongue is Vainer than my Heart, and my Outward Ceremonies and Adornments more for the Foolish World, than any Pleasure I take therein, for the World Respects nothing but Golden Out-sides, whereas my Happiness is, that I can be Content with any Fortune, so Heaven would but Spare the Life of my Friends, for Fortune can neither Affright nor Surprize me, although she be so Powerful, as to Advance and Ruin whom she pleases; but though she hath Power over the Body, and Estates of men, yet she hath none over the Souls, or Minds of some men, I say Some, as Wise, and Honest men, for Knaves and Fools alter their Minds according to Fortunes Frowns or Smiles; but my Noble Husband's Constancy and Patience can neither be Altered with the one nor the other, for he is one and the same both in Prosperity and Adversity, by whose Example I have Learn'd Patience, and am Constantly,

Madam,
Your Faithful and Unfeigned Servant.

LETTER 168

Madam,

If the Lady P.R. be as much in Heaven's Favour, as she is in Nature's and Fortune's, she is not only Happy, but Blessed, for Nature hath given her Beauty and Wit, and Fortune hath given her Riches and Honour, and if Heaven give her Grace to Use those Well, she may be Crowned the Glory of her Sex; But as Beauty, Wit, Honour, & Riches, are like Load-stones, to draw Love, Admiration, and Respect, so they draw Envy and Malice; she hath many Suters, but whether they be all Lovers I cannot tell, nay I dare say, she cannot tell whether they be True Lovers or not, yet no doubt but they all Swear they are, for Suters and Courtly Lovers make no Conscience of Oaths; wherefore if she have a Judgment answerable to her Wit, she will chuse a Husband Wisely, and not Fondly, a Man rather for Merit, than Person, or Wealth, for Wit rather than Title; for a Woman that Marries a Fool, a Knave, or a Shark, is as Unhappy as a Man that Marries a Scold, a Whore, or a Slut. But you will say, these three later are only amongst the Meaner Sort of Women; I answer, I wish the Better Sort were free from those Vices; but there be many Cleanly, Patient, and Honest Women that are Poor, and Humbly Born, when those of Higher Birth and Greater Wealth are not so, for all are not Sluts out of Poverty, but through Miserable Covetousness, and some out of Laziness; 'tis true, I never heard Great Persons call'd Scolds, but High Spirits, but the High Spirits have Sharp Tongues; and for Adultery, Idleness and Delicious Feeding is apter to make Wanton Minds in the Better Sort, than Painful Labour, and Spare, or Coarse Diet in the Meaner Sort. But leaving this Discourse, as also the Lady P.R. to her Lovers, and those to their Fortune, I rest,

Madam,
Your faithful Friend and Servant.

LETTER 169

Madam,
You were pleased in your last Letter to tell me, that Learned men are held now in as much Derision and Scorn, as Poets and Souldiers were some twenty years since, 'tis a sign that Ignorance hath gotten the Mastery, and that Learning is beaten out of Schools and Colleges, and 'tis no wonder, since the Protectors of Learning, as Royalty, Nobility, and Gentry, are Beaten out of Power; but these are Punished now, for Undervaluing the Poets and Souldiers, a Poet and a Captain were names of Derision, they would look upon a Poet, as a Poor, Sneaking Fellow, and upon a Commander, as a Man out of Fashion, which was a sign they had lived Long in Peace; indeed, a Poet and a Captain were accounted names of such Reproach, as Men thought it a Disgrace to be seen in their Companies, especially Young Fluttering Gallants, who would Shun them more than the Pox, and your Grave Formalists would cast a Despising Smile on them, and Busie Statesmen did think it were fitter they should

be Banished, than Live in a Commonwealth, although a Commonwealth could neither have Pleasure nor Security without them, and in Danger they would have Desired, nay Flatter'd the Souldiers to Guard them with their Courage, and to Direct, and Advise them with their Skill, also they would have Intreated the Poet to Grace their Triumphs; and if it were not for the Poet, they could neither have Masks to Please their Eyes and Ears, nor Playes to Feed their Thoughts, and Entertain their Time; but though they Despised the Poet, yet they would Steal the Poets Wit, although they could not Steal his Worth, to Court their Mistresses, or to Entertain Visitors: Thus they did Basely Steal, Proudly Scorn, Vainly Despise, Maliciously Detract, Foolishly Laugh at Poets and Souldiers, who yet are Persons that are most Honoured by Renown, and Best Entertain'd by Fame, Fame placing them in the Chiefest Places in her Palace, for Souldiers and Poets are Fames Nobles, and so Greater Men to After Posterity, and more Honoured, than Bare Titles in the Present Age; and of all Degrees there have been and will be Poets and Souldiers, from the Palace to the Cottage, and they are so beloved of Fame, as Fame Advances those whom Poets Favour; but those that do Despise, or give not an Honourable Respect to those Persons wherein lives Wit and Courage, let them Live in Fear, and Die in Oblivion, and I believe your Ladiship will say Amen to it, as not only being a Lover of Merit, but a Possessor, for which I am,

Madam,
our Ladiships Honourer, Admirer, and Servant.

LETTER 170

Madam,
Mistress D.O. and Mistress G.B. were th' other day to Visit me, where Mistress D.O. told for News, that Sir B.C. had Changed his Religion, whereupon G.B. said, she was Sorry for that, for she did verily believe he could not Change for a Better than he formerly Profess'd; then she ask'd D.O. to which Religion he was Turned, for there were but four that ever she could hear of, *viz*. the Gentil, the Jewish, the Christian, and the Mahometan, and, said she, in every one of these Religions were Different Opinions, and those Opinions almost Innumerable, yet they were not Different Religions; wherefore D.O. said she had been Mistaken, for it was only a Different Opinion from the Opinion he Profess'd before; G.B. said that was no wonder, for many did Change their Party for Interest, and it was

to be Observed, that what Opinion a King or Chief Governour did Profess, the most part of their Subjects did the same, and so many Strangers that did but dwell in their Territories, either for Safety, or Traffick, or Example, but Natives Changed out of hope of Preferment, as some for Honours, Offices, and Commands, others to Enjoy their Estates, and to save Fines, or Taxes, or the like, some through Perswasion of Friends, some for Fashions sake, and some for fear of Banishment or Death: Thus some for Fear, and some for Favour, some through Covetousness, and some for Humor, changed their Opinions in Religion, but few for Conscience, and none for Reason, for Opinions in Religion are all built upon Faith, wherein Reason hath no Place, at least no Foundation; but if any Changed for Conscience, said she, it were the Meaner, and most Ignorant sort of People, who are most apt to Fear, for Moral Conscience, said she, is the most Tender Effect of a Fearful Passion, but Divine Conscience is an Effect of Grace, which the Common People hath but little of: Where-upon Mrs. D.O. told Mrs. G.B. that her Discourse proceeded from an Uncharitable Mind; Mrs. G.B. answered, her Discourse proceeded from the Observation of the course of the World, and from the Actions of Mankind, which she thought were the Best Informers of their Inward Dispositions, but if D.O. had Observed otherwise, she desired her to tell; D.O. said, she did not take so much notice of the World of Mankind; then said G.B. you did not well to Judg me; And hereupon D.O. ask'd her of her Opinion, as whether she thought Sir B.C. was not in a Dangerous Condition; G.B. ask'd her, whether she meant Dangerous to his Soul, Body, or Estate; D.O. said, for the Salvation of his Soul; Truly, answered G.B. I do believe, that the Great Omnipotent God is Good, Wise, Powerful, Knowing, Fore-seeing, and Just, as not to Damn a man for that which he could not possibly know, or for that which Nature made him to do, neither was he Ignorant, as not to Fore-see what Man could, or would do, and if Man could do nothing without Gods Permission, Gods Mercy would not Permit, or Suffer Man to Damn himself, for that would be to Make Man to that End, Knowing it before, as Fore-seeing it, and if he gave Man a Free-Will, that were to give away one of his Attributes, and so to make Man Great, and himself Less, and only to Impower Man to Damn himself; or for God to Make Man, and then Damn him, whereby to shew his Power, would neither stand with God's Justice nor Goodness; but certainly God could shew his Power other wayes, than by Damning those Creatures he Made, or Makes; and that God be as much, if not more Glorified by the Damned as by the Blessed, is but an Odd Belief, that Gods Glory should Arise from Torments, as if God had no other way to be Glorified, this would not Express Justice so much as Severity, if not Cruelty, as first, to Fore-see the Evil, then to make the Creature, and at last to Suffer that Evil, and to Damn the Creature for the Evil; neither, said she, can that Rational Part that God hath given me, perceive how it can stand with his Goodness and Mercy, or his Wisdom and Glory, to Suffer more Devils, than to Make Saints; neither doth it stand with his Wisdom and Power, to have more Enemies than Friends, for Wicked men and Devils are said to be the Enemies, and Good men and Saints to be the Friends, and Servants of God; but most Men have Blasphemous Opinions, as to make God either Cruel, or Ignorant, as not to Fore-know, or else to Make to Damn. But the Lady W.N. who was also Present at their Discourse, prayed Mrs. G.B. to Break off, since Man was so Ignorant, as he Knew not himself, yet would Pretend to Know God, and his Attributes, Counsels, Laws, Rules, and Decrees, also whom he Loved, and whom he Hated, who should be Damned, and who should be Saved, what Angels were in Heaven, and what Devils in Hell, who Served him a Right, and who Served him a Wrong way; also Man is so Presumptuous, as to Assimilize God, as also to Pretend to know what God sayes, making him to Speak like Man; also to Express him to have Passions; but if God be Absolute, and Incomprehensible, it is an High Presumption to Assimilize God to any Creature; besides, it is Absurd and Ridiculous to Compare that which is Incomprehensible, for if he cannot be Conceived, how shall he be Express'd? Also to say God's Goodness and Humanity is such, as to Bow to Man, since Man cannot Fully, or Knowingly Rise to Him, for 'tis Ridiculous to think that God's Great Omnipotency, or Incomprehensibility, can either Bow, Submit, or Humble it self; for God cannot Lessen himself, no more than Heighten himself, for he cannot be More nor Less, there are no Degrees in God, nor Contractions, nor Dilatations, for he is all Fulfilling; Indeed he is that which no Creature can tell, but something that is too Great and Mighty to be Declared, his Works are only a Glimpse of his Might; yet Proud Men call themselves God's Friends; O Foolish and Conceited Men! O Great and Incomprehensible God! Thus, Madam, I write the Several Discourses which these three Ladies had, by which Relation, I, and my three Visitors, have as it were, Visited you; but lest our too long Stay should be Troublesome, I take my leave for this time, and rest,

Madam,
Your faithful Friend and Servant.

LETTER 171

Madam,

My Life is so Solitary, my Mind so Peaceable, my Thoughts so Quiet, and my Senses so Lazy, as I have nothing to write to you, but to tell you I am Well, and I hope you are so too, according to the Old fashion'd Style of Letters. 'Tis true, if my Life were Active, my Mind Busie, or Factious, my Thoughts Wandring, my Senses Inquisitive, I might find out some Subject, or make some Business to write, but since I am neither Factious, Busie, Inquisitive, nor Active, my Letters will be like a Bladder fill'd with Wind, and not like a Bag fill'd with Gold or Silver; or they will be like Paper that is only fill'd with Cifres, without any Figures; But although my Letters may be as Cifres, yet you, to whom I write, are the Chief Figure in my Thoughts, which Expresses Thousands; indeed, you are as Infinite it self, for your Merits are Numberless, and there is no End of your Goodness, for which Eternal Happiness will be your Reward in Heaven; But, Madam, I love my self so well, as I would not have you there yet, for I would have you in this World as long as I Live, which without you would seem to me as the Description of the Infernals, whereas now your Life is as an Heaven to my Life, which is the Joy and Happiness,

Madam,
Of your Faithful Servant.

LETTER 172

Madam,

I Am so full of Fear, as I write this Letter with great Difficulty, for all this City hath been in an Uproar, and all through a Factious Division betwixt the Common Council, and those they call the Lords, which are the Higher Magistrates, the Common People gather together in Multitudes, Pretending for the Right of their Privileges, but it is thought the Design is to Plunder the Merchants Houses, and the Churches, by the last they seem to Regard, and Covet more the Goods of the World than Heaven;[1] indeed the World makes men apt to Forget Heaven, as loving Mammon more than God; the truth is, they have Plunder'd one of the Chief Magistrates, and were hardly kept from Plundering the Bishop, which Act Expresses their Covetousness, and Divulges their Designs; and this

---

1 Grant discusses the incident but does not identify it (138–39).

Disorder causes the Trumpets to Sound, the Drums to Beat, the Souldiers to Arm, and the Women to Weep, and to make it the more Fearful, the Great Bell, which is only Rung in time of Danger, either in cases of Fire, or War, or Mutinies, or the like, sounds Dolefully, all which makes me Tremble Fearfully, and that which increases my Fear the more, is, that my Maids being possess'd with the like Fear, come often to me with Masker'd Faces, and tell me Divers, and Different Reports, some, that the Army is coming to Destroy the City, and others, that the Souldiers have liberty to Abuse all the Women, others, that all in the City shall be put to the Sword; the Best Report is, that all shall be Plunder'd, but for this last, my Husband and I am safe, for we are Plunder-Free, having had all our Goods and Estate taken from us in our own Country, so that now we have no such Goods or Wealth as is worth the Taking; the truth is, we are rather in a Condition to Plunder, than to be Plunder'd, so that if they will but spare our Persons and Lives, I fear not our Goods, the only Misery is, that we cannot well go out of this City, by reason we have here some Credit to take up Monies, or Provisions, in time of Necessity, for my Husband hath Lived here so Long, as he can Challenge the Privilege of a Burger, and therefore we may rise up with the Tumult, and cry out Mutinously for our Rights and Privileges. But for all this I am Extremely Afraid, insomuch that at every Noise I hear, if I be not with my Husband, I run to find him out, so that I write this Letter but by Starts, yet my Husband endeavours to Allay my Fears, telling me, that the Beating of Drums, and Blowing of Trumpets, and Arming of Souldiers, is the Way and Means to Quiet this Mutiny, and to keep us in Peace and Safety, but for all that, I hear my Husband say, that it is a Scurvy Business, and a Dangerous Example; Howsoever, I leave all to his Prudence and Care; for I believe, if he did perceive any great Danger, he would Remove me out of the City, but then he must Go with me, for I will not Part from him, regarding not my Safety when he is in Danger, and I had rather Die with him than Live after him. But, Madam, hoping the next Letter to you will be more Comfortable, and that all will be as Quiet and Peaceable as it was, I rest,

Madam,
Your faithful Friend and Servant.

Madam,

You were pleased in your last Letter to Express how the Lady C.D.[1] did read some of M.Ns.[2] Playes, and that she read the Passionate Sad Parts so Whiningly, that where it should have moved Compassion, it caused an Aversion; Truly, Madam, Women for the most part, Spoil all Good Writing with Ill Reading, and not only Women, but most Men, for I heard a Man who was a Great Scholar,[3] and a Learned Man, having Read much, and one that Pretended to be a Good Poet, and Eloquent Orator, Read Mr. W.Ns.[4] Excellent Works quite out of Tune and Time, neither Humouring the Sense nor Words, but always persisting in the same Tune, which was Dull, and Flat, and made my Sense of Hearing as Dull as his Reading, but yet it was better than if he had made a greater Noise in his Reading, for that would have put me beyond all Patience, Grating, or Wounding my Ears, which would have Discomposed my Thoughts extremely, for my Thoughts live so Peaceably and Silently, and take such Delight therein, as they Hate a Noise; but in truth I never heard any man Read Well but my Husband, and have heard him say, he never heard any man Read Well but B.J.[5] and yet he hath heard many in his Time, but I know my Husband so Well, that he is like Skilful Masters of Musick, which can Sing and Play their Parts at the first Sight, so my Husband at the first Reading will so Humor the Sense and Words of the Work, as if he himself had Made, and Writ it, nay, I have heard him Read some Works, that have been but Mean and Plain Pieces, so Well, as to give a Grace to the Author, and to make his Work Sound Harmoniously, like as an Ill Instrument Well Played on, whereas others put Rare Instruments out of Tune; wherefore knowing the Difference, as what Harmony or Discord Reading makes, I am so Affected with fear of Unskilful Readers for my Poor Works, as when I Look upon them, I cannot choose but Mourn for their Danger of Disreputation; yet to Pacifie my Grief, I imagine that every several Person likes his own way of Reading Best, and so will not Dislike my Writing, for want of Well

---

1 The lady C.D. is probably Christiana, countess of Devonshire, a cousin by marriage of William Newcastle, who lived nearby at Chatsworth.

2 Margaret Newcastle (i.e., Cavendish).

3 Philosopher Thomas Hobbes, who was tutor to Cavendish's children.

4 William Newcastle, the husband of Cavendish.

5 Ben Jonson, dramatist and a friend of William Newcastle's from the 1620s and 1630s.

Reading. But for Fear I should Anger your Patience to Read so Long a Letter, I take my leave, and rest,

Madam,
Your Faithful Friend and Servant.

LETTER 174

Madam,
The Lady F.N. and her Pretty Young Daughter had th' other day a Quarrel, insomuch as her Mother intended to Whip her, but she Disputed so well for her self, as her Mother Forgave her Fault, and the chief Cause of the Forgiveness was, that she told her Mother, she had rather be Racked as a Traitor, than be Whip'd as a Slave, although, said she, I have neither Committed Treason, nor Deserved Thraldome or Slavery; besides, said she, I am Ten years of Age, too Old to be Whip'd, almost Old enough for an Husband; but whilst the Daughter and Mother were Disputing, in came the Father, and Sir W.S. who found her Weeping, but they Comforted her, saying, they came Purposely to Save her; she told them, that as long as she was in her Mothers Power, she was subject to be Whipped; Sir W.S. asked her, if she would Live with him, since she was Displeased with her Mother; she said, yes, if he pleased to take her; but her Father said, he would not Agree to that, unless he would make her his Wife; Sir W.S. said, she was too Young for a Wife;[1] the Father told him, that Three or Four years would make her Old enough; he said, not for him, for he would neither be a Nurse, nor a Tutor, for he knew Women were not Capable to be Instructed, until they were Thirteen or Fourteen years of Age, and then they must have some time to Learn, Seven years at least, neither can they Keep themselves as they ought; but when I Marry, said he, I will Marry a Wife of such an Age, as hath been Instructed both to know Good and Evil, to know Evil by Relation, and Good by Practice; such a one as can be a Companion, and is not a Nursling; such a one as can Converse Rationally, and not one that can speak a Witty Word or two by Chance, as Children do; such a one as may bring me Strong, Healthful Children, not Children that will be Children all the time of their Lives, if they Live, as being Infirm, Weak, and Sickly; or else do Die as

---

1 Margaret and William Cavendish were friends of John and Mary Evelyn. John had wed Mary when she was eleven and William composed wry verses on the topic of John and his young wife for that occasion. For a transcription, see James Fitzmaurice, "The Cavendishes, the Evelyns, and Teasing in Verse and Prose."

soon as they are Born, and from the Womb, go into the Grave; and to have a Wife that is fit for Breed and Conversation, she must be Two or Three and Twenty at least; the truth is, said he, I had rather Marry a Wife of Fourscore, than of Fourteen, for I could take more Content to Admire Antiquity, or to Listen to an Aged Sybil, or Read in an Old Chronicle, than to Play with a Baby, to Listen to a Parrat, or to Read the Horn-book, there being so much Difference between Youth and Age; but when I Marry, said he, I will Marry a Wife that's near to my own Age, for if I Marry a Wife much Younger than my self, I shall be Jealous of her, and if I Marry one much Older than my self, my Wife will be Jealous of me, so as we shall be Unhappy either wayes; besides, in Unequal Ages Men and their Wives are apt to Upbraid one anothers Age, but when their Age is Equal, neither hath Cause to Dislike each others, and for the most part in Equal Ages are Equal Loves, and Fearless Lives, as neither of them is Jealous, and if we have Equal Strength and Constitutions, we shall not Out-live one another Long, nor Wish one anothers Death, nor grow Weary of one anothers Life; but I will, if you will Consent, Keep your Daughter as a Baby, or a Toy for a Closet, but not take her for a Wife, to Govern my House and Family; by my Faith, said her Father, she shall be no Toy, if I can help it, but if you will take her for a Wife, I will give her ten Thousand Pound, and if I have no more Children, I will Double, or Treble it; said Sir W.S. I am Content, for though she be too Young to Govern my Family, I am Old enough to Dispose of her Wealth, and for Society and Conversation, I know no better Companion, no better Governour, nor no better Friend than Mony, it is Beloved of every one, but Loves no man, so as I shall not Fear Mony will Cuckold me, it will rather Bawd for me, and so for Love to Mony I will take your Daughter to Wife; Whereat her Father said he should have her, and so much Mony too. And so leaving them to Conclude the Match, I rest,

Madam,
Your faithful Fr. and S.

LETTER 175

Madam,
In your last Letter you Advised me to Write a Book of Orations,[1] but how should I Write Orations, who know no Rules in Rhetorick, nor

---

1   *Orations* by Cavendish was published in 1662.

never went to School, but only Learn'd to Read and Write at Home, Taught by an Antient Decayed Gentlewoman whom my Mother kept for that Purpose? which my Ill hand (as the Phrase is) may sufficiently Witness; yet howsoever, to follow your Advice, I did try to Write Orations, but I find I want Wit, Eloquence, and Learning for such a Work, and though I had Wit, Eloquence, and Learning, I should not find so many Subjects, to Write so many Orations as will Fill a Book, for Orations for the most part, are concerning War, Peace, and Matters of State, and Business in the Commonwealth, all which I am not Capable of, as being a Woman, who hath neither Knowledg, Ability, nor Capacity in State Affairs, and to Speak in Writing of that I Understand not, will not be Acceptable to my Reading Auditors: Nevertheless, to let you see how Powerful your Perswasions are with me, I will send you those two or three Orations I have Written for a Trial, if you Approve of them, I will Write as many as I can find Subjects to make Orations of, and if I can get so many as will make a Book, I will set them forth in Print, although I have no Hopes, nor Confidence in that Work, for I fear it will be Lost Labour, and Wast Time; but I am in all Times,

Madam,
Your faithful Friend and Servant.

LETTER 176

Madam,
Some Ladies th' other day did Visit me, and in their Discourse they spoke of the Duke of D. the Marquess of C. the Earl of F. and Vicount G. but I observed that in their Discourse they only gave them the Title of a Lord;[1] 'Tis true, a Lord is a Noble Title, but yet the fore-mentioned Titles be of Higher Degrees, by which they ought to be Mentioned or Named; truly, in my Opinion, those Men or Women that do not give every Person their Highest Titles, are either Ill-bred, Foolish, or Spiteful, for it is through Envy, or a Low, Base Nature, to Detract, or Take from any one his Just Rights and Dues, but Noble, Generous, and Heroick Persons, will rather give more than what is Due, than Lessen ones Due Rights, which shews, such Persons have more Civility than others have Justice; the truth is, it is a kind of a

---

1 Both Cavendish and her husband took titles seriously and made remarkable gains in status during their lives. His claim to being a prince and hers to being a princess are sometimes ridiculed but are supported by a letter from the Garter-King-at Arms (*Historical Manuscripts Commission*, Part II, *Portland Papers*, vol. 2, 142).

Cosenage, or Theft, to keep back the best Part of a Title, as to mention several Degrees of Men, and not to give them their due Titles of Honour; but if they should be so Uncivil to Knights and Doctors, as to Dukes, Marquesses, Earls, and Viscounts, there would be many Quarrels in this Nation; for a Knight would take it for an Affront to be call'd Master, and not Sir, and so a Doctor; but the most Ridiculous thing in this Nation is, that when any one asks a Poor Tradesman, as a Cobler, he will say, Pray Sir how doth your Lady? or, Remember my Service to your Lady, meaning the Coblers Wife, which is as much in Extremes this way as th' other; But this Nation is apt to Run into Extremes, in which I leave them, and rest,

Madam,
Your faithful Friend and Servant.

LETTER 177

Madam,
You were pleased to Tell or Express in your last Letter, that I was Accused for some Words I had spoken concerning G.K. and L.O.[1] which Words were Prejudicial to their Great Affairs, and Dangerous Designs, as Doubting their Successes, and Slighting their Proceedings; I confess I did Doubt of their Successes, and did not Approve of their Proceedings, but yet I did not Slight them, for then I should not have Mentioned them; and truly those Words I Spoke, were not through an Evil Design, or a Malicious Nature, but out of a Deep Consideration of the Evil that was likely to Ensue both to their Honour, and Disadvantage of their Affairs, and the Present and Future Condition of their most Approved Friends and Faithful Servants; and as for Doubting their Successes, indeed my Fear was the Ground of my Doubts, for perceiving no Visible Power, yet hearing of Present Action and Dangerous Adventures, and Hazard of their Persons, it made me rather Fear a Treachery, than Hope for a Victory, and I Declared my Opinion, by reason I had a near Relation to them, hoping it might make them Circumspect, and Cautious in their Adventures, as to Consider

---

1   L.O. could be the stepson of Cavendish, Henry, who was styled Lord Ogle. It is possible that G.K. is an anagram involving Kingston, i.e., Henry Pierrepont (Ogle's brother-in-law). Sara Heller Mendelson believes that the letter is a defense by Cavendish of herself after she became entangled in a secret mission to England undertaken in February of 1658. William was "rebuked by Hyde and the King.... but the chief blame was attached to Margaret for her presumptuous interference" (*The Mental World of Stuart Women: Three Studies* [Amherst: U of Massachusetts P, 1987] 39–40). Mendelson does not attach names to L.O. and G.K.

their own Weakness, and their Enemies Power, and not Rashly to Venture Hand over Head, or rather Heels over Head, but to let Wisdom Counsel before Courage Fights, for though Hellish Furies, or Spiteful Fortune, may Disturb Human Wisdom for a time, yet Human Wisdom constantly Followed, doth Charm Hellish Furies in the End, Binding them within a Circle of Fear, and it makes Fortune's Wheel turn to Wisdoms own Bias; but had I Spoken Harsh, or Sharp words, they might well Forgive me, because Love and not Hate Produced them, for many times False Hearts Produce Dissembling Words, in a Flattering Style, whenas a True Heart sends forth Stormy Words, being Driven out by a Violent Passion of Fear; wherefore I Appeal to their Justice to Acquit me from an Evil Construction of my Good Intention. Neither were these Words Spoken in a Publick Assembly, but in my Private House, and to some Particular Persons, and every ones House is, or should be a Privileged Place, out of which Informers ought to be Banished, rather than the Owners Condemned or Accused; but what I said, I desired should be Told, for the Reasons before Mentioned, that my Opinion or Words might Alter their Designs, for I did not desire my Words should be according to the Old Saying, A Private Speech in a Sleepy Ear. But sometimes some may Speak so, as not only to desire their Speech should lie in a Sleepy Ear, but to be Buried under a Silent Tongue, & those Speeches ought not to be Digged up by the Memory, lest their Wandring and Restless Ghosts, or Spirits (for Words are Incorporeal) should Affright the Present Times, or some Particular Persons, which, if their Incorporalities were not Molested with Repetitions, would Rest Quietly in the Pit or Grave of Oblivion; but if I have said any Words that have Displeased those Persons you Mention, which are my Dear and Near Relatives, pray them to Pardon me, since it was a Superfluity of Love, which Overflow'd the Banks of Discretion, and made my Words Float on the Seas of Affection, without the Ballast of Judgment, or Guide of Prudence, which being Tossed on the Billows of Fear, and Storms of Imaginary Danger, I am likely to be Drown'd in Sorrow and Tears, as being Driven against their Displeasures, unless their Friendship and near Relation Save me, and bring me to the Harbour of their Favour, which my Faith tells me they will, or otherwise tell them I will never Believe them more; But howsoever, I rest,

Madam,
Your faithful Friend and Servant.

LETTER 178

Madam,

I shall not Trouble you now to buy the Round of Feathers that came out of France, for I have one made here in this Town both Cheaper and Better than those were; but I have sent as many several Messages, or Letters, concerning the Cap and Feathers, as I have heard a Lady did to her Husband, being in the Chief City, and she in the Country, who sent to him to buy her a Hat and Feather, the next Week she sent to buy her a Hat, but not a Feather, the third Week, to buy her a Feather but not a Hat, the fourth Week she would have neither Hat nor Feather; but I have bought a Cap, and many Feathers, not only that they are in Fashion, but for Use, for the Hanging, or Falling Feathers shadow my Face from the Burning Sun, and Fan a Gentle Air on my Face, that Cools the Sultry Heat, so that were it not a General Fashion, it should be my Particular Fashion in Summer time; Indeed, Feathers, in my Opinion, Become Women better than Men, for Women are more of the Nature of Birds than Beasts, not only for their Hopping and Dancing, which Resembles Flying, but because they are more Useless Creatures, for most Birds are of no Use but to Sing, and some to Prate, they are neither Useful for Labour nor War, as most Beasts are; 'tis true, Vulturs, Ravens, Crows, and such like Birds, will be at the end of a Battel, but 'tis only to Feed on the Dead Carcasses slain in the Battel, like those that Feed on the Slanders of their Sex; Also Feathers are Light, not for Shining, but in Weight, and so Women have Light Natures; Feathers are Unsteady and Restless, so are Women both in Body and Mind; indeed Feathers and Muffs are not so Seemly for Men as for Women, for how can a Man Guide his Horse, or Use his Sword, when his Hands are in a Muff? yet it was all the Fashion the last Winter for Men to wear Muffs, tied to a long String about their Necks, the Muffs hanging at the lower end of the String, and when they had an Occasion to lay by their Muffs, they flung them behind their Backs, which seems like as Poor, Beggarly Souldiers Knapsacks, or as Tinkers Budgets, and the String about their Neck seems like as if they were going to be Hang'd for Stealing some Bread and Cheese, or for Robbing an Apple-Orchard, or for Stealing Ragged Linnen off the Hedges, or some such Petty, or Worthless things; But Men are as Inconstant in their Fashions as Women, if not more, so as it is to be hoped they will Change to a more Manly Fashion than Muffs, and a more Handsome Fashion than Boot-hose tied up to their short Breeches, which Boot-hose about the Knees appear like Wens, and Swell'd Sores ready to be Lanced, to let out the Corruption that is Gathered therein; truly, to me it would appear more seemly for Women to wear Swords, than Men to wear Muffs, for Women, though Weak, and Unskilful to Handle and Use a Sword, yet had they Courage, they might make a shift to Assist an Assaulted Friend, or to Protect their Honour against Violation, whenas a Muff doth as it were Tie up a Mans Hands, and is a Hinderance either to Assault or Defend. But Women have no Occasion to wear Swords, for they are Protected by the Civil Laws of all Nations, besides, all Noble Gentlemen are Guards to the Female Sex, and for the Assistance of Friends, there be few that are Assaulted in their own Houses, and Women are not suffered to Fight in the War; neither are they Chosen for Seconds, nor is it fit they should be in Drunken Quarrels; and as for Thieves, it is an Old Saying, Thieves are too Strong for True men, for Thieves will seldom Assault One, under Two or Three, not but that Women ought to do their Endeavour to Assist a Friend in Distress, though they were sure to do them no Good, but their striving to Help must do them no Hurt, by hindering them to Help themselves; as for Example, some Women that see an Enemy Assault their Husbands, Sons, Father or Brother, or are by when they Quarrel with any other Man, will in a Fright take hold of their Friends, thinking to Pull them from Hurt, whenas that holding may be the Cause of their being Kill'd, as not being suffered to Defend themselves. Thus may their Loving Fear be the Cause of their Death; but I have wandered too far, from Feathers and Women, to Swords and Death; wherefore leaving all to Fates and Fashions, I rest,

> Madam,
> Your faithful Friend and Servant.

LETTER 179

Madam,

I Hear by your last Letter, that the Lady H.W. doth Entertain a Maid-servant that hath lately Served in my House, and therefore desires you to write to me, to send her word whether she was a Good Servant when she Served me, and whether she was Trusty and Chast; first, she must Excuse me, for I will not Dispraise a Servant out of my Service, unless it were as a Punishment to some Notorious Faults; for Servants may be Better and Worse in Several Services, according to the Several Imployments, or Places, or Labours they are Imployed in; for some Servants may be very Proper and Fit, Industrious, and Prudent in some sorts of Places or Labours, as to be

Excellent Servants, and in others be very Ill Servants, so as it may be the Fault of the Master or Mistress not to Imploy them Properly, or that perhaps such Places which are Proper for such a Servant are Supplied; and perchance a Servant may See his own Errours, and Repent the Faults Committed in one Service, as not to do the like in another, so as it may be Injustice for a Master or Mistress to Dispraise a Servant, which may prove to his Ruin, as to hinder him from a Good Service; Neither ought a Master or Mistress to give a Servant an Undeserved Praise, for that were to speak Untruth, besides, it would be a Cheat to Prefer a Servant with a False Report, or to Cozen a Master with a Servants Undeserved Praise, like as Tradesmen do put off Ill Commodities upon their Word, that they are Good, and the Buyer relying upon the Sellers Word, as believing him to be a True Speaker, is Cozened; nay, if the Wares be Good, Praise is their Due, but yet Sellers must Speak their Praise but of that which they have found Good and Serviceable in them; wherefore the best way is to let every Master or Mistress prove their Servants by their Services. The next is, the Lady H.W. would know whether she be Trusty and Chast? As for Trust, I Intrust my Servants as Little as I can, but just what of Necessity I must, for there is an Old Saying, that in Trust lies Treason, and I will not Tempt, or Inable them to be Traitors, if I can Avoid it; As for the Chastity of my Servants, I do not Inquire what Constitution they are of, but what Service they are fit for in my Houshold Affairs; neither am I Porter, or Spy of my Maids Lower Parts, it is too Foul an Office or Imployment for any Mistress; but if I hear they do not Demean themselves as Good and Honest Servants ought, in an Honourable, Govern'd House, they have Warning to be Gone, paying them such Wages as their Bargain was. But the truth is, though my Husband is pleased to make me Mistress of his House & Houshold-servants, yet I seldom take any Servants, or turn them away, for I have an Under-Officer as my Lieutenant-General, which is the Governess of my House, & she receives my General Orders, and Executes the Particular Housholds Affairs, which belongs to the Government of a Mistress that hath a Master, which is a Husband. This, Madam, I have Related to you, although I think you well Know it your self, and may Relate it to the Lady H.W. and so taking my leave of you for this time, I rest,

Madam,
    Your Ladiships faithful Friend and Servant.

LETTER 180

Madam,

Here is a Lady in this City, who is the only Child of her Parents, and so Handsom, that when we came first hither, she was Gazed on as much as if she had been a Blazing Star, and those Churches she did Frequent were alwayes the Fullest of People, which seems, they went to Church rather to See than to Pray, more for the Admiration of a Creature, than for Devotion to the Creator, and it shews, she was the only Saint that was Regarded, for thus she was Admired and Followed; but as Blazing Stars soon Vanish, so Beauty soon Fades, although her Beauty was likely to Last, being more in Favour than Colour, for indeed she had Extraordinary Well-favour'd and Pleasing Features in her Face, but now they are Alter'd, & that in Few Years, which shews, Time was more Spiteful & Mischievous to her Face, than it Usually is to others, & as Time was Spiteful to her, so was also Fortune, for she is yet Unmarried, and begins now to be Melancholy, some say, for want of a Husband; for indeed most Maids account it a great Misfortune to live Long Unmarried, it seems they Know not, or will not Believe the Cares and Troubles that Accompany a Married Life; but perchance her Melancholy may proceed from the Decay of her Beauty, seeing her self Neglected, and not Regarded, for now when she goes to Church, not anybody takes a Particular Notice of her, by which we may observe, that Flourishing Beauties are like as Flourishing Favorites, Admired, Flattered, and Followed for the time they are in Favour; or like Conquering Generals, being Famous whilst they gain Victories, but if Fortune Frowns, they are Neglected, if not Despised, the like for Beauty when Faded; and Fortune for the most part is an Enemy to Beauty, for she doth not so often Advance the Owners, as those that are but Indifferent. But leaving Beauty to Youth, and the Lady to her Parents Care, to get her a Rich, and Good Husband, I rest,

Madam,
Your faithful Fr. and S.

LETTER 181

Madam,

The Lady B.D. was th' other day to Visit me, and whilst she was with me in came the Lady A.B. whose Hair is as White as Snow, not White by Birth, but by Time; yet her Face appears Young, which is a Wonder; but some Persons Hairs will turn White, before their Years grow Old; but whether she be Old, or in her Autumn, or Young, I will not Question, yet she made a Graceful Show, and to my Fancy seem'd very Handsom, and her Gray Head Became her Well, for she had Curled her Gray Hair as Curiously as the Youngest Woman could have done, and certainly the Lady B.D. thought she appear'd too Handsome, for I never saw any Woman appear more Envious or Spiteful in my Life, both in Countenance, Behaviour, or Words, than the Lady B.D. did against the Lady A.B. and the Lady A.B. perceiving the Lady B.D. not to be in a Good Humour, endeavoured to Gain her Favour with all the Obliging Civilities she could, but all would not do; by which we may perceive, that nothing can Cure or Abate that Peevish, and Self-loving Humour, as to desire to be Absolute above the rest of our Sex, but a Self-denial caused by a Heavenly Grace Infused into the Soul by a Divine Power, to which Divine Power I leave all our Sex, and rest,

> Madam,
> Your faithful Friend and Servant.

LETTER 182

Madam,
I Heard that the Lord D.D. declares he will Challenge the Lord E.E. to Fight a Duel, by which he declares his Present Fear, rather than his Future Intention, otherwise his Neighbours would have heard of his Fighting Actions before they had heard of his Boasting Words: but I suppose Drink Produced those Words, and not his Will; the truth is, Strong Drink, or rather the Vapor of it, is not only apt to Produce Vain Speeches, but Foolish, and sometimes Desperate Actions, for much Drink many times will cause Cowards to Fight, and then Fury Possesses the Room of Fear. But leaving the Lord D.D. to his Intended Duel, I rest,

> Madam,
> Your faithful Friend and Servant.

LETTER 183

Madam,
I Do not Wonder, that those which are Indued and Adorned with the Bounteous Gifts of Nature, should Seek, and Endeavour to Divulge them; the truth is, it were not Fit nor Well, that those Gifts, as Courage, Judgment, Wit, and Beauty, should be Buried in Obscurity; but there are

many that believe through Partial Self-love (for all Mankind have that Love) they are Indued and Adorned with such Gifts, when all their Neighbours and Friends see they are not so much Favoured, but rather Disfavoured with Defects, for each man sees each others Defects, though not their own; But I have Observed, that there is a Disagreeing between Nature and Fortune, for those that Nature Smiles on, for the most part Fortune Frowns on, as if Fortune did Envy Nature's Bounties, for though Destiny and Fate hinders Fortunes Malice sometimes, yet they more often Assist her, or rather Fortune doth Assist them, for Fortune is the Servant to Fate, by which we may perceive, that Nature hath Powerful Opposers, or Over-ruling Potents. But leaving Fate, Destiny, and Fortune, to their Decrees, Power, and Fate, I rest,

Madam,
Your faithful Fr. and S.

LETTER 184

Madam,
You Express'd in your last Letter, that Sir W.N. was to Visit you, and that you fell into a Discourse of the Humours, and Natures of Mankind; the truth is, the Nature of Mankind is like an Endless Labyrinth, past finding out; also you Express'd you fell into a Discourse of Governments, and I can tell you what I have heard of my Husband, viz. that the greatest part of the World of Mankind is Govern'd by Lies and Fables, which is, that all the World is Govern'd by Religion, and there is no Truth certainly but in Christian Religion, why then, all the Heathen, Jews, and Turks, are Govern'd by Lies and Fables, and those are much more than three Parts of the World, which shews that most of Mankind are Fools, and yet all Men think themselves Wise, for although all Mankind are so Ambitious and Covetous, as not to be Satisfied, yet all men are Satisfied with their Wisdom and Wit, thinking they have enough, for every man thinks he hath more Wit, and is Wiser than his Neighbour, and is Conceited with himself for it, and yet every man sees his Neighbours Follies; (for Follies are easie to be Seen, but Wit and Wisdom lies Obscure) whereas if every man had Wit, and were Wise, there would be no Fools; but Mankind is not only Foolish, but False, I mean most Men, in truth there is no Trust in them, concerning which I have heard my Husband say, that the Wisest thing for this World is, to Believe as Little as a man can, and for the next World, to Believe as Much as a Man can; indeed, Facility and Credulity

in this World, are great Enemies to a man's self, for they often Betray him into Misfortune and Unhappiness, at least into great Errors and Follies, for which he is never Pitied, but Scorned. But I will write you my Husbands Discourse concerning the Natures of Men, in his own words; said he, The Disposition of Mankind for the most part is such, as you shall seldom see them Smile or Laugh, but at the Follies or Misfortunes of other Men, which shews they have so much Love for Themselves, as they have no room left for Others, nay, you shall hardly Converse with any speaking of other men, but they will find some Fault or other with them, for finding Fault shews they could Mend it, and by that means they think they cry themselves up still for the Wiser, nay, you shall meet with Few Discoursing of others, but they will lay Load on them, even sometimes to Railing, though they never Offended them, which shews most Extreme Ill Natures, and if they do Commend him, it is very Coldly, saying, He hath his Faults for all that as well as other men, and the Epilogue of their Discourse is, He hath Rare Parts, but for this, and but for that, and but for the other; but if they hear any thing to a man's Prejudice, how Rejoyced they are, and will Believe it presently, though it be never so Improbable, and bring Reasons to Fortifie the Prejudice; and if it be any thing to a Mans Honour and Reputation, they will Pull it down presently by Detracting, saying it is Impossible it should be so, and Fortifie it with the best Reasons they have: Certainly they think other Mens Faults make them Virtuous, though they have ten times more Faults themselves; But surely their Faults do not Glorifie them, except others would take Warning by them not to Do the like, which I dare Answer for, they will not. But every Man hath his Weak and his Strong Side, and if he do Compare himself with another, he doth it not Justly, for he Compares his Strong Parts with the other mans Weak Parts, and it seems Truth when so Compared, and makes him Proud, but did he Compare his Weak Parts with the other's Weak Parts, and his Strong Parts with the other's Strong Parts, truly I doubt then he would be much out of Countenance. But some have no Strong Parts to Compare, and yet will Rail on others, and that is Craftily done, to Pull down others, to make them Equal to themselves, and then they are as Fine men as any; but I will, said he, End my Discourse with a Saying of that Noble Sir Philip Sidny, concerning those that will find fault with others; says he, Hath a man any Good thing in him? Love him for that, for there are many that have none, and One Virtue, or Good Quality, is worth a Thousand Vices, and I can make a Benefit of his Good, and leave his Vices to him to Mend, without Playing the part of his Schoolmaster; which was most Wisely, Nobly, and

Honourably said. By this, Madam, we may perceive, though Mankind is Generally Bad, yet some Particulars are Wise, Witty, Good, and Noble, and I wish for the sake of Mankind all were so, but though this cannot be hoped, yet I am,

> Madam,
> Your faithful Friend and Servant.

LETTER 185

Madam,

The War is likely to be Continued, and I am Sorry for the sake of our Sex, not only that Women are Shiftless in time of Misery, as in Misfortunes, but that they live in Torment, not in their Bodies, but in that which is far Worse, in their Minds, for Fear is the Torment of the Mind, insomuch as it is more Happy to be Dead, than to Live in Fear, it Rakes the Mind, and makes the Body Restless, and this Fear I mention, is not so much for Themselves, as their Friends that Hazard their Lives in the Wars; for though Worthy men go to the Wars with Joy, hoping to gain Honour, yet Women Depart from those Friends with Grief, for fear of their Death, and in their Absence they never enjoy a Minutes Rest or Quiet, for there is not only a War in the Mind, as betwixt Hope and Doubt, but a Tyrant, which is Fear, for Fear is an Absolute Conquerour, and a Tyrannical Possessor of the Mind, Plundering the Mind of all Content and Happiness, Banishing all Hopes, and then Inhabiting it only with the Worst of Passions, as with Grief, Sorrow, and Impatience, making Despair Governour thereof. And this, Madam, by Woful Experience, I have found my self, praying I may never be the like again, for I had rather live as I do, in a Peaceable Banishment[1] with my Husband, although Accompanied with Pinching Poverty, than to be Possess'd with Fears in my own Native Country; but those that never had the Sweetness of Peace, or have not known the Misery of War, cannot be truly and rightly Sensible of either. Wherefore leaving at this time what is Past, and making the best use of the Present, I rest,

> Madam,
> Your very faithful Friend and Servant.

---

1   Cavendish is at odds with her husband on the topic of exile and war as a possible remedy.

LETTER 186

Madam,

The other day the Lady E.E. and the Lady A.A. were to See me, and they Discoursing of several Subjects, at last fell into a Discourse of Baseness and Wickedness; said the Lady E.E. I would choose rather to be Wicked than Base, for I would rather Steal a Man's Purse than Steal his Wit, and I had rather Deny a Friend, than Betray a Foe, and to Fight for my Bread, than to Flatter for my Meat, to Kill a Man's Person, than Detract from his Fame; also I would rather be a Whore than a Bawd, though I were sure to have the Pox for my Hire; said the other Lady, I am not of your mind, but I had rather be Rude, than Base or Wicked, for I would rather choose to Tell a Bold Truth, than a Civil Lie, to Deny Plainly, than to Promise Feignedly; and they ask'd me, of which mind I was, I said, I would neither be Wicked, Base, nor Rude, but I would take no Affronts, but rather Affront a Rude Person if I could; they said, put the case I was Forced to be Wicked, or Base? I answer'd, I would not be Forced, neither with Pain, nor Death; said they, this was Easie to Say so, but Hard to Do it; I replyed, it was true, but yet there have been Examples, that Resolution and Patience have Overcome Torment and Death, and said I, I hope Well of my self, although the Proof doth lie in the Trial. Thus, Madam, we pass our Time with more Words than Deeds, for we did nothing but Talk; and lest I should Weary you with the Repetition of our Discourse, I take my leave, and rest,

        Madam,
           Your faithful Friend and Servant.

LETTER 187

Madam,

My Imployment continues as yet, which is, to read Plutarch's Lives, and amongst the rest, I find Described the Life of Cato Uticensis, whose Story, if true, makes me love the Memory of this Cato, for his Courage, Honesty, and Wisdom, and for the Love to his Country; but yet I cannot Allow his Death for the Love of his Country, for surely he Mistook the Principle, and Ground of his Love; for put the case Philip King of Macedonia had been alive when his Son did Conquer Persia, and he seeing his Son follow the Fashions of the Persians, should have Kill'd himself for the Change of Fashions, from the Macedonians to the Persians, (although it was from a Worse to a Better) or he should have kill'd him-

self, if the Laws and Customs of Macedonia should have been Changed
into the Laws and Customs of the Persians, although it might have made
the Kingdom of Macedonia Flourish the more, and be more Happy and
Peaceable; or put the case of a man that hath been Born and Bred in this
Country, and should chance to be carried into Turky, as there to live,
should Kill himself for Changing Countries, although he neither Changed
his Religion, nor lived in less Safety, Peace, or Plenty, and had all his
Friends near, and round about him; or if one of the States should make
himself Monarch, all the rest should Kill themselves, having as much
Plenty, and Prosperity, and more Safety than they had, this would seem
Strange, and like a Lunacy, as a Defect of Reason, indeed a mere Madness.
The same is with Cato, for he perceiving his Country was like to be
Govern'd as a Monarchy, which was before a Republick, Kill'd himself,
although he knew the old Government was so Corrupted, as it caused
great Riots, Tumults, Seditions, Factions, and Slaughters, Killing and
Murdering even in the Market-place, so as it could not be Worse what
Chance soever came, but was Probable a Change of Government might
make it more Peaceable and Safe; wherefore Cato did not Kill himself for
the Peace and Safety of his Country, but for the Government, as choosing rather to have it Governed Ill by the Old way, than to have it
Govern'd Well another way; but if the Change of Government had been
likely to Alter their Religion, to Destroy their Natives, to Torture their
Friends, to Disperse the Ashes of their Dead Ancestors, and to Pull down
their Monuments, and his Country to be Enjoyed, Possess'd, Ruled and
Governed by Strangers, he had Chosen Well, to have Voluntarily Died,
rather than to Live to see those Miseries,[1] Calamities and Destructions, but
he knowing his Country fell unto the Government of a Noble Native,
who had Conquer'd many Nations to Inlarge it, and Brought in much
Wealth to Inrich it, and many Vassals to Serve it, and had not only
Courage, but Power and Skill to Protect it, Prudence and Justice to Rule
and Govern it, and Clemency and Tenderness to Love it, and yet Cato to
Kill himself, because Caesar was to be Chief in it, was strange; yet howsoever Cato did Nobler to Kill himself, than those that Killed Caesar, for
Cato's Death shew'd only a Dislike to the Change of the Government,
and not a Hate to the Man that Governed, whereas the Murderers of
Caesar shew'd more an Envy to the Governour, than a Dislike to the
Government; But the Wisest men may Err sometimes, so did Cato in his

---

1 Cavendish is thinking of the Civil Wars in which the tombs of her family, the Lucases, were
   desecrated. See letter 119.

Death in my Opinion; Wherefore leaving Honest Cato to Honourable Fame, I rest,

> Madam,
>> Your faithful Friend and Servant.

LETTER 188

Madam,

To give you a Relation of the Four Rich Widows, as you desired me in your last Letter, is, that one of them seems Grave and Formal, the other Jolly and Merry, the third Sad and Sighing, the fourth seems neither Formal, Merry, nor very Sad; The first Mourns Ceremoniously, and all her Family, the second Mourns after the French Mode, the third Mourns Dolefully, as to sit in Darkness, the fourth Regards not what Mourning she wears; the first keeps an Hospitable House, and Entertains all Company, the second goes to all Publick Meetings, and is Entertained, the third Receives Condoling Visits, the fourth follows her dead Husbands Will, and endeavours to Execute his Living Desires, which he would have Performed when Dead; the first Pretends to be a Wise Widow, the second a Brave Widow, the third a Sorrowful Widow, the fourth a Good Widow. Now to give my Opinion of them, I cannot, for Women cannot be Judged of, their Natures being past finding out, for a Woman cannot Guess at her self, should she Study all her Life time; the truth is, our Sex is so Various and Inconstant, that the Length of Time cannot Prove us, no not Death it self, for a Woman may Die in a Humour, which had she Lived, she would have been in another. But leaving the Four Widows to their Different Humours, and our Sex to their Inconstant Natures, I rest,

> Madam,
>> Your very faithful Friend and Servant.

LETTER 189

Madam,

The Four Rich Widows I formerly mentioned in a Letter to you, give me leave now to tell you, one of them is Married again, and another of them is Dead; the Sighing, Weeping Widow is Married to a man that was an Under-officer of her Former Husband's, but I know not why she should Marry him, unless out of Charity, for he is miserably Poor, neither hath he such Worth and Merit as her former Husband had, also he is reported to be Debauch'd, if so, it is likely he will love his Pleasures better than his Wife, and will maintain them with her Estate; wherefore 'tis Probable, she will have as much cause to Weep and Mourn for her Second Marriage, as for the Death of her First Husband. But the Good Widow is Dead, and in the time of her Sickness I went to Visit her, and being with her, I told her I was sorry she was so Ill, she answer'd me, that she was never so Well since her Husband Died, for I account my self Well, said she, when my Mind is free from Trouble, although my Body be Sick; for when my Body was in Health, my Mind was Sick with Discontented Thoughts, that Nature should make me of a Longer Life than my Husband, but now, said she, I am near a Perfect Health both in Mind and Body, for in Death there is no Sickness, and this Sick Body of mine, is but as a Medicine to a Perfect Cure; I told her, it Proved her Love to her Husband was a Firm Love, as to Continue to Death; I hope, said she, to Continue in Death as much as to Death; but, said she, my Love to my Husband was not only a Matrimonial Love, as betwixt Man and Wife, but a Natural Love, as the Love of Brethren, Parents, and Children, also a Sympathetical Love, as the Love of Friends, likewise a Customary Love, as the Love of Acquaintance, a Loyal Love, as the Love of a Subject, an Obedient Love, as the Love of a Servant, a Moral Love, as the Love to Virtue, an Uniting Love, as the Love of Soul and Body, a Pious Love, as the Love to Heaven, all which several Loves did Meet and Intermix, making one Mass of Love, but Death seized on this Treasure of Love, and left me Poor, and having no more such Love in Store, it made my Life to Pine away, like those that Starve for Want, but now, said she, Death hath Invited me to a Feast of Joyes; with that she turned her head and Died. As for the other two Widows, *viz.* the Formal and Grave, and the Merry and Gay Widow, they are neither Married nor Dead, they Prefer a Courtship before Marriage, and will use all means to keep back Death; the Formal Widow loves to be Courted incognito, the Gay Widow takes a Pride to have Publick Courtships, both taking Pleasure in Variety of Lovers, or rather Flatterers. By this you may know that the one Widow hath done Foolishly, the two others Wickedly, the last Died Lovingly. But leaving those two to Amorous Imbraces, the third to Repentance, and the fourth to Death, I rest,

Madam,
Your very faithful Friend and Servant.

LETTER 190

Madam,

Give me leave to tell you, that I write this Letter with no Small Difficulty, for though I sit so near the Fire, as I have Burn'd a part of my Clothes, yet the Cold is so Furious, as it doth not only Freez the Ink in the Standish, but in the Pen I am writing with, so that I am but a Cold Writer, nay, the very Thoughts seem to be Frozen in my Brain, for they move very Slowly, as if they were Stupified, only my Love to your Ladiship keeps Warm in my Heart; indeed, your Love doth help to maintain the Fire of Life; I know not how Cold it is at the Poles, for I never was there in Person, but in my Imagination[1] yet, it cannot be Colder there, than it is here at this present time; for my part, I could almost think, that this Cold hath Travell'd from the Poles hither, but this thought of mine would be Contradicted through two Reasons, the One, that Cold Moves Slowly, although to bring Reason against Reason, it seems Probable that Cold is very Quick, for it catches every Mankind by the Fingers, and by the Noses, as Soon as it comes near them, even as Soon as Burning Fire would do, and much Sooner; the Other Reason is, that Cold in the Long Journy would get itself a Heat, and so Wast by the way; but leaving these Reasons, Though the Senses know not from what Places, or Parts, Cold comes, or what it Causes, yet they know that we have here at this time Cold with all its Potent Strength, as an Army of Flakes of Snow, with Ammunition of Hail for Bullets, and Wind for Powder, also Huge Ships of Ice, which Float in the Main Sea, and Stop up all the Narrow Rivers; also Cold and its Army Shooting forth the Peircing Darts, which fly so Thick and Fast, and are so Sharp, as they Enter into every Pore of the Flesh of all Animal Creatures, whereby many Animals are Wounded with Numbness, and Die Insensibly, although Mankind bring what Strength they can get against Cold, as an Army of Furs, where every Hair stands out like a Squadron of Pikes, to Resist Cold's Assault; and Ammunition of Coals serves for Bullets, and Ashes for Powder, with great Loggs for Cannons, Billets for Muskets and Carbines, Brush Faggots for Pistols, where the Bellows as Fire-locks, make them fly up in a Flame; also great Pieces of Beef for Ships for Men of War, with Cabbage for Sails, Sawsages for Tacklings, Carrots for Guns, and Marrow-bones for Masts, Ballasted with Pepper, and Pitch'd or Tarr'd with Mustard, the Card and

---

1   Cavendish anticipates a passage in *The Blazing World* (1666, 1668) in which the heroine visits the North Pole.

Needle being Brewis and Neats Tongues, the Steers-men Cooks, besides many Pinnaces of Pork, Mutton, and Veal, and Flying Boats, which are Turkies, Capons, Geese, and the like, all which Swim in a Large Sea of Wine, Beer, and Ale; yet for all this we are Beaten into the Chimney-corner, and there we sit Shaking and Trembling like a Company of Cowards, that dare not stir from their Shelter; and many in the Sea-fight have been Drowned, from whence some have been taken up Dead-Drunk, then carried and Buried in a Feather-bed, where, after a Long Sleep, they may have a Resurrection, but how they will be Judged at that time they Rise, whether Damned with Censure, or Saved by Excuse, I cannot tell. Thus, Madam, I thought it was the part of a Friend to give you a true Relation of our Cold Condition, but in all Conditions or Extremities I shall alwayes be,

Madam,
Your faithful Friend and humble Servant.

LETTER 191

Madam,
If you were here in this City, now all the ground of the Streets is covered with Snow, you would see the Young men and their Mistresses ride in Sleds by Torch-light, the Women and the Men dress'd Antickly, as also their Horses that Draw their Sleds, and then every Sled having a Fair Lady, at least to her Lovers thinking, sitting at one end of the Sled, dress'd with Feathers and Rich Clothes, and her Courting Servant like a Coachman, or rather a Carter, Bravely Accoustred, driving the Horses with a Whip, which draw the Sled upon the Snow with a Galloping pace, whilst Footmen run with Torches to light them; but many of these Lovers, not using to drive Horses so often as Court Mistresses, for want of Skill over-turn the Sled, and so tumble down their Mistresses in the Snow, where-upon they being in a Frighted Hast, take them up from that Cold Bed, and then the Mistress appears like a Pale Ghost, or Dead Body in a Winding sheet, being all Covered with white Snow, and the Sled, when the Mistress is Seated again, instead of a Triumphant Chariot, seems like a Virgins Funeral Herse, carried, and Buried by Torch-light, and her Feathers seem like a Silver Crown, that Usually is laid thereon, also the Sled is Drawn then in a Slow, Funeral Pace, for fear of a second Fall. By this Custom and Practice you may know, we have here Recreations for every Season of the Year, and as the Old Saying is, that Pride in Winter is never Cold, so it

may here be said, that Love in Winter is never Cold; indeed, I have heard say, that Love is Hot, and to my Apprehension it must be a very Hot Amorous Love that is not Cold this Weather. But leaving the Hot Lovers in the Cold Snow, I rest, by the Fire-side,

                    Madam,
                         Your very faithful Friend and Servant.

LETTER 192

Madam,
Although I am as Unwilling to stir from the Fire-side this Cold Weather, as Criminals are to go to their Execution, (for indeed the Sharp Cold is to me as a Sharp Ax, and the Peircing Motions like Points of Swords) yet my Husbands Perswasion, which is as Powerful on me, as the Powerfullest Authority of States to particular Persons, Forced me out of the City, as without the Walls, to see Men Slide upon the Frozen Moat, or River, which Runs, or rather Stands about the City Walls, as a Trench and Security thereof; and I being Warm Inclosed in a Mantle, and Easily Seated in my Coach, began to take some Pleasure to see them Slide upon the Ice, insomuch as I wished I could, and might Slide as they did, but yet I would Slide as one of the Skilfullest, and most Practiced, and with a Security the Ice was so Firm as not to Break; but since I neither had the Agility, Art, Courage, nor Liberty, I returned Home very well Pleased with the Sight, and being alone to my self, I found I had a River, Lake, or Moat Frozen in my Brain, into a Smooth, Glassy Ice, whereupon divers of my Thoughts were Sliding, of which, some Slid Fearfully, others as if they had been Drunk, having much ado to keep on their Incorporeal Legs, and some Slid quite off their Feet, and Fell on the Cold Hard Ice, whereof some Sliding upon Imaginary Shoes, with the Imaginary Fall were tossed up into the Air of my Brain, yet most of my Thoughts Slid with a good Grace and Agility, as with a Swift, and Flying Motion. But after I had sat by the Fire-side some time, the Imaginary Ice began to Melt, and my Thoughts Prudently Retired, or Removed, for fear of Drowning in the Imaginary River in my Brain. And so leaving this Imagination, I profess my self really,

                    Madam,
                         Your faithful Friend and Servant.

LETTER 193

Madam,

Th' other day a man was brought to me, to be seen for a Wonder, that being above an Hundred Years old, had all his Senses Free from the Defects of Age; but I believe he made himself Older by his own Report, than he was, being a Poor man, and got Mony by Shewing himself, and to make him appear Older, he let his Beard Grow down to the Small of his Wast, so as he was a Mountebanck for Beard, as some Italians are for Drugs; the truth is, his Beard was the Stock of his Livelihood, for he was Fed & Maintain'd by it, his Chin, like Fertil Land, did yield a Goodly Crop of Hair, but whereas Crops of Corn or the like, must be Mowed or Reaped before a Profit can be made, his Profit was to have his Unreaped or Unmowed, which is, to be Unshaved; But in my Opinion, there is nothing so Ill-favour'd as for men to wear great Beards, it is neither Becoming nor Cleanly, but Misbecoming and Slovenly, and it is as an Alms-basket, or the like, for Crums, or as a Tub for Drops of Drink; indeed men that wear Great Beards had need to Perfume them well, or else they will Smell of Scraps, Tappings, and Grease, after Eating and Drinking, and if they be Amorous men, they will hardly Gain a Mistress with Kissing; besides, Long Beards make Men look like Goats; yet howsoever, a Great Long Beard was Beneficial to the Poor Old man; and so leaving him to it, or his Beard to him, I rest,

Madam,
Your faithful Friend and Servant.

LETTER 194

Madam,

My Aguish Indisposition hinders me from taking that Pleasure I Used to do this Carneval Time, which is Shrovetide, for this is the most Pleasant and Merry time in all the Year, in this City, for Feasting, Sporting, and Maskarading; as for Feasting, Fasting is the Cause, for by reason Lent is a Spare time for Diet, the People in this, and so in many other Places, do as it were, Forestore their Stomacks, like those that do Fore-store their Provisions Foreseeing a Dearth, insomuch as they Eat not according to their Appetites, but according to the Time, by reason Lent is only for Fish, or other such Cold and Spare meat, and therefore they Prudently will Surfet of Flesh this Shrovetide, that they may not Covet Flesh, as to have a Longing desire thereto; also their Sporting is after the same kind and like for the same End, by reason they are to Pray as well as to Fast, like as those that will, or think it Lawful to Commit what Sins they can, or please, before a Confession, Penance and Pardon; But truly, these are Harmless Sports, consisting only in several Attires, or Accoustrements, as to wear Vizards, &c. and some of the Women do Accoustre themselves in Mens Habits, and the Younger sort of Men in Womens Habits, where the Women seem to be well Pleased, and take a Pride to be Accoustred like Men, but the Men seem to be more out of Countenance to be Accoustred like Women, as counting it a Disgrace to their Manhood, although they do not seem so, being dress'd in the most Ill-favour'd dress that can be Devised, to Imitate Devils, but whether they Imitate them Rightly for outward Form, I know not, for I believe they never were in Hell to Learn, or Know how Devils are Formed, or Bodied, or Accoustred, I believe they may Sooner, and more Aptly Imitate their Wickedness than their Figures; but these Sports I went abroad to See, being Perswaded to go forth, by reason it was very Fair Weather, and Sun-shiny Dayes, although to my Sense of Feeling, I had Frost and Snow within me, or was as if I had been Shaken with a Cold North-wind, having a Cold Fit of an Ague upon me, which Cold and Stormy Indisposition of the Body, did Dull, and Darken the Mirth of Pleasure, as Dark Clouds do the Light of the Sun, for Health and Sickness are like Fair and Foul Dayes. But the sorts or kinds of Sports are done for this Year, and all the Men, Women, and Children, were Marked the next day, which was Ash-wednesday, with a Black Mourning Cross on their Forheads, I know not whether it be to Cross out their Former Sins, or a Barricado to Keep out Following Sins, although I fear it is not in the power of a Cross to keep back Sin, I know not what it can do to keep back Punishment, but they all seem to be very Devout in Frequenting the Churches. Yet this is but the Beginning of Lent, but towards the later End, I suppose they will be as if they were half, or three parts Tired, not so much with Fasting as Praying, for though they eat not Flesh meat, yet they eat oftener other Good meats, as Fish, Spoon-meat, Sweet-meats, and the like, also they have the liberty to Drink more Wine; indeed most Christians all the Lent time, as also on many Fasting dayes in the Year, live for the manner of Diet somewhat like the Pythagoreans[1] or Gentils; But I, being not well in Health, have the liberty to Eat what I will or can; and so leaving the Generality to their Lent-diet, I rest,

> Madam,
> Your faithful Friend and Servant.

---

1   Pythagoras forbade his followers to eat meat and, curiously, beans.

LETTER 195

Madam,

To tell you what Pastimes this City hath, they be several Sights and Shews, which are to be seen for Mony, for even Pastime is Bought; for at several times of the Year come hither Dancers on the Ropes, Tumblers, Jugglers, Private Stage-Players, Mountebanks, Monsters, and several Beasts, as Dromedaries, Camels, Lions, Acting Baboons, and Apes, and many the like, which would be as Tedious to me to Relate as to See, for I would not take the pains to See them, unless some Few; amongst the rest there was a Woman brought to me, who was like a Shagg-dog, not in Shape, but Hair, as Grown all over her Body, which Sight stay'd in my Memory, not for the Pleasantness, but Strangeness, as she troubled my Mind a Long time, but at last my Mind kick'd her Figure out, bidding it to be gone, as a Dog-like Creature; and though I am of so Dull and Lazy a Nature, as seldom to take the Pains to See Unusual Objects, yet here coming an Italian Mountebank, who had with him several persons to Dance, and Act upon the open Stage, also one which did Act the part of a Fool, and that all to draw a Company of People together, to hear him tell the Virtues, or rather Lies of his Drugs, Cures, and Skill, and to Intice, or Perswade them to Buy, and to be Cozened and Deceived, both in Words, Drugs, and Mony; I saw this Fool Act his Part so Well, that many of the People bought more Drugs for the Fool's sake, than for the Apocryphal Physician's, which was the Mountebank; indeed, Madam, a Fool's Part, as it is the Pleasantest, so it is the most Difficult to Act, I say, to Act it Well, for it doth require more Ingenuity and Wit than any other Part Acted on the Stage, for though the World is full of Fools, yet there are not many Feigned Fools, for most men endeavour to seem Wiser than they are, but Feigned Fools endeavour to seem Foolisher than they are; But where there is one Feigned Fool in the World, there are a thousand Feigned Wise men, and where there is one Professed Mountebank, or Jugler, there are thousands that are so, but will not be Known, or Thought to be so. Upon this Profess'd Mountebank's Stage, there were two Handsom Women Actors, both Sisters, the one of them was the Mountebank's, th' other the Fool's Wife, and as the Saying is, that Fools have Fortune, his Wife was far the Handsomer, and better Actor, and Danced better than th' other; indeed she was the Best Female Actor that ever I saw; and for Acting a Man's Part, she did it so Naturally as if she had been of that Sex, and yet she was of a Neat, Slender Shape; but being in her Dublet and Breeches, and a Sword hanging by her side, one would have believed she never had worn a

Petticoat, and had been more used to Handle a Sword than a Distaff; and when she Danced in a Masculine Habit, she would Caper Higher, and Oftener than any of the Men, although they were great Masters in the Art of Dancing, and when she Danced after the Fashion of her own Sex, she Danced Justly, Evenly, Smoothly, and Gracefully; wherefore in this Woman, and the Fool her Husband, I took such Delight, to see them Act upon the Stage, as I caused a Room to be hired in the next House to the Stage, and went every day to See them, not to Hear what they said, for I did not Understand their Language, & their Actions did much delight my Sight, for I believe they were better than their Wit, which, as I suppose, were but some Stale, Bald Jests, and Broken Pieces, or Senseless Speeches, taken out of some Romances, or such like Foolish Books; But after they had been in this City some Short time (for so it seem'd to me) to my great Grief, the Magistrate Commanded them out of the Town, for fear of the Plague, which was then in the City, although some said, the Physicians through Envy to the Mountebank, Bribed them out; the truth is, they had Reason, for the Mountebank was then so much in Request, as most of the People made him their Doctor, and Faen Potage (for so the Fool was named) was their Apothecary; But they being gone, I was troubled for the Loss of that Pastime which I took in Seeing them Act; wherefore to please me, my Fancy set up a Stage in my Brain, and then brought out some Incorporeal Drugs for Incorporeal Diseases, to be Bought by Incorporeal People, and the Incorporeal Thoughts were the several Actors, and my Wit play'd the Jack Fool, which Pleased me so much, as to make me Laugh Loud at the Actions in my Mind, whereas otherwise I seldom Laugh Heartily, as the Phrase is; but after my Thoughts had Acted, Danced, and Played the Fool, some several times of Contemplating, my Philosophical and Physical Opinions, which are as the Doctors of, and in the Mind, went to the Judgment, Reason, Discretion, Consideration, and the like, as to the Magistrates, and told them, it was very Unprofitable to let such Idle Company be in the Mind, which Robbed the multitude of Thoughts, of Time and Treasure; whereupon the Magistrates of the Mind Commanded the Fancy-Stage to be taken down, & the Thought-Actors to go out, and would not Suffer them to Cheat, or Fool any Longer; And so leaving my Mind Free of such Strangers, I rest,

Madam,
Your faithful Fr. and S.

LETTER 196

Madam,

Here is no News, but that the Lord N.N.[1] lives Nobly, Plentifully, and Pleasantly, which is to live Happily, although there is not any man that knows of any great means he hath to Live on, which makes it a Wonder he can Live so Well, having so Little whereupon; the Lord C.R. asked him, how it came that he Lived, and Maintained his Family so Honourably, being a Ruined man in his Estate and Fortunes? He answer'd, he had Fortunatus's Purse; said the Lord C.R. if you have Fortunatus's Purse, you may make War, and Conquer Kings and Kingdoms, for it is the Nature of that Purse never to be Empty, but whatsoever is Taken out, is Replenished again; the Lord N.N. said it was true, but, said he, the Nature of that Purse is, whensoever any Mony is offered to be taken out to make War, the Golden Pistols turn to Leaden Bullets, and Bullets without Guns, Powder, Arms, and Men can be of no Use; then, said he, you may Relieve all the Poor, and Distressed Persons, which are many in this Age; Yes, said the Lord N.N. more than can be Relieved, for that Purse, said he, hath another Nature, for if any offer to take out Mony to Give or Lend it away, above the Owners Use, it becomes Invisible, for though the Owner knows he hath it, yet he cannot find it, and the Purse is a Sensible Purse, for it knows as well as the Owner, to what use his Stores shall be Employed; Why, said the Lord C.R. you Maintain your Servants, and Near Friends; yes, said the Lord N.N. but Servants are for my Use, and Children, Brothers, and Sisters, are Part of my self, like as a Piece of Cloth that is divided into many Parts, yet is still the same Cloth, for the Dividing Alters not the Nature or Quality. But the truth is, Madam, Fortunatus's Purse is Prudence and Good Management, which keeps out Poverty from a Family, and makes a man Thrive, as making a Great Shew with a Little Substance, and such a Purse all Wise men are Masters of. But leaving the Lord N.N. and his Purse, I rest,

Madam,
Your faithful Friend and Servant.

---

1   It appears that N.N. is Newcastle and C.R. is Charles II, who used those initials. For another discussion of Charles II, see letter 33. The letter seems to be based on an incident in which the King suggested that Newcastle dined better than he (Grant, 174). The story of Fortunatus may be found in several places including in Thomas Dekker, *The Pleasant Comedie of old Fortunatus* (1600).

LETTER 197

Madam,

You were pleased in your last Letter to Desire me to write to you my Contemplations, which, should I Express, you would Understand they were very Vain; for Solomon sayes, All is Vain under the Sun, which if so, our most Pious, and Devoutest Contemplations are Vain; but my last Contemplation had the full measure of Vanity, where I did imagine my self Empress of the whole World, which World was to be Governed by my Fancy, Opinion and Approvement; and first, I would have my Counsel-Ministers of State, and Magistrates, Philosophers, both Natural and Moral, and my Court-Officers and Attendants, Poets of all sorts, so should I Govern Wisely, and Live Pleasantly, by which I Imagined the World of Men would be so United in Peace, Concord, and Tranquillity, as it would be Harmonious. But leaving these Vain Imaginations, I am really,

Madam,
Your very faithful Servant.

LETTER 198

Madam,

In your last Letter you Express'd to me, that Mr. F.R. was to Visit you, and his Discourse was bent all against Women, saying, that most of their Actions were spent in Dressing, and their Thoughts in Devising and Inventing of Fashions, and that they were Composed of Nothing but Vanity, and made up with Art, so that by their Dressing, they might be thought rather to be Artificial, than Natural Creatures; but you Answer'd him Well, when you told him he was more Artificial with Formality, than Women with Vanity, and that all Men were as much Artified as Women, and I having nothing to do, after I had read your Letter, made a Copy of Verses upon the Theme of his Discourse, I confess they are not Good ones, but such as they are, I send them you, as following.

Thou Seeming Wise man, what is that to thee,
If I to Please my self, Accoustre me
According to my Mind? Must nought be worn
That doth the Body Handsomly Adorn?
If we must nothing Artificial wear,
Then go stark Nak'd, and all the Body Bare,

For if thou wear'st a Rag, though ne'r so Plain,
Yet Artificial still thou wilt remain;
Nay, if with Fig-leaves thou dost make thy Breeches,
'Tis Artificial still, if sow'd with Stitches;
If thou dost Shave thy Beard, or Cut thy Hair,
Or Pair thy Nails, or Corns, 'tis Art, I Swear;
But if thou Artificial things think'st Vain,
Then like a Beast in Woods and Fields remain,
And feed on Grass Unmow'd, and Herbs Unset,[1]
And Fruit that's Wild, if thou but canst them get,
For Nature's not so Bountiful to give
All Creatures a Sufficiency to Live;
For if that Art did not Increase the Store
Of everything, the World would be but Poor,
Nay Beasts would Sterve, and Men with Famine Dye,
If Art did not use Skill and Industry;
But Art and Nature do so well Agree,
Like Man and Wife, they Propagators be,
And therefore Scholars, as Grammarians, miss
When they say Both the Female Gender is.
But, Lord! What Fools these Seeming Wise men are,
Or those that are Precise, and do not wear,
Nor will allow that any thing be worn
Which may the Body Handsomly Adorn,
But Rail at those that Newer Arts Attire,
And nothing but Old-fashion'd Clothes Admire,
When in those Older Clothes and Fashions too,
Art had as much as in new Modes to do.
When Women fine are Dress'd, and Curl'd their Hair,
They Rail, and say they Artificial are,
They are not Handsom, 'cause th' are Artified,
With several colour'd Ribbands they are tyed,
Worthy is only she to be Admir'd
That's only in her Natural Dress Attir'd,
And thus they Talk; but if her Dress be so,
She Naked as her Mother Eve must go.
What shall I say to these Grave Fools their Talk,
Who with an Artificial Pace do walk,

---

1 Not planted by people.

And yet Condemn the Art that Women use,
And think therein they Nature much Abuse?
They may as well Condemn the Husband's Care,
Who doth Manure his Lands to make them Bear,
Or Gardners that do Plant, or Set Sweet Flow'rs,
Or make fine Arbors, or Cool Shady Bow'rs;
Or Cooks that do dress Meat with wondrous Skill,
Which Nourishes the Body, and doth Fill;
Or Apothecaries, which do Drugs Compound,
To Help the Life, and make the Body Sound;
Or States, or Commonwealths, which do provide
What makes Good Laws the Vulgar for to Guide,
That men may live in Neighbourhood and Peace,
In which Mankind doth Thrive, & much Increase.
They may as well call all the Preachers Fools,
Because they Preach & Teach by Logick Rules.
Yet Preachers in their Pulpits do Declame
'Gainst Dressing Arts, and all our Sex do Blame
For Plaited Braids, Pendents, and Curled Hair,
And all our several Garments which we wear,
A Feather'd Fan, though't Cools the Sultry Heat,
With terrible Threats they in our Ears do beat,
Black patches on our Face, Pimples to hide,
They Rail against, and call them marks of Pride,
And every thing indeed which we do wear,
Th' Exclame against, as if their Throats they'd tear.
Sure they would have us Adamites,[1] *yet know,*
Against Bare-necks they Thundring Words out throw,
This last, I do conclude without all doubt,
'Tis that we are not Naked quite throughout;
But let them Rail at Clothes and Curling Pins,
Black Patches, Fans, and such like other things,
We are Reveng'd, for with their Firy Tongues,
They Spend their Spirits, and do Hurt their Lungs;
For sure a Man no Reason yet can show,
Nor hath Intelligence the Truth to know,
That God should be Displeased at our Dress,
As for a Patch Damnation, and no less.

---

1   A Christian sect advocating nakedness.

Would he make Souls for Devils to Possess,
And none as made his Goodness for to Bless?
'Tis not a Feather'd Fan, or Curled Hair,
Can make him Angry, when we them do wear,
For Prayers may to Heaven High be sent
With as much Zeal from Souls as Innocent,
That have their Bodies Beautiful and Fair,
Their Garments Useful, Comly, Rich, and Rare,
For Garments Rich do not the Soul Pollute,
Nor can Poor Clothes against Great Sins dispute;
Devotion in Prosperity may live,
And praise God for the Gifts that he doth give;
As for Example, Job in's Happy State
Was as Devout, as when Unfortunate,
When he was Rich, and all in Purple Clad,
As often to his God Recourses had,
And Abram Rich, who lived like a King,
He many Offerings to his God did bring.
Thus Rich men be 'as Devout, as those that are
Both Mean and Poor, and rather Foul than Fair.
Devotion may in Palaces be found,
As soon as in a Cell under the Ground,
Or Cottage that is Poor, Thatch'd, Mean, and Low,
Wherein the Dwellers no Religion Know,
For they not having Means for to be Taught,
Do neither Seek, nor Practise what they ought,
And Deadly Sin in Poor mens Hearts may Dwell,
As oft as in Rich mens whose Wealths Excell,
And had but Poor men Wealth, they soon would grow
So Proud and High, as not themselves to Know.
And if Rich men can Serve their God as well
As those that in Low Poverty do Dwell,
Why should they Quit their Wealth, and choose to Live
With Poverty, that nothing hath to Give?
Doth all Devotion in Shav'd Heads still dwell?
Is there no way to Heav'n but through a Cell?
Must Tubs, as Pulpits, only be for Prayer,
Or must to Zealous Night-caps we Repair?
Hath none the Grace, or Spirit of God but those
Who all are clad in Puritanical Clothes?

Their very Looks and Gate with Art is Drest,
The Picture of Hypocrisie Exprest;
'Tis not the Outside makes the Soul Divine,
No more than Earth doth make the Sun to shine;
Extremes in all Religions are not well,
It Keeps from Heaven, and Draws down to Hell.

But now I send you these Verses, Madam, you must not let F.R. See, nor Hear them, for if he knows they were made upon his Discourse, he will leave off Railing against the Generality of our Sex, and fall only on Me, so as it will draw the whole Malice upon Me, by reason I have Answer'd in the Behalf of the Generality; also I have call'd him a Seeming Wise man, which will Anger him more, for it is almost as bad as if I should call him a Fool, for a man takes it for as Great an Affront to be call'd a Fool, as a Woman doth when she is said not to be Handsom. But howsoever I leave my Poem to your Discretion, to be Disposed of as you Please, and rest,

Madam,
Your faithful Friend and Servant.

LETTER 199

Madam,

You were pleased to desire me to send you word how the Poets were Feasted, and I my self amongst the rest, which was thus; Nature sent the Muses to Invite all the Poets to a Banquet of Wit, and Invited also me a Poetess, or rather Poetastress; I went, and entred into a Large Room of Imagination, Hung with Imaginary Hangings of Conception, wherein were the Pictures of Ideas, in which Room were a number of Poets met, as Nature's Guests, which when I Saw, I was extremely out of Countenance, as being all Men, and never a Woman but my self, insomuch as I knew not how to Behave my self, but at last, holding up my Head, which was bent downwards through Bashfulness, I saw my Lord one of the Chief Guests amongst them, which Sight gave me Confidence, insomuch as I went to him, and stood close by him, but the Muses to Oblige one of their Sex, came to me, and Saluted me, and bid me very Welcom, and after they had Saluted me, they Crowned every Poet there with Poetical Bayes, and Placed every one in a Chair of Celestial Flame, which had you seen, you would have thought we had been in so many Firy Chariots ready to Ascend up to the Heavens; then was every one Placed round about the Table, and we took our Places according to every ones Poetical Inspiration, but the Table we were set to, was a strange Table, for never was seen the like, it was made of all the Famous Old Poets Sculs, and the Table-cloth or Covering was made of their Brains, which Brains were Spun by the Muses, for they are Spinsters of Mens Brains, as the Fates are of the Lives of Men; but these Old Poets Brains were Spun into Cobweb Threads, as Soft and Thin as Air, and then Woven into a Piece, or Web, and Old Time was the Weaver which Weaved this Web like Damask or Diaper, in Works and Figures of Golden Numbers. Thus we see Nature Transforms Sculs into Tables, and Brains into Table Coverings, the Napkins for the Hands was Pure Fine White Paper, all over-wrought with Black Letters, and the Edges round about were Gilded; also there were upon the Table, Plates, Salt-sellers, Knives and Forks, the Plates were made of the Films or Drums of Sensible Ears, and the Knives that were to cut the Meat laid thereon, were Orators Tongues, the Trencher Salt-sellers, which were set by every Plate, were made of the Chrystalline part of Observing Eyes, and the Salt that was put therein, was made of Sea-water, or Salt-tears, which usually Flow from a Tragick Vein, the Forks that were to bear up the Meat to the Tast of the Understanding, were Writing-pens; The Table being thus Covered and Ordered, and the Guests set round, ready for the Feast, in came the Muses with Basons of Water, fetch'd from the Well, or Spring of Helicon, for the Poets to Wash before they did Eat, and after they had Wash'd, the Muses carried those Basons forth, and then brought in many several Dishes of Poetical Meats, Placing them on the Table; the first was a Great dish of Poems, Excellently well Dress'd, and Curious Sawce made of Metaphors, Similitudes, and Fancies, and round the Sides or Verges of the Dish, were laid Numbers and Rimes, like as we use on Corporeal Dishes and Meats, to lay Dates, or Flowers, or Slices of Limmons, or the like; then was there a Dish of Songs, brought by the Lyricks, it was very Delicious Meat, and had a most Sweet Relish, it was Dress'd with a Compounded Sawce of many several Airs, Notes, and Strains; then were there two Dishes of Epigrams, I think one of them was Martial's, for they were Powdered, or Brined Highly with Satyrical Salt, the other Dish was so Luscious with Flattery, as I could not Feed much thereon; then there was a Dish of Epithalamiums, but that Meat was Dress'd so Strong and Rank, as it was Nauseous to me; then there was a Hash of Anagrams, Letters, and Names, Hashed, or Minced together, but I did not like it; then there was a Dish of Funeral Elegies well Drest, but it was so Sad and Heavy Meat, as I durst not Feed much thereon;

then there was a Dish of Comedies, Excellently well Drest, with Scenes, the Sawce was Compounded, but very Savoury, being Compounded of divers Humors, and the Dish Graced or Garnished with Smiles and Laughter; the next dish to that were Tragedies, but those were Drest as we Dress Corporeal Shoulders of Mutton, or Venison, in the Blood, Stuff'd with Sighs, as the other with Herbs, and Salted with Tears. Then came an Olio, or Bisk of Characters, and after that was a Dish of Morals, which is a Meat more Wholsome than Pleasant, the Chief Sawce was Temperance, but it was mix'd with other several Virtues and Passions; then was a Dish of Natural Philosophy, a Dish I love to Feed on, although the Meat is very Hard, and not Easily to be Digested; it is Drest with Divers and Different Compounds and Ingredients, as the four Elements, and all manner of Vegetables and Minerals, the Gold is Cordial, and the Iron or Steel is Strengthening, as also Opening Obstructions, which is very Wholsom; then there were Joynted, or rather I may say Chop'd, Animals, as Blood, Bones, and Flesh, all Chop'd, Stew'd, Boiled, and Bak'd together in their own Fat or Grease; this Dish was so Great and Full, as it might have Fed Numbers, indeed it was an Infinite Hash, and an Infinite deal of Meat; then there was a Grand Sallet of Rhetorick, with Oyl of Eloquence, also a Bag-pudding of Sciences, made of Mathematical Cream, Logistical Eggs, and Astronomical Spices, which were Strewed as Thick as the Stars of the Skie; Likewise a Great Pie of Arts, Made, or Rais'd by Prentices, and Bak'd in the Oven of Time, Heated with the Fire of Labour, and was seven years a Baking, the Crust was Hard, Strong, and Thick; then there was a Quelquechose of Rallery, but whatsoever the Meat was, the Sawce was Naught, for it was made of Ingredients, as bad as Poor People Dress their Corporeal Meat with, as Lamp-oyl, Dead Vinegar, Rotten Pepper, and Stinking Garlick, as Foolish Jests, Dull, Spiteful Replies, Rude Familiarity, often Repetitions, and Reproaches, so as there was Sweet, Bitter, Sour, and altogether Mix'd, of this Dish I Tasted not, I was Sick at the Presence of it; as for the Desert, it was Musick of all sorts, Sweet, and Harmonious; the Drink we had at this Feast was Animal Spirits instead of Sack, and Vital Spirits for Rhenish Wine, but when we had Feasted as much as we would, or could, we Rose from the Table, saying a Grace of Thanks to Nature, and intending to take our Leaves, but the Muses perswaded us to walk up to the Top of Pernassus Hill, to Digest our Feast, lest we should Surfet, and when we came up to the Top of the Hill, we saw round about a most Pleasant Prospect of Nature's Works, but because we should see Farther than her Ordinary Work, the Muses gave every one a Prospective Glass, where we saw other Worlds, Creatures, and Celestials, but some saw not so Far, or so Much as others, not but that the Prospective Glasses were all of an Equal Goodness, but some had not so Good an Eye-sight as others; and after we had walked down the Hill, every one took his leave of the Muses & Departed, but the Lyrick, and the Comick Muse did so Imbrace and Kiss my Lord, as they made me almost Jealous, for though all the Muses made Civil and Obliging Addresses to him, yet not so Pleasant, and so Galliard as these two were, and there-fore I made the more Hast to Depart, that I might Separate my Lord from them, and so returning home to my House, I rest,

> Madam,
> Your Ladiships faithful Friend and Servant.

LETTER 200

Dear Sister Pye,
Distance of Place, nor Length of Time, cannot Lessen my Natural, or rather Supernatural Affection to you, for certainly my Love for you is more than a Sisters Love, nay, such a Love, as when I Lived with you, it could not choose but be somwhat Troublesome, by reason my Love was Accompanied with such Fears, as it would neither let you Rest, Pray, nor Eat in Quiet, for though it was a Watchful Love, yet it was a Fearful Love, for I remember I have oftentimes Waked you out of your Sleep, when you did Sleep Quietly, with Soft Breathing, fearing you had been Dead, and oftener have I laid my Face over your Mouth, to feel if you Breath'd, inso-much as I have kept my Self Waking, to Watch your Sleeps, and as Troublesome I was to you concerning your Feeding, as I was in your Sleeping, for I was Afraid that that which was to Nourish you, should Kill you, and I remember, I was so doubtful of every Meat you did eat, as you were used to tell me, I was Sancapancha's Doctor;[1] Neither could I let you Pray in Quiet, for I have often Knock'd at your Closet door, when I thought you were Longer at your Prayers than Usual, or at least, I did think the time Longer, so as I could not forbear to ask you how you did, and whether you were Well, and many the like Impertinencies which my Extraordinary Love Troubled you with, of which Trouble you are now Quit, living so far asunder; But though I am too far off to Watch, yet I pray

---

1 In Cervantes's *Don Quixote*, Sancho Panza is in danger of starvation because his doctor pro-tects him from so many foods.

for your Health and Long Life, and though I thought it was impossible I could Love any Creature better than you, yet I find by Experience I do, for since I am Married, I Love my Husband a Degree above you, yet howsoever, my several Affections are like God and Nature, both Infinite, and if Love Lives in the Soul, and the Soul never Dies, my several Affections may be Eternal. But you may say, if my Love was so Troublesome to you, what is it to my Husband? I must tell you, I have some more Discretion now than I had then, and though Extraordinary Love will hardly Allow, or Admit Discretion, yet Reason doth Perswade Love, and brings many Arguments not to be Impertinently Troublesom; but though I do not ask my Husband so many Impertinent Questions as I did you, yet my Love to him is not less Watchful, Careful, and Fearful, but rather more, if more can be, and all the Powers and Endeavours of my Life are ready to Serve him and you, only he must be Served first, which I am confident you will take no Exception at, but Approve of, for you are a Wife, and know what the Love to a Husband is, and so leaving you to your Beloved Husband, I rest,

Your most Affectionate Sister.

LETTER 201

Dear Sister Ann,
I Cannot Advise you to Marry, unless Men's Souls, Minds, and Appetites, were as Visible to your Knowledge as their Persons to your Eyes, for though there may be much Deceit even in Outward Forms, or Aspects, yet not so much, but (if there be Defects) there will be some Appearance, but the Defects of the Mind, Soul, or Appetites, may be so Obscured, as not to be Perceived till you find you are Unhappy by them; indeed there is so much Danger in Marrying, as I wonder how any dare Venture, yet there is less Danger for Women than Men, by reason a Man may receive a Fix'd Disgrace both to himself and his Posterity, by the Wifes Adultery, where the Wife can receive no Dishonour if she be Honest and Chast; but though she can receive no Dishonour by her Husband's Adultery, yet she may be very Unhappy by his Opposite Disposition, Cross Humours, and Unruly Passions, which Antipathy may not only be a Hindrance to the Peace of this Life, and Tranquillity of the Mind, but Indanger the Glory of a Future Life, for Mankind is apt from the Troubles of their Minds, to Curse Fortune, and to Murmur against Heaven, unless they have a Supernatural Patience; besides, Men are most apt to run into Vices in a Discontented

Humor, and are alwayes Wandering Abroad to Divert their Home-Disquiets, not that they need to go out of Doors to Seek Vice, for Vice Dwells in most Houses or Families, but that by going into many Houses or Families, they may take Infection from every one, for Vice many times is Multiplied by Acquaintance, I mean General Acquaintance, not Particular Societies; but I speak not this, as Believing you can be Infected, being Secured by the Antidote of Virtue, the Spirit of Grace, and the Balsam of Honour, which Nature, Heaven, and Education gave you; but though you cannot be Infected, yet should you seek Diversion by much Company, being of the Female Sex, you might be Suspected; Neither will I have you think by this Discourse, as if I did not Approve of Marriage, for if you do, you Mistake me, there being no Life I Approve so well of, as a Married Life, were as much Sympathy Joyns Souls, and Affection Hearts, as Ceremony Joyns Hands; but to live with Antipathy must needs be very Unhappy, and if you be so, there is no way to Help yourself, for if you be once Tied with the Matrimonial Bond, there can be no Honourable Divorce but by Death, for all other Divorces are Marked with some Disgrace, either more or less, and the Least Disgrace is too Much; wherefore, if you Marry, choose a Husband rather by the Ear than the Eye, for the World seldom gives an Undeserved Praise, but often Detracts from the Deserver, for it seldom gives Merit its Due; But the Safest Way is to Live a Single Life, for all Wives, if they be not Slaves, yet they are Servants, although to be a Servant to a Worthy Husband, is both Pleasure and Honour, for true Affection takes more Pleasure to Serve than to be Served, and it is an Honour to Obey the Meritorious; but where there is a Hazard in the Choice, and a Security in not Choosing, the Best is to be Mistress of your self, which in a Single Life you are. But whether Married or not Married, my Wishes and Prayers are, that you may be as Happy as this World can make you, and in that I shall be a Sharer with you, as being

Your very Loving Sister.

LETTER 202

Sweet Madam Eleonora Duarti,[1]
The last Week your Sister Kath'rine and your Sister Frances were to Visit me, and so well Pleased I was with their Neighbourly, and Friendly

---

[1] Daughter of a Portuguese merchant living in Antwerp. The brother was Gaspar. Evelyn visited the Duarte residence in 1641 (Grant, 136).

Visit, as their Good Company put me into a Frolick Humour, and for a Pastime I Sung to them some Pieces of Old Ballads; whereupon they desired me to Sing one of the Songs my Lord made, your Brother Set, and you were pleased to Sing; I told them first, I could not Sing any of those Songs, but if I could, I prayed them to Pardon me, for neither my Voice, nor my Skill, was not Proper, not Fit for them, and neither having Skill nor Voice, if I should offer to Sing any of them, I should so much Disadvantage my Lord's Poetical Wit, and your Brother's Musical Composition, as the Fancy would be Obscured in the one, and the Art in the other, nay, instead of Musick, I should make Discord, and instead of Wit, Sing Nonsense, knowing not how to Humour the Words, nor Relish the Notes, whereas your Harmonious Voice gives their Works both Grace and Pleasure, and Invites and Draws the Soul from all other Parts of the Body, with all the Loving and Amorous Passions, to sit in the Hollow Cavern of the Ear, as in a Vaulted Room, wherein it Listens with Delight, and is Ravished with Admiration; wherefore their Works and your Voice are only fit for the Notice of Souls, and not to be Sung to Dull, Unlistning Ears, whereas my Voice and those Songs, would be as Disagreeing as your Voice and Old Ballads, for the Vulgar and Plainer a Voice is, the Better it is for an Old Ballad; for a Sweet Voice, with Quavers, and Trilloes, and the like, would be as Improper for an Old Ballad, as Golden Laces on a Thrum Suit of Cloth, Diamond Buckles on Clouted or Cobled Shoes, or a Feather on a Monks Hood; neither should Old Ballads be Sung so much in a Tune as in a Tone, which Tone is betwixt Speaking and Singing, for the Sound is more than Plain Speaking, and less than Clear Singing, and the Rumming or Humming of a Wheel should be the Musick to the Tone, for the Humming is the Noise the Wheel makes in the Turning round, which is not like the Musick of the Spheres; and Ballads are only Proper to be Sung by Spinsters, and that only in Cold Winter Nights, when a Company of Good Huswifes are Drawing a Thread of Flax; but as these Draw Threads of Flax, so Time Draws their Thread of Life, as their Web makes them Smocks, so Times Web makes them Deaths Shirts, to which, as to Death, afterwards those Good Huswifes are Married, and lie in the Bed of Earth, their House being the Grave, and their Dwelling in the Region of Oblivion; and this is the Fate of Poor Spinsters, and Ballad-Singers, whenas such a Singer as you, such a Composer as your Brother, such a Poet as my Lord, are Cloth'd with Renown, Marry Fame, and Live in Eternity, wherein Death hath no Power, Time no Limit, and Destinies Shears are Useless; but though I am willing to Sing an Old Ballad, yet not to Dwell in

Oblivion, for I love your Company so well, as I would Live in Eternity with you, and would be Clothed as you, with Renown, for no Fashion'd Garments Please me so well, and though the Stuff or Substance is not the same with yours, the Substances being as Different as the Several Qualities, Faculties, Proprieties, Virtues, or Sweet Graces, and the like, yet I will have as Good as I can get, I will Search Nature's Ware-house, or Shop, and though I cannot have a Piece or Measure of Silver Sound, or Broccaded Art, yet certainly I hope to get a Piece or Measure of Three-poil'd Philosophy, or Flower'd Fancy, for though my Lord hath taken many several Pieces or Packs out of Nature's Shop, and hath Inhaunced the Prices, yet he must not Ingross this last Commodity to himself; 'Tis true, he hath Ingross'd two Commodities, as Weapons, and Riding, out of Art's Shop, the Hand-maid of Nature, yet sure he will be never able to Ingross all the several Kinds, and divers Sorts of Wares that Nature and Art yet have in their Store-houses. But I perceive that you three, as my Lord, You, and your Brother, do Traffick so much with Nature and Art, as I shall be but as a Pedlar; Howbeit, it is better to have some Dealings than none at all, and I will rather Trade with Toyes, than Starve for want of a Living, and in order to make my self Capable, I have bound my self Prentice to my Lord, and am willing to Serve out my Time, but my Lord is so Generous, as to give me my Freedom, and I must also desire you to give me at present so much Freedom, as to Subscribe my self,

Madam,
Your very faithful Friend and Servant.

LETTER 203

Madam,
You ought not to take it Ill if I do not Obey your Commands, in Speaking to A.F. to Grant your Requests, by reason I think those Requests would Prejudice you, should they be Granted, so that if I Speak as you Desire, I must Plead against your Good, and my own Conscience, which I will never do, although I were sure to have your Hate, for I had rather you should Hate me for the Love and Esteem I have for you, than you should Love me for doing an Unfriendly Part or Act, for I Prefer your Good before your Love; neither must you take it Ill that I send your Present back to you again, for it did appear to me like a Bribe; besides, I desire to keep my self free from such Obligations, your Love being all that I desire, and more worth than all the Service of my Life, should I Live

Long, and Act Much; But if you think I have Omitted your Commands, out of an Evil Design, or Malice, Splene, or Spite, you do me wrong, for you should find me, if I were able to Serve you, neither Cross, Negligent, nor Unwilling, but most Industrious, Ready, and Joyful to your Service, nay, were it to Ingage my Life; wherefore whatsoever you Conceive of me, yet I have this Satisfaction in my Conscience, that I am, was, and will be as long as I Live,

> Madam,
>> Your Ladiships faithful Friend and Servant.

LETTER 204

Sweet Madam C.H.

I am sorry to hear that you are Parted from your Parents through a Discontent, which is in the way to Disobedience, and let me tell you, that Unnatural Unkindness is many times the Death of Natural Affection; our Parents are our Makers, and will you Rebell against your Maker? your Father is your Earthly God, and your Mother your Earthly Goddess, to whom you ought to Kneel down, Pray, Worship, and Obey, and not to Murmur, Cross, or Neglect them; all the Endeavours of your Life are due to them untill you have a Husband, nay, a Husband must not hinder you to Assist them to the utmost of your Power, which Power 'tis likely will be according to your Husbands Will, but a Good Wife most commonly hath the Power of her Husband's Will, and he is a very Ill Husband that will not Condescend to his Wifes Reasonable Requests, for a Good Wife will Request nothing but what is within the Limits of Reason. Thus Married, or Unmarried, you must Endeavour your Parents Good and Contentment, otherwise you will raise Clouds of Grief in your Parents Minds, from whence may Rain Showers of Curses on your Life, which may cause Floods of Misfortunes, wherein all your Future Happiness may be Drowned; for it is to be Observed, that in Curses especially, which Proceed from Parents, lies an Obscure, but Potent Power, from whence fly Shafts, whereof every one is Headed with a Curse, and where it Wounds, it leaves the Head Behind it; wherefore to Avoid them, Return to your Parents again, Ask Pardon for your Fault, Promise Obedience, and Desire their Blessing, and in so doing, you will be a Friend to your self, and a Comfort to them, and believe this Advice is given you by her who is

> Your very loving Friend.

LETTER 205

Noble Sir,

I Am of your Opinion, that most of Mankind are of Lazy Dispositions, and love not to Trouble themselves in Publick Affairs, but though they be Lazy to the Publick Good, yet they are Active and Industrious to and for their Private Pleasure, or their Particular Designs; and though Mankind are Lazy to the Publick Good, yet they are oftentimes Active to the Publick Hurt, either for their Ambitious and Covetous Ends, or many times through Envy and Malice to some Particular Person who is more Eminent than the rest, for rather than they will Suffer One to Over-top All, they will Ruin All to Pull down that One; the truth is, Men are not like Beasts, to Work to a General Profit, but like Drones, to Rob the Particular Labours in the Commonwealth; neither is it amongst Mankind as amongst Beasts, for amongst Beasts there are more Bees than Drones, but amongst Mankind there are more Drones, as I may say, than Bees, that is, there are more Unprofitable, than Good Commonwealths men; But Nature seems to be in Fault that Mankind is so Bad, for if it were only Custom, the Evil would be but in some Particular Nations, and not throughout the whole World as it is; but as Nature hath not made all Creatures alike, for all Flies are not like the Bee, nor all Worms like the Ant, nor all Beasts like the Sheep, nor all Birds like the Nightingal; so indeed Mankind is of a mix'd Nature, and as it were a Composition of all other Animal Creatures, for one may perceive the Natures of other Animal Creatures mix'd in Man, and there is no Motion that belongs most Properly to other Creatures, but Man can Imitate it, nay his very Shape is a Mix'd Shape of all other Creatures, for though he hath not directly four Legs, as Beasts, yet his Arms are something like Legs, and Birds have but two Legs, only Birds Legs are set in the Middle of their Bodies, and Mens are set Below their Bodies, and though Man hath not Fins as Fishes, yet his Arms serve him for the same Use, as to Swim, and so of every Particular Part with the Whole you may find some Mixture, either more or less, of all other Creatures Shapes, as well as Dispositions; and by this Natural Mixture and Composition of Man, you may Compare every other Creature to Man, and Man to every other Creature; and since Man is a Creature made partly of all other Animal Creatures in Mind and Body, as Passions, Humors, Appetites, Senses and Shape, 'tis no Wonder if he be more Various than other Creatures are; but some Men have a Higher Composition than others, as having some Mixture of Celestial Parts, Ingredients, or Influences, with their Terrestrial, yet those are but Few, and a Degree nearer to the Nature of

Gods than other Men, and amongst those Few, Sir, you are one, for which I Admire you, and rest,

> Sir,
>> Your Humble Servant and Affectionate Sister in Law.

LETTER 206

Madam Eleonora Duarti,

The last time I was to Visit you, we fell into a Discourse of the Elixar, and the Philosophers Stone, you being of the Opinion that Gold might be made by the Art of Chymistry, I of the Opinion, it could not be made any other wayes than by the Natural way, as in the Earth. But it may be questionable, whether Gold is made by an Increasable way, or whether it was made all at first, and that there is no more than what was made when the World was made, for I cannot find a Reason against it, but that Gold may be as the Sun, which is Undecayable, and not Increasable, for it is to be Observed, that what is not Decayable, is not Increasable, otherwise it would be Infinite in this World, or Universe, which World, or Universe, hath no Room, or Place for Infinite, and the Sun which is Undecayable, Produces no other Suns, neither doth it Multiply it self, nor Alter from it self; the like of Gold, we cannot make Gold to be no Gold, for Pure Gold cannot be turned into Dross, or into other Dust, whereas all other Creatures, as Minerals, and so Vegetables, and Animals, may, and do Transmigrate, except the Sun, Moon, and Stars, and I do verily believe, it is as Impossible to Fix the Elixar, as to Fix the Sun. But the Difference betwixt the Sun and Gold, for the matter of Outward Form, as well as Several Effects, is, that the Sun is one Entire Body, which is Spherical, and Gold is in many several Parts, which lies in many several Places in the Earth; but Stars which are of the like Undecayable Nature as the Sun, are also in Several Bodies, and at Several Distances, and yet they are Stars nevertheless, and all seem to be as of one Kind or Sort, only some are Fix'd, and others Moveable; so Gold is Gold though in Several Parts, and Several Distances, only I think none is Fix'd, but what cannot be found, for though Gold is not Moveable in it self, yet it is subject to be Moved, and so may the Fix'd Stars, for any Reason to the contrary that ever I heard; And as for Effects and Influences, as the Sun and Stars have several Effects and Influences upon other Creatures, yet we cannot perceive that other Creatures have Effects or Influences upon the Stars or Sun; so Gold hath an Influence, and Works several Effects upon other Creatures, but none upon Gold, I mean in Altring or Changing its Nature, so that Gold seems to me to be the Sun, or Stars of the Earth, which Men in these Ages Adore, as the Heathen did the Sun, and by their Practice one may believe men Commit Idolatry to it; and in comparison to Gold, all other Metals are like Meteors, which do Shine like Stars, but their Light goes oftentimes out, leaving a Jelly, or Slime, as Dross. So other Metals may be Changed from what they were, as from one Metal into another, or from being Metal, but Gold cannot, at least could not as yet, be Altred by the Art of Man, so as it seems that Gold is of as Durable a Nature as the Sun or Stars; neither can I readily believe Gold can Increase, or Multiply it self, no more than the Sun or Stars, for any thing we can perceive; neither can I readily believe, that Gold can be Increased by the Art of Man, as by Chimistry, by reason Artificial Limbicks are not like the Natural Limbick of the Earth, nor the Fire that Chymists use is not like the Fire of the Sun, or the Constant Fire in the Centre of the Earth; wherefore it is not Probable, that Art should Increase Gold by a Small Artificial Limbick, and a Wasting, Uncertain Fire, which must be alwayes Renewed, and Blown, and if it be Improbable that Art can Increase, or Multiply Gold, it is less Probable that Art can Create Gold or any other Creature, though Chymists Pretend they can, they may Imitate Nature by Art, but not Create as Nature doth; as for Natural Poets, who are far beyond Artificial Chymists, their Creation of Fancies is by a Natural way, not an Artificial, and if Gold could be Created as Fancies, Chymists would be Rich, and not so Poor as Poets are, but surely it is impossible for Art to do as Nature doth, for Art neither Knows, nor can Comprehend, at least not put in Practice, the Subtil, and Intricate Motions, Divers Temperaments and Substances put together; neither doth Art know the Timing of Motions and Mixtures, to Create so as Nature doth, for some Creatures in Nature require more Curiosity than others, and some more Several, and Subtil Mixtures than others, and some require Longer Time and Pains than others, so as Man may as well believe he can Create a World, as Create Gold, or any other Creature, as Animals and Vegetables, as Chymists believe they can do by their Art; Men like Painters, may Draw to the Life the Figures of Creatures, but not Create Living Figures, or Real Creatures; 'tis true, Art may Hinder, or Oppose, or Hasten Nature's Works, to a more Sudden Maturity, but not in an Unnatural way; and as for Opposing, or Hindring Nature, Man may Set a Slip, or Kernel, or Seed, and when it is Fix'd, or hath taken Root, Man can Pull it up, and Dissolve it, so as not to be capable to Grow and Increase, nay, man can Dissolve it from its Nature, and Turn it into some other Nature, yet it is Natural for such Dissolvable Creatures to be Transformed into other things, so as it is but a Natural way; but Man cannot Create by Art, for that were an Unnatural way, Man may Increase and Multiply, not only his own Kind, but all Increasable things, but they must be done after their Natural way, or else Man cannot Increase and Multiply. Some, as Chymists, Conceive, or Imagine (for it is but Imaginable) that there are Seeds, or Slips, or Branches of Gold, which may be Producible as Plants are, but I know not where they should find them, nor do I believe if they should Search for them, they would find them, first, as not knowing where they lie, for what Man can Search all the Earth, or Fathom the Earth, or Dig to the Centre of the Earth? next, they do not Know those Branches, Slips, or Seeds to be such; thirdly, if they did Know them, and Had them, yet they Know not how, or when, or where to Set, or Ingraft those Slips or Branches, or to Sow those Seeds, or to Order them in their Limbicks; but I perceive they would make their Limbicks their Increasable Grounds, and every Limbick should be as an Acre of Ground, or a Field, indeed every Still would be worth a Lordship, nay, a Kingdom; fourthly, Man knows not the Time those Slips, Branches, or Seeds, require to be brought to Maturity, for all Creatures are not brought to Maturity in the same distance of Time; as for Example, Animal Creatures, some are Produced in a Month, some in no less time than a Year; so for Plants, some are at Maturity in a Few Hours, at least Dayes, and others not under an Hundred Years, as Oaks; so for any thing we know, Gold could not be brought to Maturity under an Hundred Years, nay a Thousand, Hasten Nature what they can, and nothing can be Hastened in an Unnatural way; nay, in some Creatures Art cannot Hasten Nature, as Animals cannot be Hastened to Perfection sooner than their Natural Time, Art may cause Abortion, as to make the Womb cast forth the Burden before the Natural Time of Birth, but not to bring it to Perfection, and if Man, which is Decayable and Increasable, yet is Ten Months, or say Seven, e're he comes to Maturity, well may Gold, which seems of an Unalterable, or Undecayable Nature, be Seven Ages; and though the Elements seem to be both Decayable and Increasable as Mankind is, yet not the Fix'd, or Celestial Elements, for though Fire Begets Fire, when Fuel is put to it, and goes out for want of Fuel, or may be Quenched out, (for if it did Increase and not Decrease, it would Burn all the World) and though Water be Increasable (although not so Increasing as Fire) as also Decayable, as to Evaporate from its Nature, for else it would Drown the World, yet I do not perceive the Sun or the Earth to be Increasable or Decayable, for if the Sea and Earth did Multiply, the Terrestrial Globe would grow so Big, as the Sun could not Compass it in a Year, and it might grow so Big as not to be Compassed in Many Years; but we observe by the Motion of the Sun, that it is neither Decayable nor Increasable, for if it were Decayable, the Compass of the Sun would be in a Less Circle, as to Compass the Terrestrial Globe in Less than a Year, but whatsoever is not Decayable, is not Increasable, and whatsoever is Increasable is Decayable; and since we find by Experience that Gold is not Decayable, as not to be Changed from its Principal Nature, *viz.* from being Gold, it may be faithfully believed it is not Increasable, otherwise there would be a World, nay Worlds of Gold. Thus, Madam Eleonora, I cannot perceive in my Reason, that Gold can be either Created, or Multiplied by Art, wherefore in my Opinion, Chymists may Break their Limbicks, and Quench out their Fire, and Endeavour to get Natural Gold a Provident way, and not to Impoverish themselves with Art. But leaving them to their Brittle Limbicks, and Quenchable, or Decayable Fire, their Great Expences, and Little Profit, I rest,

Your very Loving Fr. and S.

LETTER 207

Reverend Sir,
I Give you thanks for your Visit, although I made little Profit thereby, for whereas I should have sat and Listened to your Discourse, out of which I should have Learned much Good, both for my Understanding and Course of Life, I was so full of Discourse my self, as I neither gave you time to Speak, nor my self to Hear; indeed it was not so much a Discourse as Words, for in a Discourse there is some Coherence, whenas a Number of Words may be Spoken without any Coherence therein; after that rate I believe I Entertained you, for which I ask your Pardon, which you may the Freelier give me, because I am a Woman, & it is according to our Nature to Speak more Words than Sense, and so well we Love Speaking, as Men might think we had rather to be Damned, at least Condemned, for Talking, than be Praised, or Saved for Silence; yet give me leave to say somewhat in my own Behalf; though I am full of Words when I do Talk, yet I do not give my self Liberty to Speak often, for were the Years of my Life Divided, not Half a part of Four had been Spent in Speech; but howsoever, what I

do Speak is too much, for the truth is, Women should never Speak more than to Ask Rational Questions, or to give a Discreet Answer to a Question Asked them, unless it be in their Huswifry, and then they may take Licence to Speak as much as they will, or at Child-bed Gossipings they may have the Privilege of the Tongue, but other wayes or times, they ought to be Sparing of Speech, especially in Company of Men, but the truth is, our Sex doth not love to be Tongue-tied; but lest I should Express too much the Nature of our Sex, by Speaking too much of them, although I speak now but to your Eyes, not to your Ears, for Letters are more a Discourse to the Eyes than Ears, I will take my leave for this time, only Subscribe my self,

> Sir,
> Your very loving Friend and Servant.

LETTER 208

Worthy Sir,
You may think it a Presumption and an Incroachment upon your Profession, to give my Opinion of Mrs. Ts. Disease, but it is neither Presumption, nor Confidence of my Judgment, that causes this Writing to you, but an Affection to your Patient, who deserves my Concernment concerning her Malady, which Forces me to write to you my Opinion, which is, that I do believe her Pain and that which Accompanies it, is Caused through an Inward Heat, which Rarifies the Humors into a Fluent Distillation, also it Rarifies the Blood, making it to Flow, or Overflow, for Cold is not so Active, but Congeals & Thickens, as we shall see when any Body is let Blood, the Blood whilst it is Hot, runs Freely forth of the Veins, and remains Thin and Fluid when it is out, but when it hath stood some Time, and begins to be Cold, it Thickens, and Congeals to a Cake; so when any hath used Exercise, which Heats, and Thins the Blood, the Colour appears in the Skin, Caused by the Flowing to the Outward Parts; the like in Hot Weather, whereas in Cold Weather, or when the Blood is not Heated, the Skin appears Pale and Lank; wherefore my Opinion is, that her Pain Proceeds from Heat, for it is to be Observed, that all Inflamations are Painful, as all Sores or Swellings that are Inflamed, whereas those Sores that are not Inflamed, or those Swellings we call White Swellings, are not Painful, also for the Gout, the Pain is caused through the Inflamation; but mistake me not, I mean all Pulsive Pains, for there be many other Pains, as some which are caused through Wind, and those Pains are Painful Stitches, and most commonly caused from Hot Humours,

as Bilious Choler, or some Salt Flegm, also Headaches are caused for the most part from Hot Vapours, or Rheums, the Stone in the Kidnies and Bladder is caused through Heat, so that most Pains are caused through Heat, unless it be Child-bearing Pains, and such like; and these Considerations make me believe that Mrs. Ts. Pain in her Back is Produced from Heat; for although it be an Intermitting Pain, and not Constant, yet it may nevertheless be Produced from Heat; as for Example, the Gout is not a Continual Pain, but it is only Painful when the Inflamed Humor falls on the Joynt, yet for the most part it alwayes Falls or Resorts to one and the same Place, wherefore I believe Cooling Medicines must be her Cure, for I do not perceive that Purging, Sweating, and Dry Dieting, which are all Heating, do her any Good, but she seems rather the Worse, and Trial is the True Touchstone of Experience. But you may use the Old Saying to me, which is, Physician Cure thy self; I answer, that all Preachers do not Practise what they Preach, and some may give better Counsel than take Good Counsel, also Solomon sayes, that a Wise Saying may pass through a Fool's Mouth, and the best Physicians when they are Sick, Rely not upon their own Skill for themselves, but will send for other Physicians, for no man can Judg well of himself, either for Health, Sickness, or any other thing, by reason Partial Self-love, Fearful Doubts, Flattering Hopes, Bribe, Corrupt, or Terrifie the Judgment; but setting aside my own Judgment as Weak, either for my self or others, and Relying on yours in Case of your Patient, I rest,

Your very Loving Friend.

LETTER 209

Worthy Sir,
I Received your Letter, and Glad to see you write, that you doubt not of Curing Mrs. T. of her Painful Disease; as for the Numbness in her Hand, Thigh, Leg, and Foot, give me leave to tell you my Opinion, which is, that it Proceeds not from a Coldness but a Dryness, for if it were only a Stupifying Cold, her Sweating would have Rarified and Evaporated that Congeal'd Cold, or her Purging would have Carried or Driven out that Gross, Cold Humor, or her Dry, Strict Diet would have Consumed that Obstructed Cold, or Cold Obstruction, but she hath felt that Numb Disease since she hath used those Remedies, at least, it is more Apparent, which shews, it Proceeds not from Cold, but Dryness, which Inward Heat and Dryness causes a Cold outward Effect, for Numbness and Deadness of

Parts Proceed from Divers, and Different Causes, as from Cold, either Outwardly taken, by the Cold Weather, or Climat, or Clothing, or the like, or by Inward Cold, as by Overcooling Meats, or Drinks, or Cold Obstructing, or want of Blood, or too much Watry Humors, which Quench out the Natural Heat, and this Numbness is easily Cured. Another Numbness Proceeds from Obstructions of the Inward Parts, or Veins, either by Clammy Humors, or by Burnt and Adust Humors. Another Numbness Proceeds from a Driness of some Particular Parts, which being Insipid, cannot be Active, or Move according to their Functions, or Faculties, or Proprieties, and a Ceasing of Motion is Death. Another Numbness Proceeds from some Cold, or Thick Gross Humors that fall upon the Sinews or Muscles. Another Numbness is caused through Excessive Heat, which hath Burnt out the Natural Heat. Another Numbness Proceeds from a Decay of some Noble Parts, and this Numbness is Incurable. But the Reason why I think Mrs. Ts. Numbness Proceeds from Dryness, is, that she hath been of a very Spare Diet three or four Years, Eating and Drinking but once a Day, and that not Much, her Meat being for the most part Rost Mutton, and when she was with Child, she did Eat so Little, & Seldom, as sometimes not in two or three Dayes, as I have often wondred how she could Live, and Nourish her Child within her, which Excessive Fasting must needs Dry, and so consequently Heat her, for though Fasting may Cool after Excess, Wasting the Superfluities, which would otherwise cause too many Vapors, or Corruption, which Corruption, or Vapors, might cause an Unusual, or Unnatural Heat, yet in Scarcity, or where there be no Superfluities, Fasting doth Heat, the like doth Sweating; and thus Mrs. T. finding her Stomack Weak, or rather Ill Digesting, to Strengthen or Ease it, hath Overheated, or Dried the other Parts of her Body, and hath fill'd her Body, or rather her Thread-Veins, with Thin, Sharp, Salt, Bitter Humor, which Humor Proceeds from Heat, and Heat and Dryness many times Proceed from those Humors; where-fore there should be Applyed such Remedies as to Draw out those Pernicious Humors which are Corroding, Burning, and Drying, and there-fore I pray Use Cooling and Moistening Remedies, lest in striving to Cure one Disease, a Worse be Produced, but Cooling and Moistening will not only Cure her Numbness, but the Overflowing of her Natural Flux, which is caused through Heat, which Over Rarifies the Blood, and makes it Flow when it should Ebb, like as a Double Tide; But I leave all to your Better Judgment, Skill, Practice, Observation, and Wisdom, and rest,

Your very loving Friend.

LETTER 210

Madam,

I Hope you will not be Angry, that I do not take your Advice to Leave the Country, and Live in the City, for I have so many Reasons which perswade me not to do it, as this Letter cannot Compass, yet lest I should Offend you, I'l set down some Few: The first is, that it is more Agreeing with my Humor to live in the Country, for Naturally my Humor is a Solitary, Musing, and Contemplating Humor, and my Delight is, to Write those Fancies and Conceptions which my Contemplation doth Produce; all which would be Disturb'd with the several Noises that are made in Populous Cities. The second Reason is, the Preserving of my Health, for I have not a very Strong Body, nor a very Healthful Constitution, although, I thank God, not any Particular Disease, yet so I am, as I do not find my self so Healthful as I wish I were, and therefore a Great and Populous City is not so well agreeing with my Health,[1] as the Sweet, and Fresh Air in the Country, where the Sun and the Wind have Freedom and Power to Disperse, and so to Destroy Malignant Vapors. The third Reason is, that my Husband had an House in the City, but by the Occasion of the Civil Wars, his Estate being Torn in pieces, amongst many Parts which are quite taken from him, and his Posterity, the said House is one, so that we have no House for the present in the City to Live in;[2] But if I had one, truly, Madam, I should not be willing to Live there, for I am so much pleased with a Solitary Country Life, that I cannot bring any Argument to my self, which can Induce or Perswade me to a City Life, which is but a Gossiping, and Vain Life, where there are in Conversations more Idle Words Spoken, than Good Works Done, and more Mony Spent than their Estates are able to Pay; and if I Lived there, and should not Speak Idely, and Spend Vainly, as others do, I should be out of the Fashion, and there is an Old Saying, Better be out of the World than out of the Fashion; But your Chief Argument to perswade me to Live in the City, is, that in a Great and Populous City there are many Learned and Witty Persons, with whom I might Converse, whose Conversation would Increase my Knowledge,[3]

---

1   Dr. Mayerne, her physician, blamed her sedentary life for "superfluity of black bile" (Grant, 105). See letter 130.

2   This appears to be a letter written from Nottinghamshire after the Restoration. Cavendish and her husband eventually owned a townhouse in Clerkenwell that they used for their spring, 1667, visit to London.

3   Cavendish, of course, made a visit to the Royal Society in London some three years after the publication of *Sociable Letters*.

Better my Understanding, Quicken my Wit, and by Practice Refine my Speech or Language; Truly, Madam, the Advantage would be Great if I could Alter the Nature of our Sex, as not to Speak much, but that is Impossible, for all Women, and so I amongst the rest, are more apt to Talk, than to Learn with Attention, so that I should rather Discover my Imperfections by the Superfluity of my Discourse, than gain Applause by my Wit, for I, in my Conversation, Speak, as I may say, without Thinking, or rather Considering, but when I Write, I Think without Speaking; wherefore the Wisest way for me is, rather to Write than to Speak, for then my Speech will not Disgrace my Writings; for most men Judge their Acquaintance rather according to their Words than their Works, and those are most Applauded that are least Known, for the least Errour either in Discourse or Behaviour makes not only the Person of less Esteem, but all the Labours of their Life, were they never so Exact, Wise, or Heroick; wherefore it is a Madness to desire to Converse with much Company, especially for those that desire to keep up a Fame once gotten, unless it be in Publick Actions or Employments; neither doth that last, unless their Actions are like Pyramids which rise still Higher and Higher. But for the most part Man's Nature is so Ambitious as to desire to do Wonders, not contenting themselves with a Mean, and then their Building proves like Babels Tower, full of Confusion. But, Madam, I only desire to keep up those small Mole-hills I have made, that is, the Reputation of my Books, whereas if I did appear to the Publick World, I should be found a Blind Creature as a Mole is, not Blind of the Eyes of my Head, but my Understanding, which is Worse. And as for Conversation and Company, give me leave to tell you, Madam, I do not want a Wise, and Witty Companion, so long as my Lord Lives, neither can I want Friends so long as you both Live, which I pray God to continue to many Years, for these are the constant Prayers of,

> Madam,
> Your faithful Friend and humble Servant.

LETTER 211

Madam,
As I began this Book with those Letters to you, so I will End it, hoping you will Pardon me for Mixing some other Letters with those to your self, for the Assurance and Belief of your Pardon Perswaded me to do it, they are only to my Near and Dear Relations, and Kind and Obliging Friends. But, Madam, I know your Nature and Friendship is such, that what is Fit

and Convenient for me to do, you will Approve, and upon that ground, I am Confident you will not be Angry with me, that I do not Joyn the Answers to those Letters, wherein you were pleased to Propound several Philosophical Questions to me to Resolve, to this Book, for truly, Madam, they are so many, and my Answers to them so Long, that if I should have Joyned them to these, it would have been as a Type, or Resemblance of Infinite Nature, and I am careful not to be too Tedious, or Wearisom to my Readers. Besides, the said Letters containing nothing but Philosophical Questions and Answers, are not so Fit or Proper for this Book, wherein are only Described Humors; wherefore I am Resolved to put your Philosophical Questions and my Answers in a Book by themselves. 'Tis true, many of your Questions are Subtiler than I have Wit to Answer, but according to my Duty, and the Laws of Friendship, I have done as much as I was able, and more I hope you do not Expect, and therefore, though I have not Answer'd them so well as I should have done, and have more reason to fear rather to be Censured, than to hope for any Applause for Publishing them, yet I am satisfied that I have Answer'd your Desire, for I had rather the World should Condemn me for a Fool, than you for the Breach, or but a Neglect in Friendship, for as long as I Live I shall Prove my self,

Madam,
Your constant Friend and faithful Servant.

FINIS.

Here on this Figure Cast a Glance,
But so as if it were by Chance,
Your eyes not fixt, they must not Stay,
Since this like Shadowes to the Day
It only represent's, for Still,
Her Beuty's found beyond the Skill
Of the best Paynter, to Imbrace,
Those louely Lines within her face,
View her Soul's Picture, Iudgment, witt,
Then read those Lines which Shee hath writt,
By Phancy's Pencill drawne alone
Which Peece but Shee, Can justly owne.

Cavendish in Roman dress in a niche.

[Reprinted by permission of the Huntington Library.]

Appendix A: The Context of Family

1. Letters from Margaret Lucas to William Cavendish and Selections from his Poems in Reply (1645)

[Margaret Lucas was in her early twenties when she met William Cavendish, then marquis of Newcastle at the court of Queen Henrietta Maria. Margaret was a Maid of Honor, who had followed the Queen into exile in France after the tide of battle turned against the English King, Henrietta Maria's husband, during the English Civil wars. William was a defeated general on the side of the King and against the Parliament, but he was also a successful playwright and a coterie poet, whose songs were set to music and had appeared in popular songbooks. During the time of his first marriage, he developed a reputation as a ladies' man, which followed him to court. The letters below, which may or may not be in order of composition, give a good indication of the nature of the courtship that took place between Margaret and William during the summer and fall of 1645. Reputation and rumor were a constant concern for the couple, who decided to marry against the advice of friends and contrary to the wishes of the Queen. Some of the letters printed here are quite literary and even elevated in tone (letters 9 and 13), recalling the complexity and wit of metaphysical poetry. Indeed, Margaret may be responding in kind or in a sort of parody to some of the high-flown poetry that William wrote about her and sent to her.[1] Other letters are quite down to earth in their sense of practical politics, as is the case in letter one, which suggests that nobody ever can be assured of having the favor of the King and Queen. So, too, letter fourteen, in which Margaret reminds William that certain aspects of his passion will have to wait for fulfillment until after the two are married. At the same time, Margaret shows that she has a sense of humor and can gently tease the man she loves about his waking her up with a letter delivered before dawn (letter 4). Her assertions of modesty accord with the forms as well as the spirit of the age, especially when one realizes that she was accused of being socially ambitious by some of his friends. Perhaps because of such accusations, she gives William every opportunity to back out of the marriage even as she reaffirms her love for him. William, who was shaken by his defeat on the battlefield, was revitalized during his courtship of Margaret, if his poetry to

---

1   That poetry may be found in Douglas Grant, ed., *The Phanseys of William Cavendish* (London: Nonesuch, 1956).

her is any indication. That defeat was caused at least in part by court politics, and many of his poems show delight in love as well as contempt for
political maneuver. Struggle for position within the court is taken to be
utterly trivial, and even Henrietta Maria, an old friend and ally of William[1]
is no more than Jermyn's Jermyn, a lackey to a lackey ("Song"). At the
same time, William can offer a friendly joke about the Queen thinking that
he and Margaret could somehow be of help to that Royal enemy, the
Parliament ("Love's Thoughts"). Margaret and William were at last married
by John Cosin at the chapel of Sir Richard and Elizabeth Browne in Paris
in December of 1645.[2]]

Lucas's Letters to Newcastle

LETTER I

My Lord,
There is but one accident, which is death, to make me unhappy either to
my friends or fame or your affection, though the last I prefer equal to the
first. But I fear others foresee we shall be unfortunate, though we see it
not our selves, or else there would not be such pains taken to untie the
knot of your affection. I must confess, as you have had good friends to
counsel you, I have had the like to counsel me and tell me they hear of
your professions of affection to me, which they bid me take heed of, for
you had assured yourself to many and was constant to none.[3] I answered
that my Lord Newcastle was too wise and too honest to engage himself to
many. And I heard the Queen should take it ill that I did not make her
acquainted before I had resolved. I asked, "Of what?" They said, "Of
[your] resolution to [him]." I asked if I should acquaint the queen with
every complement that was bestowed on me, with many other idle discourse, which would be too long to write. But pray do not think I am
inquisitive after such frivolous talk, for I avoid company to avoid their discourse. For the King and Queen's favour, my lord, I think you will never
be in danger of losing it, for I never heard that any body perfectly had it.

---

1   See the third letter from Christiana Cavendish, below.

2   In a twist of fate, the daughter of Sir Richard, later Mary Evelyn, would one day worry that
    her own husband was attracted to Margaret. For more on Mary Evelyn and Margaret
    Cavendish, see the final section in the introduction to this book.

3   "You ... was" and other such practices with subject-verb agreement were common in the
    seventeenth century.

For my lord Jermyn,[1] I think you know yourself too well to seek so low, though I will not say but policy sometimes makes use of inferiors. But it is the glory of the inferiors to neglect when they get the advantage of their superiors. They that told you of my mother has better intelligence than I. And sure, my lord, I threw not myself away when I gave myself to you, for I never did any act [so] worthy of praise before. But 'tis the nature of those that cannot be happy to desire none else should be so, as I shall be in having you and will be so in spite of all malice in being, my lord, your most humble servant,

Margaret
Lucas

Pray lay the fault of my [hand]writing to my pen.

LETTER 2

My Lord,

I did not desire to deliver up the interest I had in you out of any constancy in me but out of a consideration of you. Me lord, me lord Widdrington[2] in his advice has done as noble and a true affectionate friend would do, yet I find I am infinitely obliged to you whose affections are above so powerful a persuasion. My lord, if I do not send to[3] you, pray excuse me, for if I do they will say I pursue you for your affection. For though I love you extremely well, yet I never feared my modesty so small as it would give me leave to court any man. If you please to ask the Queen I think it would be well understood. I thank you for the fear you have of my ruin, who cannot be happy in nothing more than being my lord,

your most
humble servant
Margaret
Lucas

---

1   Henry Jermyn, earl of St. Albans was a trusted confidant of Queen Henrietta Maria.

2   William Widdrington, first baron Widdrington (1610–51) was a close friend of William.

3   Invite to come for a visit. William was in Paris at The Louvre and Lucas at the Court of Henrietta Maria in the Palace of St. Germain, about thirteen miles away.

LETTER 3

Pardon me if I have writ any thing that is not agreeable. But, if I be careful in things that may arise to the scandal of my reputation, [it] is for fear of a reflection because I am yours. For, though it is impossible to keep out of the reach of a slandering tongue from an envious person, yet 'tis in my power to hinder them from the advantage of a good ground to build their discourse on. For know, me lord, Saint Germain is a place of much censure and thinks I send too often. Me lord, I am sorry you should think your love so much transcends mine, but sure 'tis as uncomely to see a woman too kind[1] as to see a man too negligent. But, me lord, I know you are a man of so much honour that I may safely rule my actions by your directions and believe my time best spent when you please to command,

> me lord, your
> most humble
> servant,
> Margaret
> Lucas

LETTER 4

My lord,
I think you have a plot against my health in sending so early, for I was forced to read your letter by a candle light for there was not day enough. But I had rather read your letter than sleep, and it doth me more good. My lord, I hope you are not angry for my advice of St. German. I gave it simply for the best. As for Mr. Porter, he was a stranger to me, for before I came in to France I did never see him, or at least knew him not to be Mr. Porter or my lord of Newcastle's friend.[2] And, my lord, it is a custom I observe that I never speak to any man before they address themselves to me, nor to look so much in their face as to invite their discourse. And I hope I never was uncivil to any person of what degree so ever. But tomorrow the Queen comes to Paris they say, and then I hope

---

1   Too free with sexual favors.

2   Endymion Porter (1587–1649) was often asked to intercede at court on behalf of friends and family (Gervas Huxley, *Endymion Porter: The Life of a Courtier* [London: Chatto and Windus, 1959] 195).

to justify myself to be, my lord, the most humble servant to you and your servants,

Margaret Lucas

If you cannot read this letter blame me not, for it was so early I was half asleep.

LETTER 5

My lord,
There is none could be more sorry to part with any thing they love so well as I do you, but it was my affection to you, not to myself, as made that desire [for marriage] to leave me. I consider none so much as to be displeased or dislike any thing in you for any consideration of what others can say, for that you think to be best shall please me most. My lord, I have heard they that have many suits to prosecute[1] of their own seldom prefer[2] any other, or if they do, so slightly as not to be regarded. Wherefore I believe my lord Jermyn has too many employments of the Queen's for to dispatch yours. It was said to me you had declared your marriage to my lord Jermyn. I assured it was more than I could do. But here is so many idle discourses as it would weary me to tell them and you to hear them. I wish myself better not only for my advantage but that I may be worth your acceptance, which I shall endeavor to be the more because I am, my lord,

your most humble
servant
Margaret
Lucas

LETTER 6

My lord,
Your verses are more like you than your picture, though it resembles you very much. But here[3] art has not been so good a courtier as it used to be.

---

1   Requests to make (of the Queen, in this case).

2   Put forward.

3   It appears that Margaret sent a portrait miniature of herself in response to one sent to her by William.

My lord, the only blessing I wish for here is I may deserve your affection, which is invaluable. I have sent this here in obedience to your commands, which I shall always be ready to execute with that observances as becomes my lord, your most

humble, servant,

Margaret Lucas

LETTER 7

My lord,
Pray believe I am not factious, especially with you, for your commands shall be my law. But suppose me now in a very melancholy humor, and that most of my contemplations are fixed on nothing but dissolutions. For I look upon this world as on a death's head for mortification. For I see all things subject to alteration and change and all our hopes as if they had taken opium. Therefore I will despise all things of this world, I will not say all things in it, and love nothing but you, that is above it. But I should be lost to those thoughts if I did not meet some of you to restore me to myself again. My lord, I hear the Queen comes to Paris this next week to the solemnities of Princess' Mary's marriage,[1] and I am in dispute wither I should come with her, if I can get leave to stay. My reason is because I think it will stop the source of their discourse of us when they see I do not come. But I shall not do any thing without your approbation, as becomes your most humble servant,

Margaret

Lucas

My lord, let your eye lament your poetry.

LETTER 8

As grace draws the soul to life, so nature, the pencil of God, has drawn your wit to the birth, as may be seen by your verses — though the subject[2] is too mean for your muse. The medium and species of my sight and understanding are flatted to all things in respect of what comes from you,

---

1   On November 5, 1645, Marie-Louise de Gonsague-Nevers married Vladislav VII of Poland.

2   Margaret, herself.

and more united and contracted than is represented from your lordship. I should be sorry [if] your affection should be as broken as the case of your picture. It can be no ill omen of my part.[1] I know not what it may be of yours. I hope it is not ravenlike to give warning of death, but I wish life only to be still, my lord, your

humble servant,
Margaret Lucas

LETTER 9

My lord,
I thank you for the token of love you sent me, for I must confess I want it, were it but to return it on yourself again. Or although I give you all the love I have, yet is 'tis too little for your merit. Or could I wish for more love than ever was or shall be, yet my wish could not be so copious but you would be still as far beyond it as your worth is above other men's. My lord, I am sorry you should bid me keep the verses you sent, for it looks as though you thought I had flung those away you sent before. Surely I would keep them were it with difficulty, and not to part with your muses so easily. And believe me, I will part with nothing that you shall command me to keep or with the name of being, my lord, your most humble servant,

Margaret
Lucas

My lord, the Queen comes not till Friday, if then.

LETTER 10

My lord,
I am a little ashamed of my last letter more than of the others. Not that my affection can be too large but I fear I discover it too much in that letter, for women must love silently. But I hope you will pardon the style because the intention was good. My lord, I can believe nothing but what is in honour of you, and beseech you to believe that I have ever truth of my side, though naked. Therefore I never said any such thing as you mentioned in your letter of your picture, nor never so much as showed it to any creature before

---

1   In my view.

yesterday, that I gave it to mend. But I find such enemies that whatsoever can be for my disadvantage, though it have but a resemblance of truth, shall be declared. I hope my innocence will guard me, but sure, my lord you have many friends though I have many enemies, or else this is a counseling age. But if I shall prejudice you[1] in the affaires of the world or in your judgment of your bad choice, consider and leave me. Or I shall desire to live no longer than to see you happy, which am so much, my lord,

> your most humble
> servant,
> Margaret Lucas

It is not usual to give the Queen gloves or any thing else but, my lord, if you please I will give them her.

LETTER 11

My lord,
I am sorry you have metamorphosed my letter and made that masculine that was effeminate. My ambition was to be thought a modest woman and to leave the title of a gallant man to you. For nature would seem as defective to give a woman the courage of a man as to give a man the weakness of a woman. But surly, my lord, I shall be content to be anything you would have me to be, so I am yours. My lord, I am sorry you have such a defluxion[2] in your eyes. I fear your writing may draw down the rheum too much, though I rejoice at nothing more than your letters. But instead of joy they would bring me sadness if I received them at such a disadvantage as to hurt them. And let me entreat you to laugh[3] no more at the letters of her who is so much, my lord,

> your humble
> servant,
> Margaret
> Lucas

---

1   Cause people to have prejudice against you because I am your wife.

2   Flow.

3   In the manuscript, it is unclear whether the word is "lafe" or "lase." Battagelli chooses "lase" and glosses the author's intent as "lose no more time."

LETTER 12

My lord,

I may very well take all your faults to me and yet be excusable for what is yours, though not for my own. And 'tis no mercy to sign a pardon where there has been no offence. I must confess my discretion did never appear so much as by my affection to love a person of so much worth as yourself. And yet, me lord, I must tell you I am not easily drawn to be in love, for I did never see any man but yourself that I could have married. My lord, if my descent did not hinder me more than the visits I receive in my chamber, I may, by the favour of Mr. Stuart, be one of the Queen of Spain's maids without dishonour to her person. I never knew the vice of envy but I must have a large proportion of grace to arm me against it if I had a rival in your affection, especially an enemy's daughter.[1] But were I sure you should hate me as I hope you love me, yet I will be, my lord,

> your most
> humble servant,
> Margaret Lucas

The Queen takes no note of anything to me.

LETTER 13

My lord,

I wonder not at my love but at yours, because the object of mine is good. I wish the object of yours were so, yet me thinks you should love nothing that were ill, therefore if I have any part of good 'tis your love makes me so. But loved I nothing else but you, I love all that is good, and, loving nothing above you, I have love's recompense. My lord I have not had much experience of the world, yet I have found it such as I could willingly part with it. But since I knew you, I fear I shall love it too well because you are in it. And yet methinks you are not in it because you are not of it. So

---

1 It is difficult to sort out the references to actual people in this letter. Grant says that he tried and failed to identify Mr. Stuart (*Phansies*, 125). It may be that much like Dorothy Osborne who jokes with William Temple about rivals, Margaret first mentions a possible rival to William (Mr. Stuart) and then suggests one for herself (the "enemy's daughter"). In any event, she feels that the status of her family (her "descent") has been found wanting by men like Widdrington and jokingly suggests that she might give up being a Maid of Honor to the Queen of England in order to accept that position with the Queen of Spain, whose court would not contain his friends and her enemies.

I am both in it and out of it, a strange enchantment. But pray love so as you may love me long, for I shall ever be, my lord your most humble servant,

> Margaret
> Lucas

My lord, they say the Queen comes to morrow.

LETTER 14

My lord,
It may be the trial but it 'tis not true love that absence or time can diminish, and I shall as soon forget all good as forget you. Me lord, you are a person I may very confidently own unless moral merit be a scandal. But, me lord, there is a customary law that must be signed before I may lawfully call you husband, if you are so passionate as you say, and I dare not but believe. Yet it may be feared it cannot last long, for no extreme is permanent. But howsoever unworthy I am in myself, I am estimable as I am one that is,

> me lord, your
> most faithful and
> humble servant,
> Margaret Lucas

LETTER 15

My lord,
Were I much sicker than I was, your kind care would cure me. I am a feared it were an ambition to desire much of your love, knowing myself of little dessert. And yet methinks it should be no sin when the desire is good. My lord, I sent a letter by my maid. I should be sorry if you thought any line can come from you could be any other way than pleasing to me. For that is only troublesome which is foolish or impertinent, with which you will never be taxed nor your judgment—unless now in choosing me. But being as your choice makes it good, and so I shall value myself, which else I should not. And esteeming myself the more for being, my lord, your most humble servant,

> Margaret Lucas

LETTER 16

My lord,
I have received your letter, which seems to satisfy me against the noise of a court. But when I read your lordship's justification under your own hand, I consider 'tis all the satisfaction can be given from a person of honour. But now having so great an injunction as is laid upon me in the name of a brother,[1] which has so great a power, together with your lordship's excuse, that having some occasions of my own this week that will draw me to Paris, of which I believe your lordship may hear of, my lord, your humble servant,

M.L.

LETTER 17

My lord,
There is nothing will please me more than to be where you are, and I begin to admire Paris because you are in it. My lord, the reason I had to conceal our affections was because I thought it would be agreeable to your desire. But for my part I would not care if the trumpet of fame blew it throughout all the world, if the world were ten times bigger than 'tis. For it would be an advantage to me and my judgment. And though I am guilty of faults I may be ashamed to own, yet since they are known in heaven I care not what can be known on earth. And I doubt not but heaven doth approve and will give a blessing to my affections to you. But setting aside all my faults, I shall never leave to have that virtue as to be, my lord, your most humble servant,

Margaret Lucas

LETTER 18

My lord,
I should be sorry if your business be not according to your desire, and pray, me lord, consider well whether marrying me will not bring a trouble to yourself. For believe me, I love you too well to wish you unhappy, and I had rather lose all happiness myself than you should be unfortunate. But

---

1   William's brother was Sir Charles Cavendish.

if you be resolved, what day so ever you please to send for me I will come. My lord, I know not what counsel to give concerning the Queen, but I fear she will take it ill if she be not made acquainted with our intentions. And if you please to write a letter to her and send it to me I will deliver it that day {we be marred} you send for me.[1] I think it no policy to displease the Queen, for though she will do us no good she may do us harm. I have sent my maid about some business and she and my lady Browne shall agree about the other things you speak of. I understand the persuasion of some against your marriage. Sure they would not persuade you but for your good. But if you think you have done unadvisedly in promis[ing] yourself to me, send me word and I will resign up all the interest I have in you, though unwillingly. But what would I not do for any thing that may conduce to your content. For hereafter if you should repent, how unfortunate a woman should I be. I have been very ill of three[2] days, but health cannot be so pleasing to me as knowing myself to be, my lord,

your most humble
servant,
Margaret
Lucas

Pray, me lord, do not mistrust me for telling of anything that you have commanded my silence in, for though I am a woman I can keep counsel, but have not power to offer the imaginations of others.

{Pray remember I have enemies}
Pray consider I have enemies.

LETTER 19

My lord,
It can be in nobody's power to use me ill if you use me well. I have not been with the Queen as yet by reason I am not well, but I hear she would have me acknowledge myself in a fault and not she to be in any. But it will be hard for me to accuse myself and to make myself guilty of a fault when I am innocent. But if it be the duty of a servant to obey all the commands of mistress, though it be against myself I will do it — if it be but to

---

1   Material deleted by the author is placed in curly brackets.

2   The original spelling of "three" is "thee," perhaps a slip of the pen.

bring myself into use of obedience against I am a wife. For the hindrance of our marriage, I hope it is not in their power. I am sure they can not hinder me from loving, for I must be and will be and am, my lord, your admiring, loving, honouring, humble and obedient servant,

Margaret
Lucas

LETTER 20

My lord,
My health will be according as I imagine your affection, for I shall never be sick so long as you love me. My lord, I hope the Queen and I am friends. She sayeth she will seem so, at lest, but I find if it had been in her power she would have crossed us. I heard not of the letter, but she sayeth to me she had it in writing that I should pray you not to make her acquainted with our destines. My lord, since our affections is published it will not be for our honours to delay our marriage. The Queen does intend to come on Monday. If not, I will send you word. I will wait on her first to Paris and then I am at your service to be commanded as, my lord, your most humble servant,

Margaret Lucas

LETTER 21

My lord,
I desire nothing so much as the continuance of your affection, for I think myself richer in having that than if I were a monarch of all the world. My lord, I hope the Queen and I shall be very good friends again, and may be the better for the differences we have had. It was reported here that you would be with us before we could be with you, and be assured I will bring none to our wedding but those you please. I find to satisfy the opinion we are not marred already we must be married by one of the priests here, which I think Cosin to be the fittest.[1] We shall not come till Monday, if then but there is no time can alter my affection. I know not what it can do [to] you[rs] for I am perfectly, my lord, your most humble servant,

Marg Lucas

---

1   John Cosin (1594–1672), Anglican chaplain to the Royalist exiles.

Love's Consideration of his Mistress' Picture

When view'd your picture, so divine,
And did consider every line,
The figure and each mingl'd color,
That life itself could not be fuller
So pencil'd by the painter's art
That at my eyes it struck my heart.

And all Love's passions it did move
That ever yet was known in love.
Then thought to touch that part, then this,
And then to steal a gentle kiss.
But check't those thoughts as sin and then
Turn'd all to eyes, look't on 't again.

The more I look't, that urg'd each thought
To think a kiss now not a fault,
Nor rudeness in my lips at all
On your twins tempting lips to fall,
Since their magnetic power did draw
Mine to them by love's, Nature's, law.

When kist, then sigh'd and drop't a tear
Because my touch found you not there.
'T was not your picture I did see
Drawn by the painter, but in me
By first impressions. And this new
Picture those motions did renew.

Those species cousining,[1] gliding pass,
Like Sisyphus in his water glass.[2]
But truly all things do obtain

---

1   Ghosts or illusions which trick.

2   William probably means Tantalus, who was placed in Hades up to his neck in water, which
    would recede when he tried to drink. The image of a man in a water glass unable to drink,
    of course, is a strange image such as might be found in metaphysical poetry.

Nothing but motion in our brain.[1]
Since touch not pleas'd but only sight,
I'll wink, so please my touch delight.

Love's Thoughts

Thus I doe think 'tis strange I never heard
From my dear love so long. Is the way barr'd?
Or doth the state of France think it their gain
By parting us the better to beat Spain?
Or else our sacred Queen thinks our intent
Something against her by us for Parliament?
For else we sure should meet. Is there no hope?
Doth Digby hinder it now from the Pope,
Or doubts our meeting may perchance miscarry
The Grand Duke's sister with our Prince to marry.
Mademoiselle or Prince of Orange's daughter?[2]
What is the cause we met not? Who's the author?
It is so long, so long ago since met.
I doubt[3] you will me utterly forget.
It is now how long? It is, let me see,
Since I had a letter or did hear from thee,
I vow it is, protesting here I may,
'Tis since I heard from you, 'tis one whole day.
Oh, gods, oh gods, how it doth grieve my soul.
Longer than six month's day at either pole.
Methuselah from 's death to 's youth and prime
To this long day was not a minutes' time.
Adam his days to this poor dust and earth
So sort to ours as strangl'd in his birth.
From the creation,[4] reckon day and night,

---

1   William invokes a notion of the time, which suggests that thought is nothing but matter in
motion in the brain.

2   This passage alludes to Henrietta Maria's attempts to find a wife for her son Charles, later
Charles II. Two candidates were "La Grande Mademoiselle," daughter of the duke of
Orleans, and a daughter of the Prince of Orange. The reference to the Grand Duke's sister
is obscure.

3   Fear.

4   From the creation until now.

When god commanded, "Now let there be light."
Not so much time consum'd as in our day.
Nor nature in that made so much decay.
Pray you then come or write or send that, that
We may do something, but if I know what
I am a villain. What I think of thee
Is still too big to be exprest by me.
Here by our love I swear that it is true,
Methinks, so long since I did hear from you
That almanacs are false, so lay them by,
And all that tells me other ways do lie.
They say 'tis but a day, but doth enrage
Me so because to me it is an age.
We'll have new ephemerides[1] and make
Love's almanacs from them for our each sake,
And hour glasses, whose last dropping sand
Heap hills of hours, nay, for years shall stand,
When parted. But when met, time shall stand still.
Observing us and waiting of our will.

Hymen's Anchorite[2]

Like an old soldier in Queen Venus' wars,
My wounds of love turn'd all to mangl'd scars,
Love's broken spear and bowed sword do meet
As offrings at your sacred altar's feet.
My discharged pistol, rusty arms, though strong,
Dismounted cannon here doth lie along.[3]
And all Love's magazine, that's thought divine,
I sacrifice here at Love's flaming shrine.
As all sweet powders, essence, sweet balls, oils,
Rich clothes, feathers, ribbons, and all Love's spoils
I here give up. All poetry renounce,
Gainst fanci'd rhyme or verse I here pronounce.
Though your maim'd soldier, Venus, scorn to beg

---

1   Almanacs, with a pun on ephemera, short lived May flies.

2   Hymen was the classical god of marriage and an anchorite was a hermit.

3   These opening lines anticipate Rochester's "Disabled Debauchee," but that poem continues
     in an altogether different vein.

So much of you to buy a wooden leg
Nor pension from Love's country, I'll be script
Stark naked first, so to my parish whipt.[1]
You have a shrine but are no saint, they say.
I have a Hymen's saint to whom I'll pray.
A glorified body she doth hold,
So purslane-like,[2] so crystal pure her mold,
As not a spot of sin on her doth fall.
Most thinks she's free of what's original.[3]
There dropping Hymen's beads with homage bow
And sacrifice my pious heart, there vow
Your holy anchorite to be alone
Within your marriage walls, thus two's made one.
And so with holy rites more pleasure have
Than soles that's damn'd for it, yet ours we'll save.
So have two heavens by infused grace,
See you here and so God there, face to face.[4]
Beatifical vision, thus we'll do,
Sav'd by you here and in the next world, too.

A Song

All my misfortunes they are gone
Now we are one.
Despise the greatest monarchs' frowns
And all their crowns,
And trifling of all. What's mankind?
Like various wind.
Like boys that feathers blow, these be
Compared to thee.

---

1 Begging by war veterans and those posing as war veterans was often a nuisance, and such beggars were often driven from town to town. The home parish was responsible for its own
poor. See A.L. Beier, *Masterless Men: The Vagrancy Problem in England, 1560–1640* (London:
Methuen, 1985).

2 Purslane, an herb found in kitchen gardens of the time.

3 Original sin.

4 Newcastle mixes a biblical allusion with a sexual pun: "For now we see through a glass,
darkly; but then face to face." 1 Corinthians 13:12.

Elizabeth Cavendish Egerton and her husband.

[Reprinted by permission of the New York Public Library.]

What's court's dissembling? Let them lie.
Or what's Digby?[1]
Or greatness of our great French Queen?[2]
Or Mazarin?[3]
Or our Queen? Do all she can,
Jermyn's Jermyn.
Not picking straws,[4] he, she, or he,
Compared to thee.

[Source: *The Phanseys of William Cavendish, Marquis of Newcastle, Addressed to Margaret Lucas*, ed. Douglas Grant (London: Nonesuch, 1956).]

2. A Letter from Elizabeth Cavendish Egerton to Jane Cavendish Cheyne (1659)

[It is sometimes suggested that Margaret Cavendish did not get along well with two of her stepdaughters, Jane Cavendish Cheyne and Elizabeth Cavendish Egerton, countess of Bridgewater. There were, however, many tensions within the family, and in the letter below Elizabeth describes her dismay regarding the speed with which her brother Henry has assumed the title of earl of Mansfield after the death of her eldest brother, Charles.[5] Clearly Elizabeth hopes that the widow of Charles is with child and that the child will be a boy. If this were true, then Henry's assumption of the title would have been invalidated. At the same time, Elizabeth seems to know that the widow was not pregnant, and that hunch was right.]

Ashridge [Hall] the 18th of September, 1659

My most dear sister,
I am sorry to hear you have not been well but hope you are better, and for God's sake keep yourself warm. I never heard the like of how earnest[6] my

---

1   Sir Kenelm Digby (1603–65), Chancellor to Queen Henrietta Maria.

2   Anne of Austria (1601–66) was Queen of France.

3   Cardinal Mazarin (1602–61), a favorite of the French Queen.

4   Perhaps tooth picks.

5   See the introduction to Betty S. Travitsky, *Subordination and Authorship* (Tempe: Arizona Center for Medieval and Renaissance Studies, 1999) for more on the life of Elizabeth.

6   Grave or serious.

brother's Mrs. is, for as yet I cannot call her by any other name though he is pleased to write his name to me "H. Mansfield." And I received a letter from my sister Mansfield [widow of the elder brother, Charles], who sayeth her midwife discourages her very much, for she fears she is not with child so 'tis not positive as yet. So as yet I shall forbear answering his letter. It [Henry's letter] was sealed with 3 seals upon a piece of paper, upon the seal with three sails with the snake. I conceive it was because my sister Mansfield's letter was sealed with three seals of K Bunl[1] as if it had been broken open, so I believe Mr. Barbarry had sent it to him [Henry] & so he [Henry] opened it and reseal[ed it]. For my sister Mansfield used to seal with fleur-de-lis. Truly though I know [from] my dear sister Bolingbrooke by her letter that he [Henry] did writ his name Mansfield, yet it put me into a passion of weeping to see another hand with that name and Mansfield and not his [Charles's] child and he not have a child. A girl of his would have been some comfort. I do not perceive he [Henry] hath written so to any of you but to me. For he thinks it angers me by reason I gave counsel to her [the widow of Charles] to come up. Truly I think if he was not so hasty it would have been much better for it would not have been stolen from him [goods stolen from the house by servants after the death of Charles], and if a boy yet should come it will be much to his [Henry's] dishonor. We [Elizabeth, countess of Bridgewater, and her husband John] are so much from repining at his [Henry's] honor that 'tis happy we have a brother to hold up the family and the greater our family is the greater honor 'tis to us. And we must give God thanks both for our father [William Cavendish, duke of Newcastle] and mother [Elizabeth Bassett, Newcastle's first wife] and not [consider various honors] a birthright to ourselves, for from them we come: so should my brother own it. For he is in that family he was borne and to be [remain]. In his letter was only he was [he stood alone as the new heir to William Cavendish].

Glad to hear by Mr. Brenoyt's letter weekly that so my son and mine are well. And so this is word for word [the contents of Henry's letter]: "Truly out of Gods great goodness to me I have been better than I did expect. Next week I believe I shall take a scorbutecal course of physic[2] by doctor Crib's directions. He is my very good friend. My wife presents her humble service to you and my Lord, to whom I present mine and am ..." And so ended his letter. This was his letter. When I see you, I will show it you. I know not [but that] he may mean [what] is better than he did expatiate by

---

1   Not identified.

2   Medicine given to treat scurvy.

the honor and estate, but I take it as he wrote it. His health I hope without two senses in it. My Lord presents his humble service to you both. Ours I pray to my brother Cheyne. Your blessing I pray to all mine and service to all your sweet babes and I beseech God bless you. With this [set of blessings] you go withal.[1] And send you have a better going with it than you have had [last few words of the letter cut off at this point].

[Source: Huntington Library manuscript MS EL 8048.]

3. Letters from Christiana Cavendish, Countess of Devonshire, to William Cavendish (1630s)[2]

[Christiana Bruce Cavendish, countess of Devonshire, was an attractive widow and the cousin by marriage of Margaret's husband, William Cavendish. In letter one printed below, Christiana flirts with William even as she asks after the health of his first wife, Elizabeth Bassett Cavendish. In this letter and in others, Christiana gives him medical advice and in so doing is not unlike Margaret, who frequently offers such counsel in Sociable Letters. Both Christiana and Margaret confess that they are not medical doctors, but the fact is that many aristocratic women were well versed in home remedies and were major sources for health care in the seventeenth century. In each instance, the confession is ironic, for Margaret and Christiana both challenged medical doctors as the sole authorities on the treatment of illness (see Sociable Letters, letter 208).

Christiana was William's ally at court in London while he remained in Nottinghamshire at his home at Welbeck, not far from hers at Chatsworth. William, at the time that these letters were written, was hoping to become Governor of Charles, prince of Wales. The governorship was an important and well-paying court office that he finally obtained, though in due course lost. In the letters, Christiana spends some time describing what is going on at court but does so circumspectly and sometimes in code. Thus, she refers to King Charles I as "the captain" and Queen Henrietta Maria as "the ensign." In the 1640s and during the Civil Wars, letters of this sort were sometimes intercepted and published so as to discredit the writers. Although the consequences of an intercepted letter were less serious in the 1630s, when these letters were written, one still had to anticipate that a letter could fall into the wrong hands. Women

---

1   In addition.

2   A note in pencil on letter 1 reads "1634."

Christiana Cavendish, countess of Devonshire.

[Reprinted by permission of the North Carolina Museum of Art.]

often played important roles in court politics, as Margaret Cavendish implies at various points in *Sociable Letters*. In *Sociable Letters*, she shows distain for such activity, but she, herself, was accused of influencing her husband's political position just prior to the Restoration.[1]

Christiana was a woman of considerable standing in seventeenth-century England. She was a patron of literary men, and her household at Chatsworth included the philosopher Thomas Hobbes, who was tutor to her children. She was also quite active in politics, and George Monck, later duke of Albemarle, may have used her as an intermediary in beginning his negotiations for the return of King Charles II to England. After the Restoration in 1660, Charles II frequented her house at Roehampton in London.]

LETTER 1

My lord,

I hope it is for your secret sins and not your declared sickness that you undergo so great a penance.[2] Since you can so easily submit to a voluntary martyrdom, I wish I could translate my faults to have them comprehended within your sufferings, so little compassion have I of your comfortings. Yet I am not so destitute of pity to deny you to a better advice than I believe you take to your self. That is that in this season that draws toward winter you should give over so rough a course [of medicine] as is prescribed you. It will be sure to have you weak, and I fear rather change your sickness into another than bring you the remedy you expect. If the spleen be your disease for whatever cause abates strength, I believe your lordship will and shall improve that fantastical sickness. You will laugh that I assume skill like to a physician. Wherein my judgment fails, your lordship I know will allow me the liberty women use to take to speak their own thought to little purpose. If I were so never to attend one, perhaps those busy impertinences would equal all other vexations you have brought upon yourself. News I have none, and which is strange I had there none of at court. My lord Cottington[3] seems to be as strange to the place they have destined for him as if it were the first day he was betrothed, which puts some in doubt. I think it affected modesty.

---

1 Grant, 171.

2 Perhaps not being able to visit Christiana in London.

3 Cottington was a friend of William, who became Chancellor of the Exchequer.

I hear of no change of officers If at this defect you find greater qualms, send not so far as Doctor Moore. I have excellent cordials at our lordship's service as is

your very humble servant
C. Devonshire

[On the back] Commend my humble service to my lady. I fear she is most to be pitied, that is tied to the observation of so ill company as I believe your lordship at this time, for I hear you refuse the visits of fair ladies. I am very sorry Sir Charts finds cause of complaint.[1]

[Source: University of Nottingham Libraries, Portland Papers, Pw 1.56.]

LETTER 2

My lord,
I know not whether I shall prevent[2] the captain. If I doe fall short of the carrier,[3] yet the news I meet withal in this place your lordship shall receive. It is enough if they may let it appear I attempt to obey you [in] the worst of all sacrifices. Your lordship sees ground for a faire conjecture that my lord Cottington wins ground. It is said the bishop has kist the King's hands. Of that I am not certain but his peace is made. My company seems to be so welcome to these good people that they allow me no time to acknowledge [any] other duty than what I owe to them. This I will assume your lordship must excuse me and assume you are attended upon with the best of affection that can be presented to you, from all your humble servants here together,

C. Devonshire

[Source: University of Nottingham Libraries, Portland Papers, Pw 1.62.]

---

1 Sir Charles, brother to William, is also sick.

2 Arrive before. "The captain" is probably code for the King. See ensign below.

3 Miss the person who brings the mail.

LETTER 3

My lord,

I am forced to present you with hasty lines because I would not pass over this messenger [and] because I cannot promise myself suddenly the like opportunity. I am not able to give your lordship so perfect and exact relation of the little time I have wasted here as you are of yours that have leisure to observe how it is disposed of. For hitherto, I have not commanded more than a thought of what is mine and that seldom in a crowd of thoughts can be preserved entire. I no sooner arrived in this place but I was engaged in a feast, and the strivings to exceed I fear will never suffer it to determine [the best feast] until your lordship come to give it the height of perfection and that may slack this ambition.[1] I find few changes at court, little friendships, and great emulations, more that strives than there's rewards for. The young prince is sweet and mild. I believe as fit to court as conquer, and with those recreations the youth employs to amuse him he is extremely well used by their majesties.... Now I hear you are designed for to receive the custody of the prince, to which I give, as little credit. Goring got up his rest upon it and I believe you will not pursue the competition. Last night my lord chamberlain made a huge feast, and a very fine one tomorrow is the ensign's[2] pastoral, then she retires, and then of hope we shall be becalmed. It is her court makes the pueril.[3] I dare not descend to particulars except I had characters.[4] Writ by lady fancy has one active part would enlarge your science. If you were a spectator, his majesty goes as yet the twelve of February to Newmarket.[5]

> Your lordship's most humble
> Servant
> C. Devonshire

---

1 William had given two lavish feasts for King Charles I in the early 1630s, to which Christiana may allude.

2 Apparently code for the Queen, see Captain above.

3 Juvenile (French), i.e., Charles, Prince of Wales.

4 Secret code.

5 A town famous for horseracing.

[Margin:] I cannot send your lordship the recipe of this extract of crystal.[1] The doctor will not communicate the secret. If you lordship use it, let it be a quarter of a spoonful in a glass of beer, as much as you can well drink at a draught. If you like it, I shall send you as much as you please. It is the greatest cooler that ever I took. Drink not above three days together. These pots of jelly: command as many as you please. Present my love and service to my lady. My hearty wishes of much happiness to all yours.

[Source: University of Nottingham Libraries, Portland Papers, Pw 1.63.]

---

1   Chemical salt as with crystal of alum.

Appendix B: The Context of Women's Letters

1. Letters from Dorothy Osborne to William Temple

[Much of the courtship conducted between Dorothy Osborne (1627–95) and William Temple is preserved in letters that were first published in the nineteenth century, though only her side of the exchange survives. The letters cover a wide range of subjects and offer commentary on a number of marriages that took place during the two-year period before she and Temple themselves were wed. In her views of love generally and of her own case in particular, Osborne is by turns romantic and pragmatic. At one point, she agrees with Temple that love is a sort of "friendship perfect" (letter 28), while at another she firmly states that she would never marry a man who was only worth 200 pounds a year (letter 56). She sometimes teases Temple in a comic sort of way, as with the story of the man who wanted to marry her in the event of his wife's death. The man died and so, says Osborne, Temple might want to marry the rich widow who is due to come on the marriage market (letter 21). Osborne's brother at first opposed the marriage between her and Temple but later became her "friend," that is advisor and agent in the marriage negotiations (letter 56). Her brother made sure, at her direction, that she would obtain the best possible terms in her jointure, for a jointure insured that a wife was given adequate support in the event of her husbands' death. Osborne wrote a total of 77 letters to Temple as part of their courtship, letters that were not intended for publication but that were nevertheless carefully written. She and Temple were married in 1654.]

From LETTER 21

Were my face in no more danger of changing than my mind, I should be worth the seeing at threescore, and that which is but very ordinary now would be counted handsome for an old woman. But, alas, I am more likely to look old before my time with grief. Never anybody had such luck with servants, what with marrying and with dying they all leave me. Just now I have news brought me of the death of an old rich knight[1] that has promised me this seven years to marry me whensoever his wife died,

---

1   One of the lower orders of aristocracy.

and now he's dead before her and has left her such a widow it makes me made me mad to think on't — £12,000 a year jointure and £20,000 in money and personal estate — and all of this I might have had if Mr. Death had been pleased to have taken her instead of him. Well, who can help these things? But, since I cannot have him, would you have her? She will marry for certain, and though perhaps my brother may expect I should serve him in it, yet, if you give me commission, I'll say I was engaged beforehand for a friend[1] and leave him to shift for himself. You would be my neighbor if you had her, and I should see you often. Think on't, and let me know what your resolve. My lady has writ me word that she intends very shortly to sit at Lely's for her picture for me.[2] I give you notice on't that you may have the pleasure of seeing it sometimes whilst 'tis there. I imagine 'twill be so to you, for I am sure it would be a great one to me and we do not use to differ in our inclinations, though I cannot agree with you that my brother's kindness to me has anything of trouble in't. No, sure I may be just to you and him both, and to be a kind[3] sister will take nothing from my being a perfect friend [to you].

From LETTER 28

'Tis most true that our friendship has been brought up hardly[4] enough and possibly it thrives the better for't. 'Tis observed that surfeits[5] kill more than fasting does, but ours is in no danger of that. My brother would per-suade me there is no such thing in the world as a constant friendship. People, he says, that marry with great passion for one another, as they think, come afterwards to lose it they know not how, besides the multi-tude of such as are false and mean it.[6] I cannot be of his opinion, though I confess there are too many examples on't. I have always believed there might be [in marriage] a friendship perfect like that you describe, and methinks I find something like it in myself [for you]. But sure 'tis not to

---

1 Here "advisor and agent in a marriage negotiation."

2 Parry identifies the lady as Diana Rich. Sir Peter Lely was an important portrait painter. Temple, living in London, could visit the artist's studio, while Osborne, situated in the coun-try had to wait until the portrait was finished and delivered to its owner.

3 Here "affectionate."

4 In difficult circumstances.

5 Overeating.

6 Intend to be false from the onset.

be taught. It must come naturally to those have it, and those who have it not can ne'er be made to understand it.

You need not have feared that I should take occasion from your not answering my last [letter] not to write this week. You are as much pleased, you say, with writing to me as I can be to receive your letters. Why should you not think the same of me? In earnest, you may and if you love me you will, but then how much more satisfied would I be if there were no need of these and we might talk all that we write and more. Shall we ever be so happy?

Last night I was in the garden till 11 o'clock. It was the sweetest night that e'er I saw. The garden looked so well and the jasmine smelt beyond all perfume. And yet I was not pleased. The place had all the charms it used to have when I was most satisfied with it, and, had you been there, I should have liked it much more than ever I did. But that not being, it was no more to me than the next field and only served me for a place to roam in without disturbance.

From LETTER 56

Who would be kind[1] to one that reproaches one so cruelly? Do you think in earnest I could be satisfied the world should think me a dissembler, full of avarice or ambition? No, you are mistaken. But I'll tell you what I could suffer: that they should say I married where I had no inclination because my friends thought it fit rather than I had run willfully to my own ruin in pursuit of a fond passion of my own. To marry for love were not reproachful thing if we did not see that of ten thousand couples that do it hardly one can be brought for an example that it may be done and not repented afterwards.

★   ★   ★

But to come to my beagle [another suitor in marriage] again, I have heard no more of him, though I have seen him since we met at Wrest[2] again. I do not doubt but I shall be better able to resist his importunity than his tutor was. But what do you think it is that gives him his encouragement? He was told that I had thoughts of marrying a gentleman that had not above two hundred pound a year, only out of liking to his person. And

---

1   Here "feel love for."

2   Wrest in Bedfordshire was the country house of Anthony Grey, the earl of Kent.

upon that score his vanity allows him to think he may pretend[1] as far as another. Thus you see 'tis not altogether without reason that I apprehend[2] the noise of the world, since 'tis so much to my disadvantage.

★ ★ ★

'Tis not that I expect by all your father's offers to bring my friends to approve it [the marriage]. I don't deceive myself thus far, but I would not give them occasion to say that I hid myself from them in the doing of it nor of making my action appear more indiscreet than it is. It will concern me that all the world should know what fortune you have and upon what terms I marry you that both may not be made to appear ten times worse than they are. 'Tis the general custom of all people to make those that are rich to have more mines of gold than are in the Indias and such as have small fortunes to be beggars.

[Source: *Letters form Dorothy Osborne to Sir William Temple, 1652–54*, ed. Edward Abbot Parry (London: Sherratt and Hughes, 1903).]

2. Letters from Aphra Behn to John Hoyle

[According to Virginia Woolf, Aphra Behn (c. 1640–89) was the first woman to make a living by writing. Behn, who sometimes was known by the coterie name Astrea, composed more than a dozen plays that were performed on the public stage and afterwards printed. She also published translations from French as well as original poetry and fiction. It is widely believed that the letters included here offer a testimony to her love for a lawyer named John Hoyle, though the letters are less transparently autobiographical than might seem to be the case at first glance. Behn no doubt felt a good deal of confusion about her love for the notoriously unfaithful Hoyle, but at the same time she played the part of a love-sick woman, comically exaggerating her confused feelings especially in the first letter. The letters were not written for publication, but Behn probably understood that, like letters by other important people, these might find their way into print.

The sixth letter, as with Cavendish's letter 173 from *Sociable Letters*, is interesting in that it mentions the reading aloud of a play in an informal,

---

1 · Put himself forward.

2   Fear.

social setting. Other letters show the relationship between Behn and Hoyle in its pleasant times (letter 5) and when it was deeply unhappy (letter 8). There were a total of eight letters, from which the four below are extracted.]

LETTER 1

You bid me write, and I wish it were only the effects of Complaisance[1] that makes me obey you; I should be very angry with my self, and you, if I thought it were any other Motive: I hope it is not, and will not have you believe otherwise. I cannot help however wishing you no Mirth, nor any Content in your Dancing Design; and this unwonted Malice in me I do not like, and wou'd have conceal'd if I cou'd, least you shou'd take it for something which I am [not] nor will believe my self guilty of. May your Women be all Ugly, Ill-natur'd, Ill-dress'd, Ill-fashion'd, and Unconversable; and, every moment of your Time there be taken up with Thoughts of me, (a sufficient Curse;) and yet you will be better entertain'd than me, who possibly am, and shall be, uneasie with Thoughts not so good. Perhaps you had eas'd me of some Trouble, if you had let me seen or known you had been Well; but these are Favours for better Friends; and I 'll endeavour not to resent the Loss, or rather the Miss of 'em. It may be, since I have so easily granted this Desire of yours, in writing to you, you will fear you have pull'd Trouble on — but do not: I do by this send for you. — You know what you gave your Hand upon; the Date of Banishment is already out; and I cou'd have wish'd you had been so Good-natur'd as to have disobey'd me. Pray take notice therefore I am better natur'd than you: I am profoundly Melancholy since I saw you; I know not why, and shou'd be glad to see you when your Occasions will permit you to visit.

Astrea.

LETTER 5

Though it be very late, I cannot go to Bed; but I must tell thee,[2] I have been very Good ever since I saw thee, and have been a writing, and have

---

1   Being agreeable.

2   In this letter, Behn shifts from "you" to "thee/thou" to show that the letter writer feels especially confident and intimate with the recipient.

seen no Face of Man, or other Body, save my own People. I am mightily pleas'd with your Kindness to me to Night; and 'twas; I hope, and believe, very innocent, and undisturbing on both sides. My *Lycidas* says, He can be soft and dear when he please, to put off all his haughty Pride, which is only assum'd to see how far I dare love him ununited. Since then my Soul's Delight you are, and may ever be assur'd I am, and ever will be yours, befal me what will; and that all the Devils of Hell shall not prevail against thee; Shew then, I say, my dearest Love, thy native sweet Temper; Shew me all the Love thou hast undissembl'd; then, and never till then, shall I believe you love; and deserve my Heart, for God's sake, to keep me well: and if thou hast love (as I shall never doubt, if thou art always as to Night) shew that Love, I beseech thee; there being nothing so grateful to God and Mankind, as Plain-dealing. 'Tis too late to conjure thee farther; I will be purchas'd with Softness, and dear Words, and kind Expressions, sweet Eyes, and a low Voice.

Farewel, I love thee dearly, passionately, and tenderly, and am resolved to be eternally,

> *My only dear Delight, and*
> *Joy of my Life*, thy
> Astrea.

LETTER 6

Since you, my dearest *Lycidas*, have prescrib'd me Laws and Rules, how I shall behave my self to please and gain you; and that one of these is not Lying or Dissembling; and that I had to Night promis'd you shou'd never have a tedious Letter from me more, I will begin to keep my Word, and stint my heart and Hand. I promis'd tho' to write; and tho' I have no great Matter to say more, than the Assurance of my eternal Love to you, yet to obey you, and not only so, but to oblige my own impatient Heart, I must, late as 'tis, say something to thee.

I stay'd after thee to Night, till I had read a whole Act of my new Play too; and then he [unidentified] led me over all the way, saying, Gad you [Hoyle] were the Man; And beginning some rallying Love-discourse after Supper, which he fancy'd was not so well receiv'd as it ought, he said you were not handsome, and call'd *Philly* [perhaps the duke of Buckingham] to own it; but he did not, but was of my side, and said you were handsome: So he went on a while and all ended that concern'd you. And this, upon my Word, is all.

Your Articles I have read over, and do not like 'em; you have broke one, even before you have sworn or seal'd 'em; that is, they are writ with Reserves. I must have a better Account of your Heart to Morrow, when you come. I grow desperate fond of you, and would fain be us'd well; if not, I will march off; But I will believe you mean to keep your Word, as I will for ever do mine. Pray make hast to see me to Morrow; and if I am not at home when you come, send for me over the way, where I have ingaged to Dine, there being an Entertainment on purpose to Morrow for me.

For God's sake make no more Niceties and Scruples than need, in your way of living with me; that is, do not make me believe this distance is to ease you, when indeed 'tis meant to ease us both of Love; and, for God's sake, do not misinterpret my Excess of Fondness; and if I forget my self, let the Check you give be sufficient to make me desist. Believe me, dear Creature, 'tis more out of Humour and Jest than any inclination on my side; for I could sit eternally with you, without that part of disturbance: Fear me not, for you are (from that) as safe as in Heaven itself. Believe me, dear *Lycidas*, this Truth, and trust me. 'Tis late, Farewel; and come, for God's sake, betimes to Morrow, and put off your foolish Fear and Niceties, and do not shame me with your perpetual ill Opinion; my Nature is proud and insolent, and cannot bear it; I will be used something better, in spight of all your Apprehensions falsly grounded. Adieu, keep me as I am ever yours.

Astrea.

By this Letter, one would think I were the Nicest[1] thing on Earth; yet I know a dear Friend, goes far beyond me in that unnecessary Fault.

LETTER 8

Why, my dearest Charmer, do you disturb that Repose I had resolved to pursue, by taking it unkindly that I did not write? I cannot disobey you, because indeed I wou'd not, tho' 'twere better much for both I had been for ever silent: I prophesie so, but at the same time cannot help my Fate, and know not what force or credit there is in the Vertue we both possess; but I am sure 'tis not good to tempt it: I think I am sure, and I think my *Lycidas* just: But, oh! to what purpose is all this fooling? You have often wisely considered it; and whatever Resolutions I make in the absence of

---

1   Most punctilious.

my lovely Friend, one single sight turns me all Woman, and all his. Take notice then, my *Lycidas*, I will henceforth never be wise more; never make any Vows against my Inclinations, or the little-wing[']d Deity. I do not only see 'tis all in vain, but I really believe they serve only to augment my Passion. I own I have neither the Coldness of *Lycidas*, nor the Prudence; I cannot either not Love, or have a Thousand Arts of hiding it; I have no Body to fear, and therefore may have some Body to Love; But if you are destin'd to be he, the Lord have mercy on me; for I am sure you'll have none. I expect a Reprimand for this plain Confession; but I must justifie it, and I will, because I cannot help it: I was born to Ill Luck; and this Loss of my Heart is, possibl[y], not the least part on't. Do not let me see you disapprove it, I may one Day grow asham'd on't, and reclaime, but never, whilst you blow the Flame, tho' perhaps against your will. I expect now a very wise Answer; and, I believe, with abundance of Discretion, you will caution me to avoid this Danger that threatens. Do so, if you have a mind to make me launch farther into the main Sea of Love; Rather deal with me as with a right Woman; make me believe my self infinitely belov'd. I may chance from the natural Inconstancy of my Sex, to be as false as you wou'd wish, and leave you in quiet; For I am satisfi'd that nothing, but the thing that hates me, cou'd treat me as *Lycidas* do's; and 'tis only the vanity of being belov'd by me can make you countenance a softness so displeasing to you. How cou'd any thing, but the Man that hates me, entertain me so unkindly? witness your excellent Opinion of me, of Loving others; witness your passing by the end of the Street where I live, and squandering away your time at any Coffee-House, rather than allow me what you know in your Soul is the greatest Blessing of my Life, your dear *dull* melancholy Company; I call it dull, because you can never be gay or merry where *Astrea* is. How cou'd this Indifference possess you, when your malicious Soul knew I was languishing for you? I dy'd, I fainted, and pin'd for an Hour of what you lavish'd out, unregardless of me, and without so much as thinking on me! What can you say, that Judgment may not pass? that you may not be condemn'd for the worst-nature'd, incorrigible Thing in the World? Yield, and at least say, My honest Friend *Astrea*, I neither do love thee, nor can, nor ever will; at least let me say, you were generous, and told me plain blunt Truth: I know it; nay worse, you impudently (but truly) told me your Business wou'd permit you to come every Night, but your Inclinations would not: At least this was honest, but very unkind, and not over civil. Do not you, my Amiable *Lycidas*, know I wou'd purchase your sight at any Rate; Why this Neglect then? Why keeping distance? *But as much as to say,* Astrea, *truly you will make me love you, you will make me fond of you, you will please and delight me with your Conversation, and I am a Fellow that do not desire to be pleas'd, therefore be not so civil to me; for I do not desire civil Company, or Company that diverts me.* A pretty Speech this; and yet if I do obey, desist being civil, and behave my self very rudely, as I have done, you say, this two or three Days — then, Oh, *Astrea*! where is your Profession? where your Love so boasted? your Good-nature, &c.? Why truly, my dear *Lycidas*, where it was, and ever will be, so long as you have invincible Charms, and shew your Eyes, and look so dearly; tho' you may, by your prudent Counsel, and your wise Conduce of Absence, and marching by my Door without calling in, oblige me to stay my Hand, and Hold my tongue; I can conceal my Kindness, tho' not dissemble one; I can make you think I am wise, if I list; but when I tell you I have Friendship, Love and Esteem for you, you may pawn your Soul upon't: Believe 'tis true, and satisfie your self you have, my dear *Lycidas*, in your *Astrea* all she professes. I should be glad to see you as soon as possible (you say *Thursday*) you can: I beg you will, and shall, with Impatience, expect you betimes. Fail me not, as you would have me think you have any value for

Astrea.

I beg you will not fail to let me hear from you, to Day being Wednesday, and see you at Night if you can.

[Source: *The Histories and Novels of the Late Ingeneous Mrs. Aphra Behn, Together with the life and Memoirs of Mrs. Behn, Written by One of the Fair Sex* (London, 1696), Huntington Library Rare Book 58250.]

Appendix C: The Context of English Letter Writing and the English Essay

1. From Angel Day, *The English Secretary*

[Little is known about Angel Day, including his dates of birth and death. Samples from *The English Secretary* (1586) are printed here because of the book's enormous popularity and its influence on letter writing in seventeenth-century England. Margaret Cavendish, casting about for a new *genre* in which to write and possibly taking note of Day's volume, realized that letters might work as a vehicle for literary expression. Letter writing is, indeed, a venerable literary form, dating back to Roman times with Pliny the Younger and to the Renaissance with Erasmus. The fact that much of the New Testament is made up of letters composed by St. Paul, of course, helps to give the form *gravitas*. The letters contained in *The English Secretary* often were employed as templates for actual correspondence, but they also were read for their wit. Their convoluted writing style probably owes something to John Lyly's *Euphues* (1578), but that style made little impression on Cavendish. Rather, she would have enjoyed the ironic voice that is often apparent (letter 2) and no doubt appreciated the sardonic jokes found elsewhere (letter 3).]

LETTER 1. From Of Epistles Amatory

Good Mistress,[1]
I am bold, though a stranger, to make these letters messengers at this present of my good meaning towards you. Wherein you may please to think that I go not about by pretence of a most entire and hearty good will which I profess to bear you to make present surmise thereupon that on so bare an assertion you should immediately credit me. I prize your worthiness at far greater value and weigh your good allowance so much as I only desire that by your favourable liking I may entreat to have access unto you, not doubting but by my being in your presence I shall so succinctly by apparent proof maintain the efficacy of that I now protest and give you so good occasion to deem well of me as you shall have no reason to repent you that upon so honest and loving a request you have conde-

---

1 A respectful form of address meaning "woman in charge."

scended to my entreaty. Whose health and prosperity tendering in all things as mine own, I send you with my letter a token of that great affection I bear you, which I most heartily pray you to accept of and wear for me. And even so do continue,

Yours, if you please to accept of me &c.

LETTER 2. An answer to the above

Sir,
Your message is unto me as strange as yourself, who are unto me a stranger, and what your good meaning unto me is I know not. For giving of hasty credit to your assertions, as you seem not to challenge, it so was I never hitherto of myself [was] so hasty to do it, having eftsoons[1] been taught that of fairest speeches ensueth[2] often the foulest actions. I cannot condemn your purpose, because I intend the best of your dealings, and howbeit I am in no point so restrained.[3] But in all reasonable sort that may be, any access may be granted. So when you shall by further notice sufficiently make apparent that with modesty I may doe it, I shall be willing so far forth as my years and present being may minister occasion in any thankful requital that may be to yield myself unto you. Till which time I return your token again, and my hearty thanks unto you by this bearer.

Your friend as one unacquainted
hitherto may be &c.

LETTER 3. An example consolatory, pleasantly written to one who had buried his old wife

The posting news hitherward of the late decease of my good old Mistress your wife hath made me in the very going away of my ague[4] fit to strain myself to greet you by these letters. In the inditing[5] whereof, I many times prayed in my thoughts that I were as readily delivered of this my tertian

---

1 Repeatedly.

2 Follow.

3 Obliged.

4 Fever.

5 Writing.

fever[1] as yourself are in my opinion delivered by such means of a hateful and very foul encumbrance. I doubt not, sir, but you do now take the matter heavily, being thereby dispossessed as you are of such an intolerable delight as wherewith you were continually cloyed by the nightly embracement of so unwieldy a carcass. I have, I must confess, very seldom known you for anything to mourn. Nevertheless, if by such means you be happily constrained to change countenance, I have prepared a golden box wherein I mean to consecrate all the tears you shed for that accident to Berecynthia, the Beldame[2] of the Gods, as a relic of your great kindship[3] and courtesy....

[Source: *The English Secretorie* (London: Thomas Snodham, n.d.), Huntington Library 600338.]

2. Francis Bacon, "Of Marriage and the Single Life"

[Francis Bacon (1561–1626) is included in this volume because Margaret Cavendish probably had him in mind as she composed letters that are essentially essays. Bacon had read essays by the French writer Michel de Montaigne and adapted their form for use in English. It also is useful to compare the male-centered views of Bacon on marriage to those of Cavendish, who frequently offers a woman's perspective on the topic. Cavendish is sometimes as terse and general as Bacon (*Sociable Letters*, letters 4 and 5) and sometimes gets into more depth and detail (letters 32 and 55). She also deals specifically with unusual marriages (letter 42). While Bacon considers the happiness that is brought by children, he does not, as Cavendish does, have anything to say about pregnancy (letter 47). While she looks carefully at what can happen in marriages that go bad (letter 35 and 36), he does not take up that subject. Her range is wider than his.]

Of Marriage and the Single Life

He that hath wife and children hath given hostages to fortune, for they are impediments to great enterprises either of virtue or mischief. Certainly, the best works and of greatest merit for the public have proceeded from unmarried or childless men, which both in affection and means have mar-

---

1   Fever peaking every other day.

2   Old woman. Berecynthia is the goddess Cybele whose worship in Rome involved licentiousness.

3   Kindness.

ried and endowed the public. Yet it were great reason that those that have children should have greatest care of future times unto which they know they must transmit their dearest pledges. Some there are who though they lead a single life yet their thoughts do end with themselves and account future times impertinences. Nay there are some other that account wife and children but as bills of charges. Nay more, there are some foolish, rich, covetous men that take a pride in having no children because they may be thought so much the richer. For perhaps they have heard some talk: "Such an one is a great rich man," and another except to it, "Yea, but he hath a great charge of children," as if it were an abatement to his riches. But the most ordinary cause of a single life is liberty, especially to certain self-pleasing and humorous minds, which are so sensible of every restraint as they will go near to think their girdles and garters[1] to be bonds and shackles. Unmarried men are best friends, best masters, best servants, but not always best subjects, for they are light to run away and almost all fugitives are of that condition. A single life doth well with church men, for charity will hardly water the ground where it must first fill a pool. It is indifferent for judges and magistrates, for if they be facile and corrupt, you shall have a servant five times than a wife.[2] For soldiers I find the generals commonly in their hortatives[3] put men in mind of their wives and children. And I think the despising of marriage amongst the Turks maketh the vulgar[4] solider more base. Certainly wife and children are a kind of discipline and humanity. And single men though they may be many times more charitable because their means are less exhaust, yet on the other side they are more cruel and hardhearted (good to make inquisitors) because their tenderness is not so oft called upon. Grave natures, led by custom and therefore constant, are commonly loving husbands as was said of Ulysses, "Vetulam suam praetulit immortalitati."[5] Chaste women are often proud and froward[6] as presuming the merit of their chastity. It is one of the best bonds both of chastity and obedience in the wife if she thinks her husband wise, which she will never do if she find him jealous. Wives are young men's mistresses, companions for middle

---

1 Belts and devices to hold up socks.

2 The servant will rule the household as if she were a wife.

3 Calls to duty.

4 Ordinary.

5 Ulysses "preferred his old wife to immortality."

6 Difficult, unpleasant.

age, and old men's nurses, so as a man may have a quarrel to marry when he will. But he was reputed one of the wise men that made answer to the question when a man should marry: "A young man not yet, an elder man not at all." It is often seen that bad husbands have good wives, whether it be that it raiseth the price of their husbands' kindness when it come or that the wives take a pride in their patience. But this never fails, if the bad husbands were of their own choosing against friends consent. For then they will be sure to make good their own folly.

[Source: *The Essays or Counsels Civil and Moral and Wisdom of the Ancients* (London: William Pickering, 1845).]

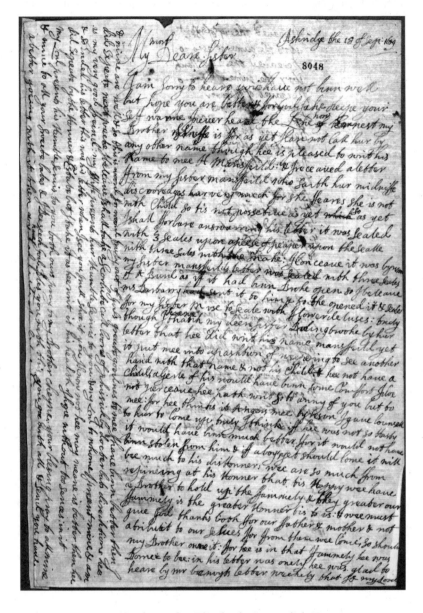

A manuscript letter by Elizabeth Cavendish Egerton.

[Reprinted by permission of the Huntington Library.]

Bibliography

Modern Editions

Bell in Campo and The Sociable Companions. Ed. Alexandra G. Bennett. Peterborough, ON: Broadview Press, 2002.

The Blazing World and other Writings. Ed. Kate Lilley. London: Pickering, 1992.

The Convent of Pleasure and Other Plays. Ed. Anne Shaver. Baltimore: Johns Hopkins UP, 1999.

The First Duke and Duchess of Newcastle-upon-Tyne. [Ed. Thomas Longueville.] London: Longmans, Green, and Co., 1910.

[*The Lotterie.*] James Fitzmaurice."'The Lotterie': A Transcription of a Manuscript Play Probably by Margaret Cavendish," *Huntington Library Quarterly* 66 (2003): 155–67.

Paper Bodies: A Margaret Cavendish Reader. Ed. Sylvia Bowerbank and Sara Mendelson. Peterborough, ON: Broadview Press, 1999.

The Phanseys of William Cavendish, Marquis of Newcastle, Addressed to Margaret Lucas. Ed. Douglas Grant. London: Nonesuch, 1956.

Observations upon Experimental Philosophy. Ed. Eileen O'Neill. Cambridge: Cambridge UP, 2001.

The Critical Heritage

A Collection of Letters and Poems. London, 1678.

Ballard, George. *Memoirs of British Ladies Who Have Been Celebrated for Their Writing or skill in the Learned Languages, Arts, and Sciences.* London, 1775.

Evelyn, John. *Diary and Correspondence of John Evelyn.* Ed. William Bray. Vol. 2. and Vol. 4. London: J.M. Dent, n.d.

——. *The Diary of John Evelyn.* Ed. William Bray, prefatory note by George W.E. Russell. Vol. 2. London: Everyman, 1907.

Evelyn, Mary. *Diary and Correspondence of John Evelyn.* Ed. William Bray. Vol. 4. London: Henry Colburn, 1857.

Hamilton, Anthony. *Mémoires de la Vie du Comte de Gramont.* 1713. Trans. and ed. Peter Quennell, London: George Routledge and Sons, 1930.

Jusserand, J.J. *The English Novel in the Time of Shakespeare*. London: T. Fisher Unwin, 1890.

Lamb, Charles. "Mackery End." *The Essays of Elia*. 1823. New York: J.M. Dent, 1906.

Langbaine, Gerard. *An Account of the English Dramatick Poets*. Oxford, 1691.

Makin, Bathsua. *An Essay to Revive the Antient Education of Gentlewomen*. 1673. Los Angeles: Augustan Reprint Society, 1980.

Osborne, Dorothy. *Letters from Dorothy Osborne to William Temple*. Ed. G.C. Moore Smith. Oxford: Clarendon Press, 1928.

Osborne, Dorothy. *Letters from Dorothy Osborne to Sir William Temple, 1652–54*. Ed. Edward Abbot Parry. London: Sherratt and Hughes, 1903.

Pepys, Samuel. *The Diary of Samuel Pepys*. Ed. Latham and Matthews. Vols. 8 and 9. London: Bell and Sons, 1974.

Rowton, Frederick. *Female Poets of Great Britain*. 1853. Detroit: Wayne State UP, 1981.

Walpole, Horace. *A Catalogue of the Royal and Noble Authors of England, Scotland, and Ireland*. Vol. 3. London: J. Dodsley and J. Graham. 149.

Woolf, Virginia. *The Common Reader*. London: Hogarth, 1929.

—. *A Room of One's Own*. London: Hogarth, 1929.

Modern Secondary Sources on Cavendish

Battigelli, Anna. *Margaret Cavendish and the Exiles of the Mind*. Lexington: UP of Kentucky, 1998.

Blaydes, Sophia B. "Nature is a Woman: The Duchess of Newcastle and Seventeenth-Century Philosophy." *Man, God, and Nature in the Enlightenment*. Ed. Donald C. Mell, Jr., Theodore E.D. Braun, Lucia M. Palmer. East Lansing, MI: Colleagues, 1988. 51–64.

Bowerbank, Sylvia. "The Spider's Delight: Margaret Cavendish and the 'Female Imagination.'" *English Literary Renaissance* 14 (1984): 392–408. Rpt. in *Women and the Renaissance, Selections from English Literary Renaissance*. Ed. Kirby Farrell, Elizabeth H. Hageman, and Arthur F. Kinney. Amherst: U of Massachusetts P, 1991.

Clucas, Stephen, ed. *A Princely Brave Woman: Essays on Margaret Cavendish, Duchess of Newcastle*. Aldershot: Ashgate, 2003.

Cottegnies, Line and Nancy Weitz, eds. *Authorial Conquests: Essays on Genre in the Writings of Margaret Cavendish*. Madison, NJ: Fairleigh Dickinson UP, forthcoming.

Ferguson, Moira. "Margaret Lucas Cavendish: 'A Wise, Wittie, and Learned Lady.'" *Women Writers of the Seventeenth Century*. Ed. Katherina M. Wilson and Frank J. Warnke. Athens, GA: U of Georgia P, 1989. 305–40.

Findley, Sandra and Elaine Hobby. "Seventeenth-Century Women's Autobiography." *1642: Literature and Power in the Seventeenth Century*. Ed. Francis Barker et al. Colchester: U of Essex P, 1981. 198–209.

Fitzmaurice, James. "Fancy and the Family: Self-Characterizations of Margaret Cavendish." *Huntington Library Quarterly* 53 (Summer 1990): 199–209.

Gagen, Jean. "Honor and Fame in the Works of the Duchess of New-castle." *Studies in Philology* 56 (1959): 519–38.

Gallagher, Catherine. "Embracing the Absolute: The Politics of the Female Subject in Seventeenth-Century England." *Genders* 1 (1988): 24–39.

Grant, Douglas. *Margaret the First*. London: Rupert Hart-Davis, 1957.

In-between: Essays and Studies in Literary Criticism 9.1 and 2 (2000).

Lilley, Kate. "Blazing Worlds: Seventeenth-Century Women's Utopian Writing." *Women, Texts, and Histories, 1575–1760*. Ed. Clare Brant and Diane Purkiss. London: Routledge, 1992. 102–33.

MacCarthy, B.G. *The Female Pen: Women Writers and Novelists, 1621–1818*. 1946–47. New York: New York UP, 1994.

McGuire, Mary Ann. "Margaret Cavendish, Duchess of Newcastle, on the Nature and Status of Women." *International Journal of Women's Studies* 1.2. 193–206.

Mendelson, Sara Heller. *The Mental World of Stuart Women*. Amherst: U of Massachusetts P, 1987.

Minz, S.I. "The Duchess of Newcastle's Visit to the Royal Society." *Journal of English and Germanic Philology* (April 1952): 168–76.

Nicholson, Marjorie Hope. "'Mad Madge' and 'The Wits.'" *Pepys' Diary and the New Science*. Charlottesville: U of Virginia P, 1965.

Paloma, Delores. "Margaret Cavendish: Defining the Female Self." *Women's Studies* 7 (1980): 55–66.

Payne, Linda R. "Dramatic Dreamscape: Women's Dreams and Utopian Vision in the Works of Margaret Cavendish, Duchess of Newcastle." *Curtain Calls: British and American Women and the Theater, 1660–1830*. Ed. Mary Anne Schofield and Cecilia Macheski. Athens, OH: Ohio UP, 1991. 18–33.

Perry, Henry Ten Eyck. *The First Duchess of Newcastle and Her Husband as Figures in Literary History*. Boston: Ginn and Co., 1918.

Rogers, John. *The Matter of Revolution: Science, Poetry, and Politics in the Age of Milton*. Ithaca: Cornell UP, 1996.

Romack, Katherine M. "Margaret Cavendish, Shakespeare Critic." *A Feminist Companion to Shakespeare*. Ed. Dympna Callagan. Oxford: Blackwell, 2000. 21–41.

Salzman, Paul. "Narrative Contexts." *Bacon's New Atlantis*. Ed. Bronwen Price and Simon Wortham. Manchester: Manchester UP, 2002.

Sarasohn, Lisa. "A Science Turned Upside Down: Feminism and the Natural Philosophy of Margaret Cavendish." *Huntington Library Quarterly* 47 (Autumn 1984) 299–307.

Smith, Hilda. *Reason's Disciples: Seventeenth-Century English Feminists*. Urbana: U of Illinois P, 1982.

Suzuki, Mihoko. "Margaret Cavendish and the Female Satirist." *SEL, Studies in English Literature* 37 (Summer 1997): 483–500.

Todd, Janet. *The Sign of Angellica: Women, Writing, and Fiction, 1660–1800*. London: Virago, 1989.

Tomlinson, Sophie. "'My Brain the Stage': Margaret Cavendish and the Fantasy of Female Performance." *Women, Texts, and Histories*. London: Routledge, 1992. 134–63.

Trease, Geoffrey. *Portrait of a Cavalier: William Cavendish, First Duke of Newcastle*. London: Macmillan, 1979.

The Seventeenth Century 9.2 (Autumn 1994). [Special issue on the Cavendish Circle.]

Turberville, A.S. *A History of Welbeck Abbey and Its Owners*. London: Faber, 1938.

Whitaker, Katie. *Mad Madge, The Extraordinary Life of Margaret, Duchess of Newcastle, the First Woman to Live by Her Pen*. New York: Basic Books, 2002.

Wiseman, Susan. "Gender and Status in Dramatic Discourse: Margaret Cavendish, Duchess of Newcastle." *Women, Writing, History: 1640–1740*. Ed. Isobel Grundy and Susan Wiseman. London: B.T. Batsford, 1992. 161–77.

Women's Writing 4.3 (1997). [Special issue on Cavendish.] Also at <http://www.triangle.co.uk/wow/04-03/wow-04-03.htm>.

Other Works

Barker, Jane. "The Unaccountable Wife." *A Patch-work Screen*. London, 1723. Rpt. in *First Feminists: British Women Writers, 1578–1799*. Bloomington: Indiana UP, 1985. 175–79.

Beier, A.L. *Masterless Men: The Vagrancy Problem in England, 1560–1640*. London: Methuen, 1985.

William Camden. Remains concerning Britain. London, 1614.

Cary, Elizabeth. *The Tragedy of Mariam, The Fair Queen of Jewry*. Ed. Barry Weller and Margaret W. Ferguson. Berkeley: U of California P, 1994.

Cavendish, Margaret. *Nature's Pictures*. London, 1656.

Cerasano, Susan and Marian Wynne-Davies, eds. *Renaissance Drama by Women*. London: Routledge, 1996.

Day, Angel. *The English Secretary*. London: Thomas Snodham, n.d. [Huntington Library 600338.]

Day, Robert Adams. *Told in Letters: Epistolary Fiction Before Richardson*. Ann Arbor: U of Michigan P, 1966.

Daybell, James. *Early Modern Women's Letter Writing, 1450–1700*. New York: Palgrave, 2001.

Egerton, Elizabeth, countess of Bridgewater. *Subordination and Authorship in Early Modern England: The Case of Elizabeth Cavendish Egerton and her "Loose Papers."* Ed. Betty S. Travitsky. Medieval and Renaissance Texts and Studies 208. Tempe, AZ: Arizona Center for Medieval and Renaissance Studies, 1999.

Evans, G. Blakemore, ed. *The Riverside Shakespeare*. Boston: Houghton Mifflin Co., 1974.

Ezell, Margaret J.M. "'To be Your Daughters in Your Pen': The Social Function of Literature in the Writings of Lady Elizabeth Brackley and Lady Jane Cavendish." *Huntington Library Quarterly* 54 (Autumn 1988): 281–96.

Fitzmaurice, James. "The Cavendishes, the Evelyns, and Teasing in Verse and Prose." *Journal of the Rocky Mountain Medieval and Renaissance Association* 16 and 17 (1995–96): 161–86.

Fitzmaurice, Susan M. *The Familiar Letter in Early Modern English*. Amsterdam and Philadelphia: John Benjamins, 2002.

—. "Tentativeness and Insistence in the Expression of Politeness in Margaret Cavendish's *Sociable Letters.*" *Language and Literature* 9 (February 2000): 7–24.

Guibbory, Achsah. "Imitation and Originality: Cowley and Bacon's Vision of Progress." *SEL, Studies in English Literature* 29 (1989): 99–111.

Historical Manuscripts Commission. Portland Papers. Vol. 2. London: Stationary Office, 1893.

Howell, James. *Epistolae Ho-Elianae.* London, 1650.

Lord, George De F. *Poems on Affairs of State.* New Haven: Yale UP, 1975.

Nichols, John. *The Progresses, and Public Processions of Queen Elizabeth.* 3 vols. London, 1788.

Parker, Kenneth. Introduction. *Dorothy Osborne: Letters to Sir William Temple, 1652–54.* Burlington, VT: Ashgate, 2002.

Sanderson, Sir William. *A Compleat History of the Life and Raigne of King Charles.* London, 1658.

Shakespeare, William. *Love's Labours Lost.* Ed. H.C. Hart. 3rd ed. The Arden Shakespeare. London: Methuen, 1930.

Slaughter, Thomas P., ed. *Ideology and Politics on the Eve of the Restoration: Newcastle's Advice to Charles II.* Philadelphia: American Philosophical Society, 1984.

Starr, Nathan Comfort. "*The Concealed Fancies:* A Play by Lady Jane Cavendish and Lady Elizabeth Brackley." *PMLA* 46 (1931): 802–38.

Suetonius Tranquilis, Caius. *The Historie of Twelve Caesars.* Trans. Philemon Holland. London, 1606.

Travitsky, Betty S. *Subordination and Authorship in Early Modern England.* Tempe: Arizona Center for Medieval and Renaissance Studies, 1999.

Wilkins, John [bishop]. *A Discovery of a New World.* 4th ed. London, 1684.

Wroth, Lady Mary. *The Poems of Lady Mary Wroth.* Ed. Josephine Roberts. Baton Rouge, LA: Louisiana State UP, 1983.

Internet Sources

The Margaret Cavendish Society Bibliography. <http://jan.ucc.nau.edu/%7Ejbf/CavBiblio>.

Renaissance Women Online. <http://www.wwp.brown.edu/texts/rwoentry.html>.